How to
COPE
with the
HIGH COST
of
LIVING

DIANE R. BLAIR

Acknowledgments

Many specialists in various areas of living costs contributed information and advice in the compilation of this book. The authors especially appreciate the help of William S. Jarrett for editorial guidance; writer seamstress Suzanne Olson for her contribution on economies in sewing, repairing, and altering family clothing; Jane Harmon for research on health services, drug and toiletries costs, and housing costs; George Freund, former test-car driver and auto-club consultant, for guidance on the selection, operation, and servicing of cars; Betty Preston for surveys of protein and other food costs; Gerald Cook for research on housing and mortgages; Richard Margolius for advice on legal services and landlord-tenant issues; Elaine Jessen for research on appliance purchasing and operating costs; librarian Helen Anderson Burnham; Alison Davis for gardening counsel; Robert B. Oliver, Jr. for advice on wood stoves; hair stylist Joseph Giacomantonio; master carpenter William Loos; Robert Sager for furniture refinishing information; Howard W. Levine and Joseph Dicola for advice on hardware and paint; Albert Drager for advice on home heating; Barbara Dickinson for her careful manuscript typing and copy-editing services... with the deepest thanks of all to the authors' constantly helpful wives, Meg Kidder Brown and Esther Margolius.

Contents

(continued on next page)

Your Master Plan for Making Ends Meet

With the cost of just about everything still on the rise, Americans have responded with healthy flexibility. More and more of us are willing to curb at least some spending when confronted with excessive prices. We are learning to get along with less.

Household budgets have been getting the fat trimmed out of them; most families find they have at least some nonessential expenditures that can be reduced or eliminated. Many families are even devising whole new modes of existence—not necessarily living less well, but living quite differently. Surprisingly, it is turning out to be not half bad.

We have been staying home more instead of burning up the highways, enjoying one another's company, and uncovering new dimensions in family and community life. And we are planting backyard gardens and harvesting vegetables that taste better than any we ever bought at the supermarket.

The Plan's Specifics

Coping with long-term inflation means that you must give the same careful, serious attention to handling your money that you give to earning it. The following strategies should enable you to achieve this all-important end.

Food is a flexible expense—flex it. Food purchasing is perhaps the one skill most worth cultivating because it is so susceptible to daily economies. Between 25 and 30 percent of a middle-income family's spendable income (after taxes) goes for food. But the amount varies remarkably. Some families spend as much as one-third less for food than others in the same neighborhood and still enjoy tasty, nutritious meals.

Housing is your major expense—control it. Those housing costs that you can most effectively control are heating and utilities, repairs and maintenance, and, very possibly, property insurance. The total of these costs comprises approximately half of your total housing outlay.

Car expenses—trim them. The average family's third largest expense is their car, outranked only by food and housing. Traditionally, the principal cost in owning a car has been depreciation—its annual loss in market value. You can reduce this, of course, by keeping your car longer. Even though repair prices keep going up, it is usually not true that repairing an older car costs more than buying a new one. However, gasoline now looms as large, or larger, than depreciation for many owners. You can reduce gas consumption and other operating costs by keeping your engine tuned, by adopting conservative driving habits, and by combining trips around town.

Clothing—learn how to dress for less. For too many people clothing is an ego trip. Belt-tightening means not giving in to whim or fancy; shopping "underground" outlets for bargains; and perhaps sewing some of the simpler garments your family wears. There are ways to spend less on laundering and dry-cleaning and come up smelling like roses.

Medical protection—buy the optimum. Though medical care is the nation's fastest rising family expense, the basic problem probably won't be solved until we have a national health care program. Meanwhile, your best defense is to buy the most complete insurance available—not the cheapest but that providing the fullest service. Acquire it on a group basis if you possibly can.

Credit? Get on a cash basis. With the prevalence of revolving charge accounts, credit cards, and installment plans, many families have taken on a needless habitual extra living expense in the form of finance charges. These have true rates running around 18 or 20 percent (less for new cars). Rates tend to be especially high during a period of tight money, the inevitable iron handmaiden of inflation.

Budget—but keep it realistic. A functional budget has two parts: a spending *plan* and a spending *record*. High costs make a mutually-agreed-upon spending plan necessary for pinning down exactly which needs and desires represent your family's real values. Without a record of how it gets spent, such bouncing costs as food, car, and household operation can drain away your money before you realize what's happening to it. Your budget need not be rigid, nor do you have to imitate the spending patterns of others. If you compare your plan with your actual spending record every six months or so, you'll see where you may need to revise your budget, pushing up some estimates and reducing others, as the prices of various regular expenditures increase or stabilize.

How This Book Can Work for You

This is a book for every resourceful family that wants to maintain its standard of living in the face of rising costs. It describes what you can do for yourself to make do for less and become more self-sufficient.

It will help you rethink your relationship to the many goods and services you buy. It can show you how to cope creatively—to avoid being hassled on the one hand by pressures to spend for things you don't need, or can make or do for yourself, and on the other by the continuously increasing prices of those things.

Much of the money-saving information in these pages is practical, do-it-yourself advice, such as how to make a wide variety of home repairs, how to bake bread that's fresher, tastier, more wholesome—and less expensive. In other areas, such as purchasing insurance, this book will help you decide which of a choice of options can best help you beat inflation and still meet your needs and those of your family.

A guide to the many ways of living better for less, this book shows you how to trim your expenses immediately in all sorts of ways. Its effect on your finances is cumulative—the incremental product of countless major and minor suggestions that will help you save. It will help you hang in there when times are tough.

How to Cope With the High Cost of Living will open up new vistas in your life. You may even find yourself getting involved in a number of activities that you never thought to try before—simply because you had no idea that they were so easy, economical, and fun.

In the process you're sure to come out ahead.

How to Feed Your Family Inexpensively

Food costs have gone up more than any other major item in your budget—almost 80 percent from 1967 to 1976. The 30 percent leap from 1973 especially caused many housewives to wonder whether a time would come when they could no longer be able to feed their families adequately on the money available to them.

One result of this anxiety is that many families who had become accustomed to fast and often impulsive shopping and easy preparation of convenience foods, often with little reference to financial or even nutritional values, showed a surprising flexibility. Thus, in recent years many Americans reduced meat consumption, cut down on sugar and sugar-using products; battled the price of coffee by curtailing use, and likewise chose to pass up other price-climbing products.

Consumers have shown particular flexibility in finding protein alternatives to high-priced meat. This hasn't always been easy; some of the "alternatives" also skyrocketed in cost. One compromise has been increased attention to combining moderate amounts of high-quality protein with the less-costly grain products.

There are hundreds of individual methods people are using to rein in food expenses—from cutting down on meat to taking brown-bag lunches to work. Here are especially productive ideas and tips you can use to save when you shop for food. This section also tells you how to get started in gardening, to produce better-tasting food at far lower cost; how to make bread easily; and what you should know about home canning and freezing.

Ways to Cut Your Grocery Bill

Cost-conscious consumers have discovered dozens of ways to cope with high food prices. Here's a summary of the most popular and most effective methods.

Wider Shopping

The most significant trend is to more comparison-shopping. In 1954 only 59 percent of shoppers visited more than one supermarket in a month, Burgoyne, Inc., a research company, reports. By 1975, 90 percent were shopping more than one. The average shopper now visits almost three different markets a month in her search for quality and specials. While most people still have one favorite market, the natives are getting restless. Almost one out of four changed favorites during the year.

Broader shopping can pay off. When prices go up sharply, stores often run more "specials." As this is written, you could pay anywhere from 88 cents to $1.49 for chuck roast; from 69 cents to $1.24 for a five-pound bag of flour.

Use specials on meats, poultry and produce to plan a week's menus in advance. Take advantage of the specials on "dry groceries" (canned and packaged foods) to build up a modest inventory at home at reduced cost.

Selecting the Store

While consumers are shopping more stores, obviously you can't get around to all to "cherrypick" the specials. Best strategy: look for the store that has the best meat or poultry specials for the week. These main-dish items usually take 25–30 percent of your food dollar.

Buy in Bulk

Families are buying ground beef in bigger packages at lower prices—not only the popular three-pound but five- and even six-pound packs. They're also buying frozen fish in five-pound cartons, using the individually wrapped fillets as needed, and frozen vegetables in two-pound pour bags.

Remember also to comparison-shop for non-food items, such as laundry detergents, dog food, and paper napkins, as they can result in worthwhile savings.

Save with Coupons

While consumers questioned in surveys preferred reduced prices to special deals, cents-off coupons have become widely used. But on trading stamps, shoppers almost unanimously said they would prefer reductions of two cents on the dollar (usual cost of stamps to retailers).

You now can redeem S&H stamps for cash. You can get 50 cents for each one-quarter book (300 stamps)—$2 for each full book of 1,200 stamps. If no S&H office is available locally, you can mail them to Sperry & Hutchinson, 30-30 Kemper Road, Cincinnati, Ohio 45266.

Save with Leaner Beef

One of the most significant trends has been public acceptance of leaner beef from grass-fed younger cattle. More such beef has appeared in stores at lower prices than for Choice-grade beef which has more marbling (streaks of fat). In fact, the amount of fat on retail cuts ranked with high prices as a major consumer grievance, a survey found.

Try the House Brands

Younger families especially have turned more to house brands, and for staple clothing needs as well as foods. Younger shoppers are more likely than older ones to try lower-price brands.

Check the Drained Weights

As prices have risen, alert shoppers have become more conscious of "drained weights"

—how much solid food they get. In general, the smaller the vegetable or fruit, the more actual food is packed in the cans. Thus, you can expect more actual yield from canned peas, lima beans, corn, tomatoes, okra, beets, cut green beans and cut asparagus, pineapple and fruit cocktail than from pears, peach halves, asparagus spears and other whole vegetables which need more room in the can to avoid bruising. While you really can see what a can yields only when you open it, one crude test of relative amount of solids is to shake the can and listen.

Buy the Food, Not the Appearance

Whether in meat or produce, fancy appearance may command a higher price without a corresponding yield in nutrition or even eating quality.

For example, red-skinned apples are priced almost entirely according to the amount of red. But the color has no effect on taste. Small apples in three- or four-pound bags cost less than the larger ones sold by the piece or in cardboard trays.

Russeted pears, oranges with greenish skin, grapefruit with rusty splotches, onions more lopsided than round—all usually sell for less but have the same nutrition.

Similarly, jumbo asparagus spears often cost 30 percent more than medium size. In canned asparagus, large spears cost more than cut pieces with the tips; canned cut green beans less than whole beans.

In beef, the attractive-looking marbled Choice grade with bright red lean and creamy white fat not only costs more but actually has less protein and vitamins than the darker-looking lower grades.

In buying fish, too, white-meat species such as flounder and haddock often cost twice as much as dark-meat fish such as pollock and hake.

Check the Ingredients

More people are reading the lists of ingredients on packages and canned foods to see what they're really getting. By law the ingredients must be listed in order of predominance. Thus, you may observe that in one brand of spaghetti-and-meat dinner, the chief ingredient in the meat sauce is water,

followed by tomato paste and ground beef. In another brand, the first ingredient may be tomatoes followed by beef.

Or you may find that one brand of "Beef with Gravy" lists beef as the first ingredient, while another, revealingly called "Gravy with Beef" lists gravy first in the ingredients as well as in the name.

Compare Different Forms

Alert consumers are learning also to compare different forms of the same food; for example, the relative cost of fresh, canned and frozen green beans at a particular time.

Save with Standard Grades

Value-wise consumers are learning to buy standard grades of foods (B and C) instead of Fancy or Grade A. The higher grades mainly provide somewhat more tenderness, and more attractive and uniform appearance —which is lost anyway when you cook things together as in a casserole, soup or stew. Grades B and C actually are the same nutritionally as the costlier "higher" grades. Since the lower grade designations usually don't appear on the labels, the best policy may be to bypass the "fancy" canned goods.

For example, the color of the "lower" grades of tomatoes—the most widely used canned vegetable—is not quite as red and not as many of the tomato portions are in whole or large pieces as in grade A.

Save on Shortenings

Food fats in general have gone up sharply in price. You save considerably by buying the cheapest vegetable shortening. They have much the same cooking properties. Lard usually is the cheapest shortening of all. In margarines, all brands no matter what the price must meet the same federal standard requiring at least 80 percent edible oils and 5,000 units of vitamin A per pound. Some processors add additional ingredients.

Save by Slicing

You can earn money at home by doing your own slicing and cutting. Often stores charge 10 or 15 cents more for the same cut of meat or the same chicken cut into stewing pieces or parts. Thus, you may find stores charging $1.19 for boneless chuck but $1.35 for the same meat sold as stew beef. You also can save by slicing bacon from the slab, swiss steaks from pot roast, pork chops from loin roast, pork steaks from shoulder, ham slices from whole ham or end.

The disparities are even more remarkable on cold cuts and cheese. As shown in the table of comparative protein costs later in this chapter, you may pay at the rate of $1.29 a pound for sliced bologna in small packages but $1.09 for bologna sold by the chunk.

Save on Eggs

Buy brown or mixed-color eggs if cheaper in your locality instead of white eggs. They're the same inside. Use large eggs during spring and early summer; switch to mediums and pullets in the late summer. If the price difference between two sizes is less than 7¢, the larger-sized eggs are a better buy than the smaller ones.

Smart Milk Buys

To save money on milk, use reconstituted nonfat dry milk for cooking and drinking. If your family prefers a richer product for drinking, mix equal parts of fluid whole milk and reconstituted nonfat dry milk. You can also use evaporated milk in cooking. To substitute it for fluid milk, combine equal portions of the evaporated milk and water.

Save on Coatings, Sauces

Save on crumb coatings for chicken and fish and enjoy convenience too by making a mix based on flour and fine bread crumbs, and storing in a tightly covered container. Grating your own cheese saves almost half. Make salad dressings at home using low-cost dry seasonings. Make your own "granola" cereals with oats and dried fruits.

Combat Waste

You may be able to save almost as much by stopping waste as by comparison shopping. A study by the University of Arizona found families put 9-10 percent of their food money in the garbage. Over half was "straight" waste such as uncooked portions of meat,

Cutting Poultry

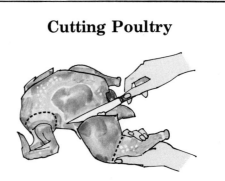

Cut skin between thigh and body. Pull leg away from body and cut between hip joint and body. Cut at knee joint. Pull wing away from body and cut at joint as shown by dots. Repeat for other leg and wing.

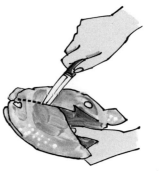

Place body of the bird, neck end down. Divide body by cutting along the breast end of the ribs to the neck as shown by dots. Repeat on other side. Cut through joints to separate breast and back.

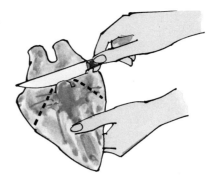

To divide breast into two pieces, use sharp paring knife to cut around bottom end of breastbone following curve of bones. For back, bend back in half to break at joint; cut to separate into two pieces.

unused bread and vegetables. The rest was remains of cooked dishes. New York State extension home economists think some of the big loss results from overestimating how much a family will eat at meals. Better to start with smaller portions, provide seconds if wanted.

Other ways to save: Cook vegetables in as little water as possible, but save any excess liquid in a jar in the refrigerator, as well as that from canned vegetables, for making soups. Cook potatoes in the skin instead of pared, to preserve food value and avoid waste. Save even small amounts of leftover vegetables. Store in the freezer; a week's accumulation will be right for soup. Also save small portions of meat and gravy poultry bones for soup or stews.

Food Stamps

As food prices have risen, more families have become eligible for food stamps. These often are moderate-income families, especially those with several children, who otherwise are self-supporting but whose income may lag behind price increases or who may encounter temporary difficulties such as a medical crisis or work cutback. Even though applications rose in the mid-1970s, more than half the families who could have the stamps still did not apply. On the other hand, controversial uses of stamps developed, in the case of college students.

The purpose of the stamps is to make sure that low- and moderate-income families are able to buy at least a nutritionally adequate diet. Eligibility is determined by income and number of people in the family. Also taken into account are taxes, special medical expenses and other unusual expenses as for child care. The families pay part of the cost of the stamps according to need.

One especially productive use of food stamps by some families has been to buy starter plants and seeds for home vegetable gardens. With an investment of $30-$40 in stamps, they have been able to produce several hundred dollars' worth of food. Government regulations do permit the use of the stamps for seeds and plants to grow food for home consumption.

You can find out if you're eligible, even in an emergency situation, by getting in touch with your local department of social services or welfare office.

What You Get From Canned, Frozen Vegetables

As an aid to comparing values, here are relative yields of some widely sold processed produce items (adapted from U.S.D.A. material):

	Can Size	No. Cups	Frozen Package	No. Cups
Asparagus, cut	14 oz.	1½	10 oz.	1¼
Beans, green or wax, cut	15½ oz.	1¾	9 oz.	1⅔
Beans, lima	16 oz.	1¾	10 oz.	1⅔
Beets, sliced, or whole	16 oz.	1¾	—	—
Broccoli, cut	—	—	10 oz.	1½
Carrots, diced or sliced	16 oz.	1¾	10 oz.	1⅔
Cauliflower	—	—	10 oz.	1½
Corn, whole kernel	16 oz.	1⅔	10 oz.	1½
Kale	15 oz.	1⅓	10 oz.	1⅛
Okra	15½ oz.	1¾	10 oz.	1¼
Peas	16 oz.	1¾	10 oz.	1⅔
Spinach	15 oz.	1⅓	10 oz.	1¼
Summer squash, sliced	—	—	10 oz.	1⅓
Tomatoes	16 oz.	1⅞	—	—

What Are You Paying for Protein?

Protein is the main nutrient responsible for building and maintaining tissues. It forms a part of enzymes and hormones that regulate body processes, and supplies energy.

Protein may be one of our most essential nutrients, but it is also the most expensive one we buy. Daily protein needs vary among individuals, but typically they range from 13 grams for an infant to 55 for a young man. As the table of comparative costs shows, various foods differ considerably in their protein value, from over 200 grams per pound to as few as 38.

Even among similar foods, such as fish, the protein yield may vary. Note, for example, the higher protein value of whole bluefish compared to flounder, and of turkey compared to broilers.

The prices in this list will vary in different areas and from time to time. Thus, the position of adjacent items may change, but not significantly over a period of a few months. You can easily figure out new costs as prices change simply by dividing the number of grams of protein per pound into the new price per pound.

The list reveals other nutritionally and financially useful facts. You can pay anywhere from 58¢ per 100 grams of protein in canned mackerel to $3.56 per 100 grams of protein in whole flounder, and (as this was written) as little as 96¢ for 100 grams of protein in turkey to as much as $3.78 for the same amount of protein in bacon.

Even for the same foods, protein costs can vary surprisingly, depending on the form in which you buy them. Note the difference in protein costs between lunch meats bought in chunks and those bought sliced, or whole broilers compared to parts.

It is not advisable to limit your meals to these foods. The most palatable and nutritionally safe way to hold down protein costs is to *combine* animal foods with plant foods that are high in protein. Because many Americans consume two to four times as much meat as the body can use, one way to save on your food budget is to lower your family's protein intake to the government's Recommended Daily Allowance of two servings. Also, because all excess protein eaten is stored as fat or burned as energy by the body, protein is a source of energy more cheaply provided by carbohydrates.

Although there is no established proof that eating less saturated fat will prevent premature cardiovascular disease, which kills 250,000 Americans yearly before age 65, many of the nation's heart specialists believe it might help. Cutting down on the total amount of meat consumed will also cut down on the amount of saturated fat.

Nonfat dry milk is another low-cost source of whole protein, useful not only for reconstituting and blending with fresh milk but also for extending the protein value of many cooked dishes. We haven't included whole milk itself on the list, but it, too, is a relatively cheap source of complete protein. A quart of whole milk at 40¢ has about 35 grams of protein, or a little over $1.14 per 100 grams.

Comparative Protein Costs*

	Typical Price Lb.	Grams Protein Per Lb.	Cost of 100 Grams Protein**
Soy granules	$1.02	216.0	$ .47
Canned mackerel	.61	87.5	.70
Dry split peas	.79	109.3	.72
Peanut butter	.98	114.3	.86
Beef liver	.79	90.3	.87
Eggs, dozen large	.76	73.2	1.04
Canned beans with pork	.29	27.7	1.05
Broilers	.67	57.4	1.17
Cottage cheese	.72	61.7	1.17
Tuna, canned, flakes	1.28	109.8	1.17
Hamburger	.97	81.2	1.19
Liverwurst, bulk	.89	73.5	1.21
Bologna, bulk	1.09	89.0	1.22
Perch fillets, frozen	1.07	87.5	1.22
Turkey (under 16 lbs.)	.84	65.9	1.27
Bluefish, whole	.61	47.7	1.29
Chicken breasts	.99	74.5	1.33
American cheese, loaf	1.40	105.2	1.33
Cod fillets, frozen	1.35	79.8	1.35
Beef chuck, with bone	.97	71.6	1.35
Chicken legs	.80	51.2	1.56
Ham, cured, with bone	1.22	68.3	1.79
Luncheon meat, canned	1.26	68.0	1.85
Liverwurst, sliced	1.38	73.5	1.88
Round steak, no bone	1.68	88.5	1.90
Bologna, sliced	1.29	65.4	1.97
Halibut steaks	1.89	94.8	1.99
Corned beef hash	.81	39.9	2.03
Frankfurters, all meat	1.25	59.4	2.10
Salami, sliced	1.69	79.4	2.13
Beef rump roast, boned	1.73	78.9	2.19
Boiled ham, sliced	2.39	103.5	2.30
Lamb, leg	1.73	67.6	2.56
Sirloin steak	1.87	71.7	2.61
Lamb, shoulder chops	2.00	58.9	3.40
Flounder, whole	.89	25.0	3.56
Bacon, sliced	1.88	38.1	4.93

* of one pound of food as purchased, including any waste, as in the case of whole fish and chicken.

** 100 grams is a convenient way to show relative costs of protein in unlike foods but is not a standard serving of protein. Nutritionists use 20 grams and recommend two servings per day. Thus the 216 grams of protein in a pound of soy granules will provide 10 servings while the 38.1 grams in the bacon will yield not quite 2.

Meat: The Biggest Slice of Your Food Dollar

Meat is the food item to watch most closely. Meat, poultry, and fish together take about 35¢ of your family's food dollar.

As a result, more and more people are looking for protein sources that are less costly but still nutritious and tasty. This chapter contains a comprehensive list of comparative protein values in various meats and alternatives. Some of the relative costs of protein may surprise you.

The present top grades of meat, called U.S. Prime and Choice, put a premium on the amount of fat streaks called marbling. The fat makes the meat juicy and seemingly more tender, especially when it's cooked rare.

But more marbling means additional feeding of cattle, and this extra feeding starts a chain of events which much of the public no longer wants or can afford. For one thing, the additional feed used to fatten cattle has at times intensified grain shortages; this in turn raises the price of beef. Moreover, while this costlier fat beef may be juicier, it's also higher in calories and cholesterol.

Ironically, the cheaper "Good" grade beef, because it has less fat per pound or given weight, has more protein, iron, and B vitamins than "Choice" grade.

About 60 percent of beef sold at retail today is Choice grade. In many stores you may not be able to find Good or Standard grade beef at all. Some stores sell the lower grades under such names as "Budget" or "Economy" beef. In a few areas where stores are required by law to show the official grades, beef is available (in some stores) under the Good or Standard names. But even if the lower grades cost just a little less, they still represent better value for many cooking purposes.

Smart shoppers know that the best ways to save money on meat are to plan your purchases carefully so you can use everything you buy, take advantage of meat bargains, and use recipes that make meat go farther.

Other shopping tactics that can help you manage your meat money:

Chicken vs. Hamburger

To determine the best value in these two major staples, here's a rule of thumb: figure that a pound of broilers is the equivalent of three-quarters of a pound of hamburger in yield (3 servings). If chicken is 55¢ a pound, hamburger at 75¢ a pound would be an equally good value, since each has a cost-per-serving of 18.5¢.

Hamburger-Lean Meat Ratio

Since lean, chopped beef may have only 18 to 22 percent added fat, it would be worth about 14 percent more than ordinary hamburger, which may contain 30 percent fat. Often it sells for as much as 20 percent more. Thus, ordinary hamburger, despite its higher fat content, usually is the better value.

The Sum of the Parts

Supermarket managers are frequently amazed that people will pay 10¢ a pound more for quartered chickens, or buy three-legged or two-breasted packages, when they could buy two whole chickens at the same price. Similarly, a package of chicken cutlets can cost $1 more a pound than a whole chicken that you cut and bone yourself. A loin roast may cost $1.09 a pound, but loin chops will run $1.69.

If a broiler is 52 percent meat, figure that legs and thighs are 53 to 55 percent meat; breasts, 63 percent; backs, 42. If the whole bird is 55 cents a pound, drumsticks are worth about 68 cents a pound; thighs, 73; breast halves, 78. Most markets charge more than this.

You also get more for your money buying a whole ham, instead of parts. You can still have it cut into parts at the store if you want. When buying half a ham, make sure you get the full half, not just an end which has had some of the center slices removed. Keep in mind that the butt is more economical than the shank but is more difficult to carve.

Take a Turkey to Dinner

If turkey costs up to 5¢ a pound more than chicken, it is probably a better value because of its higher yield of edible meat. You do even better by buying a larger turkey to be used later or shared. Turkeys that weigh over 16 pounds often cost 10¢ to 15¢ less and yield an average of 55 percent roasted meat compared to 50 percent for small-sized turkeys.

You pay more for a self-basting turkey. Since the oil solution often is 3 percent of the weight, you pay a turkey price for vegetable oil and water along with the extra price for the self-basting turkey.

Comparative Costs of Lean Meat

Since it is not the price per pound of meat but the cost of the lean that is important, note in the table (below) that you can pay anywhere from 21¢ to $1.28 for three ounces of lean. These prices will change from time to time, and may even be affected by store "specials", but as they change you can use this table of percentages to update the true costs of three ounces of lean meat.

Note that the *lower* the percentage figure, the *less* meat you need for three ounces of lean. Thus, you need only 25 percent of a pound of veal cutlets, but 35 percent of a pound of whole ham; 48 percent of a pound of broiler, but only 40 percent turkey.

Type of Meat	Price Per Pound	% of Pound Needed for 3 Ounces of Cooked Lean*	Cost of 3 Ounces of Lean
Beef liver	$ .79	27%	$ .21
Hamburger	.97	26	.25
Perch fillet, frozen	1.07	29	.31
Broilers	.67	48	.32
Turkey	.84	40	.34
Chicken breasts	.99	35	.35
Ham, whole	1.22	35	.43
Haddock fillet, frozen	1.52	29	.44
Beef chuck, bone in	.97	45	.44
Pork picnic	1.09	46	.50
Round steak	1.68	34	.57
Rump roast of beef, boned	1.73	34	.59
Pork loin roast	1.39	50	.70
Sirloin steak	1.87	43	.80
Rib roast of beef	1.89	45	.85
Pork chops, center	1.99	45	.90
Veal cutlets	3.89	25	.97
Lamb chops, loin	2.79	46	1.28

* Percentages derived from U.S. Department of Agriculture data; prices will vary in different areas and at different times.

The ABC's of Meat Extenders

Families seeking to stretch expensive meat in times of high prices should know that while all the usual meat extenders, or substitutes, do not contain the same amounts of protein, they do make contributions to the diet.

How They Contribute

Nutritional scientists rate protein according to the quality and quantity of essential amino acids present. In layman's language this translates into complete protein from animal sources—eggs, milk, meat, and fish—and incomplete protein from vegetable sources—dry beans, nuts, and cereals. What is often lost in the translation is the very important fact that food proteins complement each other. For example, a peanut butter sandwich with a glass of milk provides a protein-rich meal. The amino acids missing from the peanut butter and bread are picked up in the milk.

You can take advantage of this complementary action by using the right substitute to make meat go farther. Textured soy protein, rice, oatmeal, and other cereals not only extend the volume of a meat loaf, but make protein contributions as well. Adding an egg, dry milk powder, or wheat germ gives the protein content another boost.

Since the complementary action applies to vitamins and minerals too, it's easy to see why nutritionists are so keen on a mixed diet with meals planned around a wide variety of foods. The good news—in budget terms—is that not all protein has to come from the meat in the entree.

Among the most useful grain, legume, and nut products for combination with meat and other expensive protein foods are soybean products, wheat germ, white beans, lima beans, mung beans, peas, lentils, chick peas, and ground nuts, including their processed products, such as peanut butter. These foods are not only high in protein, but the body utilizes their protein efficiently.

Oatmeal, while it has less protein than the foods listed above, still is fairly high in protein. Thus, oatmeal is a nutritious as well as inexpensive extender. Pasta products—noodles, macaroni, and spaghetti—also are medium-high in protein.

Rice—even brown rice—is relatively low in protein. Parboiled or converted rice is a little richer in protein and other nutrients than is common polished rice. Barley has more protein than rice, but not as much as beans and other legumes.

You can easily see what is best to use in combination with expensive meat: Nonfat dry milk powder, eggs, textured soy protein, and wheat germ, because they are rich in high-quality protein and are easy to mix into meat loaf and patties. They also can be used for fish and poultry coatings and to add to gravies, soups, and other dishes.

Soy protein has all the essential amino acids but not in the right amounts. Combining soy protein with other foods—such as eggs, milk, sesame seeds, and brazil nuts—will balance its deficiencies.

Grain products, too, are low in some amino acids that happen to be available in cheese. Thus, cheese is especially useful for combining with grain products.

Often, two varieties of plant foods can supplement the missing, or low, amino acids in each other. Some of the traditional non-meat dishes of various nationalities achieve such balance; for example, the Italian *pasta fagioli* (beans with spaghetti), and the Spanish rice and beans. Various types of beans and ground nuts, which may lack only one or two essential amino acids, can be balanced with grain products as in pasta fagioli, tacos, non-meat chili dishes, corn tortillas and beans, rice and split peas, rice and vegetable curry, and so on. Even the traditional Boston baked beans with nut bread becomes a whole protein dish.

Soy Products

Since soy products have become widely used as an extender for small portions of meat, or as an alternative to meat, it is worth knowing the difference between various soy products on the market. You can pay as little as 65¢ a pound and as much as $2 for similar soy products of 50-percent protein value. The lower-price products usually are plain soy derivative; the higher-priced ones are called "meat supplements". The latter often merely have additional spices and caramel coloring, and are packaged in meal-size pouches for pseudo-convenience.

In comparing costs, note that soy granules and soy powder may be less expensive than soy protein, but the granules are only 50 percent protein and the flour may be 35 or 50 percent, depending on the kind. *"Soy protein" is 90 percent protein*. Ordinary dry soybeans are harder to find in many stores but often are available in health food stores, although at relatively high prices. They have 1½ times as much protein as other dry beans but also have eleven times as much fat. Soy grits are like soy flour but more coarsely ground. Soybean curd sold in some stores is much lower in protein value than other soy products—only 8 percent.

In recent years, as meat prices have boomed, supermarkets themselves have blended hamburger with textured soy protein and sold it under various names, such as "patty burger", "superburger", but most often as "soyburger". Store-mixed soyburger should cost significantly less than all-meat hamburger. Many stores sell hamburger mixed with 25 percent soy protein for 15¢ to 20¢ a pound less than hamburger itself; for example, 69¢ a pound compared to 85¢ to 98¢ for hamburger. But some stores have sold the mixture for only 10¢ less than the price of all-meat hamburger thus keeping for themselves a disproportionate amount of the saving.

What about the food value? The hamburger-soy mixtures contain approximately the same nourishment as all-meat hamburger. A recent test by the Hyde Park Co-op in Chicago found that a mixture of 70 percent hamburger and 30 percent soybean derivative had a protein level of 17 percent compared to 18.5 percent for an all-meat hamburger.

As with other extenders—including oatmeal and bread crumbs—the hamburger-soy mix also tends to be juicier, since the extenders help retain the meat juices (in a meat loaf, for example).

Food manufacturers have also developed their technology to the point where soybean derivatives, synthetic flavorings, coloring and vitamins are combined to make what tastes and looks like beef stroganoff, chicken à la king, bacon, and other meat-like foods. Foods that resemble other foods in appearance, taste and texture are called *analogs*. Some people call them imitation, or fabricated foods, but the word "analogs" does not downgrade them. They can be worthwhile replacements for meat.

Most of the analogs now arriving on the market are vegetable-protein substitutes for meat—most often soy protein. However, many of these fabricated foods are still relatively expensive. Some of the highest prices asked are for bacon-like garnishes, which actually cost over $3.50 a pound when one calculates the true price of the small jars.

In general, the most economical way to use soy products and other extenders is to purchase the basic soy derivatives, such as plain soy granules or soy flour, and blend them with other basic foods, such as ground meats, omelets, soups and non-meat dishes. Soy flour can be substituted for a portion of the basic flour in bread recipes to raise the protein in the loaves—but too much imparts a soy flavor that will overpower the taste of the grain products in the mixture.

Meat pinch hitters

Trim your food budget by serving meatless meals once or twice a week. Eggs and cheese are excellent sources of protein. In fact, either can stand on its own to provide many of the nutrients found in meats—at less cost. You can plan nutritious, satisfying main dishes using as little as ½ cup cheese or 2 eggs *per serving*. A puffy omelet, poached eggs with cheese sauce, and the old favorite grilled cheese sandwich are all delicious and nutritious entrees. Look through your favorite cook book for sandwiches, main dish salads, soups, and other main dish recipes using eggs and cheese.

You can also occasionally substitute dry beans, split peas, and lentils for meat. Not only are these vegetables economical sources of protein but they also give your menus tasty variety.

How to Find the Best Produce

According to recent reports by the U.S. Marketing Research Service, Americans have been eating more vegetables in recent years. One reason is the effort to stretch costly meats by combining them with larger amounts of vegetables.

Fresh produce is usually cheapest in season, especially when it is grown nearby (see chart opposite). Out of season, canned produce items are cheaper than frozen.

Fancier versions of the same items may raise prices inordinately. Thus, you may find that when a 10-ounce package of frozen broccoli spears sells for 35¢, you may pay 46¢ for the spears in a butter sauce, and 57¢ for the spears in hollandaise sauce.

Buy by Weight

Some produce, such as cabbage, is sold by the pound, while some, like lettuce, is sold by the unit, or piece. You need sharp eyes, and preferably scales, when you buy produce by the piece. We have found, for example, that you get anywhere from 14 to 44 ounces of lettuce at the same 49¢, or 59¢ for a cantaloupe that yields a low of 30 ounces to a high of 40 ounces—a difference of 33 percent.

One city, Chicago, requires that all fruits and vegetables prepackaged by the retailer must be marked with the price per pound, net weight, and total selling price. This is the fairest way to sell produce in order to assure each consumer equal value. Otherwise, an early shopper may be able to pick out a three-pound head of cauliflower for 89¢, while a late shopper may pay the same price for a 1½-pound head.

Several other states and areas also sell most produce by weight, either by law or custom—Los Angeles County, some sections of Colorado, and Wisconsin.

Pick Your Own

High farm costs have spurred more farmers to open up their vegetable fields and fruit orchards to the public to fill plastic bags with produce at reduced prices. It's not necessarily easy work but it saves; in fact, it can save as much as half the retail prices. Some families now follow the seasons—picking cherries at nearby farmers' in July, and pears and apples in August and September. In some parts of Michigan, you can even rent an apple tree of your own, as well as go into the fields in season to pick vegetables. And some orange grove owners in Florida will now rent out orange trees.

Some regional pick-it-yourself programs are now coordinated by state agriculture departments. You can find out which farmers in your area permit picking-your-own by calling the County Extension Service at your county seat. Pick-your-own farms also advertise occasionally in local papers or on radio. In any event, you can spend as much time as necessary and pick as much as you want. Picking seasons usually begin in early summer with such crops as asparagus, broccoli, cabbage, cantaloupes, corn, green beans, lettuce, and many others. Before making the trip to a pick-it-yourself farm, however, call ahead to make sure the crop hasn't been completely harvested, or isn't late reaching maturity.

Farm Markets

In some cities, farm markets are also attracting more consumers in the search for ways to restrain high food costs. Such large farm markets usually provide space for a number of nearby farmers and distributors to sell their own produce, poultry and eggs directly to consumers, usually in relatively large quantities. Savings over store prices may range from 10 to 50 percent. Experienced shoppers recommend selective shopping and making qualitative comparisons among the different stands and against regular supermarket prices, because not all farm market items are actually cheaper.

Wholesale Markets

An increasing number of families now band together and dispatch several of their members once a week or so to the so-called terminal produce markets to buy wholesale, or at least near-wholesale. You can usually find wholesale firms who will sell directly to consumers by looking in the Yellow Pages under "Produce" or "Produce Dealers." If you can't find a local wholesale or terminal market, you can get a list of the government's "Terminal Market Inspection Offices" by writing to the Fresh Products Standardization and Inspection Branch, Fruit and Vegetable Division, U.S. Department of Agriculture, D.C. 20250.

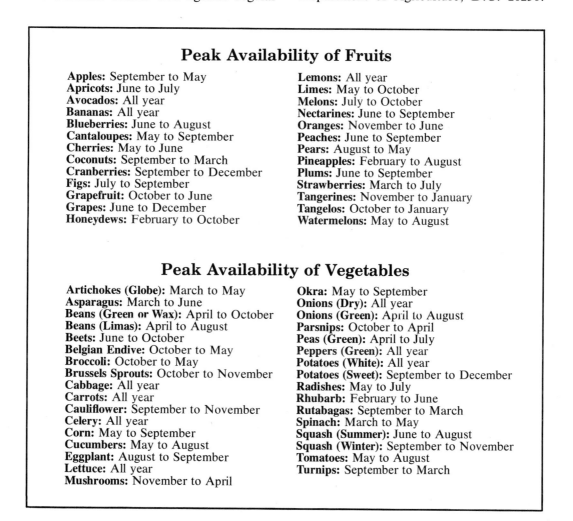

Peak Availability of Fruits

Apples: September to May
Apricots: June to July
Avocados: All year
Bananas: All year
Blueberries: June to August
Cantaloupes: May to September
Cherries: May to June
Coconuts: September to March
Cranberries: September to December
Figs: July to September
Grapefruit: October to June
Grapes: June to December
Honeydews: February to October

Lemons: All year
Limes: May to October
Melons: July to October
Nectarines: June to September
Oranges: November to June
Peaches: June to September
Pears: August to May
Pineapples: February to August
Plums: June to September
Strawberries: March to July
Tangerines: November to January
Tangelos: October to January
Watermelons: May to August

Peak Availability of Vegetables

Artichokes (Globe): March to May
Asparagus: March to June
Beans (Green or Wax): April to October
Beans (Limas): April to August
Beets: June to October
Belgian Endive: October to May
Broccoli: October to May
Brussels Sprouts: October to November
Cabbage: All year
Carrots: All year
Cauliflower: September to November
Celery: All year
Corn: May to September
Cucumbers: May to August
Eggplant: August to September
Lettuce: All year
Mushrooms: November to April

Okra: May to September
Onions (Dry): All year
Onions (Green): April to August
Parsnips: October to April
Peas (Green): April to July
Peppers (Green): All year
Potatoes (White): All year
Potatoes (Sweet): September to December
Radishes: May to July
Rhubarb: February to June
Rutabagas: September to March
Spinach: March to May
Squash (Summer): June to August
Squash (Winter): September to November
Tomatoes: May to August
Turnips: September to March

Are You Buying Cheese or Water?

As meat has become more expensive, so has cheese. In fact, the increase in the cost has been even higher than for meats, and much more than for the milk.

The reason, of course, is increased demand. Not only has cheese gained recognition as a concentrated high-protein food useful for supplementing the nutritive value of various non-meat recipes, it has also become a popular snack food. Moreover, cheese has been increasingly manufactured into blended and highly processed types (with added water) for greater spreadability.

As the table shows, different cheeses may have anywhere from 32 to 60 percent water, which the labels often euphemistically call "moisture." As the table also indicates, you get the most protein for your money in bulk standard cheeses—such as American, cheddar, and domestic Swiss—and not in packaged processed cheeses.

Cottage cheese, even with its high moisture, however, is the best value in terms of protein. Cottage cheese protein costs about one-third that of cream cheese.

In shopping cheese, watch for differences in product names such as "pasteurized process cheese," "cheese food," "cheese spread," and "imitation process cheese spread." While the basic cheddar and Swiss cheese from which these processed varieties are made cannot, by definition, contain more than 39 to 41 percent water respectively, cheese "food" may have almost 59 percent. "Imitation cheese spread" even more.

Many of the cheese "spreads" that come in small jars have 52 percent to 60 percent "moisture," with correspondingly reduced protein value, despite their high true costs of $1.66 to $1.76 a pound.

Spreads labeled "imitation" have high water content too—often 62 percent. But at low prices of under $1 a pound, they still may represent good protein value because of their low butterfat (only 5 percent) and their high proportion of nonfat milk.

Protein Costs of Various Cheeses

	Price Per Lb.	Maximum Moisture	Gms. Protein Per Lb.	Cost of 100 Gms. Protein
Cottage cheese	.59	80%	61.7 gms.	.95
Neufchatel, plain	.98	65	42.6	$2.30
Flavored, 4 oz. jar	$1.18	65	42.6	$2.77
Cream cheese, natural	.98	55	36.3	$2.70
Whipped	$1.26	55	36.3	$3.47
Process "spread" American, loaf	.84	46-50	*	*
5 oz. jar	$1.76	50	*	*
4¾ oz. spray can	$1.66	55	*	*
American, bulk	$1.30	43	105.02	$1.24
Wrapped slices	$1.38	43	105.2	$1.31
Cheddar, natural, mild	$1.49	39	113.4	$1.31
"Food," wedge	$1.45	44	89.8	$1.61
Spread, container	$1.92	52	*	*
Swiss, domestic, bulk	$1.69	41	124.7	$1.35
Wrapped slices	$1.93	41	124.7	$1.54
Parmesan, grated	$2.59	32	163.3	$1.59

*not available

**100 grams is a convenient measure for comparing protein in different cheeses, but is not necessarily a serving.

How to Spot the Better Buys in Heat-and-Serve Foods

The proliferation of canned and frozen foods has created a shopping puzzle for consumers. In many cases processors have taken traditional, basic processed foods such as canned beans or parboiled rice, added some minor ingredients or flavorings, but raised prices disproportionately. For example, you can pay as little as 6 cents for the protein in a five-ounce serving of ordinary canned beans, but twice as much for the equivalent protein in such versions as "barbecue beans" and "beans and franks."

If you need to use such convenience foods, and sometimes such uses are helpful, the money-saving trick is to buy the simplest version and add the additional ingredients.

In almost all cases, canned heat-and-serve foods are less expensive than frozen. Of the frozen foods, the best values usually are orange juice concentrate and peas. These are cheaper than their fresh counterparts and often even cost less than the canned versions.

Other frozen convenience foods that may cost slightly more than home prepared versions but may serve a time-saving purpose are pot pies, and frozen or refrigerated biscuit, yeast roll, pancake, and cookie doughs.

The other most-widely bought frozen convenience foods include pot pies, heat-and-serve dinners, macaroni and cheese, and french fries.

Frozen pot pies are not as high in protein and other nutrients as home prepared versions based on standard recipes. But because they often are used by stores as a sale feature they represent relatively good value in the frozen convenience group. Although more of a snack food than a full meal, the pot pies provide about 70% of the amount of food at about 50% of the price of heat-and-serve dinners.

The relative value of heat-and-serve dinners often depends on the type. Exotic versions such as "Polynesian" dinners often cost twice as much as the standard meat loaf and poultry dinners.

The widely sold frozen macaroni and cheese dinners are as good value, usually, as the dried versions but both these cost more than the even more-convenient canned macaroni and cheese.

The popular frozen french fries must be considered only a convenience or labor saver since their cost is approximately twice that of home-prepared french fries. The frozen french fries are, however, least costly of the frozen and other ready-to-eat potato products such as potato puffs, sticks, chips, etc.

Here are money-saving tips on three widely used "heat-and-serve" products.

Soups

All through this chapter, you'll observe that prices of various foods may have little relation to their nutritional value. This is true, too, of canned soups, a mainstay of moderate-income families. We found that some lower-price soups have relatively little nutrition while some costlier ones are relatively cheap for the nutrients provided.

Canned soups do not, of course, provide as much nutrition at low cost as do home-made soups prepared from your own stock utilizing liquids from vegetables and leftover vegetables, meats, etc. But of all "heat and serve" foods, canned soups are most reasonable for the nutrients provided.

We based our comparison on the analysis of one leading brand. But other brands can be assumed to have similar values.

Some soups are good buys in protein, providing in one cupful as much as a third or more of the nutritionally-desirable twenty grams of protein for a meal. The best nutritional buy we found is Split Pea with Ham. It provides protein at a cost per 100 grams of 93 cents, and is high in other nutrients.

Others of the popular soups in order of increasing cost of the protein are: Chicken Broth ($1.40 per 100 grams); Green Pea ($1.08); Beef ($1.40); Bean with Bacon ($1.40); Pepper Pot ($1.84); Vegetable Beef ($2.03); Scotch Broth ($2.53); Chicken Noodle ($2.58); Minestrone ($2.63); Beef Broth ($2.82); Chicken Vegetable ($2.86); Chicken with Rice ($2.88); Beef Noodle ($3); Turkey Vegetable ($3.46); Vegetarian ($4.20); Cream of Mushroom ($4.38); Cream of Celery ($6); Clam Chowder—Manhattan Style ($6).

Protein is not, of course, the only nutrient in canned soups. But the costlier nutrients often associated with protein such as B vitamins and iron often will have the same relative values in different types of soups.

Revealingly, some of the "cream" soups, while priced low, really are expensive for the nutrients provided although they are useful for casseroles. The value of any cream-style or other low-protein soup can be increased inexpensively by adding nonfat milk powder.

Condensed soups are a better value than soups which already have water added.

Pasta Products

Fancier versions of these popular canned products are noticeably more costly. For example, you pay more for spaghetti in the shape of an "O"; thus, ordinary "spaghetti with meatballs" offers more protein at a lower cost than "spaghetti O's with meatballs". Either gives you more protein for the money than "spaghetti O's with sliced franks". In general, you get most protein for your money in ordinary canned spaghetti and cheese, followed (in order of increasing cost) by macaroni and cheese; macaroni (or spaghetti) and beef; Italian-style spaghetti; and spaghetti with meatballs.

Bean Products

Ordinary pork and beans are the best buy, followed (in order of increasing cost of the protein) by Barbecue Beans, Beef and Beans, Beans and Franks, and Chili with Beans. As an example of the saving to be realized by mixing your own ingredients, you will pay less by buying the frankfurters and beans separately than you will for the same ingredients pre-mixed in a can.

How to make yogurt

If you enjoy the flavor, you can prepare yogurt at home that is just as delicious, nutritious, and far less expensive than the commercial product. Use fresh pasteurized homogenized whole or low-fat milk or powdered milk. Make nonfat yogurt with 1½ times the amount of milk solids recommended on the package for reconstituting nonfat dry milk (using warm water to speed up the process.)

The first time, use commercial yogurt as a starter—¼ cup starter to 1 quart milk. Mix up subsequent batches with some of the previous batch as your starter, but once a month better use commercial yogurt again, because contamination of the home culture is almost inevitable. Break up the starter with a fork, mixing in a little of the milk. Pour the rest of the milk into a clean glass or ceramic mixing bowl and, using a fork or wire whip, thoroughly beat in the starter to get a smooth consistency.

Before you incubate the mixture for fermentation attach a cooking thermometer to the side of the bowl, being sure the bulb doesn't touch its sides or bottom. Place the mixture in the oven and heat slowly to 100°. Checking the thermometer, maintain the temperature between 90° and 105° by reheating the oven briefly until the mixture turns the consistency of junket—about three hours. (Some oven pilots maintain the correct temperature range.) Chill immediately.

Yogurt can be stored two or three weeks, covered, in the refrigerator, but it gradually becomes thin. You may prefer to make a fresh batch once or twice a week.

If the culture didn't thicken, the incubation temperature was so high the bacteria were killed, so low they couldn't grow, or the starter may have been old. If yogurt made from nonfat dry milk does not taste right, you might try heating it (reconstituted) to 180°, then cooling it to 110° before adding the starter. Once you have perfected making plain yogurt, try adding your favorite fruits. Gently stir slightly sweetened crushed fresh or frozen fruit into the yogurt.

The Cost of Your Daily Bread

Because of worldwide demand for grains and big exports which triggered large price increases on flour, bread has become a real cost problem. The price jumped a startling 30 percent just from 1973 to 1976.

The Problem

A family of four or five might very well spend $5 or $6 a week nowadays just for bread, which is a significant portion of the $50 or $60 a week such a family typically spent for food in 1976. You can't tell the amount you get by the size of the loaf. Some loaves are what are called "balloon" bread, meaning that they are baked in a larger pan so the loaf is lighter and softer. You can squeeze such a loaf to a fraction of its size.

Too, the many sizes, varieties, and brands on the shelves make buying without comparing weights and prices hazardous to financial health. The form in which you buy bread also affects its price drastically.

Money-Saving Findings

In a 1976 survey in one locality, it was found that you could pay anywhere from 37 cents to $1.01 for a pound of bread, with the cheapest a store's own brand in a large size, and the highest, various types of rolls.
• The healthier the name, the higher the price. For example, breads called "natural" may cost more than other whole-grain breads. Dict or "slender" breads cost more but may be only sliced thinner. Similarly, you may pay 5 to 20 cents more a pound for special breads with such nourishing nomenclature as "egg" bread, "buttermilk" bread, "cheese" bread, "potato" bread, and "butter" bread. But you may not get much more than if you bought standard white bread. A baker can put as little egg as he wants into "egg" bread.
• The best money value actually is the standard enriched white loaf. The nutritional advantages of whole wheat bread, at least most commercially-baked loaves, are some-what exaggerated and may not be worth the extra cost, personal preferences aside. Most recipes for whole-wheat bread actually use white flour along with the whole wheat since whole wheat by itself doesn't have enough gluten to make a light-textured loaf.

Thus, the nutritional differences between the enriched white loaf and the standard whole-wheat loaf are smaller than many people believe. The white has, for example, 2 grams of protein and 19 milligrams of calcium per slice; the whole wheat, 2.5 and 23. Thanks to enrichment, iron and B vitamin values are about the same.
• The more specialized the item, the larger, usually, the saving on house brands. Thus, the difference may be 8 cents a pound for standard white bread, but 23 cents a pound for brown 'n' serve rolls.
• Try to buy immediate and even near-future bread needs at sales. In times of inflation, stores often use such items as bread which have gone up sharply, for specials.
• You know, of course, about the day-old bread and cake bargains, and savings-minded consumers always check that table at the supermarket. But even more variety and larger quantities are available at thrift outlets maintained by larger bakers in most sizable towns. Check the yellow pages for bakery addresses; phone the bakery for address of its nearest outlet. You'll save on cakes and often on cookies, but the main feature is bread. Large families who have to hold down expenses often buy a week's supply and put it in the freezer. Savings often are 25 to 50 percent. The bread usually is no more than 48 hours old.
• Read the label for a statement of the amount of milk solids in a loaf of white bread. A relatively high percentage, such as 4 percent or even 6, is desirable. The added milk not only improves the calcium content of the bread but the wheat protein in combination with milk provides a higher quality of protein. Also look for the word "enriched" on the label—this indicates the bread has iron and B vitamins added.

Bread Made Easily

If one had to choose a symbol of what this book is all about, it would have to be a loaf of homemade bread. Although you save only a modest amount each time you bake instead of buy, you are dealing directly with soaring prices with your own two flour-covered hands. Home baking adds up to real savings in the course of a year, as the heads of big bread-eating families will attest. At the same time you are raising your standard of living, because homemade bread is so much more delicious than commercial bread. The two are hardly comparable in the realm of food. Baking bread at home is a national trend, touchstone of the back-to-basics way of life many Americans seek.

The Better the Ingredients...

Once you make the decision to bake bread there's no point in trying to save money on ingredients. The best are priced only slightly higher than the inferior. Enriched all-purpose white flour, the main ingredient of most yeast breads (like the recipes that follow), gives your family proper day-in-day-out nutrition; it is the equal of whole wheat flour in nutritive value.

Easier Than You Think

There's nothing precise or finicky about baking bread—no tricks, no mystique. Just follow the recipe. It's really quite simple, and there's a wide margin for error. Although it takes a certain span of time to bake bread, during much of it the yeast is doing the work. Once you've mixed the batter and set it to rise, all subsequent steps can be sandwiched in among other chores.

You can even start bread one day and finish it the next. Place the batter in the refrigerator before the first rising. The cold holds the yeast in suspended animation. Next morning let the mass return to room temperature, set it to rise, and continue on.

Batter can be mixed in any bowl, of course, but bread dough seems to rise best in a big bowl that has been warmed ahead of time. It should be covered with a dish towel to protect the dough from drafts.

Whether you put it to rise in the pilot-light-warmed oven or over a pilot light atop a gas range, on a shelf in the unheated oven of an electric range above a large pan of warm water, or in a warm room, the temperature of the dough is crucial. Too much heat can make the yeast so hyperactive it actually kills itself; too little heat can suppress the rising. If you want to avoid guesswork, insert a cooking thermometer into the dough so you can take a peek at it once or twice during rising—being especially careful to avoid a draft. The thermometer should register between 80° and 85°.

Let dough rise until it is double in bulk. It is ready when you can lightly press two fingertips quickly ½″ into the dough and the indentations remain.

The Need for Kneading

A big batch of dough, enough for four loaves, is a challenge to knead, as you fold it, flatten it with the heels of the palms, give it a quick quarter-turn and fold it again, repeating the process over and over. The lightly floured kneading surface (preferably a long, wide board kept just for this purpose), your floured hands, and the dough itself all stay dry as long as you keep the dough in motion—usually.

If you roll it out on the board, begin working it and find the dough's too sticky, don't panic. Toss it back in the bowl, wash and dry your hands, scrape off whatever adheres to the kneading surface using a table knife and a dry cloth or paper towel. Lightly reflour the kneading surface as well as your hands (or oil them if you're kneading dough for dark bread). Then work a little more flour into the dough until you reach a consistency you can just handle without its sticking. Now, *keep the mass moving* as you

knead. But go easy on the added flour or you'll make your dough too heavy and your bread will be crumbly—if not crummy.

Into the Oven

You can bake in many sorts of containers— even tin cans will do, or flowerpots. Heavy-gauge steel pans are traditional, but many home bakers prefer Pyrex baking pans, which enable them to check the color of the entire loaf while it's baking (reduce oven temperature 25° below what the recipe specifies if you bake in glass). Try to avoid baking on a damp or humid day unless the heat is on in your kitchen. High humidity seems to inhibit the action of yeast.

Test to see when bread is done by drawing out the oven shelf and knocking on top of a loaf with your knuckles. If you get a resounding thump your bread is ready to come out. Turn it onto racks to cool—and chain a guard dog to a leg of the kitchen table to keep the family away!

Freeze with Ease

People who bake oftener than once a week save time by freezing bread dough (if the freezer maintains zero temperature or colder). Freeze dough just before the final rising. Wrap it air-tight and use it within a month or two. Thaw slowly in the refrigerator overnight. Bring to room temperature, knead, set to rise, and bake.

Fresh-baked bread can be frozen as soon as it's cool. Store loaves tightly sealed in moisture-proof wrap for as long as three months in the freezer if it maintains 0°. Defrost right in the freezer wrap at room temperature to keep the bread from drying out, then place it in a 400° oven for a dozen minutes to bring back that fresh-baked flavor and aroma. Or if you're in a hurry, wrap a frozen loaf in foil, puncture the top of the foil several times with a carving fork to let the steam out, and bake at 400° for about 20 minutes.

The recipes that follow have been tested (at sea level). The baking times are correct. If your oven is reasonably accurate, the bread you bake will astound and delight you and your family.

Care in measurement

When preparing a bread batter (it is not technically called "dough" until it's ready to knead), spoon the flour into the measuring cup and level it with the back of a knife without shaking it down. This is the way to measure all flours and meals (a "meal" is a coarser grind of flour).

White Bread

5¾ to 6¼ cups all-purpose flour
1 packet active dry yeast
2¼ cups milk*
2 tablespoons sugar
1 tablespoon corn oil margarine
2 tablespoons salt

Combine in big mixer bowl *just* 2 cups *only* of flour and the yeast.

In separate saucepan heat together milk, margarine, and salt until barely warm (115°-120°), stirring as the margarine melts. Add to flour mixture in big mixer bowl. Beat with mixer on low speed for ½ minute, scraping sides of bowl with a rubber spatula. Beat 3 minutes at high speed.

Stir in by hand enough of the balance of flour to make a fairly stiff batter. Turn onto a lightly floured bread board (or any freshly scrubbed smooth surface) and knead until pliable and silky (10 or 12 minutes). Make into a ball.

Place in a pre-warmed, lightly greased bowl and turn dough over to grease the top surface. Cover with a damp cloth and set in a warm (80°-85°), draft-free place to rise until double in bulk (about 1¼ hours).

Punch down the dough and turn onto a lightly floured surface. Divide the punched-down dough into equal parts.

Shape each part into a round ball, cover and let rest 10 minutes. Roll out or press with hands to flatten and roll up into loaves, carefully pinching the seams and tucking

*If you regularly bake white bread in quantity, you can lower the cost per loaf by substituting reconstituted dry milk powder.

A gift of bread

Men have taken to bread baking at home, finding in it a release from pent-up tension while producing a product that garners praise from all. It feels great to be told, "That loaf of bread you gave us was terrific!" Fresh homemade bread is one of the time-honored neighborly gifts. In some places the new family moving in is presented with a loaf of just-baked bread as a sign of welcome.

---

under the ends. Place in two greased 8½"x 4½"x2½" bread pans. Cover and let rise in a warm place until doubled (45 minutes to an hour). Preheat oven 10 minutes to 375°.

Bake until golden brown, about 45 minutes. Test for doneness by rapping on the crust with the knuckles for a hollow sound. If the crusts seem to be browning too fast, cover loosely with foil for the last quarter-hour of baking. Remove from pans onto wire racks to cool.

Recipe makes two loaves, each of them 20 ounces.

Whole Wheat Bread

4 to 4½ cups whole wheat flour
2 packets active dry yeast
1¾ cups milk
⅓ cup packed brown sugar
2 tablespoons corn oil margarine
2 tablespoons salt

In big mixer bowl, combine *only* 2 cups of the flour with the yeast.

In a separate saucepan, heat together milk, brown sugar, margarine, and salt until warm (115°-120°), stirring down the melting margarine. Add to dry ingredients in big mixer bowl.

Beat with electric mixer set at low speed for ½ minute, scraping side of bowl with rubber spatula. Beat 3 minutes with mixer on high speed.

Stir in by hand (preferably with a wooden spoon) enough of the rest of the flour to make a fairly stiff batter.

Turn onto lightly floured surface and knead until pliable but elastic (5 or 6 minutes). Shape into a ball and place in pre-warmed lightly greased bowl; rotate dough once to grease both top and bottom. Cover with damp cloth and let rise in a warm (80°-85°) place until doubled (one hour or more).

Punch down dough and turn onto a lightly floured bread board. Cover and let rest approximately 10 minutes.

Make into a loaf. Place in greased 8½" x4½"x2½" bread pan. Cover and let rise in a warm place until doubled (30 minutes or more). Preheat oven 10 minutes to 375°.

Bake for 35 to 40 minutes. Remove from pan and cool on wire rack.

Recipe makes one big loaf, 36 ounces.

Dark German Rye Bread

3 cups unbleached white flour
½ cup unsweetened cocoa powder
2 packets active dry yeast
1 tablespoon caraway seed
2 cups water
⅓ cup molasses
2 tablespoons corn oil
   margarine
1 tablespoon sugar
1 tablespoon salt
3½ cups rye flour

In big electric mixing bowl combine white flour, cocoa powder, the active dry yeast, and caraway seed.

Heat together water, molasses, margarine, sugar, and salt until warm (115°-120°), stirring to help the butter melt. Add to dry mixture and beat with electric mixer on low speed for ½ minute, constantly scraping side of bowl with a rubber spatula. Then beat 3 minutes with mixer at high speed.

Stir in by hand 3 to 3½ cups of the rye flour, enough to make a batter that is light but not stiff.

Turn onto a lightly floured bread board and knead until smooth (6 to 8 minutes). Cover and let rest 20 minutes.

Punch the dough down and divide in half. Shape into two round loaves and place on greased baking sheet or in two 8″ pie tins. Lightly brush tops with cooking oil. Cover and let rest in a warm (80°-85°), draft-free place until doubled (45 minutes to an hour).

Preheat oven to 400° (*fuel-saving tip: preheating any oven can't take longer than 10 minutes*). Bake for 25 minutes to half an hour. This recipe makes two loaves, each of them 24 ounces.

Short on time?

When you're in a hurry for some fresh bread to accompany a meal, if you flatten the loaf over a wider-than-usual surface of a cookie sheet, it will take less time to bake. Likewise, if you shape the dough into small, individual loaves or rolls, it will bake a great deal faster than it would as one or two big loaves.

Cornell Bread

3 cups tepid water
2 packets active dry yeast
2 tablespoons honey
6½ to 7 cups unbleached
   enriched white flour
½ cup full-fat soy flour (from a
   health food store)
¾ cup nonfat dry milk powder
3 tablespoons wheat germ
1 tablespoon salt
2 tablespoons corn oil

Mix water, yeast, and honey in a big bowl and let stand in a warm place 5 minutes.

Sift together flour and dry milk; stir in wheat germ.

Add salt to yeast mixture plus half the flour mixture. Beat batter 2 minutes with a mixer or 80 strokes with a wooden spoon.

Add oil. Beat in remainder of flour mixture by hand, adding more flour, if necessary, to make a fairly stiff dough. Turn onto a lightly floured surface and knead 10 minutes or until dough looks silky and elastic.

Place in pre-warmed greased bowl (preferably ceramic) and turn once to oil both sides of dough. Cover the bowl with damp cloth and let the dough rise, free from drafts, in a warm place (80°-85°) until it has doubled, about 45 minutes.

Punch down dough, pulling in the edges toward the center, and turn over in bowl. Cover again and let rise 20 minutes in a warm place.

Turn onto lightly floured surface and cut dough in two equal parts. Cover and let rest for 10 minutes.

Roll or press one ball of dough at a time into a long, ½″-thick rectangle. Roll up, sealing the edges and tucking under the ends. Place in greased bread pans. Cover and let rise in a warm place until doubled in bulk, about 45 minutes.

Preheat oven 10 minutes to 350° and bake 50 minutes to one hour. Cover pans with foil if tops start to get too brown. Bread is ready if it sounds hollow when tapped. Brush tops with melted butter just before removing from oven to give loaves a soft, golden crust. Cool on racks.

This recipe makes two loaves, each of them weighing 21 ounces.

Italian Bread

> 7½ to 7¾ cups enriched all-
>   purpose white flour
> 2 packets active dry yeast
> 2½ cups warm water (110°)
> 1 tablespoon salt
>   yellow cornmeal
> 1 tablespoon cold water
> 1 slightly beaten egg white

In big electric mixer bowl combine just 3 cups *only* of the flour and yeast. In saucepan combine warm water and salt. Add to the dry mixture in mixer bowl. Beat with electric mixer at low speed for ½ minute, scraping the sides of the bowl constantly with a rubber spatula. Beat 3 minutes with mixer at high speed.

Stir in by hand enough of the rest of the flour to make a very stiff batter. Turn out on a lightly floured bread board and knead until dough is as smooth and elastic as you can get it (20-25 minutes). Shape into a ball and place dough in a pre-warmed, lightly greased bowl. Turn dough over to grease other side of ball. Cover with a damp cloth and place in a draft-free, warm location (80°-85°) to rise until double (up to 1½ hours).

Punch down the dough. Turn out on lightly floured bread board. Divide in half, cover, and let rest 10 minutes.

For long Italian loaves, roll out each half of dough to a 12''x15'' rectangle. Starting with long edge of dough, roll tightly, sealing as you go and slightly tapering the ends of the rectangle.

Place seam side down on greased baking sheet sprinkled with yellow cornmeal. Cover and let rise in a warm place until double (45 minutes to an hour).

Before baking set a large shallow pan on oven rack at lowest level and fill with boiling water. Preheat oven 10 minutes to 375°.

Add 1 tablespoon cold water to slightly beaten egg white; brush loaf tops and sides. Cut diagonal slits in the top of the bread with a sharp knife.

Bake about 20 minutes, sheet on mid-oven rack (above rack with pan of boiling water); rebrush with egg white-water mixture. Bake an additional 20 minutes until golden brown. Cool on wire racks.

Recipe makes two long loaves, each of them 24 ounces.

Old-Time Oatmeal Bread

> ½ cup warm water (110°)
> 2 packets active dry yeast
> 1¼ cups boiling water
> 1 cup quick-cooked rolled oats
> ½ cup light molasses
> ⅓ cup corn oil margarine
> 1 tablespoon salt
> 5¾ to 6 cups enriched
>   all-purpose white flour
> 2 eggs, beaten
> 1 egg white, slightly beaten
> 1 tablespoon cold water
>   Quick-cooked rolled oats

Pour the active dry yeast into the warm water and stir to soften.

In large electric mixing bowl combine boiling water, oats, molasses, margarine, and salt; cool until lukewarm. Stir in just 2 cups *only* of the flour and beat thoroughly with electric beater or by hand, preferably with a wooden spoon. Add softened yeast and the 2 eggs; beat again thoroughly.

Stir in enough of the remaining flour for a soft batter.

Turn onto a lightly floured bread board and knead until pliable and silky (10 or 12 minutes). Make into a ball.

Place in pre-warmed, lightly greased bowl and turn dough upside down to grease top and bottom. Cover with a damp cloth and place in a draft-free, warm place (80°-85°) to rise until double in bulk (about 1½ hours).

Punch down the dough and turn onto lightly floured bread board. Divide in equal portions. Cover and let rest for 10 minutes.

Sprinkle bottoms and sides of two well greased 8½''x4½''x2½'' bread pans with rolled oats.

Shape dough into loaves and place in pans. Cover and let rise in a warm place until doubled (up to an hour).

Mix slightly beaten egg white with 1 tablespoon cold water and lightly brush tops of loaves with mixture; sprinkle with oats.

Preheat oven 10 minutes at 375°.

Bake until golden brown, about 40 minutes. If crusts seem to be browning too rapidly, cover loosely with a sheet of foil for the last 15 or 20 minutes. Remove from pans onto wire racks to cool.

This recipe makes two loaves, each of them 24 ounces.

Guide to Your Own Vegetable Garden

In the battle against high food prices, some 50 million households have put in backyard gardens. Many families new to home farming enjoy the truly fresh bounty so much more than they thought they would, they eat more vegetables than usual—improving nutrition and cutting down on the amount of other foods they have to buy. Children (and many an adult) who previously turned up their noses at vegetables pitch right in when the very ones they've seeded and weeded are set before them.

How Much Can You Save?

There are many variables, but the average suburban garden, 15 x 25 feet, carefully planted with high-yield, minimum-space vegetables, should produce around $350-worth of "money crops." Much of what isn't consumed in the course of the season can be frozen or canned.

Neither Hard nor Costly

Vegetable gardening requires almost no skill. Getting your hands down in the warm soil of Planet Earth is balm to jangled nerves.

If the family pitches in together, initial soil preparation and seeding take only one long weekend, or a couple of short ones, of concentrated effort. After that, a total of two to four hours of weeding and watering a week is about all that's required.

For a small subsistence plot, the average gardening family, assuming it owns the few necessary tools, spends $20-$25 for everything—seeds, transplants, stakes, ground limestone, fertilizer, and tiller rental.

Clean, sharp high-quality tools lessen gardening labor. Cheap ones bend or break; non-oak handles give you splinters. If you haunt garage sales, you can pick up used tools cheap, and today, alas, old is often better than new. If you have to buy new ones, *here's what you'll need and about how much you'll have to spend to get good tools:*
• Spading fork, $6.50 (unless you rent a rotary tiller; rental $10)
• Steel bow-type garden rake (with at least a 60″ handle if you're tall), $5.75
• Common hoe, $4.25
• Wheelbarrow, $8-$20, depending on capacity, for a one-wheeler; or a two-wheel garden cart with which you can haul more weight but only over relatively smooth terrain, $15
• Garden hose, $7.25 per 50-foot length if made of rubber ($5.25 if made of plastic)
• Sprinkler or soil soaker, $7

Fencing-In

A garden that is likely to come under attack from marauding small animals or be walked across by little wandering children and dogs had better be enclosed with a two-foot-high 1″-mesh "chicken wire" fence, sometimes called "galvanized netting," about $6.00 per 150-foot roll. Much easier than nailing up such a fence is to staple it to wooden posts previously driven into the ground around the garden plot. Borrow a stapler if you don't own one.

You'll also need a ball of strong twine, 60¢, and two stakes for laying off rows. A trowel is useful but not essential.

Planning Your Patch

If possible, try to locate your garden near the house, so you can slip out and pull a few weeds or yank a radish whenever the mood strikes you. Rabbits, woodchucks, and deer, which can wipe out a garden overnight, tend to steer clear of a place where people are coming and going. The ground should be level or slightly sloped (preferably toward the south) and should have good drainage. If the location you have in mind does not get a full six hours of sunshine daily all summer long, choose another site.

What if you don't have a backyard, or yours doesn't get all-day sun? It's quite likely you can still have a vegetable garden. Thousands of towns across America are letting part-time farmers cultivate plots on town lands for nominal fees to residents.

The beginner's common pitfall is planting too big a garden, one that becomes too much to tend as springtime's enthusiasm gives way to midsummer neglect under the broiling sun. If this is your first, settle for a little one. You can still grow a wide variety of vegetables by planting short rows or by planting a few feet of one variety and continuing on in the same row with another. One hill of summer squash, for example, will produce more than most families can use.

Plot your garden on a big sheet of paper, one-half inch to the foot. If your land slopes, run the rows across the hill following its contours. Otherwise, run your rows north and south, planting tall growing vegetables at the north so shorter ones won't fall in their shade.

How to Buy Seed

Well before winter's end—as early as the previous autumn—start sending out postcards to seed companies requesting their catalogs. Be warned, they're often out of them by the end of March. Match the seed varieties that appeal to you in the catalogs against a special list of the best varieties to grow in your area based on highest quality

and (for some vegetables) greatest disease resistance. Call and ask for this important list by looking in your phone book under "United States," then "Agriculture, Dept. of" and find "County Agricultural Agent" or "Co-operative Extension"—either of which may also be in the regular listings.

Seed company sampler

W. Atlee Burpee Company
18th Street & Hunting Park Avenue
Philadelphia, PA 19132; *or*
Clinton, IA 52732; *or*
Riverside, CA 92502

Northrup King & Co.
1500 Jackson Street, N.E.
Minneapolis, MN 55413

D. R. Mayo Co. (*seeds for the South*)
P.O. Box 10247
Knoxville, TN 37919

Gurney Seed & Nursery Company
(*seeds for cold climates*)
Yankton, SD 57078

Henry Field Seed & Nursery Company
Shenandoah, IA 51601

The Chas. C. Hart Seed Co.
Wethersfield, CT 06109

Burgess Seed & Plant Company
P.O. Box 218
Galesburg, MI 49053

Farmer Seed & Nursery Company
Faribault, MN 55021

Although many home gardeners spend hours riffling through seed catalogs in anticipation of spring, most rely on seed packet racks that appear toward winter's end in garden centers, hardware, and variety stores. During a period of shortage of favorite varieties, if you find exactly what you want on the rack, at least you have the seeds in hand, which is preferable to a "sorry, temporarily out of stock" response to your mail order.

Rather than buying one packet each of several different varieties of, say, corn, and then using perhaps only a few seeds from each packet in a small garden, consider sticking to one or two top-recommended varieties that produce well where you live, planting a short row or two, or a part of a row, every weekend for a month or more after the soil becomes warm. This will give your family a continuing sequence of harvests—and you will use up all your seeds.

If you intend to plant a lot of any one vegetable, buy the more economical ¼-lb or ½-lb packages, which are a lot less expensive per seed than individual packets. But don't bother with so-called "taped seed" it's too expensive for the little effort in thinning it saves.

Choosing What to Grow

Pound for pound, juicy red sun-sweetened tomatoes return the most value for your time, money, and effort of any home-grown vegetable—especially compared with what you pay at the market for those poor pale pink imitations.

Other perishable vegetables like corn, peas, and green beans should also be at the top of your list, because, fresh-picked from your garden, they have a flavor and succulence unmatched by supermarket produce.

Keep your space requirements in mind, however. A small plot will provide food for many a feast if it is planted with such crops as lettuce, green beans, summer squash, broccoli, chard, tomatoes (staked), peas, and cucumbers (both of which can be grown on a fence). By comparison, corn, melons, and winter squash need a lot of room.

Broccoli, cabbage, cucumbers, and melons are considered comparatively difficult to grow because of their need for more or less constant control of disease and insects. Loose-leaf lettuce is easier to grow than heading (iceberg) varieties.

For a tiny plot here's a fail-safe list of vegetables that grow from seed as soon as the soil is workable:
  radishes
  beets
  carrots
  peas
  lettuce
  beans—must wait until soil is warm

In his excellent book *How to Grow Your Own Vegetables,* published by Meredith, 1973, author Mike Kressy suggests this "Beginner's Special" for a 10x20-foot plot. Working across the 10-foot width from north to south:
  corn, 2 rows
  zucchini, yellow squash, cucumbers, 1 hill each
  pole beans, 6 poles-worth
  eggplant, 1; tomato plants 4, staked
  peas, 2 rows; followed by carrots and beets
  chard, lettuce, a half row of each
  cabbage, 1 row
  scallions, parsley, radishes, ⅓ of same row each

The garden a rural couple in their middle years plant annually for their own needs yields vegetables they eat daily in season and produces a surplus for their huge basement freezer. In soil fertilized with plenty of manure from a farmer-neighbor who spreads it for them in the winter so it has time to rot thoroughly, they plant:
  green and yellow snap beans
  beets
  chard
  onions
  lettuce
  parsley
  carrots
  peas
  cucumbers
  summer squash and winter squash
  broccoli
  muskmelon (as cantaloupe are also called)
  corn
  potatoes (from sets)
  tomatoes, green peppers, and egg plant (from seedlings)

With the tomatoes, onions, and green peppers they grow, they make their own spaghetti sauce and freeze it in meal-size amounts. They've discovered the best vegetables for freezing are: corn (cut from the cob), snap beans, broccoli, beet greens, beets, chard, peppers, and tomatoes.

But fresh or frozen, "every mouthful is a joy for its superb flavor," they say, "and for the satisfaction of having grown it."

Grown from Transplants

If you are new to vegetable gardening you may not want to trust your luck growing plants from seeds indoors in early spring—though no denying, you do save money this way. Unless you have a south-facing window plus optimum conditions of temperature and humidity and a knack for watering just often enough just the right amount, you'll find it quite difficult to grow sturdy dependable "transplants" from seeds. Buying commercially grown seedlings assures you of vigorous plants less likely to fail and more likely to yield bounteously.

Purchase transplants that are stocky, of medium size, relatively young, and—look closely!—free of disease and bugs. A promising transplant has four to eight true leaves (the first "leaves" on the stalk are really the parted seed covering). For fruit-type crops like tomatoes and peppers, it is better that there be no flowers on the plants before you transplant them to your garden. It is essential that there be a firm block of soil around the roots or that the plants have been grown in individual peat pots.

Soil Preparation

Wait a day or two after a rain to check your soil if you have any serious doubts about it. Scoop up a handful and press it in your hand. If it is somewhat moist, crumbles easily, and falls away, you probably have good *friable*

loam for growing vegetables. But if it compacts in a sticky way, it contains too much clay. The remedy is the same if it feels gritty when you rub it between your fingers, mean-ing it contains too much sand. Unless you've started a compost heap, the best advice is to buy an organic substitute. The cheapest is readily available peat moss, which comes

Compost: a heap o' savings

You can keep your garden productive at rock-bottom cost for fertilizer and soil conditioners by starting a compost pile. It's simple:

Pick a spot not too near the house but not too far from the garden and within reach of the hose, preferably a shady place where the pile will stay moist. Mark off a six-foot square. Begin by throwing pulled-up weeds there. Add grass clippings and refuse from harvested plants—and don't worry, the heat generated inside the pile will destroy plant diseases and insect larvae if you have problems with them during the summer; toss it all on.

When autumn comes, fallen leaves make an ideal composting material—almost as good as manure (the best of all if it's free). Pile up the leaves next to the compost heap, run the lawn mower back and forth through the leaf pile to pulverize them and prevent matting, then add them to the compost. You can toss on vegetable waste from the kitchen, but not animal refuse like meat fat, which takes too long to break down. Sawdust and wood shavings, ashes from the fireplace, peanut husks, cheese whey—are all compostible.

Build your compost pile in layers. After the first 8"-10" of organic matter, throw on a couple of shovelfuls of garden soil to introduce decay-producing organisms. Scatter a cupful of any commercial fertilizer, and water with the hose. If your soil is too acid or if you're composting with a lot of pulverized (highly acid) oak leaves, sprinkle on a handful or two of ground limestone to sweeten the mix.

Keep adding successive layers this way until the pile is several feet high. It's a good idea to build it with slanted sides and a depression on top to catch rain and snow. Rapid decay will not occur until the following summer when the weather gets hot.

It's a long haul, but the compost should be ready to mix into the garden at the end of the summer or the following spring when you are preparing the soil and want to improve tilth as you increase nutrient—free!

highly compacted, about $7 a bale. It doesn't do anything to enrich your soil, but peat moss will give it proper texture and moisture-holding property, and your vegetables will grow better.

Don't spring for bagged manure. It's not worth the cost. But if you know someone who keeps farm animals or horses and can get it free, old rotted manure is better than peat moss, although it doesn't contain as much nutriment as some gardeners like to think; you should still figure on using fertilizer. If it is available, use plenty of manure —as much as four bushels per 100 square feet—to improve the structure of your soil. But watch out: fresh manure can burn fragile plant roots. Avoid this danger by tilling it into your plot at least two weeks before planting to give it a chance to rot.

The pH factor: Do be sure to have your soil tested if this is the first vegetable garden on your selected plot. It's a service of either your state Agricultural Extension Service or your State Agricultural Experimental Station. There may be a small charge or it may be free. Call your Agricultural Agent's office and ask where to send a sample, so that you can learn what kind of soil you have and how to improve it if it needs improving. It may not. But across whole broad regions of the U.S. the soil is too acid for best vegetable production and requires an application of ground limestone when the garden plot is prepared. Vegetables need soil that is between 5.7 and 6.9 in pH reaction—very slightly acid.

For a soil test, dig samples with a spade driven in vertically at five or six places on your plot. Take a thin slice from the side of each hole and mix these together thoroughly. Send in about a cupful of this mix in a plastic bag placed inside a box or heavy envelope. Be sure to label the plastic bag with your name and address, the depth to which the samples were taken, the types and strengths of fertilizer previously used (if known), and the general kinds of vegetables you intend to grow. Shortly you will receive a report telling you the pH factor of your soil and probably describing its texture, proportions of organic materials, and what to do to improve it. Follow its advice and you are almost guaranteed your garden will provide a better yield.

How to till: A small garden plot can be tilled by hand with a spading fork or a long-handled spade (easier on the back), the clods broken up and clumps of grass and larger rocks thrown aside. But most people spend $10 to $12 (per half day) to rent a gasoline-operated rotary tiller, because it greatly lessens the work if your soil is not too hard or too heavy. Get instructions where you rent and be sure to remember to drop the drag bar before you begin. The rotating blades pull the machine along; the height you adjust the drag bar more or less determines how deeply they dig.

Rototill 6″ to 8″ deep once up and down your plot, then a second time side to side. Rough-rake it to get rid of stones and debris. Add a 2″ layer of organic matter if your soil is too sticky or sandy and rototill this in.

Next, spread a light layer, four pounds per square feet, of commercial fertilizer (and ground limestone if required) over the plot and rake it into the top few inches of soil. Don't neglect the fertilizing. If you plan to plant your crops close together to get the most out of a small patch, and you want successive crops in the same space, your garden must be fertile. Just don't overdo the fertilizing. It will only wash away. Rake spring-cultivated soil soon after tilling to prevent excessive drying. A final raking may be necessary just before seeding. Small-seed crops like carrots need a well-pulverized surface for good germination and an even stand.

When to Plant

One of the best ways to get the most out of your garden and spread out the harvest is to plant each initial crop as early as you can without risking damage by cold. The so-called "frost-free date" in your locality is usually two to three weeks later than the average annual date of the last occurrence of 32°. The easiest and surest way to find out this date is to call your county Agricultural Agent or Co-operative Extension.

Many vegetables are so hardy, however, they can be planted a full month before the frost-free date, just about as soon as the ground can be worked in the spring. Most of those that are this cold-tolerant do better planted in cool weather and, in the

Best Times for Planting Vegetables

Cold-hardy plants for early-spring planting		Cold-tender or heat-hardy plants for late-spring or early-summer planting			Hardy plants for late-summer or fall planting, except in northern third of U.S. (plant 6 to 8 weeks before average date of first fall freeze in your locality)
very hardy (plant 4 to 6 weeks before frost-free date)	hardy (plant 2 to 4 weeks before frost-free date)	not cold-hardy (plant on frost-free date)	need hot weather (plant 1 week or later past frost-free date)	medium heat-tolerant (good for summer planting)	
broccoli cabbage lettuce onions parsley peas turnips	beets carrots chard mustard parsnips radishes endive	beans, snap okra soybeans squash corn tomatoes potatoes chard	beans, lima eggplant peppers sweetpo- tatoes rutabaga cucumber melons	beans, any kind chard soybeans squash corn cauli- flower	lettuce beets turnips parsnips collards kale

Areas in the Plains states that warm up quickly in the spring, and are subject to dry weather, call for very early planting to escape heat and drought.

southern two-thirds of the nation where summers get very hot, should not be planted after the arrival of spring. Some of these same hardy vegetables can be sown in late summer, however, for safe fall harvesting.

Above are some popular vegetables grouped according to approximate best times for planting.

How to Increase Production

In the spring if you have only one period of time or a single burst of enthusiasm for getting your plot planted, consider single plantings of such long-harvest vegetables as tomatoes, summer squash, beets, carrots, chard, peppers, broccoli, and cucumbers. If you make only one planting of corn, choose both early and late varieties to spread out the harvest. Single plantings of crops like radishes, head lettuce, and peas each produce for only a short while, however, even if you plant several varieties.

You can extend the production value of a small plot by succession planting—putting in head lettuce in the spring, for example, replanting the row in early summer with carrots, then planting leaf lettuce in late summer after the carrots have all been pulled and eaten. Or by following radishes or peas with snap beans. If you decide to do succession planting, check the kinds of vegetables and the varieties as to their adaptability to growing at particular times of the season. Peas, for instance, grow well in early spring and late fall but poorly in mid-summer.

To extend your garden's harvest, second and third plantings of crops adaptable to late summer growing, like lettuce, will put fresh vegetables on your table when other gardeners have hung up their hoes. If succession planting appeals to you, the chart that appears on the following page makes much of the idea of keeping something growing in all spaces all season long.

Succession Planting Increases Production

Spring	Late Spring, Early Summer	Late Summer
onions, leaf lettuce, beets, and carrots	tomatoes, peppers	
peas *followed by*	chard	
beets *followed by*	leaf lettuce *followed by*	Brussels sprouts
head lettuce *followed by*	carrots *followed by*	leaf lettuce
radishes *followed by*	lima beans *followed by*	peas
spinach *followed by*	snap beans *followed by*	Brussels sprouts
green beans *followed by*	cabbage or cauliflower	

In plotting your garden, all early-maturing crops can be grouped, so that as soon as one is used up and removed another takes its place. It's a good idea not to follow a crop with the same vegetable but with an unrelated one in the same row. If you're trying to get all you can from a tiny plot, try *intercropping*—planting radishes and lettuce (fast to mature) between the rows of beets and carrots (relatively slow growing); start zucchini between rows of peas, which you will take out long before the zucchini is ready to eat. Crowding the garden this way tends to keep weeds down.

How to Sow Seed

Every seed packet's instructions tell you exactly how to plant and care for what's inside—proper sowing, thinning, watering, harvesting, plus percentage of germination to expect, date of testing, and the year the seeds are to be planted. A successful gardener reads packet instructions carefully.

The time-honored way of marking newly sown rows was with the empty seed packets stuck on sticks. But you can identify your rows with indelible ink on lengths of lath.

A garden notebook: Since every seed packet carries such specific directions for growing the particular vegetable, you might consider organizing this essential information in one place by stapling your seed packets, as you acquire them, onto the pages of a looseleaf notebook. When you're ready to sow the seeds, you'd tear out the individual packets

—and restaple them emptied, for handy reference concerning the culture and harvesting of each vegetable you've planted. Partly empty packets stapled back in place would be easy to keep track of for later plantings. Your looseleaf notebook would become a guide to what's coming up where in your garden, and when. It would also help you make succession plantings accurately to get the most from your plot.

Down to earth: A heavy cord stretched tightly between short stakes makes laying out rows easy. To open furrows for large

seeds like peas, the trick is to walk backward, stepping on the cord to hold it down, dragging the tipped-up blade of the hoe along so that one corner of the blade makes a V-shaped trench. For small seeds requiring much shallower sowing, hold the hoe blade-up and drag handle along the string.

Try to space seeds fairly evenly, because too heavy a hand wastes them and costs time in difficult thinning since the seedlings will come up all bunched together. It is vitally important to sow seeds no deeper than packet specifications. Sow a bit shallower in the spring, especially in heavy soil; sow a bit deeper in lighter soil and when you make warm-weather plantings. Cover the seeds and provide good contact with the earth by very gently firming the soil over them with light pats of the palm of your hand or with the back of the blade of the hoe from a standing position.

Be sure and wait until a stretch of sunny weather has sufficiently warmed the soil before planting bean, squash, or cucumber seeds. Packet directions always say to plant such seeds in "hills." Some gardeners say a hill is a mound, others say a hill is merely a cluster of seeds sown on the flat. If your soil does not have excellent drainage, warm-season seeds often rot because of excessive moisture from spring rains unless planted in hills that are actually mounds. But if your soil drains freely, dries out quickly and the spring rains are light, you may be better off planting bean, squash, and cucumber seeds in clusters.

Keep them moist: When seeding is completed and the rows tamped, mist the plot with a hose to dampen the soil. Frequent mistings aid seed germination. Try to keep the soil constantly moist until the seedlings come poking through the ground.

How to Set Out Transplants

Earlier harvests, economy of garden space, and a longer productive season can be attained by purchasing small plants of certain vegetables for setting directly in the garden. If you live in the temperate or colder regions of the U.S., it is essential that such crops as tomatoes, peppers, early cabbage, eggplant, cauliflower, and head lettuce be grown from transplants if an early garden is your objective—with fresh vegetables to harvest well before prices drop in the stores for the same produce. (In the warmer regions of the U.S. almost all vegetables can be started from seed in specially prepared beds in the open.)

Every effort should be made during transplanting to disrupt as little as possible the growth of young plants that you've bought in flats or market packs. Pick a cloudy day for the job. Full sun can dry out root tendrils in no time. Stir a quarter-pound of ordinary (5-10-10 or 5-10-5) fertilizer into two gallons of water to have ready as a starter solution to give the little plants a boost. Dig small holes and fill them with enough starter solution to keep the soil moist around the transplants for a few days while they adjust to their new surroundings; the holes should drain before you begin transplanting.

Give the seedlings themselves a light watering before you start and transplant only a couple at a time. Use a table knife, narrow spatula, or a tongue depressor-type stick to remove tender seedlings from a flat. Be careful in lifting and planting not to disturb them any more than absolutely necessary.

Set everything except tomato transplants so that the new soil line is just a bit higher around the stem than it had been. Set tomatoes an inch or two deeper than they had been, and new beneficial root structure will grow from the buried stem.

Press each plant in place firmly but not too roughly to avoid pinching or breaking root tendrils. Press a shallow basin around the stem to collect water. Snipping about one-third off the ends of at least some of the hardier leaves is also beneficial at this time to help roots recuperate.

Protect tomato, pepper, cabbage, and eggplant transplants from cutworms with little individual walls around them cut from milk cartons or stiff paper rising two inches above the ground and penetrating an inch below soil surface.

Water newly set-out plants every day until they are well established. If the days immediately following setting-out are sunny and hot, protect the seedlings with newspapers stapled or taped into cones (these also protect if you get a sudden late frost). And don't be alarmed if some of your transplants droop right before your eyes. They'll perk up again. Individual ones differ greatly in their recuperative powers. Hardier than peppers and the highly delicate eggplant, tomato, lettuce, cabbage, and related vegetables practically always re-establish themselves swiftly.

Growing the Big Two

How to grow tomatoes: Fresh-plucked from the vine, a juicy, sun-ripened tomato is perhaps the ultimate reward in gardening. Tomatoes come in a spectacular number of varieties—cherry tomatoes and giant Beefsteak ones, tomato-paste tomatoes, orange ones, yellow ones, and pink ones, even tomatoes that look like little pears.

Since space is limited in most backyard gardens, the general practice is to stake tomatoes rather than let them sprawl (see photo opposite). Make sure you buy varieties meant to be staked, however. The stakes should be six to eight feet long and be driven two feet into the ground; they have to support a considerable weight when the fruit is ripening. Tie up the vines with thin strips of soft cloth or lengths of yarn.

There's a new way of supporting tomato plants called caging. It involves surrounding each plant with a three- or four-foot self-supporting cylinder of heavy cross-laced fencing, the type with 3″ x 4″ holes between wires. This system is said to produce higher percentages of perfect fruit because no tying of the plants is needed. The plants, intertwining the fencing, are contained and supported by it. Caging reduces wind damage.

Tomatoes grow best in fertile, well-drained soil but they'll produce in almost any kind as long as they get direct sunlight all day long. Consider planting early, mid-season, and late varieties to have tomatoes to eat straight through the summer. It's best not to transplant tomato seedlings until all danger of frost is past.

Go easy on the fertilizer. With tomatoes it's easy to fertilize too heavily. Then they go all to vine and leaf instead of flower and fruit. Two weeks after transplanting, feed with a fertilizer that says, "tomato food" or some-such on the label. Feed once more one month after planting, then don't feed again until the vines set fruit. But from then on feed every two or three weeks until the last tomato is plucked. Each feeding give every plant a heaping teaspoon mixed into the soil 8″ or 10″ from the stem.

Tomatoes do not do well unless watered properly, with heavy soakings of the roots weekly (if it hasn't rained) and more frequently if your soil is sandy or you suffer a heat wave. Tomato foliage should not be sprinkled any more than absolutely necessary when watering the garden.

Once-a-week tomato pruning consists of removing the small shoots called "suckers" that develop in the crotches where the leaf stems join the main stem. (Be careful as

you prune and when tying up the vines not to brush off any yellow flowers, each of which is a tomato-to-be.) Grasp the sucker between thumb and forefinger and bend it sharply one way, then back the other, and it will come right off without injury to the vine. This will give you one main stem to develop into the vine, but if you leave one of the early strong-looking suckers to develop, you can have a secondary stem, and this may increase the yield. Choose the first sucker right beneath the first cluster of blossoms; prune all others that appear.

Spray or dust for insects on a weekly schedule with an all-purpose insecticide (and while you're at it, spray or dust the other vine plants and the beans, but try to keep it off the leafy vegetables like lettuce). Hand-pluck any big gruesome green hornworms you see into a can and dump them down the toilet.

Sometimes tomato blossoms drop off of their own accord due to inordinately cold or hot temperatures, too much rain or sun, or excess nitrogen from over-fertilizing. Al-

though garden centers sell a hormone spray called Blossom Set to help trim your losses, there isn't much you can do about it. You just have to wait for later flowers to produce fruit; blossom-drop rarely continues.

Pick tomatoes when they are fully ripe and red (or orange or yellow). Don't ripen them on the windowsill in the sun; quality will deteriorate in the heat. Those you pick green, including those you salvage at the end of the season before the first fall frost, should be ripened at temperatures between 55° and 72°. Light will give them a bright color but is not essential to ripening. Incidentally, green tomatoes, sliced thin, are delicious fried.

How to grow potatoes: One of the greatest home-garden money crops, good quality spuds are easy to grow. They do well in any fertile soil that has good drainage but do best in a somewhat acid earth with a pH between 5.0 and 5.4, which helps them avoid potato scab; scab-resistant varieties should be planted anyway. Buy certified seed potatoes from a garden center or farmers outlet. Plant only when the soil has become warm and dry. Dig deeply and spread a band of 5-10-10 fertilizer along the bottom of a 10″deep furrow. Cover this with soil and plant sections of seed potatoes 10″ apart, 4″ to 6″ deep, each section having at least one or two eyes. Later, to avoid sunburned tubers which will turn green, hoe the earth up around the plants—and keep the weeds down.

Have a weather eye open for the nefarious potato bug, a beetle the larvae of which can eat the leaves off a potato vine in a few days. If you see one of these fat pink grubs spray with Sevin, malathion, or an all-purpose spray.

Harvesting when the ground is dry is easy, using a spading fork to dig up the tubers, but hold off until the vines have wilted. Use care in digging not to bruise any more potatoes than absolutely necessary. There will be a lot of ping-pong-ball-size ones that can be eaten right away.

Don't wash potatoes before storing them. Pick over and save only the unbruised, uncracked ones. They keep for long periods when stored in a cool dark place (between 45° and 50°) with good ventilation. Extended exposure to light can turn spuds green. Stored at room temperature they may sprout or shrivel. Don't refrigerate them either; below 45° they may develop a sweet taste (some of the starch turned to water) and turn dark when you cook them, although their nutritional value will not be diminished. Potatoes are a carbohydrate food, (plus Vitamins C and B₁, iron, and niacin), but your body uses more carbohydrates than proteins and fats put together.

Helping Your Garden Grow

How much water does a vegetable garden require? Not an excessive amount. Plants can get too much water, whether due to too much rain or too much watering, and growth will be stunted if oxygen can't reach the roots in the mud. A total lack of water for only a short period, however, can be harmful to mature plants and sudden death to young ones.

The garden should get 1″-1½″ of water per week during the growing season after seeds have sprouted. This doesn't mean sprinkling the surface until the soil is damp an inch or two down. It does mean that you or nature must provide your vegetables with enough water weekly to reach a depth of 8″-10″, enough so that if the top of the soil gets parched between rains, the root systems will be able to reach down and draw up moisture to keep the plants from drooping. Deep watering once a week grows deep roots, and deep roots support healthy, productive plants.

So set a couple of jars in the garden. Mark them with strips of masking tape at the 1½″ level. Then when you (or nature) water the vegetables, you can check the level in the jars to see when they've had enough.

The time of day you water doesn't matter much, although evening watering can leave plants damp all night, which promotes fungus.

Water economics: Because (unless you live in the Southwest) you never know how much rain to expect (or not to expect) in summer, the cost of watering your garden is an expense factor worth pondering. To get the equivalent of the necessary 1½″ of rainfall in a week when it doesn't rain, you will have to run 160 gallons of water through your garden hose for a 12 x 15-foot garden. But knowing a dry summer can run up the cost of growing your own, keep in mind the same drought conditions will probably increase the cost of vegetables at the market.

A *soil soaker,* which is a perforated length of hose or canvas that attaches to the end of the garden hose, lets water dribble slowly into the ground along its length. In many communities water bills have soared. A soil soaker uses less water than a sprinkler, from which a substantial volume evaporates into the atmosphere. If you already own a sprinkler, however, go ahead and use it, as it does provide plants with a refreshing shower and brings down their temperatures on blazing hot days. Besides, soil soakers are a nuisance to move around among the rows. It usually takes two people to move one to keep from injuring sensitive young plants or knocking off fruit.

Easy weeding: Your garden must be kept weeded. Weeds rob plants of soil nutrients, sun, and air. Some weeds harbor diseases, insects, and nematodes (tiny parasitic worms) that can return to reinfest a garden year after year.

As soon as the soil is workable after each period of rain is the best time to hoe or cultivate the garden to get rid of weeds that have sprouted. This will leave the soil loosened up so air can reach plants and the next rainfall will be readily absorbed.

When you hoe, hold the handle thumbs up even if this feels a bit awkward at first. Keep both the handle and yourself fairly upright and employ the same sweeping action you would use to sweep a floor, holding the blade of the hoe quite flat to the ground and close to your feet. This way the weed stems are cut off just beneath the surface without endangering the roots of the vegetables.

Simple thinning: Surplus seedlings should be removed before they begin competing with one another. Although many thinnings can be taken to the kitchen, the final yield will usually be greater if you thin early than if you wait and only thin vegetables that are mature enough to eat.

Thin as soon as the seedlings appear to be established. Snip them out with sewing scissors, don't pull them up. Take out every other seedling the first thinning, naturally snipping any weaker looking ones in preference to stronger ones. A couple of weeks later, as plants begin to look crowded, thin again. The final thinning should conform to the plant spacing directions on the seed packet (that you restapled in your looseleaf garden notebook). Rule of thumb: plants may touch one another but leaves should not overlap.

The word on mulch

Most gardeners new to the game don't bother with it, but laying down a layer of organic material when seedlings are 2″-3″ high—*mulching*—preserves moisture, decreases runoff, insulates the soil from hot sun or unusual cold and, most importantly, keeps weeding to something less than a chore (see the photo in the next column). Underneath cucumber or squash vines, mulch provides a clean resting place for ripening fruit. One drawback, however: When it's dried out, mulch can easily catch on fire if someone carelessly flips a lighted cigarette into the garden.

Common organic mulches are partially decomposed hay, straw, corncobs, and dry (not fresh) grass clippings. But fallen leaves chopped fine by running the lawn mower through the pile, pine needles, wood shavings, and peat moss all make good mulches. Sawdust, which can usually be hauled away for the asking from lumber mills, is an excellent mulch, although it requires nitrogen fertilizer applications to prevent plant nitrogen starvation.

Before applying a mulch, hoe out the weeds among the rows and pull those among the seedlings. After that, with mulch in place, garden care becomes a breeze. And when the season's over, if you turn the mulch under, it decomposes into compost for next year's garden.

Beating the bugs: If this is your first garden, planted where no garden has been grown before, you are probably going to be less bothered by plant diseases than by marauding insects. With some simple preventive measures you can ward off most insects, but if you come under heavy attack and can't figure out what's bugging your garden, send to the Office of Communica-

tions, USDA, DC 20250 for a copy of Home & Garden Bulletin No. 46, *Insects and Diseases in the Home Garden* (one free to anyone who asks).

You are also perfectly at liberty to consult your county Agricultural Agent. He heads the agricultural division of the Co-operative Extension Association (usually at your county seat) which, in addition to testing soil, diagnoses plant diseases, identifies weeds and insects, and suggests remedies. It also distributes informational bulletins you may request applicable to your particular region on many aspects of gardening. Its services are free, or there's an extremely nominal charge.

To have a plant problem analyzed by your Agricultural Agent:

• In preference to mailing, bring in an example at least 12″ high, if possible, *in the process of dying,* not dead. It's best if the dividing line between healthy plant and problem area is clearly visible on your specimen, because it is at this point analysis of the problem can best be made by experts.

• If you cannot come in with your sick plant (and/or your living, bottled, marauding insect), put the dying plant between paper towels in a plastic bag perforated with a few holes for air. Then pack it in a crush-proof container for mailing. But don't mail a sick plant to your ag' agent too late in the week, because it will undoubtedly sit in a hot warehouse over the weekend somewhere and expire before it reaches its final destination, making verification well nigh impossible for the laboratory.

A well-cared-for garden, says Mike Kressy in his book *How to Grow Your Own Vegetables,* will be unappealing to harmful insects if you:
• Grow disease-resistant varieties;
• Weed not only the garden itself but cut down weeds in the immediate vicinity of your vegetable patch. An overgrowth of weeds can harbor plant diseases and insect colonies that can ever so easily spread to your plants.
• Stay out of the garden when plants are wet. Waterborne diseases can be spread from plant to plant on your hands and even by your clothing brushing against the leaves of the plants.
• Pull up and remove all plants as soon as they finish bearing. Destroy diseased plants immediately.
• Adopt a friendly attitude toward beneficial birds, toads, and insects. Learn to love ladybugs, praying mantises, ground beetles (the dark brown or black ones), and dragonflies. All eat harmful insects. Ants, beetles, grubs, and other burrowing insects dig air passages in the soil and help keep it friable, at no cost to you.

Home gardeners risk disappointment if they wait too long before attempting to control harmful insects or diseases. Effective control means dusting or spraying every seven to 10 days from seedling stage to harvest. Dusting is quicker and easier, especially if you use one of those refillable plastic squeeze-can applicators, but spraying distributes the chemicals more evenly on all surfaces of the plant. Dust or spray when the air is dead calm to avoid having chemicals drift onto other edibles.

So-called "all-purpose" insecticides are the choice of most home gardeners. When you buy one of these spray or dust mixtures be sure the label says it contains one or more of such insecticides as methoxychlor, malathion, or carbaryl (Sevin), plus a fungicide such as maneb, zineb, or captan.

One way of saving money is to mix your own all-purpose spray:
1 gallon water
2 level tablespoons carbaryl
   (Sevin) 50% WP* (wettable powder)
4 level tablespoons malathion 25% WP
2 level tablespoons maneb 80% WP
Shake the spray can every once in a while as you're working with this mixture to keep the chemicals in suspension. Be sure never to use the sprayer for anything but insecticides and wash it out thoroughly after every use to diminish corrosion of its mechanism.

Bluntly stated, insecticides are poisonous to humans and animals. Read manufacturers' instructions carefully and follow them exactly to minimize the danger. Considered less hazardous but not as effective as the aforementioned chemicals are rotenone and pyrethrum, both of which are organic. Most chewing insects decamp at a whiff of rotenone. Pyrethrum routs sucking insects.

Label directions for mixing up sprays often seem to be designed for truck farmers, not home gardeners. You are told the right amount to mix for a 100-gallon tank, when your little hand pump sprayer holds only a gallon. Dr. Spencer H. Davis, Jr., a Rutgers University Plant pathologist, comes to your rescue with these conversions:
• Adding 1 pint of any liquid to 100 gallons of water is the equivalent of adding 1 teaspoon to 1 gallon of water.
• Adding 1 pound of "wettable powder" (abbreviated WP) to 100 gallons is the same as adding 1 tablespoon to 1 gallon of water.
• If the directions speak in terms of 800 parts per million, 1 teaspoon to 1 gallon of water will be about right.
• For fertilizer, or mulch or some-such, 1 ton per acre works out to approximately 1 pound per 20 square feet in the typical backyard garden.

Weeds people eat

Dandelions, as soon as the crown is putting out young leaves large enough to promote the development of chlorophyll, can be picked and cooked like any vegetable. Don't wait too long, though. Once the flower appears the leaves aren't tender and taste bitter. One of the earliest greens of the year, dandelion shoots are richer in vitamin A than most garden vegetables and contain riboflavin and thiamin, plus such minerals as calcium and iron—more of the latter than spinach. Dandelion greens taste great in salads, too, so don't pass up this bargain.

Home Canning How-To

The time you spend putting up fresh vegetables and fruits when your garden is bountiful can pay you back all year with nutritious, low-cost foods. Even though some 700 deaths from botulism poisoning have been traced to improper home canning since 1927, the risk can be eliminated if you:

• follow tested, approved methods and take no shortcuts;

• use only canners, jars, and lids made for home canning;

• never reuse lids designed for one-time use and never use chipped or cracked jars;

• never use over-ripe foods since foods change chemically as they age and lose vital acidity;

• always leave the amount of head space under the lid specified in the recipe to be sure food does not leak during processing and destroy a perfect seal;

• follow exactly the times and temperatures specified in modern recipes (some of the old ones are unsafe);

• adjust processing times to altitudes (see box on next page);

• test your seals according to instructions;

• consume home-canned foods within a one-year period and never eat any food that shows the slightest sign of spoilage.

Experts believe two simple precautions could practically eradicate botulism poisoning from home canning:

1) *Never taste questionable food from a home-canned jar that has a bulging lid, leak, off-odor, off-color, or mold.* **If in doubt, don't taste!** Less than a spoonful of food contaminated with botulism toxin can be fatal.

2) *Never serve (or taste) home-canned vegetables, meat, poultry, or fish without first boiling them for 10 minutes; boil corn and spinach a full 20 minutes.*

Three Canners. On the left is a pressure canner containing jars of cut green beans. It has a spring dial-gauge on its cover for registering pressure. On the right is a pressure canner that makes use of a weight gauge. In the rear is a boiling water-bath canner containing peaches.

Instructional Texts

If in spite of these somber warnings you decide home canning is for you, that you'll have no trouble following directions and recipes to the letter, you should begin with a good book on the subject—such as Better Homes and Gardens' *Home Canning Cook Book,* 96 pages (hardcover), $2.49 from BH&G Books, 1716 Locust St., Des Moines, IA 50336. The newly revised 29th edition of the famous *Ball Blue Book,* 112 pages (paperback), is $1 from Ball Corp., Muncie, IN 47302. Both these books clearly delineate safe canning practices for preserving fruits and high-acid vegetables, low-acid vegetables, meat, poultry, and fish, as well as jellies and jams, pickles, and relishes, plus recipes for interesting uses of home-canned foods. *Putting Food By,* by Ruth Hertzberg, Beatrice Vaughan and Janet Greene, 360 pages (paperback), is possibly the most comprehensive, up-to-date book on the subject of preserving.

Canning Equipment

It's best to get a long running start if you have never done any canning. The initial investment for canners, jars, and lids is fairly high, although you can sometimes save by purchasing out of season.

Buy only standard jars made for home canning. If you intend to can and freeze, you can buy jars designed for both purposes. Jars come in half-pint, pint, 1½-pint, and quart sizes. (USDA home economists do not recommend the half-gallon size, however.)

Danger in improper canning

Open-kettle canning, in which food is cooked in an ordinary kettle and packed in jars without processing, is unsafe. Temperatures do not go nearly high enough to destroy spoilage organisms.

Oven canning is downright dangerous. Don't try it. Not only can the jars explode, the temperature of the food in the jars during processing doesn't get high enough to ensure destruction of bacteria.

Altitude correction— water-bath canning

Add 1 minute to processing for each 1,000 feet above sea level when the time specified is 20 minutes or less. Add 2 minutes to processing for each 1,000 feet above sea level if the time called for is more than 20 minutes. **Do not raw pack vegetables for processing at altitudes above 6,000 feet.**

Two Basic Processes

Water-bath canning: For fruits, tomatoes and pickled vegetable, you can use a water-bath canner, about $7, big enough to hold seven one-quart jars. The natural acid in these foods makes them safe when jars-full are heated in boiling water for the time periods recommended in the appropriate recipes. Any big metal container can be used if it is deep enough to allow water to cover the tops of the jars by a couple of inches and still have another 2″ to 4″ of space above that for the water to boil freely. The canner needs a lid and a rack to go in its bottom.

These are the steps in water-bath canning that must be followed in conjunction with a modern recipe:

1) Fill canners with 4″ to 5″ of heated water;
2) If you use sugar syrup, prepare it and keep it warm without boiling;
3) Prepare food for canning according to recipe;
4) Fill jars and place them in canner;
5) Fill canner with boiling water 1″ or 2″ above the jars, heated to a rolling boil and covered;
6) Begin processing-time countdown according to recipe directions;
7) Adjust heat so water boils gently during prescribed processing time;
8) Remove jars when time's up.

Pressure canning: Foods naturally low in acid, which include meat, poultry, fish, and all vegetables except tomatoes, pickles, and sauerkraut, must be processed by *pressure canning.* The temperature of the food inside the pressure canner reaches 240° at 10 pounds pressure, high enough to destroy spoilage and botulism organisms that might be present. Not every pot called a ''pressure canner'' is suitable for low-acid canning, however. Some sold today designed for fast cooking have only a single 15-pounds pressure control, which won't do for canning; 10 pounds is a must. Look for a pressure canner that has a pressure gauge on its lid that is either a weighted control or a dial. A weighted one limits pressure by a pre-set control to 5, 10, or 15 pounds. It's simple, accurate, and never needs calibrating. A dial control indicates the pressure but needs checking periodically to make sure it is accurate. This is sometimes handled as a service of the Co-operative Extension Service, which you can locate by looking under the federal listings in your phone book.

A heavy 16-quart cast aluminum Underwriters Laboratory (UL)-listed pressure canner that will hold nine one-pint or seven one-quart jars in a rack costs between $36 and $40. Stamped aluminum ones are less expensive but not as sturdy.

Here are the steps in pressure canning to be followed in conjunction with a modern recipe:

1) Warm two or three inches of water over low heat in the canner;
2) Prepare food according to recipe;
3) Fill jars and place in canner;
4) Cover and lock canner and turn heat up high; reduce it when steam emerges from the vent and allow it to flow freely at a moderate rate for 10 minutes;
5) Close vent and bring pressure up over higher heat until 10 pounds of pressure is attained; then adjust heat to maintain a constant 10-pound pressure;
6) Count processing time from the moment 10-pound pressure is reached;
7) When time's up, according to the recipe, turn the heat off and allow pressure to return to normal;
8) Take pressure regulator off or open petcock before removing cover;
9) Place food on a cooling rack as soon as it stops bubbling.
10) Check seal when jars are completely cooled. A curving down in the lid identifies a sealed jar. You can also check the seal of the jar by tapping the lid with a metal spoon and listening for a ringing sound.

The temperatures reached in either a boiling-water-bath or pressure canner are not sufficiently high to kill every type of organism that can cause spoilage and food poisoning. For that reason you must boil all home-canned vegetables, meat, poultry, and fish thoroughly before tasting or eating, it must be stressed again—this is *your* life. Bring them to a rolling boil, uncovered, and boil 10 minutes longer; corn and spinach require 10 minutes beyond that.

How much makes a quart?

How many jars will be required to can 10 pounds of tomatoes? The answer depends on such factors as quality, maturity, variety, and size. But this chart will serve as a guide in helping you decide how many pounds of vegetables to buy or harvest to make one canned quart.

Vegetables	Pounds
Asparagus	2½ to 4½
Beans, limas in pods	3 to 5
Beans, snap	1½ to 2½
Beets, without tops	2 to 3½
Carrots without tops	2 to 3
Corn, sweet, in husks	3 to 6
Greens	2 to 6
Peas, in pods	3 to 6
Potatoes, new white	5 to 6
Potatoes, sweet	2 to 3
Pumpkin	1½ to 3
Squash, summer	2 to 4
Squash, winter	1½ to 3
Tomatoes	2½ to 3

Is Home Freezing for You?

A home freezer can save a significant amount of money on food bills only if you dedicate yourself to making the freezer work for you. If you intend to eat home-frozen food on a daily basis you probably can make a freezer pay off—the more so if you grow your own fruits and vegetables and/or someone in the family is bringing home fish and game.

Economics of Freezer Ownership

As this is written, freezer prices have not increased substantially. You can still get one for between $14 and $20 per cubic foot. Look for much more heavily insulated freezers to appear on the market; they will be priced somewhat higher than present ones but will operate less expensively.

Far more uprights than chest-type freezers have sold in recent years simply because they are easier to move food in and out of, and an upright takes about half the floor space of a chest model. However, when you open the door of an upright the cold spills out and the heat rushes in, a waste of energy. When the lid of a chest-type freezer is opened there's very little exchange of hot and cold air.

"No-frost" models freeze by forced circulation of zero or subzero air. This adds to operating costs and dries out food that is not properly wrapped. "Frostless" freezers, on the other hand, cut the current off every 24 hours, for a period, or cut it after every 20th door opening, and most such models introduce heat to melt frost as well. Some even have a heating element (more electricity wasted); others reverse the refrigeration process temporarily. Less expensive to operate than either of the non-frosting models is the standard freezer that has to be defrosted manually. With ordinary use, defrosting is necessary only once or twice a year, however, and the lower initial cost plus the saving in electricity make manual defrosting worth the effort for most con-

sumers. Be careful not to allow too thick a frost build-up, though; it lowers freezer efficiency and increases operating cost. Most freezers should be defrosted before the frost is ½" thick.

What It Costs to Freeze

Estimating the useful life of a freezer at 15 years, here is a rough idea of the cost per pound of freezing and storing food for one year. The example is a $200, 12-cubic-foot, manual-defrost, 396-lb.-capacity model (average 33 lbs. per cubic foot). Although electricity is figured at 5¢ per kilowatt-hour, this figure varies widely across the U.S., as do such factors influencing operating cost as frequency and amount of freezing, how often the freezer is opened, and room temperature where it's located.

Net depreciation based on 15 years at 5¼% interest compounded annually	$11.96
Return on investment foregone at 7¾% interest (yielding 8.17% compounded)	13.33
Repairs	6.00
Electricity used in freezing food	1.80
Electricity for maintaining 0°	54.76
Packaging (@ 2¢ per lb.)	7.20
Total annual cost (taxes and finance charges not included)	$95.05
Cost per pound per year	.24

Making best use of your freezer by frequent turnover of its contents will help defray the cost of buying and running one. Consuming and replacing the contents four times a year drops the cost per pound in the example above to 6¢. It doesn't cost any more to operate a full freezer than a half-empty one. And in case of a power failure a full freezer will stay cold longer.

Incidentally, your freezer should have an individual circuit to prevent interruption of power flow from other appliances plugged into the same wall socket. This is why some people prefer to locate the freezer in the cool of the cellar, with a short direct line to the main junction box—transferring food to the freezing compartment of the kitchen refrigerator for week-by-week use.

When You Buy a Freezer

Look for the Underwriters Laboratory seal of approval before purchasing any freezer, and make sure you get a good spoilage warranty in case of breakdown; these are good for three to five years usually.

How big? A general figure of six cubic feet of freezer space per family member is often used. If your freezer will be utilized mainly for storing frozen food and seldom for freezing it, as little as three cubic feet per person will do. But if you're going to depend on it for most of your food supply, if you grow much of what you eat, if you hunt and fish, you may need as much as 10 cubic feet per person.

One cubic foot of freezer space will hold about 35 pounds of frozen food if packages are regular in size, square-cornered, and stored in contact with one another; 30-35 pounds if packets are irregular in shape.

To Come Out Ahead

As utility rates rise, the cost-per-pound to freeze food and keep it frozen will also rise. You can save on electricity by keeping these freezer-use tips in mind:

• Hold your freezer at 0°, and buy an inexpensive refrigerator-freezer thermometer to check on this. Food maintained at any higher temperature loses nutritional value, taste, texture, and appearance.

• If you don't put in a vegetable garden, purchase vegetables and fruits in season for freezing when they are cheapest.

• The most expensive food item in most families being meat, this is the food freezer owners try hardest to save money on. Here are two important ways of doing so: Shop for advertised specials, being careful not to overstock on any one item of meat, poultry, or fish since you may need the space for another "special" next week; buy a side of meat wholesale and have it cut into standard cuts (unless you equip yourself and learn to dress your own meat, which can amount to some saving). Wrap the cuts for freezing

when you get home. But be forewarned that bulk meat is not always as cheap as supermarket meat since the prices per pound quoted in bulk meat ads may refer to an entire side, and you may find that it's shrunk considerably in weight after it's been dressed. You could be freezing less meat than you shelled out for. If you have a large freezer, before considering the purchase of a side of meat, send for a copy of Home and Garden Bulletin No. 166, *How to Buy Meat for Your Freezer,* 20¢, Superintendent of Documents, U.S. Government Printing Office, Washington, DC 10402.

• Be extremely wary and investigate thoroughly any food-freezer plan you become interested in before you sign a contract. The package deal that includes a freezer may be less to your advantage than buying one on your own; the food items in the plan may not meet your family's food requirements or desires. You may find a direct approach more economical in the long run. Such plans vary so much in value, not to mention ethical standards, you'd do well to check with your Better Business Bureau, friends, and neighbors before signing.

• Use your freezer not for snack foods, pastries, or ice cubes but for food items you have bought as bargains or grown yourself, for bread home-baked in quantity to save cooking fuel, for make-ahead main dishes that are cheaper to prepare in quantity with ingredients that cost less in bulk, and for ready-to-eat desserts made from your bumper crop of fresh fruits.

• Save oven fuel by roasting the biggest turkey that will fit in your oven, or roast two or more chickens at the same time. Serve the meat hot the first meal, then carve up the rest and freeze it in meal-size amounts —slices in some packets, cubes for stews, soups, and casseroles in others, and grind up what's left for hash.

• Freeze your own convenience meals if there are days in your life when mealtime is unpredictable. Freeze spaghetti sauce in Seal-A-Meal boilable plastic bags, for example, and heat it in boiling water while the pasta is cooking. Or freeze raw, thin hamburgers individually for quick-thaw near-instant frying. A wall-mounted Seal-A-Meal bag sealer costs about $17.

• But most important in making a freezer pay off is keeping it filled as much of the

Selecting Fruits and Vegetables for Freezing

Whenever selecting fruits or vegetables for freezing, remember that the quality of the frozen product can only be as good as the quality of the fresh product.

Firm, vine- or tree-ripened fruit is the most satisfactory. Ripe fruit just right for eating is your best guide for selecting fruits for freezing. Eating-ripe fruit has as its characteristics a firm texture, good color, and full flavor.

Fresh, tender vegetables from the garden are best for freezing. Gather the vegetables early in the morning and prepare for freezing immediately or refrigerate till preparation times. Store them only a short time, however, as vegetables soon lose flavor, quality, and food value. Some vegetable varieties freeze better than others, so find out from your County Extension Service which ones they recommend.

Apples	Ripe, firm, full-flavored, crisp
Apricots	Fully ripe, firm, plump, golden yellow color
Asparagus	Young; tender stalks, crisp; well-formed, tightly closed tips; about 2 inches light-colored woody base
Beans, green	Young; tender; crisp snap; long, straight pods
Beans, lima	Tender-skinned; crisp; slightly rounded, bright green pods
Beets	Young; not more than 2 to 3 inches in diameter; rounded with smooth, firm flesh
Blueberries	Ripe, full-flavored, large, dark blue color with soft, powdery bloom
Broccoli	Firm, tender stalks; tight, compact, dark green heads; not woody
Brussels sprouts	Firm, compact, bright green heads; small to medium heads
Carrots	Firm; well-shaped; dark in color; mild flavored
Cauliflower	Firm; tender; snow-white head; heavy, compact head; bright green jacket of leaves
Cherries	Tree-ripened, firm, bright red
Corn	Young; tender; even rows of plump, milky kernels; fresh, green husk
Greens	Young, tender leaves
Peaches	Ripe, moderately firm to the touch, creamy to yellow background color
Pears	Fairly firm to touch, yet beginning to soften, shiny skin
Peas, green	Bright green, well-filled pods; plump peas
Plums	Ripe, slightly soft to touch, well-colored for variety
Potatoes, sweet	Firm texture; smooth; bright; uniform skin color; medium to large
Raspberries	Fully ripened, firm, juicy, purple or red better than black for freezing
Rhubarb	Firm, tender, glossy stalk with large amount of pink or red color
Rutabagas	Roots heavy for size; firm; smooth; small or medium
Squash, summer	Young with small seeds; firm; tender rind; heavy for size; glossy
Squash, winter	Mature; fully colored; firm, hard rind; heavy for size
Strawberries	Ripe, firm, red, fragrant aroma, stem caps attached
Turnips	Heavy for size; firm; smooth; fairly round

time as possible, with foods moving in and out on a regular basis. Of course, every package should have a label naming the item, its weight, and the date it was put in. Then keep a running account that looks like this:

ITEM	Pkg. size	No. pkgs.	Date put in	Date to be used	Pkgs. used
Corn	10 oz.	16	8/76	6/77	III
Salmon steaks	2 lbs.	4	5/76	7/77	I

The rule for economical freezer use is, "First food in, first food out." This assures that you will be using frozen food at its highest state of nutrition and taste and that no packages will be mislaid in the freezer.

What to Freeze

Practically all fruits (except bananas) freeze. You can freeze them in a syrup pack, but to save money on sugar you may prefer an unsweetened fruit pack. Processing differs with various fruits. Apples, for instance, are washed, peeled, cored, and sliced into a solution of ½ teaspoon ascorbic acid color-keeper to one quart water. Blueberries, on the other hand, are washed, drained, and steamed for only a single minute, cooled swiftly and packed in cold water.

Some vegetables freeze better than others. Salad greens, celery, green onions, cucumbers, radishes and—most unfortunately—tomatoes lose their firmness and do not freeze well.

Water blanching is the preferred way of processing most vegetables for home freezing. They are simply placed in a wire mesh basket and immersed in boiling water in a big kettle for a time that is specific for each vegetable.

How to Thaw

Frozen meat, poultry, or fish is best thawed in the refrigerator. There's less moisture loss and this way the surface does not reach dangerously high bacteria levels before the food has thawed in the center, as can happen if food is simply left out on the counter to thaw. Meat, poultry, and fish can be cooked without thawing; allow about one-third to one-half more (fuel-wasting) cooking time.

What about refreezing previously frozen foods that have been allowed to thaw? Some

If the current goes off

Don't panic, but don't open the freezer door or lid during a power failure. You're in luck if your freezer is full; the food will probably stay frozen for as long as two days. If only half full, count on its staying frozen by itself only 24 hours. Foods that are only partially thawed and still have ice crystals in them can be refrozen. There will be some loss in quality, of course, and refrozen packages should be used as soon as possible. If there's been a gradual warm-up to 40° over the course of several days, don't try to refreeze, however. This is most apt to happen after the current has been off for some time. Hence, the value of a freezer alarm. Buy one that can be heard all over the house. They cost about $13, emitting a loud sound for a week, or until someone gets the electricity going again, any time the temperature inside the box rises to 24°.

It's good insurance to set up an arrangement with a dry ice supplier to let you buy 50 pounds if you ever need it. This should keep the food in a 20-cubic-foot freezer at about 15° for three to four days.

foods, fish and poultry in particular, may have been frozen previously, even though you purchase them unfrozen. If you refreeze them not much deterioration in quality will result because commercial foods are originally frozen at a prodigiously fast rate, much more swiftly than home freezing. Most partially thawed foods refreeze safely if they still contain ice crystals and are firm in the center. However, many foods—and thawed ice cream is one of them—will not regain top quality. Thawed meat pies, poultry pies or cream pies, casseroles, or vegetables should not be refrozen after having been thawed.

Packaging for the Freezer

Use only moisture- and vapor-proof materials (heavy-weight aluminum foil, polyethylene plastic bags, freezer film wrap, plastic or metal containers). The shrink-film wrap on meats you buy at self-service counters "breathes" and is unsuitable for freezer storage longer than a couple of weeks. Overwrap these packages with vapor-proof material to prevent freezer burn. Delicate foods like freshly-caught brook trout or bass can be frozen in water in sealed plastic bags. Freezing fish in ice this way virtually eliminates the danger of freezer burn. In addition, when thawed the fish will taste as fresh as the day on which they were caught.

Be sure to freeze foods as soon as they are packed. Put them into the freezer a few packages at a time. Freeze no more than three pounds per cubic foot of freezer space in any 24-hour period. (Don't freeze a quarter of beef all at once. Move it from refrigerator to freezer in small lots.) Freezing too much at once slows the rate of freezing and may inhibit quality not only of the foods being frozen but of others already in the freezer. For quickest freezing, place packages or containers against the coldest coils or walls and leave little spaces between them as they are freezing to speed up the process. Later move and restack them tightly together to conserve space. Save electrical energy by putting only cold foods into the freezer. Cool hot foods quickly by placing freshly-filled freezer containers or bags in ice water until the outside of the containers or bags feels cool. After doing this, then go ahead and freeze the food.

Care in sealing wrapped foods in an airtight way is as important as using the right container for liquids. The four sketches that follow show the best method for wrapping foods for freezing:

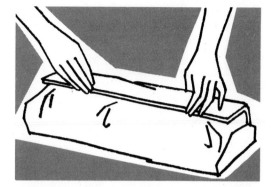

2 Make sure that the coated side of paper is next to the food. Bring wrapping sides together at top. Fold down edges in series of locked folds.

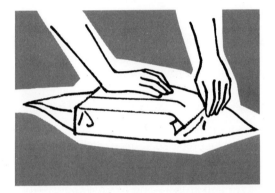

3 Press wrapping paper against food, then crease both ends to form points. Press wrapping tightly to remove any entrapped pockets of air.

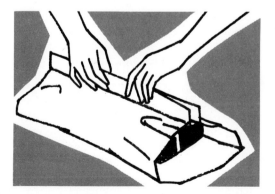

1 Use suitable wrapping paper 1½ times as long as what is needed to go around the particular food. Place food in center of wrapping paper.

4 Turn under both pointed ends. Secure ends and the seam with freezer tape. Label packages carefully with contents and date of packaging.

Cook with an Electric Slow Cooker and Save

In the old days, a pioneer woman would fill a cast-iron kettle with meat and vegetables, and leave it simmering on the back of the range while she went about her chores. Today, people use the same old-fashioned approach with a newly popular appliance—the electric slow cooker. Various types are now on the market. Some are heated by a low-wattage element under the pot. Those best suited for long cooking have coils that wrap around the pot instead of on the bottom which reduces the possibility of burning and provides a more even heat.

The Time-Saving Advantage

The ingredients of a pot roast, soup, or stew can all be prepared at once, popped into the cooker on "low" and pretty much forgotten about until the food is ready to eat. For full flavor and aroma—and to save energy—the lid should not be lifted before the food is ready to serve, except with a few recipes that call for additional preparation toward the end, like adding rice or pasta.

You can plug a cooker, set on "low," into an electric timer (the kind that turns your lights on automatically when you're away) and set the timer to start the pot at the appropriate hour to have certain kinds of one-dish meals all ready when you get home.

Nutritionally Speaking

Some makers claim slow cookers "retain healthful vitamins, minerals, and juices." Nutritionists agree, but with a condition. There's a trade-off for convenience in a loss of nutrition if consumers aren't careful in the way they use the cookers. During a low-heat cooking period of several hours a considerable quantity of the water-soluble nutrients leach out of the food into the cooking liquid. Since it doesn't boil, there is no steam and virtually no moisture loss. Thus, the homemaker who fails to use the accumulated broth because it is messy to handle or may have fat from the meat that needs skimming, is throwing away important vitamins and minerals. If the broth is not served with the meal, perhaps reduced over high heat and/or a thickener added, it should be saved for use in other soups, sauces, and gravies.

To preserve nourishment, University of Minnesota extension nutritionist Mary Darling recommends reducing the amount of cooking liquid to a minimum and even cutting the cooking time as short as possible. When a recipe calls for browning, most meats should be sautéed separately to seal in juices and enhance flavor; browning in the cooker on "high" takes far too long. Cut vegetables with a sharp knife to avoid bruising them. Place vegetables on the bottom of the cooker and set the meat on top. Cover and cook till tender.

How Slow Cookers Save Money

Set on "low"—about 200°—a slow cooker will cook all day for a few cents' worth of electricity. A cooker can, if necessary, be turned on "high" for faster cooking. Uncovered, this is a good way to reduce the broth. It will simmer on a modest 150 watts depending on the make. However, many foods have to be stirred on "high" to prevent scorching or sticking.

Cheap cuts of tough meat are made fork-tender cooked long on "low" and are more juicy when served. Slow cooking is ideal for pot roasts, stews, hens, and short ribs. It's also good for low-cost soups containing high-protein lentils and soybeans.

A slow cooker doesn't heat up your kitchen, and that saves on air conditioning in those parts of the country where houses have to be cooled in hot weather.

Cut Costs with a Pressure Cooker

A pressure cooker saves money two ways: It makes inexpensive cuts of meat tender without loss of flavor or nutrients, softening tough connective tissue much more swiftly than any other cooking method. And it uses minimal fuel by cooking foods in one-fourth to one-third the time required of most other methods, using the lowest burner setting after pressure is attained.

Moisture-heat pressure cooks potatoes, carrots, and beets in a fraction of open-pot time—peas in a mere 1½ minutes, acorn squash in 10 minutes, chicken in 15 minutes, Hungarian goulash in 20 minutes, pot roast in 40 minutes, navy bean soup in 45 minutes, plum pudding in an hour.

Air and liquid affect flavor in cooking. All air is exhausted before pressure cooking begins, and only enough liquid is used (in most recipes) to make steam. Thus flavor and color are retained and essential vitamins and minerals are preserved. Several vegetables can be cooked at the same time without swapping flavors; cooking odors of even strong-smelling vegetables are virtually eliminated, which is nice for nostrils.

How a Pressure Cooker Works

At sea level water boils at 212°. In an open pot, no matter how high you turn up the heat under it, the water doesn't get any hottter but vaporizes away in the form of steam. Turn that pot into an airtight container, however, continue heating the water, and you raise both its boiling point and the temperature of the steam generated. At five pounds pressure per square inch, its temperature reaches 227°. At 10 psi, it goes to 230°. At 15 psi, which is the pressure that most pressure cooker recipes specify, the temperature of the steam penetrating the food reaches 250°.

Many women who received pressure cookers as wedding gifts have let them sit on the shelf, having heard stories of accidents in which food spewed out the vent pipe all over the kitchen ceiling. You can minimize this risk by never pressure-cooking applesauce, rhubarb, split peas or split pea soup, cranberries, spaghetti, cereal or pearl barley; any of these foods can foam up and clog the vent. You should not fill the cooker more than two-thirds full because of the same risk of clogging the vent and developing too much pressure. But be assured that modern models made by either of the two big pressure cooker manufacturers, Mirro and Presto, conform to the safety standards of Underwriters Laboratories and have features that make them reasonably safe.

When Using the Cooker

Stay nearby when you are using a pressure cooker. Such a small amount of water is used to create the steam that if you go off and forget it, the water can steam away and the pot may be ruined. It's an excellent idea to buy an accurate kitchen timer as an adjunct to ownership of a pressure cooker. Not only is dead-accurate timing of cooking essential to prevent overcooking, but if you are called away by the doorbell or telephone, the timer bell will remind you to rush back and move the cooker off the heat.

Cookbooks used to recommend that tough cuts of meat be cooked at low pressure (five psi) for better flavor and less shrinkage, the slower penetration of heat supposedly retaining the juices and flavor. Cooked at high (15 psi) pressure, they said meats would have more of a "stew like" flavor and a fibrous texture from the driving out of the juices by the high pressure of steam. Modern pressure cooker manuals indicate that this is nonsense, but if you acquire a cooker with a variable pressure gauge you might like to experiment and decide for yourself. Such meats as pot roast, flank steak, tongue, and oxtail cook deliciously under pressure in a moist atmosphere, but no one would want to subject a steak to a steam bath.

When you cook vegetables and don't want to intermingle their flavors, place the vegetables on a rack above a small amount of steam-producing water (one-half cup in a four-quart cooker). For soups and stews, where blending of flavors is just what you want, the rack is dispensed with; and since there is little evaporation, the amount of liquid you pour in the cooker will approximate that in the finished dish.

Meats should be browned thoroughly on all sides in a little fat directly in the cooker; tongs are useful for turning it. Seasonings and liquid are then added.

To Reduce the Pressure

Some recipes call for pressure reduction immediately after the specified number of cooking minutes, and it's important that this be done rapidly to avoid overcooking. Some cookbooks advise against pressure-cooking of vegetables, saying they overcook while the pressure is dropping. This can be avoided by placing the bottom of the cooker in a cool water bath or simply by running cool water against its sides to reduce the pressure instantly—unless your cooker's instruction manual specifically says not to do so. In some recipes, the cooker is removed from the heat and the pressure is allowed to fall of its own accord. In modern pressure cookers, the dropping of the little plunger in the automatic air-exhaust vent clearly indicates when all pressure has subsided so that the pressure regulator can be taken off and the cover removed.

Is there any risk of explosion? According to the UL standard, a pressure cooker must have a safety valve that lets steam escape automatically at no more than twice its maximum operating pressure, while the cooker itself must be able to withstand five times the maximum operating pressure.

Homemakers, however, have been injured in attempting to add ingredients to a cooker shortly after it has begun to pressurize because they tried to open the kettle before the pressure was down. Even a small amount of steam pressure is hazardous; never force open a cooker unless it has cooled and is completely depressureized —the steam can rush forth and scald you, warns the U.S. Consumer Product Safety Commission. It's extremely important to read and clearly understand the precautions and safety advice in the instruction manual.

If you have to add vegetables for the last few minutes of cooking time, as you do in making a stew, let all the pressure dissipate before disengaging the lid. Then, build the pressure back up.

Buying a Pressure Cooker: Not to be confused with the bigger more expensive pressure *canners*, most top-of-range three- or four-quart cookers are priced under $20 and feature a pressure regulator that adjusts to five, 10, and 15 pounds pressure per square inch. Electric pressure cookers are more expensive but can serve as an extra burner when your range top is fully occupied.

Pressure cooker cooking

The recipe books that pressure cooker manufacturers slip into the cartons tell how to thicken the liquid in the bottom of the cooker properly if you want a sauce or gravy—by mixing flour and water together and adding it to the liquid—or you may be told to add some cornstarch. Another way to thicken? Yes, indeed. The French answer is Beurre Manie, a simple mix of equal parts of flour and butter or margarine at room temperature. A piece the size of a walnut stirred into the juice will thicken a little more than a pint—lumplessly.

Lunch to Go

In these days of hectic lunch hours and crowded, expensive lunch counters, taking your lunch to work makes a lot of money-saving sense. Whether you carry a plain brown paper bag or a fully equipped lunch box, packing delicious and attractive meals is a challenge to your ingenuity. The following ideas should help you to pack creative, delicious lunches:

• Sandwiches are, of course, the most popular lunch box feature. Conserve time and effort by making one or two weeks' supply at once and freezing them for up to two weeks. Be sure to wrap the sandwiches separately in foil, freezer bags, or clear plastic freezer wrap and label each with the ingredients and date. A sandwich plucked from the freezer before starting for work will be ready to eat at lunchtime.

• Sandwich fillings that freeze well include cream cheese, hard-cooked egg yolks, sliced or ground cooked meat and poultry, tuna, salmon, and peanut butter. *Do not freeze* sandwiches containing lettuce, celery, tomatoes, cucumbers, egg whites, jelly, or mayonnaise.

• Make sandwiches interesting by using various kinds of breads including white, rye, pumpernickel, whole wheat, French, and nut breads. Also try bagels, English muffins, and hamburger or frankfurter buns.

• Perk up your sandwiches with lettuce, onion slices, and tomato slices. To keep these vegetables fresh, wrap them separately in foil or clear plastic wrap, then add them to the sandwich at lunchtime.

• Fixing roast beef or ham sandwiches? Try slicing the meat paper-thin. You'll find that it is easier to eat four or five thin slices than one thick slice.

• Besides sandwiches, there are a host of other foods you can take along in your lunch box. Take advantage of the wide-mouth vacuum containers by packing chilled desserts, custard, pudding, tossed salads, vegetable salads, gelatin salads, or canned fruits, as well as hot soups, stews, sandwich fillings, or casseroles. The handy wide mouth makes it easy to spoon the food out of the container.

• Small plastic containers with airtight seals are great for lunch boxes because they help prevent spilled food.

• All foods taste better when kept at the right serving temperature but it's especially important to keep poultry, eggs, and mayonnaise mixtures, such as ham and potato salads, cool at all times. Also be sure to keep creamed mixtures in a vacuum container so the soups will stay hot or the puddings and custards cold.

• Freeze a can of fruit or vegetable juice overnight. It will be thawed by lunch, and will keep the rest of the food in the bag or box cool.

• To keep your tossed salad fresh, pack the salad dressing in a separate small container so it can be poured over the salad just before eating.

• Add crunch to your lunch with fresh vegetables. Carrot and celery sticks or cauliflowerettes are easy to pack. For a special treat include some sour cream dip in a vacuum container.

• Fresh fruit is a delicious and nutritious lunch-box dessert. Wrap the fruit in clear plastic wrap so that you can wrap up the core or peel after lunch. An orange partially peeled and then wrapped makes peeling at lunchtime a snap.

• Cupcakes baked in paper bake cups and frosted with butter-type frosting travel well. To protect the frosting, invert a paper cup over the cupcake.

• If even your spare time is too limited for lunch box preparation, you still may save money by carrying your lunch. Check the store for the best buys in ready-to-travel foods, such as cakes, breads, cheeses, potato chips, pickles, crackers, canned fruit, and even canned puddings, in serving-size containers.

• Lunch box equipment ranges from plain to fancy. If you frequently carry your lunch, invest in a metal lunch box with a made-to-fit vacuum bottle. Although all types of plastic eating utensils are available, you can save money and make eating easier by using metal utensils from home as part of your lunch kit. A cloth napkin rather than a paper napkin is also a worthwhile addition to your lunch box.

Do Your Own City Farming

If you live in town and have a patio, a balcony, a rooftop, or perhaps only a south-facing windowsill, you have enough room for a mini vegetable garden.

The only requirement is full bright sunlight. If you can't come up with a space that gets at least six hours of sun, nothing you can do in the way of watering, fertilizing, or tender loving care will make any difference.

How to Get Started

Start by assembling the containers you'll need. They have to be large enough to hold adequate soil for your plants at maturity—but they don't have to be anything fancy. Save money adapting plastic pails, dish pans, and wastebaskets from a variety store. Using a red-hot awl or ice pick, bore four ¼" drainage holes in these, spaced evenly around the sides near the bottoms (but not *in* the bottoms themselves).

Actually, anything you can make drainage holes in will do to hold plants, from clay pots for your windowsill to large wooden boxes for your patio, and boxes can go on casters so you can move them around. Bushel baskets painted inside and out last three or four years and look attractively rural with a full crop of lettuce spilling out the top.

If your garden area is a flat city roof, be aware that these get exceedingly hot in the sun. Protect tender roots from burning by insulating containers from the roof surface by placing them on bricks or folded newspapers.

It's important to provide good drainage inside your containers. Do so with pebbles, gravel, or crushed-up broken clay pots (though, for heaven's sake, don't bust up good ones, they're beginning to get very scarce). Spread this in the bottom to a depth of 2" in any container a foot in diameter and to a depth of 6" in larger containers.

If you're only planning on a couple of tomato plants, you can fill your containers with synthetic soil substitute, usually a mixture of a lightweight aggregate, peat moss, and fertilizer. Although manmade "soil" of this kind is free of weed seeds and plant disease organisms, a warning: it's difficult to keep watered properly. You have to keep restoring the nutrients that wash out. And because it dries out quickly, you can't go off and leave it for a weekend in hot weather without risking loss of your precious plants.

If you're serious about mini-gardening, you can save money by putting together your own highly reliable potting soil:
- One-third dark, rich, screened topsoil borrowed or begged from a country friend, or bought at a garden center if that's your only recourse;
- one-third coarse sand or a lightweight equivalent like horticultural vermiculite or perlite; and
- one-third made up half of shredded peat moss and half of dry processed manure. The latter is enough fertilizer for initial plantings. Make sure the peat moss is moist and the ingredients are well mixed together before filling your containers.

What Should You Plant?

There are a number of varieties of compact vegetables that are ideal for container gardening. New ones appear in the seed companies' (free) catalogs every year. Here are some favorites:
- Tiny Tim tomatoes, 6" high, produce clusters of bright red midget tomatoes. Fruits ripen in about 45 days and keep bearing for a long time. Best not to try growing them from seed. Many neighborhood florists stock these and other vegetable miniatures ready for transplanting; use water-soluble fertilizer mixed at half-rate as a "starter solution." You can stake them or let them sprawl out of raised containers. Be sure and pinch off suckers (unnecessary growth in the crotch where branches join the stem) if you want a single vine; or let one sucker below the first cluster of flowers develop into a second stem for a greater yield.

To help a tomato plant release its pollen, on a warm, dry day merely strike the stake. If you're troubled with blossom-drop, try to pick up a hormone spray called Blossom Set. It may help. If they've all fallen off, wait. Give the plant a chance to grow some new blossoms before you throw it away in a fit of pique.

• Golden Midget produces 4″ ears of corn on 30″ stalks in about 60 days—and none lost to the raccoons in city gardening! You can boil the ears and eat them whole, they're so tender. But be sure and plant at least two rows, no matter how short they may be, or a small block of corn, for adequate wind-pollination to take place.

• Tom Thumb lettuce forms a mini-butter-head the size of a tennis ball. You'll probably find any looseleaf lettuce easier to grow, however. Be sure to make periodic plantings starting early in the spring for successive harvesting of this vegetable all through the summer months.

• Minnesota Midget muskmelons are ready to eat when only 4″ in diameter. One vine produces a lot of fruit.

• Short n' Sweet is a delicious mini-carrot only 3″ long.

• Patio Pik, small hybrid cucumbers, should be trained onto a trellis or they'll be all over the place; keep them picked.

• Cherry Belle is a round red radish that is about the size of a cherry. Plant a few seeds every couple of weeks or so for continuous supply of them.

• Vinette is a midget green pepper; buy nursery plants.

• Dwarf Morden and Little Leaguer are two varieties of miniature cabbage that can be grown quite easily in a window box. Space them approximately 8″ apart.

• Squash calls for a big container. Aristocrat is a bush-type zucchini just right for mini-gardens.

Grow the Crop from Seeds

Although they take some looking-after, you can grow seeds indoors to steal a march on spring if you have a south-facing window that gets a lot of sun. Use readymade peat pellets available at garden supply outlets. They contain synthetic soil that swells up several times its size when you add water to the pellet.

Clean out your containers with soap and hot water and rinse them well before you line them with soil and pop in the pellets. Water and wait for them to expand, then make a little hole with your finger to the proper planting depth that is called for on the seed packet and drop in two or three seeds. Cover the seeds with peat moss and moisten them with water.

Then enclose the container in a plastic bag until the seedlings emerge. Leave the most vigorous-looking seedling and pull out the others. Water thoroughly before transplanting to a larger container after the first two true leaves develop, being careful not to disturb the roots.

Wait until a day when the plants need watering about three weeks after the two-leaf stage, then apply a level teaspoon of commercial 5-10-5 fertilizer per square foot of soil surface. Stir the fertilizer into the top ½″ of soil and water thoroughly. Repeat this procedure every three weeks. It will keep your vegetable plants growing and producing. Don't over-fertilize, however; they'll turn brown and you will have to re-pot or start again.

Water only when the surface of the soil becomes dry ¼″ down. Don't overwater or you'll rob your plants of oxygen to the roots and they'll just keel over. During a heat wave you may have to water as often as three times a week, however. Be careful never to let the plant soil dry out completely. It's very hard to get an even distribution of moisture established again. Be absolutely sure to check on soil moisture by just sticking your finger down as deep as you can every few days.

To stay ahead of any unwanted insects that may wend their way to your mini-garden, you can dust with rotenone or Sevin insecticides, both very low in toxicity. Skip edible leaves like lettuce and chard (incidentally, a great candidate for container growing because you can repeatedly harvest the outer leaves of two or three plants and have chard to eat all summer).

Cucumbers In a Flowerpot, by Alice Skelsey, $2.95 from Workman Publishing Company, Inc., 231 East 51 Street, New York 10022, is a thorough growing guide to the mini-culture of a dozen vegetables, plus herbs, oranges, lemons, limes, peaches, figs, strawberries and, unbelievably, bananas.

Reducing the High Cost of Housing

A home of one's own on a plot of land. It remains the great American dream, even though the inflated cost of houses and mortgages now requires more resourcefulness by young families to achieve the dream, and even a planned gradual approach. Some couples now remain longer in rented quarters. Others have bought into condominiums for at least a mid-term compromise and as a way to partly control leaping housing expenses. An astonishing number live in mobile homes.

Whatever the mode, the heaviest drain on the average family budget is housing. "One-quarter of income for shelter" was once the rule for getting by comfortably; today, many a couple spends 30 to 40 percent. Older couples with paid-off mortgages are watching the rise in real estate taxes with deep apprehension and keep thinking of moving. This section of the book explores important aspects of saving money on shelter that you should have firmly in mind before renting, buying, or building; before signing a lease, mortgage, or building loan.

Then it delves into some of the ways you can lower day-to-day housing operating expenses, including how to save on furnace fuel, reduce hot-water costs, tame utilities, reduce appliance costs, and lower your phone bill.

How to Deal with Landlords and Leases

Landlord-tenant relationships often become abrasive during a period of inflation—especially one like that of the 1970's—because of dramatic jumps in heating and other operating costs, and the tendency toward property neglect that becomes visible in times of high costs. This problem is heightened by the fact that more young families are being forced to turn to rental housing because of the high tags on detached houses, and the restrictions in many areas on mobile homes.

A common source of conflict is security, or "damage", deposits. In a typical complaint, one family reported that their landlord refused to make urgent repairs, even though the husband offered to do part of the work if the landlord furnished the materials. So the couple moved out, despite the fact that their lease had 15 months to go. Even though the landlord immediately rented the premises to another party, he refused to return the couple's $140 security deposit.

There is no foolproof way to insure that the landlord will return a fair amount of your security deposit, but there are several actions you can take that will help fortify your position.

Before you sign a lease, make a list of all defects found in the apartment and have the landlord sign it. Do the same when you leave. In Michigan such a check list is mandatory. It is probably the best protection you can muster, but as a practical matter it may not always be possible to get the landlord to sign such a paper—particu-larly if the lease is signed long before moving in. Even so, make up a check list of the condition of all sections of the premises, and when you move in try to get the landlord to sign it—or at least mail a copy of the list to the landlord by certified mail (and keep a copy yourself). Take pictures if possible to support your assessment of the condition of the premises.

When leaving the apartment, make up a similar check list and try to get the landlord to sign it. Also take pictures (again) to support your claim concerning the condition in which you are leaving the premises. Try to find out before you leave what charges the landlord will seek for various types of damage. You may minimize your losses by making any necessary repairs on the most expensive items yourself before moving out. If your landlord has kept what you believe is too large a piece of your deposit, ask him to provide a detailed breakdown of the charges.

Finally, if no satisfactory response is forthcoming, consider the possibility of bringing action in small claims court to recover a fair part of your security deposit. One midwestern woman was able to recover all of the $100 retained by her landlord when she proved in small claims court that there had been no damage to the premises when she left. Other frequent disputes involve termination of leases, retaliatory actions, and the "right to repair".

One trend visible in new laws in several states, notably New York and Florida, is to require landlords to pay interest on security deposits under specified circumstances, and also to strengthen requirements for return of deposits. Delaware, for example, now provides that a tenant can collect double the amount if the landlord does not return a deposit within 30 days of termination of the lease.

Two Maryland counties have created landlord-tenant offices to investigate and try to settle the rising number of disputes, and Washington and Hawaii also recently enacted a new landlord-tenant code that gives tenants more protection.

Before signing a lease, you should, of course, read it carefully. Know what it obligates you for, and if the obligations or restrictions seem too severe, be sure to get legal advice. A landlord may give you a so-called "standard" lease to sign, but even "standard" leases can be negotiated and changed. One provision to be wary of, for example, is whether you are allowed to sublet, or assign, the lease if you decide to move or plan to be away for an extended period of time. Will you need the landlord's consent? What are the conditions for obtaining it? Can you at least get a clause stating that he won't withhold consent unnecessarily? If your sub-tenant does not pay the rent, will you be liable?

You should also check the following:

• Does the lease disclose the name and address of the owner or authorized property manager?

• On what day is the rent due, and do you have any days of grace?

• Are you, or is the landlord, responsible for specific repairs and upkeep, such as painting and plumbing? What services does the landlord undertake to provide? Heat? Utilities? Garbage removal?

• What restrictions are there on alterations? Can you have your own washing machine, or does the landlord provide adequate laundry facilities? Will he let you put in an antenna or air conditioner without paying for additional wiring or other charges?

• Does the lease provide for renewal at your choice, and if so, at what rental?

• If you do make any improvements on the premises, either with or without the landlord's consent, do such improvements become his property?

• If taxes go up, can the landlord increase your rent to cover the increase, and by what percentage? The percentage increase, if any, should be stipulated in the lease, and you should determine whether your potential increase is fairly prorated according to the number of apartments on the property.

• Is there an additional charge for parking lots or garages?

• Are you required to cover a certain percentage of the floor with rugs or carpets?

• Is there adequate closet space, and are there enough kitchen and bathroom cabinets? Is long-term storage available in the building?

• Are there enough electrical outlets? There should be two or three for each room.

Read the entire lease carefully to determine if there are any clauses that you want deleted. Most leases are not printed in any logical order, and the important clauses may be buried deep within a long paragraph. To strike a clause, cross it out on *all* copies of the lease you sign. You and the landlord, or his agent, should then initial each change.

Remember: verbal statements don't count. Only what is written in the lease itself is legally binding. If, for example, the landlord promises to redecorate or provide new equipment, such promises should be made a part of the written, signed lease.

Rent-check power

Clogged drains—faulty wiring—leaking ceilings—the litany of tenant woes could go on and on, and in too many apartments it does. You complain to the landlord, but he just shrugs and says that all repairs are your responsibility.

When the landlord won't do his part, what can you do? Use your rent money to improve your living conditions.

Because of consumer pressure from tenants, a number of states now have laws that give you a right to use your money as leverage to get repairs made in your apartment.

There are two types of laws that protect you—repair-and-deduct laws and rent-withholding laws. Under repair and deduct, you can have repairs made and take the money out of your rent; under rent-withholding statutes you pay your rent money to a court and the court has repairs made.

Battling the Inflated Mortgage

The interest you pay on your mortgage actually is the biggest single expense in your housing bill. High rates are inevitable in any inflation, although they may ebb and rise from one year to another. But high rates on top of the bigger mortgages needed to buy today's costlier homes result in enormous costs. On a $25,000 mortgage at 8½ percent for 30 years you'll repay a total of $69,210—almost three times the original loan.

These steep rates have especially hampered families in the 25-35 age bracket who have become the largest group in our population. The lofty cost of mortgages is another compelling reason why young families need to seek smaller but expandable houses.

Cutting Costs

Even in an inflation it's worth shopping more widely for a mortgage among different lenders. Some families also might qualify for programs of subsidized mortgages for moderate-income homeseekers. Too, if you can make a larger down payment, you're more likely to get a little lower rate. Even a difference of one-fourth of 1 percent can save $1,530 in the total repayment of that $25,000, 30-year mortgage.

If, besides trimming the rate, you can undertake a little larger monthly payment and repay on a 25-year basis, you would further reduce your total repayment to $59,175. That's a saving of $10,000. The difference between monthly payments on 25-year and 30-year terms is not as great as people sometimes believe. A 25-year, $25,000 mortgage at 8½ percent would require payments of $201 a month compared to $192 a month for a 30-year mortgage.

Sometimes, you may find that large developers have arranged mortgages on their homes at lower rates than an individual buyer can get.

Safeguards

Make sure you get a clause in your mortgage contract letting you "prepay" without an excessive penalty if interest rates drop.

Another safeguard is to try to get into the contract as long a grace period as your state's law allows. Some states let the mortgage-holder foreclose if the mortgage is in arrears only 60 days. But reputable lenders usually wait at least three or four months if you previously were prompt. If you become delinquent for reasons beyond your control, such as unemployment or a medical crisis, many banks and other lenders will wait a year if you continue to pay the taxes and interest, and maintain the property.

Note whether the mortgage contract or accompanying promissory note impose any extra charge for late payments, and how much these charges may be. In some states, lenders have exacted late charges of as much as 2 percent per annum on the unpaid principal as long as the payment is in default. Such charges are in addition to the normal mortgage interest and could saddle a homeowner with a heavy penalty.

Also note whether the mortgage contract requires you to deposit sums "in escrow" to pay taxes and insurance. Held in your own account, this money could earn interest; held by the lender, it doesn't. An increasing number of states require that lenders pay interest on escrow accounts. If yours doesn't, obviously it's to your benefit to avoid, if the lender is willing, any requirements for escrow deposits.

The Different Types of Mortgages

There are three types of mortgages: FHA and V.A. on which maximum rates are controlled by the Government; and conventional, on which banks, savings associations, and other lenders set their own rates (although subject to various state maximums).

All lenders usually charge the same rates on FHA and V.A. loans, although closing costs and other extra charges may vary. On the conventional loans, now most-widely used, rates often do vary. Lenders who assume the greatest risks with smallest down payments, longest repayment terms, and most liberal appraisals, usually charge highest rates, and often also require larger closing fees. One government study found a nationwide variation of about one-half of 1 percent among the different types of lenders, such as savings and loan associations, banks, and insurance companies.

At one time, FHA mortgages cost less than the conventional. Today conventional mortgages often are as low. The remaining advantages of FHA and V.A. mortgages is that they permit smaller down payments and longer terms.

For V.A. loans, veterans must apply to a bank or other lender, which submits the application to the local Veterans Administration office. Direct V.A loans are made only where mortgage money is not readily available, often the more-rural areas.

Peacetime veterans are not eligible for V.A. loans. Veterans must have seen 181 days of active service during a period of hostilities. All such veterans of World War II and the Korean and Vietnam conflicts are eligible. Under the National Housing Act of 1970, the maximum guaranteed mortgage loan of $4,000 was increased to $12,500. A World War II veteran who got,

say, a $4,000 loan in 1946 is still eligible for another one of $8,500, or the full amount if he never availed himself of a V.A. mortgage.

Rural dwellers, and not just farmers, may be able to get mortgage help from another federal agency—the Farmer's Home Administration (FmHA). If you have a moderate income, and live in an area of under 10,000 population and can't get a mortgage from a commercial lender on reasonable terms, ask your county extension agent (usually located at the county seat) how you might apply for an FmHA loan. Elderly rural dwellers (62 or over) also may be eligible for FmHA loans.

Special Mortgage Situations

Subsidized low-interest mortgages are available to help low and moderate income families buy houses. Sometimes younger families, whose incomes naturally tend to be moderate, may qualify. Eligibility depends on income and number of dependents, and requirements vary in different areas. For example, in 1975, a Suffolk County, New York, family with adjusted income under $8,500 could qualify for a mortgage subsidized by FmHA. Such mortgages also are sponsored by HUD, and in some states by state housing agencies.

Usually these government-subsidized mortgages are handled by savings and loan associations, mortgage companies, and some banks. They can supply information on current availability and eligibility requirements. In the case of one of the main HUD programs, called the Section 235 Program, home seekers can qualify for a mortgage subsidy if their income is no better than 80 percent of the median income for their area as computed by HUD. If the median income for an area is $12,000, a family with $9,600 could satisfy this requirement and be eligible for Section 235.

The buyer, as of 1976, has to make a down payment of at least 3 percent of the first $25,000 plus 10 percent of any additional amount. If all the qualifications are met, HUD pays part of the interest so that the cost to the buyer may be as low as 5 percent per annum. The program can include condominiums and co-op apartments as well as one-family detached and town houses.

Variable-rate mortgages: Some states now permit mortgage lenders to require "variable" mortgages, permitting the rates to vary as general interest rates rise and fall. The permitted variation in some recently written mortgages is 2½ percent. The hazard is that you can begin with an 8½ percent mortgage and wind up with one for 11 percent. Variable-rate mortgages, which permit changes as frequent as every six months, make budgeting for housing uncertain.

"Balloon" mortgages, which include a single unusually large payment at the end of the contract, also may be hazardous to financial health. If the property owner can't manage the final big payment he may have to renew the mortgage at whatever new rate the mortgage-holder requires.

Arranging for a Mortgage

It's best to consult with potential lenders even before you buy a house and ask about the possibility of getting a mortgage loan, and what down payments and rates would be required. When you have selected your house and compared rates and fees among several lenders, the next step is to arrange the mortgage itself.

The lender's mortgage or real estate officer will help you fill out the application. Bring with you the needed financial data the officer will need. This includes: copy of the deed or purchase contract, information on type of construction, plot size, purchase price; any present debts you have, your income, wife's income, and employer; number and ages of dependents, and a list of your cash and other assets. The lender will then arrange for an appraisal.

Assuming an Existing Mortgage

If you are buying a house which already has a mortgage at a below-current rate, obviously it's to your advantage to take it over. But both the seller and the mortgage lender must be willing.

One advantage to the seller in letting the buyer take over an existing mortgage is that he avoids possible penalty charges in paying off the mortgage ahead of time. Charges can be several hundred dollars.

There are two ways in which an existing mortgage may be taken over. The preferable way, especially for the seller, is if the lender is willing to release the seller from liability on the mortgage and substitute the buyer. On an FHA mortgage, FHA's approval also is needed.

Another way to take over an existing mortgage, is if the seller is willing to let his name remain on the mortgage bond. In that case, the lender legally may demand the mortgage payments from the seller if the buyer fails to make them. Even so, sellers sometimes are anxious enough to sell the house to assume this liability for a buyer.

Thus, if you are the buyer, and the existing mortgage is a desirable one, it would be wise to stipulate in the informal "binder" you sign when making a deposit on the house that the purchase is conditioned on taking over the mortgage. Have this stipulation written into the "contract to buy."

On an FHA mortgage, if the seller is willing to be liable, FHA approval isn't needed.

Another problem in taking over an existing mortgage is that you may have a large down payment to cope with. Sometimes an eager seller is willing to take a "purchase mortgage," really a second mortgage, for part of the down payment. The buyer should be sure the rate is not so much higher that any advantage of the existing mortgage is cancelled. Or, the original lender may be willing to negotiate a new "split rate" mortgage, with part at the old rate, part at the current rate.

How Much Can You Carry?

Most reputable lenders for their own protection will try to see that you don't over-commit yourself. The usual yardstick is that your total monthly housing expense shouldn't exceed 25 percent of monthly after-tax income. "Housing Expenses" include monthly mortgage payment, and one-twelfth of annual property tax, upkeep, and insurance. Some lenders also prefer to include heating costs in the monthly total, especially in these days of steep fuel costs.

But this general guideline can vary according to number of dependents, job stability and prospects, other unusual expenses such as high medical bills, etc. A home seeker with many mouths to feed can't afford as much housing expense as a small family with the same income.

Can You Get a Bargain in a Repossessed House?

Federal agencies usually have on hand houses they have taken over because the owners didn't meet payments on their government-guaranteed mortgages.

The main agencies are the Housing and Urban Development Department (HUD) and, to a lesser extent, the Veterans Administration. In the mid-1970's HUD especially had many houses it had to take over as the result of a program of subsidized mortgages for low-income families. Many families who bought these properties with government-aided mortgages found they could not meet the payments and the repair needs.

One problem with these bargain properties is that many are in rundown areas. Some also need extensive repairs. Since the mid-1970's, HUD has required the buyer to rehabilitate these houses. A skilled do-it-yourselfer probably can do most of the necessary work.

Prices of the FHA "as is" homes depend on location, size, and cost of rehabilitation. Generally, however, they are sold for approximately the current market value. In New York in 1975, the average price was approximately $3,500.

An example of various creative efforts to make use of the repossessed houses has been group efforts by several Brooklyn, New York, neighborhood associations. With start-up help from a local church and a foundation, one group bought several of the houses for $1,500 each, had contractors make repairs, and sold the houses. The association used the proceeds for a revolving fund for additional purchases.

On properties with V.A. mortgages, if the borrower still can't continue, the lender notifies the V.A. and receives permission to foreclose. The V.A. institutes rehabilitation if needed. The property is then listed for sale with all real estate brokers.

HUD also sells its repossessed properties through real estate brokers and will try to help buyers to find financing.

Almost all large cities have such reacquired properties, and sometimes they are available in suburbs. While some properties are in rundown areas, others can make habitable beginning homes.

V.A. repossessed properties can be bought by veteran or non-vet. Payment plans are flexible, depending on the value of the property.

The FmHA usually has repossessed properties for resale in the more rural areas.

Another challenging program, but one that needs to be approached with caution, is HUD's experimental "Urban Homesteading" plan. Under this program HUD transfers repossessed rundown houses to municipal authorities in some cities. They in turn give the houses at little or no cost to people who qualify by agreeing to occupy the property for at least three years; making repairs before moving in (within eighteen months); and rehabilitating the property. But be warned that energy, determination, and capital are needed to successfully rehabilitate most houses in the "homesteading" program.

More information is available from real estate brokers or from the HUD, V.A., and FHA offices. (Check in your phone book under "U.S. Government"). You also can contact HUD by writing to Office of Public Affairs, Housing and Urban Development Department, Washington, D.C. 20410.

Two other sources for information on potential bargains in repossessed houses are your city or county real-estate or tax department (for properties taken over for delinquent taxes) and local banks (for properties taken over on non-government guaranteed mortgages). Always inspect such properties with care; have a contractor estimate probable repair costs; make sure you can get a mortgage before making a bid; make sure zoning regulations permit alterations.

Land auctions also are on the increase. These usually involve relatively large acreage in rural areas. If that's what you're seeking, you can write for lists of local auctioneers to the National Association of Auctioneers, Lincoln, Nebraska 68500.

Buying a Mobile Home

If you're considering buying a mobile home, here's a concise guide to what you should know.

Types of Mobiles Available

Single-wides: Most common type of mobile home is the single unit, typically 12 by 65 feet, providing 744 square feet of usable space. Other sizes range from 8 feet by 29-45 feet, to 14 feet by 50-70 feet.

Expandables: These have "additions," which telescope inside the home and are placed in position at the site, adding 60 to 100 square feet.

Double-wides: Two single units towed separately to the site are joined to make one large unit.

What's Included

Major appliances, furniture, and floor coverings usually are included in the price. Air conditioning and laundry equipment usually are optional.

Extras

Some extras are required by mobile home communities. They may include: steps with handrails for each door; skirting to conceal the wheels; supports or "piers" (often concrete blocks); over-the-roof "tiers" or anchors in high-wind areas.

Quality Factors

Most mobile homes built today should follow safety and health standards developed by the American National Standards Institute, (ANSI Standard A119.1). Look for this seal near the door. Some states have higher standards. So also look for your state's certification seal. Especially look for safety and quality factors: comfortable living facilities with adequate storage space; structural strength and rigidity; adequate running gear and hitch; protection against water and wind at joints, connections, and exterior openings.

Adequate fire protection is especially important. The main hazards are:
• Furnaces which weren't cleaned before the heating season; also furnaces that had been modified to use a different type of fuel than that recommended.
• Lack of an outside fuel shutoff valve.
• Metal exterior doors that became distorted under high heat, making them difficult to open.
• Too-small windows, usually jalousies, that didn't permit escape, and hard-to-remove storm windows and screens.
• Failure to use fire extinguishers.
• Uneven support by the recommended number of jacks, thus impeding door and window operation.

A diagram must be posted showing position and number of placement piers and tie-down anchors, if required in high-wind areas. A map must be provided showing the area for which the home was built in terms of snow and wind velocity load which the roof can be expected to withstand. Homes built for the "North" zones usually are sturdier than those for "Middle" or "South."

Site

Whether you can put a mobile home on your own land depends on local regulations. HUD advises not buying land until you check with local authorities. You also have to arrange for connections to electric and gas lines and water main (or have a well drilled) and sewer (or install a septic system).

You also can rent space in a mobile home park. There are over 15,000 in the nation with 15 or more homes. Some are more attractive and well-planned than others. Compare available parks and their advantages before deciding. Rents vary from $60 a month to over $120 depending on facilities, landscaping, location, and services. Such parks can be found in every state but are especially numerous on the West Coast and Florida, Michigan, and some Midwest states. Some won't accept children; some charge considerably more than others. For ratings, consult *Woodall's Mobile Home Park Directory* at your library.

Prices

In shopping for a new mobile home, compare prices on the same or similar models among at least three dealers. If you belong to a credit union you can get estimates of current prices of various models.

Depreciation is likely to be greater than on conventional fixed homes which usually *appreciate* because of the increase in land value. A five-year-old mobile home usually will sell for about 75 percent of its original price.

Warranties

Compare warranties provided by different manufacturers, especially noting how long the home is warranted, and whether all parts are covered; whether a defective part must be returned to the factory at your expense for service. Warranties may run for as little as 90 days and as long as a year. But also make your own inspection before completing the purchase. Especially look for leaks, defec-

tive plumbing, window problems.

The dealer's responsibility does not stop with selling you the home. Provisions for set-up and future service should be covered in writing at the time of sale. Best protection is to choose a reputable dealer. Check his reputation with the Better Business Bureau or local Chamber of Commerce.

Financing: Mobile homes are expensive to finance. Banks, savings associations, credit unions, and finance companies make loans for mobile homes. There are two kinds: government-insured and "conventional."

Conventional loans usually require down payments of 20 to 30 percent. Repayment can be as long as ten years, or 12-15 for government-insured purchases.

To qualify for a government-insured loan you must intend to use the mobile home as your principal residence, and have an acceptable site, either in a park or on your own land.

The home must meet HUD construction standards. It must be new or, it must have been financed with a government-insured loan when new. Total price may include furnishings and accessories as well as transportation and initial insurance premium.

Government-insured loans can go up to $12,500, or $20,000 for double-wides. Down payments may be as low as 5 percent of the total price up to $6,000 and 10 percent of any remainder. It is, of course, to your advantage to make as large a down payment as you can manage because of the high rates on mobile-home loans. But don't attempt too-high payments. Mobile-home loans involve conditional sales contracts or chattel mortgages and thus can be repossessed much like a car, and without the greater protection against foreclosure provided by traditional home mortgages.

Insurance

If your mobile home is to be financed, the lender will require comprehensive and extended coverage. If you buy for cash, you will need coverage for your own protection. Insurance may be bought through your dealer, with the lender providing the financing (at extra cost). Or you may buy it independently, which gives you a better chance to comparison shop for lowest cost.

How to Save on Energy

Motivating many an American's quickening energy consciousness is the steadily increasing cost of heating the house and hot water, cooking food, running appliances, and lighting lights. But the specter of shortages and still more steeply rising prices for fuel and power drive home the seriousness of a national problem: America's need for energy is increasing faster than the supply.

We are hard at work to change this. While intensive research and development programs are underway, the solutions are years if not decades in the future. Meanwhile, the problem confronts us now. As the hunt for new energy sources and the development of cheap, clean, safe energy alternatives begin in earnest, American families are having to learn to use the energy available to them more efficiently, to conserve it in every possible common-sense way.

This section tells how to match costs to efficiency in heating your house; how to augment furnace heat with a stove. It shows how reducing the use of hot water (and perhaps not heating it as hot) saves substantially on the fuel bill. Here are the many ways you can light your house for less and cut down on appliance overuse. Air conditioning need not take such a bite out of the budget; the section ends with money-saving ideas on house cooling.

How to Save on Furnace Fuel

For families living in the colder parts of the nation, the cruelest financial blow of the mid-1970s has been the sharply increased cost of heating their houses.

Once you've done all you can to keep the cold out and the heat in *(see page 119 on how to insulate and weatherproof your house),* your next most vital consideration is to make sure your heating plant is operating at peak efficiency.

Anything connected with repair or tune-up is best left to a professional. The delicate adjustments called for are not within the skills of most homeowners. The national average cost of an oil-burning furnace service contract is approximately $55. The best of these include emergency service, complete summer overhaul and tune-up, plus "insurance" covering repair and replacement of specific parts. The thoroughness of the maintenance your furnace receives, however, makes a big difference in how economically it performs.

Servicing your furnace: Some new homeowners neglect to have their furnaces serviced until the inevitable day they quit operating altogether. Your heating unit should be professionally checked once a year, preferably well before the start of the heating season.

You can tell if a serviceman is making a thorough adjustment of your oil burner if he uses instruments for four final tests:

The carbon dioxide content of the flue gas. The higher the carbon dioxide content, up to a certain point, the more complete the combustion.

The smoke test. It measures the quantity of solid emissions and enables the serviceman to "clean up" the fire.

The draft intensity over the fire. If the products of combustion aren't removed quickly, they tend to smother the flame.

The stack temperature. This test measures the effectiveness of the heat-exchange process by making sure not too much heat is being lost up the stack.

Not all servicemen are equipped with the instruments for making these tests and sometimes when they have them they neglect to use them. If you think you may be burning too much oil, your oil supplier will be glad to have these efficiency tests made either at a nominal fee or on a no-charge basis as a service to the community.

You can also make some observations yourself. Check the flame by uncovering the small glass port in the front of the furnace or boiler. In the widely-used gun-type high-pressure burner the flame should be orange-yellow, bushy, and evenly shaped; it should never look or sound like a blowtorch or show more than a slight tinge of smoke at the tips. The furnace should start with a minimum of "swoosh" and never vibrate. There should be no sign of smoke coming from the chimney.

If you are about to invest in an oil burner, a flame retention burner, so called, may save you some money in operation.

In the case of gas burners, the pilot light should be blue. Any carbon on the pilot mechanism should be cleaned off. If the pilot light shrinks when the burner starts, the regulator may be sluggish or a vent may be clogged or there may be a restriction in the line. If any such case, you should call the gas company service department. A layman should never touch a gas-fired furnace.

Gas heating plants usually don't need as much service as oil burners and can get along with less frequent cleanings. But they should get the carbon dioxide test recommended for oil burners.

If you have a forced air system, keep furnace (and air conditioning) filters clean. Dirty filters cause poor heat distribution (or cooling), waste fuel, and shorten equipment life. Central system filters should be changed once each heating season (and every cooling season). If you have filters in your warm-air registers, you'd do well to remove them because they block the air flow. You get greater heating efficiency if filters are used only in the furnace.

You can inspect the ducts to make sure they're not leaking warmed air. If you can reach them, leaks are easy to close with tough, highly adherent duct tape. Warm air ducts running through unheated parts of the house like the attic, crawl space, and garage should be insulated with batts or rolls of standard insulation, foil face toward the duct, and held in place with duct tape.

Conserve your cellar's warmth: The heat that radiates from the stove pipe called the stack that runs from your furnace to your chimney warms your cellar and is just as worth conserving as heat delivered to registers and convectors upstairs.

Buttoning up your cellar tight, however, poses a dilemma, because an oil furnace needs fresh air to burn properly. If it doesn't get enough air it "cokes up" and creates soot that lessens its efficiency drastically. Most houses built since World War II have several louvered vents in the cellar walls mainly installed to keep it from getting too humid in summertime. These can be closed off for winter, all but one nearest the furnace. The cellar door can be weather-stripped and cellar windows double glazed (inexpensively with a sheet plastic tacked over them inside). But keep in mind that the opening into the cellar admitting air for the furnace to "breathe" should be the same size as the cross dimensions of the flue.

Some newer houses have been built with a special duct running directly from the outside to the oil burner, so it can have all the air it needs without the necessity of leaving a vent open that would cool off the cellar. You might talk to your furnace man about having one installed.

Keeping the cellar as warm as possible helps keep the floor above warm and saves furnace fuel.

Fuel conservation checklist: Here are measures you can take.
• Turn down the heat. A computer study by Honeywell, Inc., demonstrated fuel savings in turning down your thermostat at night and turning it up in the morning well beyond the cost of the fuel to reheat the

house. The farther you turn it down the more fuel you save (see percentages that follow). (Although some tropical house plants may not thrive at nighttime temperatures as low as 55°, most house plants do better at the cooler temperatures, as you may already have noticed.)

Lowered nighttime temperature	Percent of saving in heating fuel when thermostat is lowered at night for a period of	
	4 hours:	8 hours:
70°	0%	0%
65°	2½%	5%
60°	5%	9½%
55°	7½%	14½%
50°	9½%	19½%

Whenever your house is unoccupied for even a few hours, you save fuel by turning down the thermostat. But don't keep readjusting the thermostat during the day if you feel chilly or hot; it wastes fuel. Adjust body temperature instead by keeping a sweater handy. However, there are worthwhile savings in lowering the thermostat a couple of degrees on mild days, then pushing it back up in cold weather.

• Prevent heat loss to the rest of the house by weatherstripping all four sides of the bedroom door if you like to sleep with the window open in wintertime. Best way to get a warm night's sleep in a cold bedroom is in flannel pajamas under an electric blanket which is itself at least partially insulated under a tightly woven light wool blanket that keeps the warmth radiating toward you. Electric bed coverings, operating intermittently to augment the body's heat, consume a negligible amount of electricity. On even three or four beds in the house, they cost far less to operate than running the furnace to keep the house warm all night. Just be sure family members have as much insulation *under* as over them to retain body heat. A mattress plus pad lets too much heat escape. An old worn blanket under the pad does the trick.

• Take down all the screens on the sunny side of the house when summer's over. You receive an appreciable heat gain from the sun through south-facing windows even on cloudy days in the winter. Screens can block as much as half this valu-

able solar radiation. Conversely, close draperies at night to increase insulation against the cold.

• Be sure decorative covers, furniture, or draperies are not restricting the free radiation of heat from convectors or radiators. Radiators sitting against cold walls should have a sheet of aluminum or aluminum foil behind them to reflect heat back into the room. Metallic paint, bronze or aluminum, often used on radiators, cuts down the amount of heat given off. So does glossy white paint, whereas a flat paint, the darker the better, tends to improve radiation. A coating of dust allowed to remain on radiators or convectors reduces their effectiveness.

• Hammering in radiators and convectors, and/or in the pipes leading to them, caused by too much water collecting in a steam system, can block the circulation of steam and hot water. Convectors have a little petcock on the side that may need to be opened occasionally. Water that condenses in a (steam system) radiator can be sent traveling back down the line by propping up the end of the radiator opposite the valve. If that doesn't work a furnace repairman should bleed the system of water at the boiler end. But get rid of the knock, because it is damaging to the system and means it's operating inefficiently.

• "Balance" your central heating system for economy and comfort. It's a matter of trial and error. Adjust the fins in forced hot air registers to give each room a suitable amount of heat and no more. For example, your kitchen should not need much heat at all and bedrooms can stay cool. Bathrooms and living areas may need to be warmer. Unfortunately, a steam-heat system cannot be handled the same as a forced hot air system, because radiator valves must be turned all the way on or all the way off. Radiators can be turned off in rooms that are unoccupied or underused in winter and if there's no traffic through them, the doors can be sealed off with duct tape.

• Increase heat circulation. A strategically-placed circulating fan (which draws a mere 80 watts) can increase room comfort. A duct with a small, quiet fan inside it can be easily installed in the wall of a room with a high ceiling to draw down the 10° warmer air that collects near the ceiling and blow it out at floor level.

• Close the damper in your fireplace when you're not using it so you won't lose heat up the chimney.

• Should you moisten the air in your house? You'll feel more comfortable indoors in very cold weather if the house isn't too dried out. A humidifier in the furnace plenum allows you to feel more comfortable at a lower thermostat setting. The old ploy of placing pans of water on the radiators doesn't help, now that we keep our houses at 68° or lower, because not enough water evaporates to make any difference. However, retaining humidity generated by bathing, cooking, and laundering makes sense up to a point: If you see water condensation on the inner surface of double-glazed windows, you've let the humidity get too high and may be inflicting hidden damage on the house between the walls; be sure to lower the humidity quickly by briefly opening a door or window and/or turning on an exhaust fan.

Which Fuel for You?

Difficult as it may be to decide which one is most economical, your choice of fuel is a major factor in your choice of any auxiliary heating facility you may want to invest in to trim your furnace fuel costs. *Fuels vary in their capacity to provide heat, some burning with greater efficiency than others:*

• Electricity has 100 percent efficiency in a resistance heating unit in the room where it is located.

• Natural gas burns with an efficiency of 80 percent.

• No. 2 (the common) fuel oil burns at 70 to 75 percent efficiency if the furnace is clean and tuned.

• Coal burns with about 50 percent efficiency.

• Dry hardwoods have about half the heating efficiency of coal and one-third that of furnace oil—but in the case of coal and wood a great deal depends on how the fuel is burned.

A standard cord of air-dried, dense hardwood weighs about two tons and provides as much potential heat as a ton of coal, 150-175 gallons of No. 2 fuel oil or 2,400 cubic feet of natural gas. Wood burns cleanly, with far less pollution than most fuels, and the ashes can be used in the compost heap. Wood is free for the asking in many places.

Supplementary Heating Options

The fireplace: About half the new houses in this country have fireplaces, and many

Where to get free firewood

National parks prohibit the felling of trees, but you can get permission to fell live trees or collect deadfalls from the administrator of any of our 164 national forests if you can convince him you know how to go about doing it. Some states have opened their forests, too.

Contact your local Forest Service district ranger for information on removing undesirable trees, those that are poorly formed, diseased or genetically inferior, like pin cherry. They pose a problem for the forest manager, who is glad to get rid of them because they occupy growing space for more worthwhile trees than he can raise by trying to sell them. State, county, and city parks often have trees you can cut. Find out by calling your State Forester for state parks, County Extension Agent for county parks, and City Forester for municipal parks.

Highway departments cut a lot of trees and put them somewhere. Call your town hall and find out if you can cut and haul away some of this excess wood.

You can also get free firewood from dumps and landfills. Since many local ordinances forbid open burning, the quantity of discarded trees keeps mounting on these lands so badly needed for disposal of other wastes.

Fireplace wood is also available as industrial scrap. Sawmills accumulate pieces of slab, trim, and edging that they offer at minimal cost if you pick them up. Power companies sometimes let you have logs and limbs from powerline maintenance.

Most commonly, firewood is sold by the cord, usually described as a well-stacked pile of logs 4 x 4 x 8 feet. Since few people burn logs four feet long, many sales are "face cords" of 16"-long pieces making up one-third of a standard cord.

In some parts of the U.S. firewood is sold by the ton, which is equal to about one-half cord. If you buy by the weight instead of volume, however, look for the driest wood and avoid paying for extra water content.

families have installed them as remodeling projects in older houses. Conventional fireplaces, however, are only about 10 or 15 percent efficient. In addition, once you get a good fire going, the heat creates such a draft it draws house heat with it up the chimney. However, a fireplace in the same room with your furnace thermostat, if you keep the doors of the room closed, will help to keep that room cozily warm, cutting down the number of times the thermostat turns on the furnace.

If family evening activities are centered here, it may not matter much if the rest of the house cools off—for a considerable furnace saving. The trouble is, as the fire dies down, the house heat still pours up the hot flue; the damper can't be closed until it's completely out.

The sure—but messy—solution is to put the fire out with water. The expensive solution is to install tempered glass doors (about $45; or about $135 for tempered glass folding doors with an adjustable vent) that seal off the fireplace opening when they are closed but allow radiant heat to penetrate the glass into the room. An inexpensive expedient is simply to keep a sheet of asbestos board handy that fits over the fireplace opening while the fire dies down after the room is vacated. When it's out, the damper should be closed, of course, to prevent loss of house heat up the chimney.

Double your fireplace heat

Most of the heat generated in an ordinary fireplace escapes up the chimney. At least half this lost energy can be caught and pushed into the room by substituting a "Thermal Grate" for your present grate or andirons. It consists of a two-foot row of six 2″-diameter steel tubes that suck in cold floor-level air, heat it as they curve below, behind and up over the fire, and discharge it out into the room at the top of the fireplace opening. The hotter the fire, the stronger the thermal action. The Thermal Grate is 25½″ high and 19¼″ deep. It is available from the manufacturer, The Golden Enterprise, P.O. Box 422, Windsor, VT 05089, for $93.50 (Vermont residents add 3% sales tax) plus cost of delivery (by truck). Weight, 40 pounds.

The average cost of a traditional all-masonry fireplace ranges from $1,200 up. A factory-built one is a metal box surrounded by insulation that keeps its outer shell safely cool no matter how hot the fire gets inside. Its light weight allows it to be placed directly on a wooden floor or against wooden wall framing, whereas a traditional masonry fireplace usually needs special framing and sufficient air space around it to make it safe, plus its own foundation extending below the frost line.

An installed factory-built fireplace costs one-third to one-half the price of a conventional masonry one. Prefabricated metal fireplaces are less durable, however (depending on how much they are used), than masonry ones. A factory-built unit is not difficult to install. Complete instructions come with it, and installation can be completed in a weekend by a reasonably handy person. The chimney arrives as a single package along with sections of prefabricated insulated chimney pipe, the number of these depending, of course, on ceiling height and/or distance to roof. The sections twist-lock together, negating the need for any special tools in assembly. Wood-burning factory-built fireplaces are usually available in 28″, 36″ and 42″ widths.

A fireplace of any kind requires some sort of surrounding hearth to catch flying sparks. A shallow rectangular box or steel hoop holding a depth of crushed marble or peb-

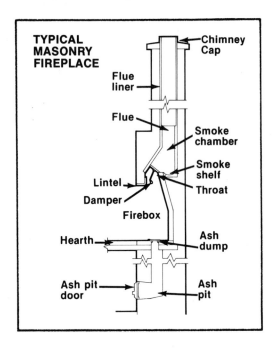

TYPICAL MASONRY FIREPLACE

Chimney Cap
Flue liner
Flue
Smoke chamber
Smoke shelf
Throat
Lintel
Damper
Firebox
Hearth
Ash dump
Ash pit door
Ash pit

bles makes an attractive one. A frame of wood holding a layer of bricks is equally effective. The hearth in front of a fireplace in a wall should extend into the room at least 16" and on either side of the opening at least 8".

The cast-iron stove: Benjamin Franklin caused a lot of arguments with his new invention, the cast-iron fireplace-stove. Franklin estimated he got 75 percent more heat from it than from a fireplace because it radiated from front, back, top, and sides. Householders, finally realizing how much heat they were losing up the flue, started closing off their fireplaces and installing Franklins in front. Folding doors that could be closed tight appeared on later models, with a sliding draft regulator, allowing hot coals to glow for hours after the fire died down.

Since the fall of 1974, the Portland Franklin Stove Foundry, Portland, Maine 04104, where since 1877 cast-iron Franklins have been made, has been having trouble getting raw materials. The price of pig iron went from $60 to $150 a ton in a single year. Today a true Franklin stove with folding doors costs about $350, to which freight charges of $10 per 100 pounds to the Midwest and $15 per 100 pounds to the West Coast must be added; the largest Franklin weighs about 350 pounds crated. There is more than a year's wait for cast-iron Franklins; only 50 or 60 per week are made.

An "imitation" Franklin stove, folding doors, fire screen grate and all, made of steel plate instead of cast iron, is available for $189.50 plus shipping from L & A Machine Welding, Box 104, Auburn, ME 04210.

Franklins are efficient, but suppose you have a plentiful source of wood: what's the easiest, most economical way to get the most heat out of it? One answer is the Norwegian Jotul cast-iron stove that features an interior baffle system that prevents heat from being lost up the chimney. It is so efficient it can run up to 12 hours on a single charge of wood. These are imported by Kristia Associates, P.O. Box 1461, Portland, ME 04014, which will send you its catalog for $1. A 24" high model 12.8" wide and 19" long costs about $190; a larger model 30" high, 14" wide and 29.5" long is approximately $320.

The Trolla cast-iron heater for wood or coal is also made in Norway. It is a thermostatically controlled (appallingly homely) stove that has been used in Norwegian homes for generations. It looks after itself: if the fire gets too hot, the damper automatically closes down; if the room gets too cool, the damper opens to allow more oxygen into the firebox—keeping the fire going a lot longer on less fuel. It also has a top-surface grill that hinges back to expose a cooking surface for use in an emergency. You can write AS Trolla Brug, Trondheim, Norway, for the name of the distributor nearest you.

Sears sells a wood-burning gravity-type freestanding heater that burns logs up to two feet long and holds the fire a good half-day without refueling. The manually-controlled model with a draft regulator in the ash pit door is about $100; same stove with thermostatic controls automatically opening and closing the damper is about $150.

How to install a stove

How to Set Up a Coal or Wood Stove is a short, explicit leaflet prepared by the Cooperative Extension Service of the University of New Hampshire and available free from your Cooperative Extension office. It lists the necessary equipment and gives step-by-step guidelines for installing a stove either in front of a fireplace opening or freestanding. Simple illustrations show proper juxtaposition of stove, pipe, and chimney.

Be sure to check your local building code before installing a fireplace, freestanding or built-in, whether you connect it to an existing chimney or install a new one. Codes provide for your protection and safety. They are enforceable and govern in disputes.

Safety tips: Inspect the flue that will serve any fireplace or auxiliary heating device you install. A flue coated with resins from former fires can catch on fire; a blocked chimney can send deadly toxic gases through the house—and an unused flue is a favorite nest-building place for birds. It is not safe to burn charcoal indoors, particularly in a stove or fireplace of the type that has a damper in its stack. Burning charcoal releases deadly carbon monoxide.

For another $40 you can add a so-called "counterflow blower" that releases heated air at floor level; a thermostat turns a 125-watt blower on only when the heater becomes hot. Sears also has a wood- (or coal)-burning radiant heater that burns up to 60 hours on one stoking of coal; 34" high and 20" in diameter. It's about $80. Both stoves are described in Sears' *Home Improvement* catalog supplement.

The freestanding fireplace is really a contemporary version of the old pot-bellied stove. It comes in bright and subdued baked-on enamel over steel—orange, red, gold, or olive. When it gets hot it radiates heat in every direction. Prices range from $135 up, plus the cost of an insulated prefabricated chimney. Both stove and chimney are light, so shipping charges are reasonable.

Space heaters: Electric space heaters are not basically an efficient heating method. Federal energy officials are critical of their use to save other fuels, pointing out that a utility company will burn up three or four times as much energy in fuel oil to provide electricity for a space heater.

But for supplementing a home heating system, as in warming a bedroom briefly on a cold morning, or a family room or cold garage, space heaters can be useful. They can save turning up the thermostat.

For some families, especially in mobile homes and in some relatively warm areas, space heaters are the only source of heat.

Be sure that any electric heater you buy at least carries the "UL" seal assuring you it has been tested by Underwriters Laboratories against shock and fire hazards. Some heaters, and especially some produced in periods of energy crisis or heater shortages, are inadequately constructed and do not have the "UL" seal.

There also are potential dangers involved in the use of gas and oil space heaters, especially to children. In fact, about half of all victims of injuries from space heaters last year were children under five, the Consumer Product Safety Commission reports.

Unvented heaters, which burn natural gas, liquified petroleum, and other fuels pose the greatest threat of carbon monoxide poisoning. They need a constant supply of fresh air to operate safely and avoid the buildup of poisonous gases.

A quick source of heat

Before you run out and buy a big power-consuming space heater, give consideration to the relatively cheap, reliable infra-red bulb. Its heat is more concentrated than a space heater's and the bulb's rays heat you directly instead of the air around you. A 250-watt infrared bulb in an overhead bathroom fixture will begin warming you the moment you step out of the shower. A couple of them over the workbench in an unheated garage will keep you toasty in all but the most severe weather.

Fire and burn problems are common to both fuel and electric space heaters. These injuries often occur when children and even adults inadvertently brush against heaters and clothing catches on fire or they are burned by the hot surfaces.

As well as the "UL" label, when buying a heater make sure it has a thermostat control so that the heater will cycle on and off to avoid overheating. The thermostat helps save fuel.

Electric models that combine radiant and convection heating by use of a fan are most efficient. Most heaters are 1320 watts. Any higher wattage might require special wiring.

Make sure any heater you buy has an automatic control to turn it off if it tips over. Especially if there are children in the family make sure the protective guard is closely-woven enough to keep a youngster from poking a finger or other objects through the grill.

Avoid using extension cords. If one is necessary, use a heavy-duty cord.

Be careful about using an electric heater in the bathroom. Accumulated moisture or contact with water and grounded plumbing fixtures could cause shocks. Never place heater near the tub or sink where it could fall into the water.

How to Reduce Hot-Water Costs

Next to heat, the most expensive energy requirement in most homes is hot water. Although some families run more than twice this amount, a typical household uses 25 gallons of hot water per member each day. At a low estimate of ½¢ a gallon to heat the water to 140°, that's 50¢ a day for a family of four. In some parts of the U.S., notably the Northeast, energy costs push that estimate twice, even three times as high.

There are ways to trim this expense, the most obvious of which is to train your family to shut off the hot water at every possible moment it isn't absolutely needed. End the habit of letting it run while soaping up hands or face; turn it off while shaving. Hot water you're not using is money down the drain.

More hot water is used for bathing in U.S. homes, however, than any other purpose. Many Americans bathe daily, even though dermatologists say once every few days is often enough for most people. A tub takes 25 to 30 gallons, and some people shower afterward to get the soap scum off. A shower alone uses far less water to get you just as clean if you don't stay in there yodeling all day. By installing a new needle-spray shower head you can cut the flow from as much as 10 gallons a minute down to four gallons a minute. Adults can save additionally by turning off the water while applying the soap (and shivering a little), but this is not a sensible idea for children, who may scald themselves getting it back on.

How hot does your water need to be? That's up to you. For every 10 degrees you lower it, your hot-water costs come down 3% The warmest anyone in the family prefers for taking showers is as high as you really need to heat your water if 1) your hot-water pressure is adequate without adding cold; 2) you're already committed to home laundering with cold water; 3) you wash dishes by hand (because dishwashers need at least 140° to do a good job). Simply have each member of the family take the temperature of their shower water the way they like it using an ordinary outdoor thermometer. The highest reading (probably about 110°) is where you set your water heater—to save.

Heating efficiently: If your water-heating costs seem high even though you're using all practical means of conservation, the problem could lie in an old tank with worn insulation that's letting too much heat escape. Or there may be an accumulation of sediment in the base of the tank interfering with transfer of heat to water. You may be able to improve performance by opening the valve at the bottom of the tank and drawing off the sediment.

The water heaters in many houses today, particularly those installed by developers when the houses were built, are mediocre "builders models" with only five-year warranties. If you replace your heater be aware that the better quality "ten-year models" are not only guaranteed to last longer but are more heavily insulated and thus cost less to operate; they provide faster recovery.

If you think you're spending too much to heat it and you run out of hot water frequently, consider installing a separate oil-fired water heater operating independently of your house heating plant. These are being installed in houses with forced-air heat.

Generally, gas-fired hot water heaters are quick and have a high recovery rate, but the continental supply of natural gas is drying up. Oil-fired ones are usually somewhat more economical and also have a high recovery rate. Electricity used for heating water, though it has a relatively slow recovery rate, is clean (and needs no flue). If it is expensive in some areas of the U.S., it is less so where a local utility offers a lower rate if you heat your water electrically—still lower if you heat your house with electricity. To save significantly, consider installing an electrical timer in the line to the heater that will shut it off at night and turn it on again in the morning early enough to bring it back up to hot by the time you arise. Just be sure the timer is rated to handle the very high wattage of the heater.

Ways to save on laundering: As energy costs continue to rise, reducing—or eliminating—hot water is the key to cutting home laundering costs. A water temperature setting of 140° is adequate for clothes washers (and dishwashers). In fact, higher settings tend to shorten the life of glass-lined tanks.

Tests have shown that all but the very dirtiest laundry comes clean in cold water, however, and does so with detergents other than those whose manufacturers make cold-water claims. Consumers Union estimated in 1974 that families might save up to $50 a year laundering in cold water. Several non-phosphate detergents containing a sodium carbonate "builder" (water softener plus cleansing agent) proved generally most effective in CU's cold-water tests, outperforming a high-phosphate detergent except in soft water.

Many families, however, still prefer hot-water washes for sanitary reasons. Certainly for washing diapers or when anyone in the family has a contagious illness, hot water is preferable; a disinfectant should be added to the wash water. A chlorine bleach is the least expensive disinfectant (though it may damage some synthetic fabrics). The high heat of a dryer also helps destroy bacteria and molds.

Water temperature switches on the newer automatic washers allow a choice of wash and rinse water temperatures for various types of fabric. (Most also have variable-fill capabilities that save on hot water.) Permanent-press and synthetic fabrics, whether they are washed in hot or cold water, if they are rinsed in hot water and spun dry at high speed, come out of the washer wrinkled. Give them a cold water rinse instead, set the spin selector on low and you'll hold wrinkling to a minimum. If they are then either hung up to dry or put through a brief "permanent-press" cycle in the dryer, such fabrics require no ironing, which is a further saving in energy. But for all other fabrics, setting the spin selector on high speed saves electricity.

If your present washer lacks such features as these but is otherwise in good condition, you can control washing time, fill level, temperature, etc. manually. It merely means having to remain nearby to adjust the controls during the wash and rinse cycles. However, if you are in the market for a new washer, bear in mind that a front-loading one uses half the hot water of a top-loader.

In general, you save both hot water and electricity by waiting until you have a full load. But while large-capacity washers save energy by handling in one load what small washers can only do in two, today's family laundry usually contains so many different fabrics and colors, smaller separate washes become a necessity. If this is the case at your house and you are considering the purchase of a new washer, you might look for a compact one since it uses less hot water to fill and less electricity to run than a half-full big washer. On the new machines, a "suds saver" does conserve hot water if you use it to wash lightly soiled laundry first in a quick cycle.

Drying economics: The best energy-saving investment for drying laundry is still a clothesline and pins. Laundry can be hung out to dry practically all year, but watch out for sudden below-freezing temperature drops in winter, because the fibers in hard-frozen fabrics may break if the wind blows.

Although an electric clothes dryer is relatively inexpensive to operate, you save money by running it only when you absolutely have to and then only with a full load (but not overloaded). Set the controls for the shortest drying cycle that will get your laundry reasonably dry; towels, washcloths, and heavy garments can be hung up indoors (or out) while still damp to cut down on dryer time. The lint trap in your dryer should not be allowed to become even partially clogged or it will lengthen drying time and increase energy consumption. The same holds true for the dryer's vent pipe to the outdoors. It should be checked and cleaned out periodically. Consider disconnecting it in the coldest months since the heat and humidity otherwise lost will reduce your fuel bill.

If you are thinking of buying a new electric dryer and your house is equipped for 220-volt circuitry, be aware that a 220-volt dryer, while it does dry faster, operates less economically than a 110-volt one. Gas dryers usually cost less to operate, but their energy cost can be further reduced if you buy one with an electric ignition or mini-pilot system instead of a full pilot. If you already own a gas dryer, you may be able to install an adapter to convert to electric ignition. A gas dryer with a full pilot uses an additional 4,800 cubic feet of gas per year, the Consolidated Edison Co. estimates.

Ways to save on dishwashing: Anyone who lets the hot water flow when washing dishes by hand may be interested to know an electric dishwasher uses less energy to do the same job—about 15 gallons of hot water and one kilowatt hour of electricity per load. If you wash dishes by hand, you might form the simple habit of flipping off the hot water after each utensil is rinsed.

A dishwasher will usually hold a family's entire day's dishes if they are properly stacked. So save time, detergent, water, and electricity by waiting to run the washer only when it is full. Use the detergent the manufacturer recommends. Laundry or other detergents can produce an excess of suds that decrease the machine's efficiency. Measure carefully. Too much detergent can etch or permanently cloud glassware. Too little won't get the job done.

Cut dishwasher electrical expense in half by turning it off before the drying cycle and opening the door to allow air to dry the dishes. This too will contribute to your heat and humidity requirement, putting at least a small dent in your fuel bill in the course of a winter. Be sure to clean the filter screen frequently. A clogged filter reduces the efficiency of the unit, costing you extra energy.

Are your water bills rising?

In various parts of the U.S. where cheap "city" water had long been taken for granted, the cost has been creeping up. Many families are now being drained for over $100 a year. One New York water district sent each of its customers notice of these cold, wet facts:

A faulty washer that will let a leaking faucet fill an ordinary cup in 10 minutes wastes over 3,000 gallons a year. A leak the thickness of a pencil lead wastes 1,000 gallons *a day*—and increases the average water bill $9 a month.

A lot sneakier is a toilet tank leak. You may not notice it at all and yet it can waste as much as 3,500 gallons a day, which really zooms your water bill. Put your ear against the front of the tank when you're sure it's full. If you hear any trickle at all, drop a little food coloring into the tank. If it shows up in the bowl before the next flush, you've got a worn washer in all likelihood. Short of a joint family determination not to use the toilet as a wastebasket for every little scrap of paper or cigarette butt, there doesn't appear to be any really practical way to reduce the amount of water needed to flush a toilet bowl adequately. Toilets in many not-so-old houses require six to eight gallons each flush. New smaller models are available that flush with as little as three gallons, but you have to buy both tank and bowl (about $75) since they work as a unit.

Mulching around plants curbs the necessity of heavy garden watering. A garden hose that springs a wasteful leak is an easy home repair with a metal connector, available at hardware stores, that hitches the two parts of the hose together either side of the leak. Summer lawn sprinkling is a luxury where water is expensive. Not watering a well-established lawn, allowing it to brown off during a period of drought, doesn't hurt the grass. The roots lie in dormancy and put up new green growth following a good soaking rain.

Taming Those Beastly Utilities

A house alight at night is consuming money in terms of kilowatt hours, a unit of power (kwh) equal to 1,000 watts of electricity. Lit continuously for 10 hours, a 100-watt bulb consumes 1 kwh. A 60-watt bulb can burn for 17 hours for the same amount of money.

Buy the bulb that fits your needs. Bulbs are rated for *lumens, watts,* and *hours* right on the package. The lumen is a measure of brightness, wattage is the amount of power the bulb uses, the hour rating is the average life span of the bulb. A 100-watt bulb with a high lumen rating burns brighter than a 100-watt bulb with a lower lumen rating, but doesn't last as long. Save money by using lower lumen bulbs where you don't need bright light to work or read by.

So called "long-life" bulbs last longer but give less light. Comparing two 100-watt bulbs, one standard and the other long-life, both use the same amount of electricity but the standard bulb lasts about 750 hours with a brightness of 1,750 lumens. The long-life bulb may last three times as long (about 2,500 hours) but will produce only about 1,470 lumens, 20% less brightness, and will dim as it ages. Obtainable at electrical supply houses and larger hardware stores, a 130-*volt* bulb used in standard household 110-volt circuitry will not burn at quite the same lumen level as a 100-watt bulb but will last much longer than a long-life bulb in those awkward to change places—stairwells, closets, and ceiling fixtures where you have to remove the globe.

Higher wattage light bulbs are more efficient than lower wattage ones. A 100-watt bulb produces more light (1750 lumens) than two 60-watt bulbs (2 x 860 lumens, or a total of 1720). Similarly, a 75-watt bulb emits more light than two 40-watt ones, about 1,170 lumens, whereas a 150-watt bulb of the same type emits 2,800 lumens—

nearly 2½ times the brightness for only twice the wattage.

A fluorescent tube consumes 75% less power to create the same amount of light as an incandescent bulb. Put another way, fluorescent tubes emit from three to five times as much light per watt as incandescent bulbs and last 20 times as long. One 40-watt (four-foot) fluorescent tube provides more light than three 60-watt incandescent bulbs.

How dimmers save dollars

Next to your major appliances, incandescent bulbs are the biggest consumers of electricity in your house. Replacing wall switches with dimmers is a simple do-it-yourself way of coping with this expense, a matter of merely turning off the house current at the entry panel, unscrewing the faceplate, detaching the old switch, and attaching the device to the same two wires. Costing about $5, a dimmer will control from 40 to 600 watts of incandescent light (but don't plug a vacuum cleaner into a socket controlled by one or you'll ruin the dimmer).

The electronic solid-state dimmer saves electricity in direct proportion to how far down the lights are dimmed. Practically all dimmers made to go in wall switchboxes are this type. When the power is dimmed 25% an incandescent bulb burns at 52% of its rated brightness; bulb life increases 11 times, a bonus saving that pays for the dimmer in time. Dimming the lights in an air-conditioned house saves money two ways. It takes about a half a watt of air-conditioning power to remove one watt's-worth of heat produced by incandescent lighting. Conservatively estimated, 10% to 20% can be sliced off the electricity bill if the lights are dimmed a mere 10% throughout a centrally air-conditioned house.

When you install dimmers you make the greatest savings in electricity by using the lowest wattage bulbs needed to adequately light whatever activity ordinarily taking place in that room demands the brightest illumination. Then make it a family rule only to raise the light level (via the dimmer control) as high as is needed for any other activity going on in the room. For sewing you need as much light as you can get, for reading somewhat less, for cards a lot less, for watching television hardly any at all, although some light in the TV room helps ward off eyestrain and headaches.

The rated life of a fluorescent tube is 12,000 hours, though it won't last nearly that long if you turn it on and off too often. Mass production has made the four-foot length the least expensive to buy, cheaper even than the two-foot tube. However, a single long fluorescent tube, although it costs more initially than two tubes half its length, takes less energy to produce the same amount of light as the two short tubes. (Similarly, one large incandescent bulb burns less electricity than several small ones that add up to the same number of lumens.)

Don't be put off by the bluish light you see coming from most fluorescent fixtures (because the original bulbs haven't yet burned out in so many cases!). Within the same general price range you can buy fluorescent tubes in "warm white", pink, "natural", gold, even red and green, and there's a magenta color that indoor plants seem to thrive under. If none of these colors suits your needs, Westinghouse manufactures a fluorescent tube that perfectly imitates sun light (its FS 20 and FS 40) for about $14—not exactly coping with the high cost of living, but a spectacular way to light a room.

Although indirect lighting is less efficient than direct lighting, the most esthetically pleasing way to install fluorescent tubes is to hide the light source. The simplest way of doing so is to mount the fixtures on the wall behind a 6"-wide shield of wood to "wash" the wall with light, or as cove lighting reflecting light from the ceiling. In the kitchen, fluorescent tubes directly illuminating work areas from fixtures mounted under wall-hung cabinets make complete use of the available light, although they may require a 5" or 6" apron in front of them to keep direct light from shining into the eyes of a short person standing at the counter.

In all these instances the rear surface of the faceboard should be painted flat white. Hiding the wiring is the hard part of such installations, however. Most communities require Romex cable (or BX) for wiring run between walls (some even require conduits). Check your local code. Cable can usually be brought up through the floor behind base cabinets from the cellar; in a one-story house, it might be snaked down from an attic junction box. But don't forget that a fixture has to be connected to a wall switch which, in turn, must be tied into an outlet or a junction box in the attic or cellar. Study up on electrical installation before attempting this sort of project. Most localities demand that if you do your own wiring, it be inspected and hooked up by a licensed electrician. Your fire insurance policy may specify the same requirement.

In bathrooms and recreation rooms fluorescent fixtures can very easily be mounted out of sight above a drop ceiling of translucent plastic panels, an excellent way of lighting an entire area evenly.

Protruding from one of the spring-clip terminals that holds a fluorescent tube in place is the starter, a tubular element about the size of a nickel in diameter. If the tube flickers before it burns steadily or if you have to flip the switch on and off several times to get it going, you may need a new starter. Neglecting it curtails the life of the tube and is wasteful of electricity. Replace the starter by turning it counterclockwise until it slips out, then lock the new one in by pressing it in and turning it clockwise. **Fixtures make a difference:** Recessed downlights with properly designed aluminized reflectors provide almost twice as much light as those with a white interior finish.

Reducing Appliance Costs

An effective family campaign for cutting the high cost of utilities ought to go beyond finding out who left the cellar light on. It should establish in the minds of all family members a sustained awareness that cold, hard cash is being spent foolishly *and fast* whenever such energy-hungry appliances as air conditioners and color television sets are allowed to operate needlessly. It should also involve a careful choice of major appliances, when you buy, to reduce both energy consumption and breakdowns.

Although the amount of energy a particular appliance consumes depends on such factors as size and efficiency, how often and for how long it is used, as well as how well it is maintained, you can make deeper inroads lowering your electricity bill by concentrating on the major appliances rather than the minor ones. Just for example, in a single hour a 300-watt color television set gobbles as much energy as an electric can opener uses in a full year of normal use.

The cost of operating an appliance relates to its wattage, the amount of time it's used, and the cost of power where you live. Taking into account that electricity rates vary widely from one locality to another, average operating costs (see chart on next page) are figured at 5¢ per kilowatt hour. Your own costs may be higher or lower depending on size of appliance, your utility's charge per kwh, amount of use, and further increases since these costs were calculated. Estimates are based on data from the Electrical Energy Association.

To get a much more accurate estimate of the annual cost of operating any appliance in your house, write down its wattage (usually found on an attached plate or stamped on the chassis). Multiply this figure by your own best estimate of the number of hours the appliance is operated per week.* Multiply that figure by 50 (the weeks in a year, assuming you take a two-week vacation). Divide this figure by 1,000 to arrive at the total kwh's the appliance uses per year. Find your local kwh rate on your electricity bill if you can, or call your utility office and ask. Multiply it times the total kwh figure and you'll have the approximate before-tax cost of operating a properly-working appliance for one year. You will also be able to figure whether an appliance that you suspect may not be working properly is wasting power.

Refrigerator-freezer savings: Keeping food cold is one of your steeper expenses but one subject to various small economies that can add up to solid savings over the course of time. Check the temperature of refrigeration

*An appliance that cycles on and off, like a refrigerator, can be roughly estimated by timing the on periods in an average hour, adding them together and multiplying by 168, the number of hours in a week.

Average Operating Costs of Common Electric Appliances

	Wattage	Average Annual Kilowatt Hours	Average Annual Operating Cost
Water heater, quick recovery	4,474	4,811	$240.55
Water heater, standard	2,475	4,219	210.95
Refrigerator-freezer, 14 cu. ft. frostless	615	1,829	91.45
Food freezer, 15 cu. ft., frostless	440	1,761	88.05
Food freezer	341	1,195	59.75
Electric kitchen range	12,207	1,175	58.75
Refrigerator-freezer, 14 cu. ft.	326	1,137	56.85
Clothes dryer	4,856	993	49.65
Room air conditioner	860	860	43.00
Color TV (tubes)	300	660	33.00
Color TV (solid state)	200	440	22.00
Dehumidifier	257	363	18.15
Dishwasher	1,201	363	18.15
Television, black & white (tubes)	160	350	17.50
Fan, attic	370	291	14.55
Air cleaner	50	216	10.80
Roaster	1,333	205	10.25
Microwave oven (depending on size)	1,450	190-300	9.50-15.00
Frying pan	1,196	186	9.30
Heater, radiant	1,322	176	8.90
Fan, window	200	170	8.50
Humidifier	177	163	8.15
Electric blanket	177	147	7.35
Iron	1,088	144	7.20
Television, black & white (solid state)	55	120	6.00
Electric coffeemaker	894	106	5.30
Automatic washer	512	103	5.15
Portable broiler	1,436	100	5.00
Hot plate	1,256	90	4.50
Radio	71	86	4.30
Deep fat fryer	1,448	83	4.15
Trash compactor	400	50	2.50
Vacuum cleaner	630	46	2.30
Fan, circulating	88	43	2.15
Toaster	1,146	39	1.95
Grill, sandwich	1,161	33	1.65
Food waste disposer	445	30	1.50
Clock	2	17	.85
Sun lamp	279	16	.80
Food blender	386	15	.75
Floor polisher	305	15	.75
Hair dryer	381	14	.70
Food mixer	127	13	.65
Heat lamp, infrared	250	13	.65
Sewing machine	75	11	.55
Heating pad	65	10	.50

first. A thermometer placed inside—elevated off the shelf or freezer bottom—will tell you if your setting is low enough to chill and freeze food properly but not so low as to overchill needlessly and waste electricity. The freezer compartment should be 0°; the food-storage compartment 38° to 40°. Store your more perishable foods at the back of the top shelf, the coldest part of the refrigerator, if this is a higher setting than you're accustomed to.

Try to take as many items for a meal out of the refrigerator with one door opening as possible; the fewer times you open the door the less electricity used. If you make the mistake of storing cooked food in it while it's still hot, your refrigerator has to work harder. But it isn't safe, especially in summer, to wait too long for foods to cool; this gives spoilage bacteria too good a chance to breed and multiply.

More than ¼″ accumulation of ice on the surfaces of the freezing compartment acts as insulation, making the compressor work harder. Dust allowed to accumulate on the coils at the back or bottom of the refrigerator wastes electricity the same way. Clean the coils regularly with a vacuum cleaner or a rag wrung out in water and ammonia.

If feasible, isolate your refrigerator-freezer from heat sources such as the range, a radiator or hot-air vent, or a sunny window, and avoid placing it in a niche where it will create its own heat buildup. The cooler the outer coils can be kept, the lower the cost of operation.

Although some large-size refrigerators introduced in 1975 reduce operating costs by use of heavier insulation (at some sacrifice of storage space), in general it does not pay to buy a bigger refrigerator-freezer than you really need because it will take more electricity to run.

Fully frost-free models cost anywhere from 17% to 50% more to operate (depending on whose estimates you use) than those that are frost-free in the refrigerator compartment only; defrosting the freezer compartment manually needs to be done only a few times a year and can usually be accomplished in less than half an hour. If you already own a fully frost-free unit, however, check your owner's manual and see if there's a switch you can activate to shut off the built-in heater intended to

prevent condensation. It wastes electricity when house humidity is low, as it is in winter or in an air-conditioned kitchen.

Sight and sound savings: Although TV, radio, and hi-fi actually take only a small percentage of the family energy dollar, television accounts for more of it than the others simply because TV is going so much of the time in so many homes, an average six hours a day across the nation. In some households with more than one set or where a set is left on practically all the family's waking hours, a fairly hefty chunk of the electric bill is going for home entertainment.

The self-evident answer is never to use TV as a radio—switch it off when no one's watching and save money.

Instant-on color sets consume electricity even when they're "off," however, a little current is still running through them to keep them warm. You can always unplug one, of course, but now some of the newer models have a switch for cutting the power completely when the set will not be used for an extended period. By taking half a minute to come on, saving some electricity, other new models make a compromise between instant-on and the longer time older sets need to warm up.

Solid-state televisions operate on half the power tube sets require. Though they seem to be able to go longer without needing repair, when they do go on the fritz solid-state sets can cost more to fix than tube-type ones—factors to ponder if you're buying.

Keeping costs down on the range: It's all too easy to waste energy by not using your kitchen range properly. Here are some ways to improve efficiency and save some money in the bargain:
• Make use of the full capacity of your oven as often as practical by cooking foods for future meals. Bake extra potatoes for hash browns, for example. When cooking on top of the range, triple recipes for such dishes as spaghetti sauce, soups, and stews that take a long time to cook. Then freeze the extra for future use in meal-size packets.
• Use only as much heat as you need to cook a dish. (We Americans tend to overcook vegetables.) Too high heat for too long wastes fuel and ruins food. When roasting, turn off the oven half an hour or so before

Can you trim your gas bill?

There's probably little you can do to reduce the cost of natural gas or propane, unless you happen to have a decorative gaslight burning continuously outside your house. If you do it's costing you more than your range. Replacing it with an electric light is the obvious answer.

Pilot lights on a conventional range (some have four) burn more than one-quarter of the gas the range consumes in the average home. Turning off the pilots and lighting the burners by other means is not worth considering because of the inherent dangers involved. But if yours are adjustable, you can check to make sure the pilots are set as low as possible not to blow out in a strong draft and no higher than necessary to ignite the burners. If you just happen to be in the market for a range, look into the new models that feature electric ignition. They cut your cost of gas by at least 25% in the course of a year and add nothing to your electric bill.

Gas is billed in either cubic feet or therms. One therm equals the heat energy of 100,000 BTUs. Although you may be paying more per therm or less, the national average was 16¢ per therm in 1975, according to the American Gas Association, but general rate hikes have been steadily pushing it higher.

serving time and take advantage of the retained heat to finish the job. Similarly, atop an electric range, turn off the burner a few minutes before the food is done and let residual heat continue the cooking.

- By using small amounts of water for range-top cooking, foods will heat faster and you'll use less energy. Turn the surface unit on high until the water in the pot begins to boil, then turn it down to the lowest setting at which water will simmer. Such minimal-water cooking retains nutrients.
- Save fuel by cooking more than one vegetable in plastic boil-in-the-bags in the same pot—but be aware of the energy waste in having to bring a whole pot of water to the boil for just one boil-in-the-bag food.
- Always defrost foods before cooking.
- By using flat-bottom pans that totally cover the heat source, you avoid wasting cooking fuel or prolonging cooking time. A tight-fitting lid keeps the heat in the pot, foods cook faster at slightly lower temperatures, and your kitchen stays cooler, which saves energy if it's air conditioned.
- When you have something in the oven, don't peek. Every time you open the oven door 25% to 50% of the heat escapes, a big waste of energy. If there's no window in your oven door, use cooking aids such as a timer, meat thermometer, or time-and-temperature charts in saving fuel.
- There's never any necessity for preheating an oven longer than 10 minutes, and then only for baking.
- If you use aluminum foil in the oven, make sure it isn't blocking vents or you'll be wasting heat. Don't place foil in the oven directly under a pan that may spill over, because it reflects heat away from the pan. A slightly larger pan or sheet of foil placed on the next lower shelf will catch the spills.
- Don't bother scrubbing pot bottoms until they shine. Dull surfaces absorb heat better. But do shine up the reflective surfaces under and around burners, or line them with foil.
- When preparing a single dish or a small amount of food for any reason, consider using your electric skillet instead of the range. You'll save some energy, unless you cook with gas and gas is much cheaper than electricity where you live. Divide a skillet with foil inserts to prepare small portions of several dishes simultaneously, *the* technique for preparing leftovers at lunchtime.
- Make sure your oven door seals tightly and does not leak heated air.
- Even though self-cleaning ovens do use a lot of energy to burn food accumulations off their inner surfaces, it is somewhat offset by their greater insulation, which saves fuel during baking and roasting. It is a saving to turn on the self-cleaning feature when the oven is already hot from having been used.
- A microwave oven is probably too expensive to be considered an investment for coping with the high cost of living, even though it uses 50% to 75% less electricity than a conventional electric range, cooking almost everything in about one-fourth the time. Trouble is, for certain types of frying and baking you would still want to use your regular range.
- Here's one last hot tip: Keep morning coffee in a thermos so you won't have to use fuel to reheat it when you want a cup later in the day.

House-Cooling Economies

In some parts of the U.S., air conditioning has become so expensive to operate many householders who own the equipment don't use it except on the most unbearable days.

Strict control of operation is the key to cutting the cost of air conditioning where and whenever it must be used. For each additional degree of cooling you allow yourself, your air conditioner requires 5% more electricity. Decide on a comfortable setting in the high seventies, then leave the unit's thermostatic controls alone, because frequent readjustment wastes energy.

Turning the air conditioner on an hour before retiring will cool a bedroom sufficiently. A room unit should be switched off when the room will be unoccupied for an hour or more. If no one is home during the day, a timer can be installed (approximately $15) to turn the unit on automatically, so your house or apartment will be cool when you get home, and shut it off late at night after you're asleep. Installation is a cinch. You merely run the power cable from the switchbox through the timer to the air conditioner. Just be sure the timer's amperage, wattage, and voltage ratings are appropriate to the air conditioner's.

Buy the right air conditioner: Matching the space it must cool to the unit's size is basic air conditioning economy. Too small a unit won't do the job. Too big a one will lower the temperature all right but may leave you feeling uncomfortably clammy because it does not stay on long enough to get rid of excess humidity. It also adds unnecessarily to your electricity bill, of course, but keep in mind when you buy one that air conditioners gradually lose their rated cooling efficiency as they get old. *In helping you choose the right size unit a responsible dealer will need to know the answers to these questions, which you should jot down beforehand:*
• What are the dimensions, including the ceiling height, of the room you want to cool?
• What do you use it for—bedroom, living room, kitchen?
• Is the room completely closed off from the rest of the house?
• What size and type of windows? Single or double glazed?

• On which side of the house do you intend to install the unit, sunny or shady?

Once you and your dealer have decided on the proper size, make sure you buy a model that will use as little electricity as possible for the volume of cooling you anticipate needing. All new models display their energy-efficiency rating (EER), which is merely the watts (energy consumed) divided into the Btu (cooling power). An EER of 6 to 7 is only fair, 8 to 9 is good, 10 or higher is excellent.

To Save Electricity: Whether you live where you can get along without it most of the summer or in an area where air conditioning is a necessity much of the year, here are some measures worth considering to reduce the cost of cooling your house:

Keep use of heat-producing appliances and incandescent lights to a minimum during daytime high-temperature hours. They add dramatically to cooling costs, as do TVs and stereos—whether or not anyone's looking or listening. Save activities that generate excessive heat, like baking, for the cooler early morning or evening hours. Try to do moisture-making chores—laundering, dishwashing, wet mopping—during the cooler part of the day too. The added humidity they create puts an extra load on the air conditioning. Use exhaust fans to get rid of moisture. Vent a dryer to the outdoors.

During the warm months, inspect, and if necessary clean, both the indoor and outdoor coils, having first turned off and disconnected the unit. Keep the filter clean (some are vacuumed, others can be washed out). Your unit will run cooler at less cost.

If you have a choice, install a window unit on the shadier side of the house or where it will be shaded by a tree or shrub. The cooler you keep the outside coils the less the compressor has to work and the greater your electricity savings.

A broad expanse of glass window-wall facing south can be protected from the sun with an "eyebrow," a wood frame over the window projecting two or three feet (depending on your latitude) spanned with 10"-wide boards set on edge inside the frame parallel to the window 8" to 10" apart. Eyebrows keep out the sun when its arc is high in the summer sky and admit it in winter to warm the house when the sun rides lower toward the south. (Energy from the sun in the form of infrared rays penetrates glass easily and turns to heat when it hits something solid, even on cloudy days.) Closing venetian blinds and/or draperies on the sunny side of the house can save far more Btu than you might imagine. Better still, of course, are awnings or shutters on the outside of the windows.

Any kind of exterior shading of sun-facing windows and outer walls of your house is worth consideration—deciduous shade trees, elevated freestanding sections of fencing, even vines. Ivy trained to grow over the western wall of a house that takes the full brunt of the long afternoon summer sun helps greatly in reducing heat conduction. But grow it only over masonry, asphalt shingles, plastic or aluminum siding; ivy can deteriorate wood siding and stucco.

Everything you have done to insulate your house for winter will keep the heat out in summer—optimum attic insulation, caulking, weatherstripping. (Caulking of window air conditioners themselves should not be overlooked.) If you have storm-screen sash, don't remove the glazed sections; leave those conventional storm windows in place that are not needed for ventilation on days when the air conditioning can be shut down. Do-it-yourself so-called "Weather or Not" extruded plastic snap-together storm window kits (about $8 per window) come with tinted vinyl sheeting to replace the clear vinyl in summertime and cut radiant heat penetration from the sun.

If you aren't using the ducting for central air conditioning, all vents should be closed in a forced-air heating system throughout the house. Seal off any rooms with duct tape that will not be occupied in summer (making sure vital fire exits are not blocked thereby). Fireplace dampers and doors to closets should be kept shut. Make sure draperies and any other obstructions are kept well away from air conditioning vents.

Why attic fans are back: Attic fans are being reevaluated as a consequence of the high cost of air conditioning. Since they have been available for several decades their advantages and limits are by now so well defined you should have no trouble deciding whether one is appropriate to your environ-

mental needs. Don't confuse the two kinds of attic fan, however. Those with enormous blades that move a lot of cubic feet per minute are made for cooling the entire house and draw air up from lower floors through louvered vents in the ceilings of rooms immediately beneath the attic space. The much smaller electric ones and wind-driven turbine roof fans (see photo above) are strictly for exhausting accumulated hot air from a sealed-off attic—but even in a thoroughly insulated house they decrease hot-air infiltration that gradually works its way through the ceiling insulation on sweltering days. They are a must for holding down air conditioning costs in the South.

On summer evenings when the temperature drops rapidly after a hot day, the indoor temperature of the average non-air conditioned house falls only half as fast, even with the windows wide open, as the outdoor temperature. Greatly increasing the amount of air moving through the house, a large ventilating attic fan can speed up the rate of cool-down. In a two-story house, only ground-floor windows are opened when the fan is turned on to cool the house fast. This can lessen the amount of cooling (and energy) required of hot-night air conditioning.

Because of the artificial breeze a big whole-house ventilating fan creates when a few windows are partially opened, those in the kitchen and family room can be the only ones opened where people are gathered in the evening after a hot day. Then these can be closed and one window partially opened in each bedroom at night.

Normally, even when attic-fan breeze is barely perceptible its cooling effect is noticeable to a lightly clad person. On cool, dry nights, sleepers may be as comfortable as if the house were air conditioned; the breeze created by a large attic fan can make dry air feel much cooler than it actually is— an effect that is largely cancelled on hot humid nights, however.

In addition, cooling down the structure of the house slows heat-up the following morning. A thoroughly insulated house that is closed up tightly soon after daybreak may stay comfortable well into the afternoon.

As an economical alternative to air conditioning, especially in the more temperate parts of the U.S., a ventilating attic fan lets existing air conditioning have a new role as a back-up system to be turned on only when the weather makes the house unbearable— for considerable savings in electricity. A whole-house ventilating fan operates on only 550 to 650 watts, as compared to 2,800 watts for the average minimal-capacity (24,000-Btu) central air conditioner. Single-speed whole-house attic ventilating fans cost around $125; two-speed units with remote control cost about $150; plus the cost of a self-closing ceiling intake louver that opens when the fan is running, plus an exhaust louver in front of the fan for attic sidewall installation.

Attic ventilating fan size is rated in terms of how much air the fan can impel in cubic feet per minute (CFM). For optimum effectiveness a fan should have a CFM rating approximately that of the total cubic feet of the interior space to be ventilated. Multiply length times width times height (in feet) of each room, hallway and stairwell (excluding basement, closets, storage rooms, and the attic where the fan itself will be located). Add up the room totals for total cubic feet.

Various factors affect the efficiency of an attic ventilating fan, such as its placement in the house and the number of corners that interrupt air flow. Since your calculations may not yield a figure that is the true equivalent of a fan's capacity, you'd do well to

choose the next largest size above your figure; the difference in fan size makes very little difference in electrical power expended. If your house is in the South, your roof completely exposed to the sun, the fan size you choose should well exceed your total cubic-foot figure. If you live in a relatively cool climate, a fan half the CFM of your total measurement is probably adequate.

The air intake in the floor of your attic should be as centrally located in relation to the whole house as possible, usually midway in a center hall. It is not necessary to have intakes in several room ceilings, because air flow through any room of the house is controlled by the amount that a window (or windows) is opened. Ultra-lightweight aluminum ventilator shutters open automatically as the fan comes on. Weatherstripping on each shutter blade quiets its closing and insulates in winter.

Cooling down the attic: On a sunny 95° day heat can build up to 150° in an attic "ventilated" only by intake air vents under the eaves and gable-end louvers. Such high heat eventually seeps down through insulation of even optimum thickness and raises the house temperature. Anyone directly under the ceiling feels the radiation. A small electric fan installed against a louvered end-wall vent or in a hole cut in the roof can solve this problem. It has been estimated that a cool ceiling allows you to set your air conditioning thermostat 3° higher when heat is not radiating from the ceiling. Since for each degree you can raise your thermostat you save about 5% in energy, a 3° difference is a 15% saving—minus, of course, what it costs to run the attic fan.

Intake air vents in most houses are adequate for drawing in outside air as the fan exhausts the hot attic air. But in some old houses a vent should be installed in the gable end opposite the fan.

Powered attic ventilators are available, thermostatically factory-adjusted, to turn the fan on at 105° and off at 95°. A 165-watt one for the roof that moves 500 CFM costs about $55. It is a moderately difficult installation for a householder, necessitating the cutting of a one-foot hole in the roof. A sidewall equivalent that mounts against an existing grille costs around $50 and is quite a lot easier to install.

Ways to Trim Your Phone Bill

As calling-up threatens to replace the near-lost art of letter writing, the telephone has become the single most costly utility in some U.S. households. Direct dialing has made it easier than ever to call long-distance, as many a family phone bill so clearly demonstrates.

The best way to reduce your phone bill, of course, is to cut down the number and duration of long-distance calls. But are you talking full advantage of all the other ways you might cut your telephone costs? Most companies, for example, offer a choice of services. The one you subscribed to originally may not be the most economical one for you now. By calling your phone company business office you can check and see which is the most appropriate service for your pattern of calling.

How to Save on Service

In some parts of the country *flat-rate* (or "unlimited-call") *service* is all that's available. For a monthly fee you can make as many calls and talk as long as you like within your specific geographical "local calling area," which usually includes towns immediately adjacent to your own. Calls outside that area, whether in or out of your state, are billed separately.

If you don't make many local calls, *message-unit service* is less expensive than flat-rate. You are allowed a specified number of "free" message units and are charged a certain amount for each one in excess of that base rate number. A message unit is deceptive, however. You pay as much for a short call to a distant point as for a longer call to a nearby point—and most phone bills don't bear the slightest clue as to how those extra message units were used, although a small number of phone companies have begun rectifying this inequity. If you call certain numbers frequently, you can gauge how much such calls are costing (once you have used up your basic allowance of message units) by calling the phone company and asking how much you pay per message unit and how many message units it is costing you to call each of these numbers. If you make a lot of multiple message-unit calls regularly, ask your phone company business office if it offers a package of more "free" message units per month at a higher base rate—called Call-Pak in some localities. This will usually be less expensive than paying for extra message units over and above the "free" ones on the basic rate. Or where both types of service are available, consider the possibility of two lines into your house, one on flat-rate service (especially economical for a family with teenagers making many local calls), the other on message-unit service. You can have a phone for each service, or both lines can work off a telephone that allows you to switch from one to the other by pressing buttons.

If you make an average of not more than a single phone call a day—the U.S. daily average is 5.36 calls per phone—*economy rate* (also called "budget rate") is available in 21 states and the District of Columbia. It's a bargain. There's no limit on incoming calls. Each outgoing call is paid for individually, usually after a designated rather low number of base-rate calls have been used up. Senior citizens find it a boon.

Across the U.S. some 1700 independent telephone companies provide *party-line service,* a good way to save if you're on a tight budget. The basic rate for a two-party phone can be as much as one-third less than a one-party line. Although occasionally you may have difficulty getting the line, if you have an emergency call to make, the law says that once informed of this the other party must hang up.

A few states offer a special *state-wide rate plan* that saves money if you have to call distant points frequently within the borders of your state. The plan is tacked onto your basic service and has no effect on local calls if you're on flat-rate.

Available only in a very few places so far is *Pick-a-Point,* which lets you make a limited number of calls to a specific phone number anywhere in the U.S. for a flat monthly fee. It's good for staying in touch with a relative or a child away at college.

If you're going to be away from home a couple of months or more, a *temporary disconnect* is a money-saver in some localities. You are billed a nominal sum for the entire period rather than your regular monthly charge, and some phone companies will even switch your incoming calls to another number in your absence.

Do You Need All That Stuff?

You may have forgotten that when you had your phone, or phones, installed you let the phone company rent you some ancillary equipment that in a time of belt-tightening you really don't need—Princess, Trimline, Touchtone phones, bell chimes, or extension phones. Some telephone company "representatives" are expert pitchmen, overloading you with fancy options that sound like peanuts at the time you agree to them but which may be costing you a small fortune over the course of years. Such rental charges don't show up on your phone bill. If you decide you'd like to trim your costs by having such equipment removed, there is usually no charge for doing so. Additionally, the rental crunch for any extra equipment you consider essential may be suspended (by some phone companies) with a one-time-only payment that wipes out the never-ending monthly charges.

Extension phones may be considered a necessity in a large house, but you can save the monthly rental charge for those extra phones by stripping down to one, with a plug on the end of its cord, and having phone jacks installed around the house for a one-time installation charge only. Then you simply carry your phone with you wherever you want to call from; anyone calling in, as you move from jack to jack, receives a busy signal.

How about plugging in your own equipment? The phone company may demand that you have it interfaced to conform to its equipment if yours does not incorporate a "connecting module". For an answering device, which operates on house current, interfacing obviates the risk of 110-volt electricity somehow getting into the low-voltage phone system and giving a repairman a jolt or worse. Since you have to pay the standard monthly one-phone rental anyway, plugging in your own phone is not economical.

An unlisted phone number is an easy extra monthly charge to beat. Merely have your phone listed under some fictitious name and let the phone company bill that name at your address, care of your name.

Economical Telephoning

It's in careful phone use, however, that you can achieve the greatest economies.

If you should reach a wrong number on an out-of-town call, instantly ask the person who answers to give you the area code and number you reached in error. Then dial "O" and report the mishap. The call won't appear on your phone bill. The same goes for a poor connection or a cutoff in mid-conversation on any long-distance call. Don't just hang up and call right back—hang up and call the operator. You'll be given a good connection and you won't be charged for the time you talked up to the moment of disconnection nor for the fact that the operator put your call through. In truth, you can save money best when you must phone long-distance by trying never to talk to an operator. You are charged the three-minute-minimum operator-assisted rate—always a lot higher than a direct-dial one-minute rate—whenever you call person-to-person, collect, from a coin telephone, as a hotel guest, by credit card, or bill to a third number. None of these calls can be dialed direct; all involve an operator.

Everyone knows, but people tend to forget, what a good idea it is to jot down the salient points you want to cover before dialing a long-distance call. Then use a kitchen timer. You may even be able to say all you want to transmit in a one-minute call—the phone companies' greatest bargain, especially for long, cross-country calls (if you live in the East, place your call before 11 p.m. and reach your party out West early in the evening; call before 8:00 a.m. if you live in the West and reach your party back East in mid morning). Available round the clock, the one-minute call is handy for confirming with parents or spouse your arrival at a point of destination or the time of your return home.

When you don't know if the person you want to reach is going to answer your ring, which is the better bet, person-to-person or dial-direct? A person-to-person call is always between five and 16 times more expensive (depending on time of day and day of week) than a one-minute dial-direct call. Thus, you can make several dial-direct calls for what it costs for a single person-to-person call to the same number. Person-to-person service is valuable when you need to talk to someone whose whereabouts is uncertain. Otherwise, dial-direct is more thrifty. Incidentally, you are always charged for three minutes on a person-to-person call whether you use up the time or not.

You can even save money when your phone goes out of order. Most phone companies now issue a credit on your bill if you are deprived of the use of your phone for 24 hours or more.

If You Can't Hang Up

The telephone is here to stay—an expensive, ingrained habit in most of us—but any family can lower its monthly phone bill by using the mails more often and calling long-distance less. Suggestion: Buy a stack of postcards at the Post Office and place it right by the phone with pens. If the family neglects to use them to communicate when there's no emergency reason for calling out of town, don't fume—get tough. Have all members of the family log their long-distance calls on a calendar hung over the phone and pay for their calls with cash or chores when the monthly bill arrives. (But don't have family members ask the operator to call back with charges, because that amounts to the same thing as an operator-assisted station-to-station call, and you'll be charged for this service.)

One-Minute (or less) Interstate Dial-Direct Phone Rate Periods							
	MON	TUES	WED	THURS	FRI	SAT	SUNDAY
8 a.m. to 5 p.m.	**Dial-direct weekday rate** FULL RATE —most expensive 1-minute rate						
5 p.m. to 11 p.m.	**Dial-direct evening rate** 35% CHEAPER than dial-direct full rate						**eve rate applies**
11 p.m. to 8 a.m.	**Dial-direct night-&-weekend rate** 60% CHEAPER than dial-direct full rate						

Each additional minute costs less than the first minute.

Dial-direct rates apply to all calls from one state to another (except Hawaii and Alaska) completed without an operator's assistance. If you run into equipment trouble completing a dial-direct call, you are eligible for the dial-direct rate even if you require the services of an operator to get through to the person you're calling. Dial-direct rates also apply to calls placed with an operator from a residence or business phone where dial-direct facilities do not exist.

What's Involved in Maintaining Your Home

To make it easier for you to decide which jobs to tackle on your own and which to leave to professionals, here are some of the common problems of maintaining a house—described more in terms of what's required in skill, effort, time, and materials than in the actual how-to of doing the jobs.

Reshingling a Roof

A leaking roof risks damage to the structure and should not be neglected. A simple patch or replaced shingle, however, may be enough. By repairing immediately you can add years to your roofing, but if you put it off, the sheathing under the shingles will rot, eventually making a new roof imperative. If your roof isn't too steep and heights don't bother you, consider reroofing your house yourself. Because two-thirds of the cost of reshingling is labor when the job is contracted for, more and more roofs are being reshingled as do-it-yourself projects. The job is more in the nature of heavy drudgery than hazard, as long as you observe elementary rules of safety.

If your roof has only one layer of shingles you can reshingle right over them. The old layer will provide extra insulation. But if you find two or more layers, check your town's building ordinances before adding another layer; new roofing can add as much as four tons to the weight of the structure. Can your house take it?

Most houses across the U.S. are roofed with type 240 self-sealing asphalt tab shingles

with a UL "C" rating, which means that Underwriters Laboratory has tested them for light fire exposure; they do not ignite easily. There are many different weights and categories of shingle, but in type 240, the industry standard, all major brands are pretty much the same price. Your main consideration then is color.

The unit of measurement in buying shingles is a "square", enough to cover 100 square feet; type 240 weighs 240 pounds. Heavier weights than this are not worth the average 50% higher price for the added years of life. Wood shingles and shakes are undeniably handsome but cost about three times as much as type 240 and because they are flammable have been declared illegal in many communities. Slate is more expensive than wood and is too heavy for houses designed to support asphalt shingle roofs.

If you decide not to reroof yourself, you would do well to get estimates from at least three roofing contractors. Check their reputations locally, ask for references for jobs comparable to your own, then call those homeowners or, better still, go by and have a look at the roofs themselves. The price varies, of course, depending on the height of the building and the necessity for scaffolding. The going price may be undercut by an unscrupulous roofer who does the job fast, uses sleazy materials, and skips town afterward so he won't have to honor his guarantee.

Type 240 shingles are guaranteed for 15 years (heavier weights, 25 years). The homeowner should get the manufacturer's guarantee in writing from the roofer and has the right to ask the roofer to spell out, in his own contract, a guarantee that his work will stand up for a specified number of years. (Ten years is reasonable for type 240 shingling.)

Once the shingles are in place the job is not finished until vent pipes and chimney have been flashed with good quality black roofing cement to prevent water penetration between the edges of the new shingles and the old roof. Copper is the ideal material for valleys, but it is expensive and getting scarce, so homeowners have turned to aluminum, no thinner than .020 gauge.

Replacing Siding

A house that has been adequately and repeatedly painted and caulked over the years usually will not need residing for many generations. The householder who is a fairly good carpenter should not hesitate to tackle residing himself, with help, but he should think twice about a two-story house because of the necessity of scaffolding (rented).

You have a wide choice of materials: boards laid up horizontally ("clapboards") or vertically, plywood, hardboard or fiberboard paneling, wood shingles or shakes, asbestos-cement shingles or siding, sheets of prepainted aluminum formed to look like clapboards, vinyl or masonry. Prices for these vary widely, of course, for a great variety of treatments.

If you're considering wood: Will you want unfinished or untreated (which needs a three-minute dip in a water-repellent preservative before installation to ensure longer paint life), preprimed or prefinished, smooth or textured, contemporary or traditional, horizontal or vertical? If you do choose wood, preprimed is strongly recommended because of its built-in protective factor. It is easily painted and generally develops fewer problems. Prefinished siding, on the other hand, is more expensive, and the homeowner must be assured it can be repainted; there may be problems in preparing the surface to accept paint. The important properties to look for in wood siding are freedom from warp, good paint retention, and ease in working. These

properties are found to a high degree in cedar, eastern white pine, sugar pine, cypress, and redwood; to a good degree in the spruces, western hemlock, ponderosa pine, and yellow poplar; to a fair degree in western larch, Douglas fir, and southern pine.

Some wood sidings are only for horizontal use, others only for vertical, and some either way if adequate nailing areas are provided. You can choose between dressed and matched and shiplapped edges. Treating these edges with water-repellent preservative is wise if the joints will be exposed to wind-driven rain.

Plywood (which is all manufactured in exterior grade now) and hardboard sheet materials come in 4x8-foot sheets and longer and are intended for vertical layup. A ⅜″ thickness is considered minimum; longer life is usually obtainable with ½″ or ⅝″ thickness. A four-foot width exactly spans three 16″-on-center studs, allowing for perimeter nailing for desired rigidity. Where horizontal joints are necessary, they should be protected by some sort of flashing. Plywood sheets come in such textures as grooved, "rough-sawn," and brushed, and usually in a choice of stain. If you dispense with the more expensive matched or shiplap edges, the joints where panels meet should be caulked and covered with a batten—or a batten running down each stud to give the look of wide-board, board-and-batten treatment. Hardboard sheeting is applied the same way.

Aluminum and vinyl siding can be applied right over old siding or sheathing. Both materials are lightweight, making for easy do-it-yourself handling; both come either smooth or textured; both can be purchased either with or without insulation backing. Their only drawbacks are that aluminum does dent; to change the color of vinyl is difficult. But neither will peel, blister, rot, rust, corrode, or support fire readily, and termites are not interested in them. Best of all, aluminum and vinyl siding both tend to cost less than other types in most areas (except the Northwest, where wood is cheaper).

Common steel-wire nails rust rather quickly and disfigure siding. The heads may show rust spots right through putty and light paint. Noncorrosive nails of aluminum, stainless steel, or galvanized steel are therefore a must in applying siding; annularly threaded ones, having greater withdrawal resistance, make for greater stability and longer life.

Masonry siding is, of course, virtually maintenance-free, but only if the initial application meets exacting standards. Application is not a do-it-yourself job, and tradesmen who can apply stucco properly are disappearing from the scene. When you can find one he's likely to be expensive.

Refinishing a Hardwood Floor

Successful floor refinishing is all in the preparation. The home handyperson can rent a drum sander, with its accompanying disk sander (for sanding the edges of the floor and hard-to-get-at places like the interior of a closet and stair treads where the big machine won't go). Rental centers rent this professional equipment for approximately $12 a day. A drum sander does take a certain amount of practice to develop a pro's technique, so think twice about starting right off on the living room floor; you may want to give yourself some on-the-job training on one of the more obscure floors in the house first. Although the process is not difficult, you'll be tired at the end of the day because the machines are heavy, even though they are counterbalanced to minimize fatigue as much as possible. Handled carelessly, however, the damage will show —a drum sander can never be allowed to revolve in one place with the abrasive surface touching the floor. You must keep moving or lift it off. The machine is never lowered to the floor, either, until the drum is spinning. The rental people will show you how to attach fresh sheets of abrasive paper that they sell, but the abrasive itself is as sharp as little shards of glass, and old work gloves should be worn for changing sheets to avoid cutting the palms of your hands.

You start with coarse-grit abrasive to take off the old surface, then switch to finer grit for smooth finishing.

When the floor is as smooth as you can get it, thoroughly vacuum and finish with a penetrating floor sealer, which may or may not include a stain, depending on whether you want to darken the floor.

Three coats of floor sealer are considered by some householders (particularly those with small children running about) to give the longest-lasting surface, one that can easily be touched up wherever it shows signs of wear. A sealer surface does not shine; it glows softly under a coat of wax. It is the least expensive way to finish a floor.

Shellac is inexpensive, but it does not wear well. Lacquer is too expensive. Bowling alley varnish is a good choice. The fast-drying easy-to-apply polyurethanes are toxic to breath in application, but coating the floor with a clear, hard, bubble-free, glossy or matte plastic this way makes it completely impervious to moisture. The floor will stand up to more hard wear than any other surface except floor sealer. It's the best choice of the hard clear finishes.

Use a minimum of three coats of penetrating floor sealer; use at least two coats of any hard clear finish. Wax all finishes, but don't bother with paste wax, because liquid waxes today are just as durable, infinitely easier to apply, and don't need buffing. But a couple of coats of wax over any floor finish are important as a final protective coating that absorbs wear and keeps the hard finish underneath looking new longer.

Making a Damp Basement Dry

Surface-water penetration usually stains the cellar walls high up. Ground-water penetration can usually be diagnosed by stains appearing at the bottom of the cellar wall, often at the joint where the wall meets the floor. The householder can undercut this joint with a cold chisel and hammer (a small sledge hammer speeds things up) wherever the water seems to be entering and fill it with epoxy cement—work that can only be done when the concrete is dry. If water pours in through a hole in the wall after a heavy rain, the hole should be chiseled out to make the cavity slightly wider than the opening (see top photo in following column) and filled with quick-setting hydraulic cement, molded into a plug and inserted just as it's about to harden. Easy enough, the job can be done while water is actually entering.

Cracks in the wall are also cold-chiseled wider behind than in front, making a cavity in which the repair material will hold fast. This repair isn't difficult either, but the best

patching material, a two-part epoxy cement, is expensive. The fumes should not be inhaled. Ventilate the immediate working area with a fan if you can't get a draft to blow through your basement.

If the walls are seeping generally, you probably will have to waterproof from the outside, but first you should try an interior coating, of which there are many brands for cement block or poured concrete foundation walls. It can be brushed on or troweled on.

Such a coating penetrates the pores of the concrete and expands as it hardens. But if there's a good deal of pressure against your cellar wall from ground water or from accumulated water after heavy rain, you have no recourse but to dig down to the foot of the foundation on the offending side and coat it thickly with liquid asphalt foundation

sealer, $5.50 per five-gallon drum (the same material as roof coating). It is a good idea to install drain pipe at the bottom of the trench and backfill it within a foot of the surface with gravel before replacing the soil if you have had a bad leakage problem.

If after all of this your basement is still damp in hot weather, the answer is a dehumidifier with humidistat. The water it extracts from the air can usually be made to flow into the house drain system if you build a rack for the dehumidifier up against the floor joists. Line the rack with foam plastic to absorb vibration from its compressor, and you probably won't be able to hear it in the rest of the house.

Plumbing Systems

Small plumbing repair jobs aren't difficult for the home handyperson. If you live in an old house you can expect to have a leak or drain stoppage once in a while (*see page 97, A Water Pipe Is Leaking!, and page 99, A Drainpipe Is Blocked!*) or a dripping faucet or toilet tank that won't shut off (*page 106, How to Fix Leaking Plumbing Fixtures*).

Making a repair or an addition to your basic plumbing systems is often possible for the mechanically-inclined householder. But be aware too that in many communities fixing or changing any plumbing comes under the code and may require the services of a professional.

The two systems are not as complex as they look. The larger pipes, which seldom need repair except in the oldest of houses, are the waste-disposal system. When one of these soil pipes gets clogged, if you can't unclog it yourself (with rented equipment if need be), you can find someone to unplug it for you by looking in the Yellow Pages. The smaller pipes carry hot and cold water in separate systems under 45 to 50 pounds pressure per square inch.

Most modern water supply systems are copper pipes, with two types in common use. One is rigid, the other soft-tempered and flexible, differentiated as "tubing". The majority of home plumbing jobs are accomplished with flexible copper tubing in the common ⅜" diameter in 15-, 30-foot, and longer lengths. Easy to bend, it is ideal for plumbing remodeling because it can be run within walls totally out of sight. Tubing is cut either with a special cutting tool (easily rented) or with a hacksaw. Bending is done by sliding a tightly coiled special spring tube-bender (also rentable) onto the tubing and bending it over a curved surface—which can be your knee.

Compression fittings, the choice of most householders tackling their own plumbing problems, are almost leakproof, and therefore the best bet for inexperienced persons. Brass ferrules are slid over the two ends of copper tubing to be joined. A brass union (like a double bolt with one head) screws into both ferrules, and the ends of the copper tubing are compressed inside as the union is tightened, making a joint that can withstand 50 psi water pressure without the need for joint compound. Use two small wrenches when working with compression fittings.

Flexible copper tubing can be connected to rigid copper pipe with a special adapter—as can copper pipe or tubing to galvanized steel pipe. But the two types of metal must be isolated, either with a one-foot section of brass pipe or via a special dielectric union, to prevent corrosion from an electro-chemical reaction taking place between the copper and the iron.

Fixing old galvanized iron plumbing isn't as difficult as most people imagine. If you can remove part 1 and figure out how to remove parts 2 and 3, you can buy an exact replacement for the defective fitting or length of pipe and reassemble everything in reverse order without trouble. Be sure to use pipe joint compound on all threaded joints to prevent leaking, and never tighten any joint too tightly. Rental centers have the standard plumbing tools you'll need, like pipe wrenches, which are used—firmly but gently—in pairs, one to grip the pipe, the other the fitting. Pre-threaded pipe in an assortment of lengths is now available in the plumbing departments of some big suburban discount houses, along with all the standard fittings—T's, elbows, unions, and reducers. Unless you're extremely careful, however, you run the risk of compounding a plumbing problem in a house built before World War II. Galvanized iron pipe in old houses is likely to have become extremely corroded and difficult to handle. Wrenches carelessly applied at one place may loosen a fitting or break open a new leak up or down the line some distance from where you're working.

Replacing a section of cast iron soil pipe calls for working with molten lead; this type of repair is considered too difficult for the inexperienced person.

Upgrading Your Electrical System

If you're having to plug too many appliances into too few sockets and keep blowing fuses, don't think that you have to rewire the whole house. Usually new circuits can be added to an existing system; it is possible for a home handyperson to learn enough about electricity to install needed new lines. In many communities you are allowed to do this work, installing sockets, fixtures, and switches yourself and stringing the wires to the service entry panel, then hiring a licensed electrician to come in, inspect what you've done, and attach the wires—for a considerable cost saving.

Your building code, a copy of which can be picked up at your town hall, will tell you what size and type of wire you are obligated to use—in most suburban localities #12 Romex, a fabric-covered wire, 20¢ a foot. Only in certain cities is flexible armored cable ("BX") required, 25¢ a foot for #12 wire.

Installing a Door Lock

This is not a difficult job for the home handyperson. The most effective auxiliary lock, popular in high-crime urban areas as a supplement to the regular door lock, is the so-called "Segal" dropbolt, or "deadfall", lockset that resists prying by gripping a heavy socket attached to the door frame. Buy the lock first, examine the instructions, then purchase the specified drill bit, unless you have the exact required size already. Don't spend money on an expensive pick-resistant cylinder because today's burglars don't bother to pick locks—they pry open doors and windows with a pinch-bar. Or they enter by clamping a lock-wrench onto the rim of the cylinder and break the lock's internal bolts. Block the gap between door and frame to foil pinch-barring by installing strips of heavy metal angle iron for the purpose. Bolt a metal guard plate over the face of the cylinder on the outside of the door. It comes in a kit with four carriage bolts and protects against lock-wrenching.

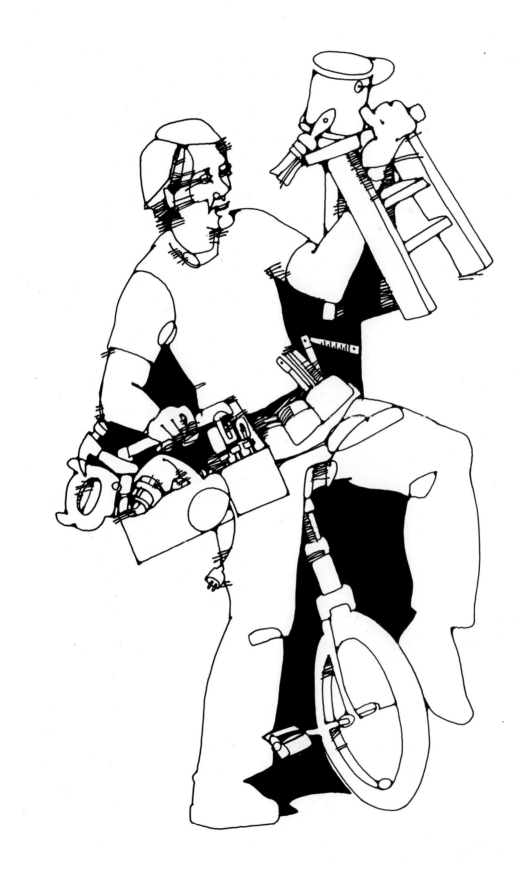

Home Improvement

We used to believe that home repairs and improvements were best left to professionals unless a homeowner was handy with tools. All that has changed with the prohibitively high rates most tradesmen charge—if they can be persuaded to take on small jobs at all. Today, we do it ourselves. And we often wind up doing a better job than "professional."

But many people still hesitate to do it themselves for fear of botching the job. Admittedly, that sometimes happens. If you make a careful study of the tools, materials, and techniques entailed, though, you'll find that you can handle a great many more repairs and improvements than you ever thought possible. Unanticipated problems are solved as they arise. Each logical step of the process falls into line as the project moves forward toward completion.

On the following pages, you'll find instructions on how to handle a variety of emergency repairs—including what to do if the electricity quits, if you smell gas, if a water pipe is leaking badly, and if your drain is blocked.

In addition, you'll learn how to make many household repairs and improvements that you should never pay someone else to do—how to replace an electrical plug, patch wallboard, replace wall tile, insulate your house, weatherstrip windows and doors, lay carpeting and floor coverings, and much more.

Painting, both exterior and interior, furniture restoration, and remodeling round out the chapter.

Six Emergency Household Repairs You Can Handle

Even if you don't consider yourself handy, there are a few common problems you shouldn't have to call a repairman to attend to—if you could find one who would. Some of these problems can be put off till *mañana*. Others demand immediate first aid.

The Electricity Has Quit!

This can happen when you turn on an iron or an electric skillet; it usually means too many appliances have been plugged into the same circuit. Or frayed insulation is allowing bare wires to touch, causing a short circuit. Result: either a blown fuse or a tripped circuit breaker, depending on which of these devices has been installed in your house to kill the power automatically when a circuit is overloaded. If you're sure it was just one too many appliances that shut down the circuit, unplug the iron or the skillet and change the fuse or reset the breaker.

The best way to be prepared for a short circuit is to familiarize yourself during *daylight* hours with each of your electrical circuits served by its respective fuse or circuit breaker on-off switch. Plotting the course of a circuit through your house or hunting the cause of a blown fuse or tripped circuit breaker are identical procedures.

First, for safety's sake, shut off the power from the street at your service entry (the terminal where the power enters the house). In some older houses, you turn off the power merely by opening the fuse-box door; other service entries have a main switch in the form of a lever on one side of the fuse box; still other boxes have removable sections of black plastic which are pulled out of the box by an attached handle. Now you can remove any fuse without danger of shock.

Remove a single fuse or flip a single circuit breaker switch to "off", then turn on the power again. Now run around the house testing the appliances, the light switches and the convenience outlets (using a lamp that you know is working); those without power are the ones on the circuit you're testing. You should have the room-by-room coverage of each circuit in your house posted at the fuse box or circuit breaker so you'll be able to find the source of the trouble more easily the next time your electrical "safety valve" closes down.

There's no way of telling whether an overload or a short circuit has tripped a circuit breaker. A *fuse* that has blown because of an overload, however, usually has a clear window through which you can see the hole in the metal strip inside. A fuse that has blown because of a short circuit will probably have a blackened window.

Finding the cause of a short circuit can be a bit tricky. Usually two bare wires are touching in the plug or cord leading to a lamp or an appliance; or the trouble may be in a swivel lamp that someone has over-swiveled once too often and the insulation on the wires inside has broken. Check the insulation you can see first before opening up possibly offending lamps or appliances looking for shorts. Sometimes you will see the short in the form of a loud popping flash that leaves a blackened area at the spot where the short occurred. But if you miss the flash you will have to hunt for it. Unplug every appliance and switch off all the fixtures throughout the circuit that you know is shorted out. Put in a new fuse. Now go around turning on one appliance or fixture at a time. When the fuse blows again you've found the faulty appliance or fixture. If no single one of them blows the fuse by itself, chances are the circuit was overloaded. Go back, plug in and turn on every appliance and fixture on the circuit so they are all running at the same time. If that blows the fuse, you've got your answer. It's overloaded, and you'll have to move one or two of the highest-wattage appliances to another circuit. (Appliances that create heat, like a toaster or waffle iron or portable heater, draw the most wattage—and cost the most to run.)

If a check of visible wiring reveals no exposed wires where the insulation has chipped or peeled off, the short is probably in your house wiring, and it's time to call in an electrician.

There's a Smell of Gas!

Immediate action is called for when gas is escaping. If you come home and smell gas when you open the door, don't light a match or flame or turn on any motorized appliance, because the slightest spark may ignite the fumes. Turn off the main shutoff valve located near the gas meter. *Every member of the household should be shown the location of the main gas shutoff and be taught to operate it.* Throw open the windows to allow air currents to carry away the escaped gas before turning the main valve back on and igniting the various pilot lights. The moment the gas is on again, pilots should be lighted as swiftly as possible. Preferably, one person should light the pilots in the cellar or utility area (after reading the direction on the plate attached to every gas-fired utility) and another person should stand ready to light the pilots in the kitchen range, making sure that the burners are turned off. After all pilots are lit, if you still smell raw gas, close the main valve again and call the utility company for a serviceman. Open up a few windows to prevent another gas build-up until he arrives. Leave suspected holes in the lines well enough alone; above all, don't light a free flame and pass it along the pipes looking for a leak. That's risky.

If a stove burner fails to ignite when the range-top pilot is lit, the burner may be clogged with particles of food. Lift-out-type burners can be washed in a solution of baking soda but must be dried thoroughly before reusing. Set them in the sun or shoot some hot air through them with a hair dryer. Non-removable burners can be cleaned with a stiff brush if you are careful not to shove the food particles inside the parts that surround the ring; check to see that nothing is plugging the flash tube running from pilot to burner; clean the orifice in the burner at the head of the flash tube with a pin. Don't turn any adjustment screws in the process of cleaning the burners.

A Water Pipe Is Leaking!

Because your water supply system is under constant pressure, a small leak can produce a flood. Every house has a main shutoff valve, usually located in the basement or utility room where the supply enters the house. Leaks that can't be turned off at a fixture can be stopped by turning this main valve in a clockwise direction. Responsible

members of the household should be made familiar with its location so they can get it turned off quickly if a bad leak develops.

A tiny leak in a copper pipe is an easy emergency repair consisting of first turning off the water running through the pipe, then wrapping it with plastic-coated cloth duct tape (see top left sketch on page 98), which is stronger and less stretchy than electrical tape and more moisture-resistant. Though black plastic electrical tape doesn't work nearly as well, it can be pressed into service if you keep a steady stretch as you wind it on. In either case, overlap each spiral after having thoroughly dried the pipe so the tape will stick.

A somewhat larger leak in a pipe can be repaired temporarily with a piece of rubber held tightly in place with an ordinary C-clamp. A small block of wood set between the rubber and the C-clamp will even out

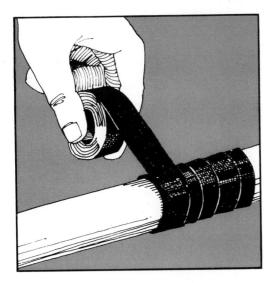

the pressure along the length of the leak. A permanent repair should follow this emergency treatment as soon as possible.

You can get a more positive grip on a pipe with a hose clamp, which is a pierced strip of flexible stainless steel with an attached buckle. You slide this buckle to

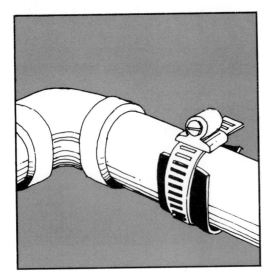

snug the clamp around the pipe over a strip of rubber, then tighten it with a screw that's a part of the buckle. It's worth keeping a couple of hose clamps on hand for this emergency since they are by far the easiest and most effective remedy for small leaks.

Best bet for a larger leak is a sleeve clamp, which consists of two curved pieces of hinged metal that screw together. But it

must fit the pipe perfectly. A section of rubber sheeting over the leak seals the hole when the clamp is screwed tightly closed.

Corrosion at joints in pipes—where a pipe is threaded into an elbow, for example —can start a leak. The remedy, after shutting off the water, is to unscrew the offending section of pipe or the fitting and apply pipe joint compound to the threads or Teflon tape made expressly for the purpose (both available at hardware stores). This will usually seal the joint when pipe and fitting are screwed back together. Use two pipe wrenches for a job like this so as to cause as little damage to the plumbing as possible. Systems of galvanized iron pipe over 30 years old can become very fragile when corrosion has set in. If joints and fittings are frozen too tight, don't force the issue. Wait for the plumber.

There's another measure for plugging a leak around a fitting that still hasn't stopped after you try pipe compound. It's an epoxy cement that hardens like soft metal. The water has to be shut off and the pipe dried before application for proper seal. Instructions are on the tube or can, but a word of warning: you can waste a distressing amount of a plumber's expensive time resorting to this expediency since the material has to be chiselled and chipped away before he can unscrew the fitting; and he is likely to use bad language while whacking off the stuff. ing off the stuff.

If you discover a large wet spot seeping through a wall or ceiling, there's no point in waiting for the plumber's arrival before tearing open whatever encloses the pipe. Go right ahead: the plumber will only have to do it when he gets there, and you may be able to apply first aid to the ailing pipe, allowing you to turn the water on again until he does arrive. Just be sure, before you start ripping, that the wet spot isn't caused by a leak in the roof—or by someone upstairs having let the tub run over.

A Drainpipe Is Blocked!

The first thing to try, when a bathroom sink becomes plugged or drains sluggishly, is to remove and clean the stopper, which in most modern fixtures is designed to trap *hair*, the main culprit here. Holding the drain handle at sink top in the "open" position with one hand, push down on the stopper and rotate it slightly to disengage it from the inner horizontal rod that raises and lowers it. If this doesn't work, try the familiar rubber plunger called a "plumber's friend" that's attached to a short wooden handle. The simple-force type works best in sinks. Run a few inches of water into the bowl and plug the overflow hole with a wet cloth or sponge. Slick a little petroleum jelly around the rim of the cup to seal the suction, then set it over the drain. Slam it down hard and yank it up alternately a few times. *If this doesn't work,* check to see if the U-shaped trap underneath the sink has a screw-in plug in its bottom. These are usually easy to remove with a monkey wrench (lacking one, try pliers), but be sure to place a pan under it to catch the stopped-up gunk. If there's no appreciable flow, reach in with a straightened coat hanger on the end of which you've bent a hook and try to dislodge whatever it is that's causing

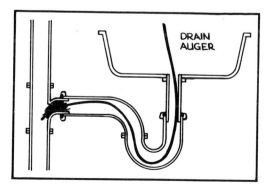

DRAIN
AUGER

the stoppage. *If this doesn't work,* try a long-cabled drain auger known as a plumber's snake; or lacking one of these, try a garden hose if you have enough length to reach the stopped-up drain from a faucet you can couple onto. Plumber's snakes (which can be rented in most localities) come in various lengths. The better ones rotate a steel shaft inside a stationary sheath. Cranking the inner cable makes a corkscrew tip engage the blockage and allows you to haul it back out. A snake works particularly well on stuck pieces of cloth. Insert it through the cleanout plug at the base of the trap; if your trap has no plug you will have to remove the entire trap, but see if you can reach the stoppage with the snake inserted at the entrance to the drain in the basin first before you go to all the trouble of disassembling the trap. Kitchen and laundry room sinks are unblocked the same way as outlined above.

A stoppage deep in your house's waste disposal system can be reached with a long snake or garden hose fed very slowly and carefully through the vent in the roof, but the latter is not recommended for amateurs because water can back up in the system from the point of the blockage and come gurgling out the drains in the fixtures. There are also drainpipe cleanout plugs usually found at the extremities of the waste system. If there's room, place a garbage can right under any cleanout plug you loosen, especially one at the bottom of a long drop, just in case the whole pipe is filled with water and gunk. Cleanout plugs are usually tight and need a good-sized wrench to open. Coat the threads with pipe joint compound before replacing, to seal the joint and to make it easier to open the plug in the future.

A toilet bowl will often respond to a plumber's helper, but sometimes a snake is required. Just keep in mind that snakes and plungers that have been in a toilet are contaminated and should not be used to unclog a kitchen sink in which dishes are washed; nor should they be used for work on your potable water supply system unless they have been properly sterilized, which means at least 20 minutes' hard boiling in a tub.

Since caustic cleaners are ineffective in unplugging blocked toilets (and can harm the vitreous surface of the bowl), a snake is usually the best choice, even though it takes a little effort to guide it up through the trap in the front of the bowl by hand. To keep from getting mucked up, shove your arm into a plastic garbage bag, because you'll have to get your hand well into the bowl to guide the snake through the trap and on into the drain.

A Windowpane Is Smashed!

Before you buy a new pane of glass, it's essential that you know the *exact* size of the opening. But put on heavy work gloves and plastic face shield first and use pliers to remove shattered remains of glass, working from the outside if feasible. Wiggle the broken pieces out of the top of the sash first to prevent having any fall on your hands while you're removing the rest. Clean away all the old putty before taking measurements. Hardened clinging putty can be softened for removal with a propane torch or, more safely but not as swiftly, with a soldering iron. It's seldom a problem, but be careful when you dig out old putty to avoid gouging the groove in the wood where the glass will seat. Sand it and seal the muntins with linseed oil to keep the oil in the putty from being drawn into the wood and becoming dried out.

glass for several openings measure them all; even the muntins in metal sash can and do vary in size. If you want to be absolutely sure the glass will fit, cut a cardboard matrix of the opening and take it with you when you go to buy the glass. A pane should be ⅛″ smaller in both dimensions than the space it will occupy, and preferably of ⅛″-thick double-strength glass.

Besides glass you'll need glazing compound or a small can of pre-mixed putty, cheap enough if you have only one or two panes to replace. If you live in a house often surrounded by small boys hitting fungoes through windows, save money on putty by buying it dry; you mix it with linseed oil. You'll also need glazier's points, and see if you can pick up a device used for setting points. Otherwise, use a screwdriver.

Dry-fit your pane of glass, then apply a thin bead of putty ⅛″ thick into the groove on all four sides to seal the glass against air and water leakage. Lay up the glass and secure it with glazier's points, two per side for small panes, 6″ apart all around for larger sheets.

Using a small putty knife, apply a sealing bead of putty. In trimming off the excess, leave the bead's outer edge flush with the

Most glass dealers sell pre-cut replacement panes for standard sizes of sash. Or they'll cut the glass for you. Measure the opening at several places both vertically and horizontally, because wood sash warps and is seldom dead square. When you buy

outdoor edge of the sash molding and its inner edge flush with the inner edge of the molding (that shows through the glass). Finish off by firmly drawing the putty knife, blade held quite flat, over the new glazing for a smooth triangular bead.

Let the putty dry for at least a week before painting it. For a tight bond the paint should extend slightly onto the glass. If you get a bit too much on the glass don't try to wipe it off; let the paint dry, then clean the glass with a single-edged razor blade.

The Roof Is Leaking!

Finding exactly where rainwater or snowmelt is entering the housetop and fixing the leak can be more difficult than you might anticipate. Unfortunately, a leak is not likely to be centered straight over the ceiling wetness, because water can cling to the underside of a rafter and travel a surprising distance before it drops off. Leaks in metal flashing can usually be stopped temporarily, but the casual handyperson should call in a professional for permanent repair or replacement of badly bent, split, or rusted flashing. Because of the way shingles overlap from eaves to roof peak, the loss of a shingle blown off in a windstorm interferes with the interlocking structure of the layering, and a patch has to be made with great care not to compound the damage.

Most leaks originate at flashings where the roof surrounds a projecting object like a chimney, vent pipe, or skylight. Less likely are leaks along the edges or on corroded surfaces of flashing lining the troughs where the roof intersects with gables and dormers. Least likely to leak is the roof surface (of a shingled roof), except as a sign that it's time to reshingle. (Nevertheless, the sharp-eyed householder inspects the roof carefully after any high wind and replaces missing shingles on the surface or along the peak.)

The best time to hunt for the source of a leak is obvious—during a heavy rain. If your house has an attic it's a simple matter. Take a bright work light with you, and when you find the hole mark it with an X. Later you can hammer a long thin nail through the roof at the X to locate the leak from outside. If a three-day nor'easter is buffeting your house you may be able to stop the leak temporarily by squirting some caulking compound into the hole and pressing it hard with your finger to spread it. You can now get an instant-patch material in a cartridge for a standard caulking gun that seals holes up to ¼" in roofing, flashing, and gutters. Cost: about $1.

If the attic has been finished with a wall or ceiling don't tear the wallboard away looking for the leak. Try to make the best guess you can at its location and take a measurement from the leak to something that will be in the same relationship to it on the outside, like the corner of a chimney or a vent pipe. Chances are that the source of the leak will be a missing or torn shingle —easy to spot when you get on the roof if you can peg its general vicinity.

A word about safety: stay on the ground until the wind dies down and the roof dries off. Wear sneakers for sure footing. Set your ladder with both its feet firmly and evenly planted well out from the side of the house. You can use a section of a second ladder as a perch for working on the roof by tying a stout rope to the top rung, tossing it over the peak using it to haul the ladder into place, and anchoring the rope to the base of a big tree or a car on the other side. Keep one hand on the ladder and the other free to operate with, whether you're working on the ladder against the house or on the one hung from the peak. Think about that drop-off behind you every moment you're up there. A roofer doesn't step back to admire his handiwork—more than once.

If possible, wait for a warm day to work on the roof when the shingles will not be brittle. Check first for shingles that are not lying flat. Slap a dab of asphalt roofing cement under any curled-up shingle and

press it flat, then hammer in a roofing nail at the edge to hold it down; put a final dollop of cement over the nail head.

If a shingle is split, but not split as far as the leading edge of the one above it, put roofing cement under it and a nail on both sides of the cut, then cover with a final coat of cement.

A badly damaged shingle for which you have no replacement can be salvaged by sliding a small sheet of copper or aluminum (coated underneath with roofing cement) as far as you can up under the shingle. You

may have to remove a couple of nails, and here's how: If the overlying shingle is brittle, bend it up only as far as you absolutely have to in order to slide a chisel underneath and pry up the nail heads. Then saw them off with the type of hacksaw that has a handle attached to one end of the blade. A prybar may work if the overlying shingle is pliable enough, but using the claw of a hammer to remove the nails may very well ruin the good shingle over the bad one.

Be just as careful replacing a shingle (don't attempt the repair if you doubt your ability, or your agility in the air; call a roofer). Remove the nails that hold it in place and slide out what's left of the old shingle. Dab some cement on the nail holes and on any crack in the underlayment that looks like it might leak. Slide the new shingle into place (see photo in next column) and nail it where the shingle above will overlap; daub cement on the nail heads. You may need an extra daub of cement to augment the self-stick strip to hold down the shingle that you had to bend up out of the way.

So-called "hip shingles" that cover the ridge of the roof are cut from regular roof shingles with tin snips or heavy shears. Leave at least an extra 3″ to slide under the adjoining hip shingle. Nail down exposed shingling that the missing hip shingle had covered and daub the nail heads. Coat the entire undersurface of the replacement hip shingle with asphalt cement before laying it in place; nail, cement the nail heads.

Occasionally wind force will make metal flashing warp and draw out of the groove or joint in the surface in which it was embedded. More often whatever was used to seal the edges of the flashing to the roof has dried out and pulled away. Mortar may have fallen out of the joint where flashing is embedded in a chimney. Butyl caulking compound is the remedy—a white rubbery material that never hardens. Apply it with a caulking gun.

Flashing that's rusted through can be patched, if the holes aren't too big, with aluminized sealer. For a tight bond, sand off the rust with a coarse sandpaper before applying. Aluminized sealer is the proper material for sealing any leak between two metal surfaces, as between a vent pipe and its surrounding flashing.

The hardest kind of roof leak to repair is a hole up out of sight under the shingles in flashing that lines the valley where angled roof surfaces meet. If the entire sheet of metal is in bad shape, best call in a professional, but meanwhile you have this expedient option good for a few months to a year: seal up the edges of the valley from top to bottom with asphalt cement, pressing it firmly against the edges of the overlapping shingles. This will stop the roof leak until the roofer arrives.

How To Get Started as a Do-It-Yourselfer

You don't have to acquire a lot of fancy equipment—even though an entire industry has sprung up in response to your needs and hardware stores are piled high with a tremendous variety of gizmos and gadgets, as well as useful tools. If you start with a basic set, then buy the tools you need as you require them, before long you'll own the equipment to tackle practically any home repair job confronting you. For that once-in-a-decade project requiring special equipment, rental centers in most localities make available (by the hour, day, or week) the same quality equipment used by professionals. Such centers are usually staffed by people who know exactly how everything operates (as opposed to the part-time hardware store clerk who may not be quite so sure when it comes to a rental) and can tell you exactly how to do a job.

There are also a great many home improvement products specially manufactured for installation by the do-it-yourselfer. Many are mass produced and can help you reach your goals more easily and quickly —but not necessarily less expensively. For example, there's no practical way kitchen cabinets can be made at home as inexpensively as they can be bought readymade, ready to install. Manufacturers of home improvement products for do-it-yourselfers advertise in home and service magazines like *Better Homes and Gardens*. All provide detailed information about their products on receipt of a postcard.

Perhaps one of your best sources of advice concerning do-it-yourself projects is your local lumber store. More than likely, the problem you're having is one that these people have helped other people solve many times. They can tell you the best material to use, the most economical way to complete a project, help you figure costs, and many other useful things.

What tools will you need?

In spite of the great variety of tools specially made for the home handyman, a basic few are all you need for most do-it-yourself projects about the house.

Look for quality, whether you buy them new or pick them up at garage sales. Professional-looking workmanship is hard to accomplish with cheap tools; well-made ones last a lifetime. Cheap ones may actually be unsafe.

Good tools deserve proper care. Cutting surfaces should be kept sharp so that tools will cut predictably. If a tool gets damaged don't put off repairing it or replacing it.

Here's a list that equips the home handyman to take on many different sorts of minor repair jobs and installation projects:

- three sizes of screwdrivers plus one phillips screwdriver
- pliers
- wood rasp
- 13-ounce-head hammer
- locking wrench
- awl
- utility (matte) knife with replaceable blades
- steel tape measure
- nail set
- eight-point-per-inch cross-cut saw
- combination try square and level
- 10" file
- hacksaw
- block plane
- 1"-wide chisel
- putty knife with 4" flexible blade
- sharpening stone
- ⅜" electric drill
- set of bits for drilling in wood or metal
- small bench vise
- safety plastic tip-up face shield
- saber saw
- orbital/straight-stroke sander
- spring-loaded staple gun

Common Household Repairs You Can Make

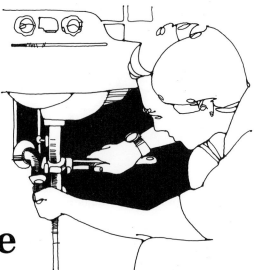

How to Fix an Electrical Cord

When the insulation begins to fray on the cord attached to a much-used appliance like an iron, the wear is easy to halt by simply binding with black plastic electrician's tape at the worn place. When something has cut through the insulation or it has worn through to bare wire, immediate repair is a vital necessity. The least that can happen is that two bare wires may touch and short out the circuit—blowing a fuse or tripping a circuit breaker—before starting a fire. The worst is that someone touching either the bare wire or the suddenly electrified housing of the appliance may get a shock that could be lethal. Under certain conditions, especially around a kitchen or bathroom where plumbing provides a perfect ground, even a very brief electrical jolt can kill. *For safety, always pull out the plug before repairing an electrical cord, lamp, or appliance; shut off power to the fuse box or circuit breaker before handling any of the house wiring.* If you harbor any doubts at all about what you're going to do, don't. Call an electrician instead.

Cords to lamps or appliances that get a lot of yanking or kinking can break inside the insulation, and you don't know where. Then the entire cord must be replaced. It's usually better not to repair but to replace a cord that gets pulled or tripped-over a lot, especially if it's old and its insulation is cracked and split.

There's quite a variance in types of appliance cord, depending on whether it's to be used under dry or wet conditions and on how much wattage it has to carry. It's best to replace a cord with the same cord the appliance came with by snipping off an inch or so and taking it to an electrical supply store for a perfect match. When you get home with the proper cord, ease of replacement depends on how far into the lamp or appliance the manufacturer has placed the terminals. If you can get at them but have trouble getting the new cord to the terminals from the outside, attach a stout string to the terminal end of the old cord. As you pull it out the string will be drawn into its place, and by pulling the string back, you can draw the new cord into the lamp or appliance and hitch it up. The white-insulated wire goes to the silver-colored screw, and the black-insulated wire to the brass screw.

Always twist the stripped ends of stranded wire together clockwise and wrap it clockwise around each terminal screw before tightening. Insulation should butt up against the screw but not be allowed to lie under it. Some replacement cords, particularly in lamps, don't attach to terminals but to other interior wires via plastic cone-shaped connectors called "wire nuts." To join two wires using a wire nut, just shove them into the spiral spring inside the nut and twist tight. If there's no strain on it, a wire nut is a safe permanent connection.

There is often a clamp of some sort inside a lamp or appliance intended to prevent any inadvertent strain on the cord from being transmitted to the interior wiring. If you don't find one, tie a knot in the cord to lie against the inner rim of the aperture through which the cord passes. Cover the knot with electrical tape to lengthen its life span.

When bare wires are exposed in any two-conductor electrical cord, the cord should be severed. Damaged outer insulation, such as you find on a toaster cord, should be trimmed back with scissors. Next, cut one wire the same 3″ or so shorter on one trimmed side of the parted cord as you cut one of the two wires 3″ shorter on the other side. This way the two splices will not lie side by side but be offset a few inches, obviating any possibility of a short occurring at the splices in the future in case the wrapping shouldn't hold. Using a pocket- or paring knife, trim off about 1″ of insulation covering the ends of the wires.

(If you are repairing an appliance cord, the insulation may be two colors. Follow the black-to-black and white-to-white coding when you splice.)

For best electrical contact, scrape the wires clean and bright before joining them. Bend the ends of the two wires together, then twist each wire tightly around the other in what's called a Western Union splice. If the cord is to be subjected to hard tugs or undue strain of any kind, it is best to solder both splices before wrapping, and here's how: Lay the splice atop the tip of the soldering gun to heat up the splice itself, then touch the (rosin-core) solder to the hot splice so that it melts down around the wires and cools to a strong joint. Tape each splice separately with plastic electrical tape. Hold the tape fairly taut for a good bond, overlapping half of each turn over half of the previous turn. Finally, encase the whole joint with a single spiral of tape.

How to Replace a Plug

Check first to see if the failure is due to the plug's not making adequate contact inside the wall outlet. Try bending the prongs away from each other slightly for a better grip. If that doesn't work, check the interior of the plug. A wire may have worked loose from a terminal screw. If the prongs are loose on their bases, nip the plug off the wire and replace it. Here's how: Cut the cord back beyond any damaged portion and slip the new plug down over the cord. Clip off

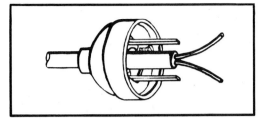

the outer insulation with scissors to expose a couple of inches of the two wires. Tie a so-called Underwriter's Knot by making a loop in both wires, passing each wire through the loop in the other wire and pulling tight. This

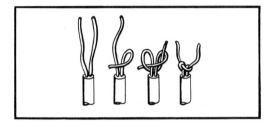

takes the strain off the wires where they attach to the terminals and puts it on the knot. Strip a half-inch of insulation from the end of each wire, being especially careful not to cut or nick any of the small wires inside. Twist the small wires four times clockwise to bind them together like the point of a waxed mustache. Pull the knot you made down firmly in the plug. Draw one of the wires around the base of either prong to its respective screw; wrap the wire around the screw clockwise; tighten the screw. The wire's insulation should come right to the

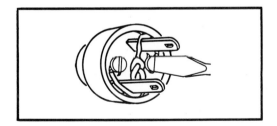

screw but not go under it. Attach the other wire the same way and slide the protective cover over the prongs.

How to Rewire a Lamp Socket

If a lamp tips over and the bulb shatters, the trick to getting the base out of the socket is to *first pull the plug out of the wall*, then either turn the glass "stamen" with pliers or press down with a tightly packed ball of newspaper and twist the base out.

Most floor and table lamps, as well as many wall fixtures, hold the bulb in an uncomplicated socket that may or may not contain a switch but comes apart quite easily. If the bulb has been flickering on and off or simply won't light even though you've tested it in a lamp you know is working, check the plug on the end of the cord first to make sure neither wire has pulled away from its terminal. Then look the cord over for the possibility of a break. If either plug or cord is damaged, follow the instructions above for repair or replacement. If they check out, the contact point in the base of socket or switch mechanism may be worn.

Assuring yourself once more that the lamp is unplugged, open the socket by looking for the embossed word "press" on the shell just under the cap. Push in at this point hard with your thumb, at the same time prying open the other side with the fingers of both hands. The cap will suddenly pop off. Draw away the metal shell and cardboard liner so that you can inspect the wires and terminals. Sometimes a wire has pulled out of its terminal. Or you may find a broken wire inside, especially if there is any swivel action in the lamp. If there doesn't seem to be anything wrong with the wiring, you should replace the socket with a new one and not try to repair it; they are quite inexpensive. If the cap is holding the lamp to-

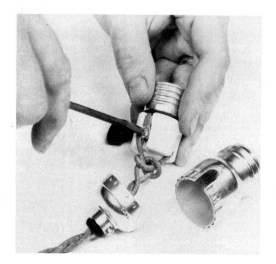

gether, leave it in place, because the new socket shell will fit it. Loosen the terminal screws in the exposed socket, free the wires and discard the socket.

In connecting the new one, reassemble the parts in the same order you removed them. Remember to wrap the wires around the terminal screws in a clockwise direction (see photo in left column). Slide the cardboard liner in place—it's the vital insulation between the wires and the metal shell—then slide the shell on and press it into the cap.

How to Fix Leaking Plumbing Fixtures

Block that drip! A hot water drop-by-drop leak that will fill an ordinary cup in 10 minutes wastes about 3,280 gallons a year, a whole year's-worth of bathing for one person (if taken as showers, which use 10 gallons less than a tub). Although the cost of the water dribbled away depends on geographical location, the cost of the fuel to heat that drip-drip-drip, if anyone's foolish enough to let it go an entire year, can amount to as much as $50.

The most common cause of dripping faucets is a worn stem washer. Kitchen, bathroom, or laundry room, all faucets are basically the same, even if they look different, so instructions will serve for any faucet.

The correct procedure: Begin by turning off the water at the shutoff valve nearest the malfunctioning faucet. If there is no shutoff valve under the fixture, you'll have to look for another valve on the gate side of the system, or close the main gate valve where the water enters the house (usually in the basement or utility room). Then turn on the faucet until the water stops dripping. Close or plug the drain under the faucet to ensure that you don't lose a vital part down the pipe.

Disassemble the faucet by 1) unscrewing the handle screw; 2) gently prying off the handle; 3) covering either the jaws of your wrench or the wide, flat cap nut on a chrome fixture with electrical tape to avoid damaging the finish; 4) remove the decorative housing called the bonnet, which may or may not be held in place by a cap nut; 5) remove the heavy packing nut with a pliers, turning it counterclockwise; 6) pull out the

spindle by hand, on the bottom of which you'll find the faucet washer held in place by a short brass screw through its center.

Washer

Unscrew it and dig out the washer with a small screwdriver or the point of a knife. Check the old washer first and see if you can make out some embossed numerals that delineate its exact size, then see if you can match it from the assortment of washers (the wasteful way most householders must buy them instead of by specific size). If the old brass screw looks shot, replace it with a new one from the box of new washers.

Now, you're ready to reassemble the faucet, but before you replace the stem, check the "seat," the surface inside the faucet against which the washer will bear; use a toothpick rather than some sharp-pointed metal tool. If the seat does not feel smooth, merely suspect it, at this point, and reas-

semble the faucet. Open and close it lightly a couple of times to be sure the washer is properly seated, then turn on the water. If the faucet still drips when it's turned off lightly, or if it starts dripping again in a relatively short time, it means the seat is corroded and channeled—as only a faucet can be that has been allowed to dribble for an unconscionably long period waiting for someone to replace its washer.

The remedy is to buy (or borrow from a neighbor) a valve seat grinder. This is an inexpensive tool that looks something like a faucet stem with a handle through one end and a round cutting wheel on the other. You insert the tool, slip the faucet's packing nut (or a matching nut on the tool itself) down over its stem and tighten it onto the faucet to hold it straight and true. Then just turn the handle of the grinder clockwise to smooth the seat; a couple of turns will do it. Some faucets have replaceable seats.

A few handy hints about fixing leaking faucets: If you can't find the proper sized replacement washer, turn the old one over. If after you get the faucet back together it still leaks from under the bonnet or around the stem, try tightening the packing nut a bit. If it still leaks, remove the handle and unscrew the packing nut. If there's a plastic O-ring, replace it; otherwise wrap the spindle with so-called "packing wicking." There's an excellent long-wearing nylon type on the market. Replace the packing nut, tightening it down firmly over the packing, then the bonnet and handle. Mixing faucets—two handles for one spout such as you find in many older sinks and washbasins—should be replaced one at a time, each faucet dismantled and reassembled separately. Otherwise you risk the frustration of getting the two stems mixed up, so that when you think you're all finished you discover that the left faucet no longer turns counterclockwise, as it properly should, and the right one clockwise.

Faucet washers are cheap, but changing them is a nuisance. A tip: teach your family to turn water off lightly. A light touch will extend the period between washer changes.

Toilet troubles are easier to correct than you might think glancing at that Rube Goldbergian contraption inside the tank—and

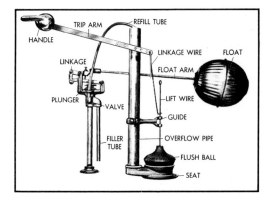

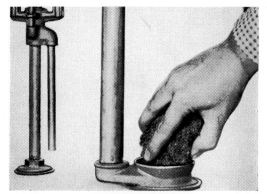

when you do look in there, handle the baked porcelain tank cover with great care; it is easily broken. Although it's possible to repair the inlet valve as explained below, if the parts are badly corroded and hard to take apart, forget it. Buy a new one. An entire ballcock assembly only costs a few dollars, and installation instructions are right on the package. But choose one of the new designs that works more quietly and wastes less water. One model (Fluidmaster) even dispenses with the float ball.

Deep down inside the flush tank that's attached to the wall behind most toilets hangs a rubber ball atop the opening to a wide pipe and held tightly in place there by the pressure of the water volume in the tank. When you flush the toilet, the long metal arm on the end of which this rubber tank ball is suspended lifts the ball free of its seat and the tank empties into the toilet bowl in one grand gravity-fed gush. (Water also runs through the narrow tube, called the bowl refill tube, into a wider vertical pipe, called the overflow tube, to replenish the water in the trap and bottom of the bowl and seal off sewer gases.)

If water flows into the tank but it does not fill up, the problem is in the tank ball. Turn off the water supply and flush to empty the tank. If the rubber still feels lively, scrub off the bottom of the tank ball with steel wool or emery paper. At the same time, to improve the seal, polish the end of the pipe it seats itself in (see photo at top of next column); polish the wire rods that lift the ball. If these rods are bent you can easily straighten them. If the guide arm they run through does not let them slip freely to make the ball drop accurately into its seat, it's a simple matter to unscrew and reposition this

arm. If the tank ball or its lift wires seem worn, replace them. Parts for toilet tanks are available at most hardware stores and any plumbing supply outlet.

If the tank fills but water still keeps trickling, first check the round object called the float ball that rides atop the water in the tank. Unscrew it and give it a shake. If there's water in it, discard it and attach a new one.

If this doesn't work, try lowering the position of the float ball in the tank by bending

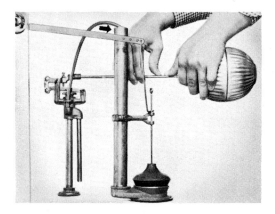

the rod it's attached to. The water should shut off when it rises to within 1½″ of the top of the overflow tube.

If this doesn't work and the water still keeps running, the problem is with the inlet valve that lets the water into the tank. At this point you have a choice: You can save money by disassembling the whole unit and replacing the washers, O-ring, or packing—quite a task—or you can go the easy route and buy a whole new inlet valve assembly (ballcock). To install it, bail and sponge the tank dry, disengage the refill tube, and undo the two thumb screws or pins that enable you to remove the float ball arm. Then, getting down on the floor, loosen the coupling nut that attaches the supply line to the tank and remove the washer and lock nut to free the pipe. Lift out the old assembly, set the new one in, and attach it loosely—new washer, lock nut, and coupling—emplaced but not tightened. Slip the refill tube into its slot, curving it over the top of the overflow tube, and reattach the float arm ball linkage. Now you can tighten the coupling at the base of the tank, and the toilet should work

If you opt for changing the washer, lift the stem and plunger in the top of the inlet valve assembly to reveal the leather packing at the base of the plunger. You may have to

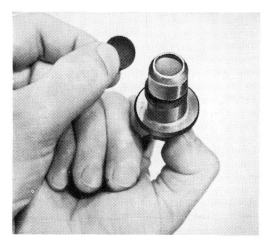

do some hard tugging on this element to force it out of its recess, or it may be held in place by a center screw. Most types also have, additionally, a washer or O-ring fitting into a groove encircling the plunger.

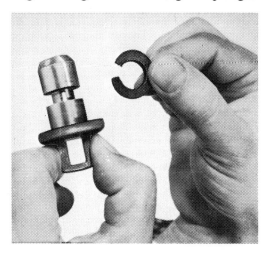

Replacing everything replaceable, while you've got the works all apart, is a good idea. Reverse the breakdown procedure to reassemble the unit.

How to Patch Wallboard

The techniques for making holes disappear in gypsum wallboard are practically the same as those for patching plaster walls, except for hairline cracks which are peculiar to plaster and which are repaired by 1) running the corner edge of a putty knife along them to clean them out; 2) brushing out the dust with a dry paintbrush; 3) wetting down the cracks with water and a sponge; 4) filling them with spackling compound mixed to the consistency of very heavy cream using your finger dipped in the spackle and running it along the cracks, pressing the spackle into place and smoothing it in one operation. Corner cracks and cracks at moldings in either plaster or wallboard are obliterated the same way.

A big problem hole in gypsum wallboard can best be repaired by enlarging the hole to a rectangular shape with a keyhole saw, perhaps with the help of a wood rasp, then cutting a piece of similar-thickness wallboard the same size as the rectangular hole and fitting it in place. Here are three different ways to hold it there permanently:

If there's a stud (vertical 2x4) in back of a moderate-sized hole, you're in luck; the new piece can be nailed to that. Bigger holes should be enlarged to enable you to nail the two sides of the new piece to two studs, the centers of which are usually 16″ apart. Nail the new piece in place making the last blow of the hammer slightly indent the surface around each nailhead. Thoroughly wet the crack with a brush and water around the entire circumference of the patch to provide a good bond.

Using a flexible 3″ or 4″ putty knife, fill the crack with spackle mixed to a consistency closely akin to putty, pliable but not runny. Scrape the excess off the surface holding the putty knife fairly flat against the wall and pressing to flex the blade. "Feather" the edges into the adjoining wall surface by drawing the spackle away from the crack in firm, semicircular sweeps of the putty knife. For a smooth final surface that may not need sanding, run a wide wet paintbrush or sponge soaked in water over the patch, following it immediately with a plasterer's float trowel barely tipped up on one long edge and passed firmly and smoothly over the patch two or three times. (Lacking a float trowel, try just smoothing the surface with a wide wet paintbrush or sponge.) Let the patch dry overnight.

If it needs sanding, use a medium-grit sandpaper to smooth and level the surface. Wear a respirator when sanding. If little cracks have appeared as the spackle has dried, don't be upset. Sand the area level and go over them again with a heavy-cream mixture of spackle. When the patch is thoroughly dry apply a prime coat or some other sealer before painting.

When there's no studding in evidence behind a large hole in wallboard, don't try to reach through to toenail a piece of wood to nearby studding. It's too awkward and almost impossible to get the backing piece placed so that it will hold the patch piece flush with the surrounding wall surface. A better method is to install a floating stud:

Wallboard patching materials

For small holes in the wall save money by avoiding ready-mixed spackle ($1.95 per quart); buy it dry ($1.25 per five-pound bag) and mix your own. It's easy. Adding a little water intermittently as you mix, you can get just the consistency you want in mere minutes. Though a bit messy, mixing it with your hands gives you the exact feel of the material. Follow directions on bag or box. You'll quickly discover that a peanut-butter-like consistency is easiest to work with for rough patching and a heavier-than-heavy-cream consistency is proper for finish coats that hide the patch and make the job invisible.

Cheaper than spackle, if you are faced with a big job, is patching plaster, which comes as a powder in five-pound bags, $1. Mixed with water, it sets up swiftly and dries in about three hours. You can slow this down by mixing it with half water, half vinegar.

Both spackle and patching plaster can be mixed with fine sand for patching a sand-finished wall.

First, saw out a rectangle of wallboard that, laid over the hole in the wall, will cover it completely with some to spare. Trace this rectangle directly onto the wall around the hole, leaning your pencil to add approximately ⅛″ all around. Trim out a rectangular hole in the wall with a keyhole saw following your pencil line. Cut a backing strip of 1x2 or 2x4 stock 6″ longer than the longest dimension of the trimmed hole in the wall. This is your floating stud. Use fast-setting epoxy glue, one generous daub at each end, to fasten it flat against the back of the wallboard spanning the hole in the wall. Hold it in place for the five minutes-plus it takes the epoxy to cure, or lay another length of wood on the outside of the wall over the floating stud and temporarily tie the two together through the hole.

When the floating stud is firmly glued in place, spread spackle across its length and butter the edges of the previously prepared patch piece; set it carefully in place flush with the adjoining wall surface. Spackle the joint all around the patch, feathering the edges, and let dry thoroughly before sanding. Seal the job with primer or sealer before painting the wallboard.

Not exactly easier, but an expedient method for closing a large hole that has no backing is to cut an oversize rectangle from a scrap of wallboard 3″ larger on all sides than the dimensions of the trimmed rectangular hole in the wall. Mark off the hole-in-the-wall dimensions on the reverse side of the oversize patch piece. Cut through the back paper surface of the patch piece on these lines, then carefully trim away the plaster to fit the hole in the wall, being very careful not to cut into the front paper surface of the patch piece. This gives you a piece to fit the hole, a patch piece with a 3″ margin of paper around it.

Spread white cement on the back of the margin and set the patch piece in place. Press the overlapping paper flat and cover with a thin coat of heavy-cream-consistency spackle, making sure to feather the edges. Sand smooth the next day and seal before painting the wall.

For a smaller hole, the simplest remedy is to trim its edges straight and flat. Then, taping a sheet of plain paper over the hole, run a soft pencil around its edges to mark an impression on the paper of its exact shape. Snip out this shape ⅛" shy of the line all the way around and tape it to the face of a scrap of wallboard. Saw out the shape or use a matte knife. Tape a 1" strip of heavy paper (or masking tape) to the back of the patch piece, one end bent over the top, the other end up around the bottom so they come together in front to form a way of holding the patch piece in one hand while you butter its edges with spackle.

Hang onto your heavy-paper handle as you insert the patch piece in place and adjust it flush with the wall surface. Trim off the paper strips with a razor blade and spread a thin coat of spackle over the whole patch. Let it dry overnight, sand it smooth the next day, and seal it before you paint it.

Small nail holes can usually be patched without trimming their edges. Lay putty-consistency spackle on with a first stroke in one direction, then firmly bearing against the putty knife blade held quite flat against the wall, make a sweep in the opposite direction that removes excess spackle and leaves a patch so flat it may not need sanding.

One rather common wall repair is patching a moderate-sized hole an inch or more across, such as is often left where a light fixture has been removed. Using a knife, enlarge the back of the hole until it is wider than the front. Thoroughly dampen the front and back surfaces around the hole with a wet brush or sponge. Now you have two choices. If there's any firm existing backing, you can saturate shreds of newspaper in your spackle, stuff them in the hole and spackle right over it, working in from the sides toward the center. But without any backing to press the spackle against, you have to create your own, and here's a trick:

Thread a length of pliable wire through the center of a piece of window screening cut to about twice the circumference of the hole in the wall. Wet the broken edges of the hole and the adjacent area for a good bond and to minimize cracking and splitting as the spackle dries. Stuff the screening through the hole, hanging onto the wire to keep the screening drawn tightly against the back of the wallboard (see top photo in next column).

Work the spackle against the edges of the hole first, then gradually in toward the center. Close the hole with a rough patch,

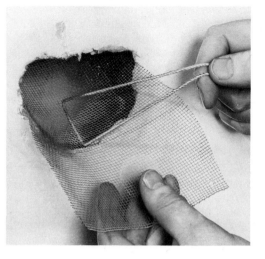

the surface of which is somewhat indented in the wall. Bridge the patch with a pencil or a piece of 1x2. Wrap the wire around it and twist tight. When the patch dries, remove

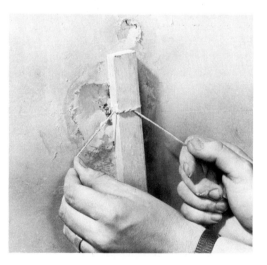

the piece of wood and snip the wires off flush with the patch. Apply a finish coat, but before you make your last couple of sweeps with the putty knife (or plasterer's trowel), dip the blade in water for a smooth final surface. Whether or not you still need to sand after the patch dries, remember to prime or seal it before painting.

How to Hang Things on Walls

Using the right fastener for the job is the first secret to successful, reliable hanging; and drilling the right size hole is the second.

In wooden walls or paneling, wood screws are the proper fastener (unless the paneling is too thin for the load and there's a risk of screws pulling out; in that case use expansion bolts). If you're going to put up a series of standards for bookshelf brackets it pays to ask your hardware dealer to help you select exactly the right drill bit for the screws you decide to use.

Most walls today, however, are hollow-wall construction, gypsum wallboard over 2x4 studding. If you have something very light to hang, an extremely fine brad or a pin driven in at a 45° angle has the least crumbling effect on the plaster sandwiched in between the two sheets of heavy paper.

Standard picture hooks can be relied on to carry weights up to 15 pounds. Press a piece of masking tape or plastic mending tape over the spot where the nail will enter the wall. This will help keep the edges of the hole from breaking down. Next, holding the bracket in place, use its two holes as guides to drill the finest possible pilot hole. Then drive the nail into the pilot hole through the bracket—carefully.

Anything heavier than 15 pounds calls for an expansion plug or an expansion anchor; while to be safe, anything really heavy calls for a split-wing toggle bolt.

Tip: Have an assortment of screws handy when you hang things on wallboard. Press an awl all the way through the wallboard before drilling for any fastener, because you may strike wood—a stud. Then you will have to switch from a fastener to a screw. Wherever you are installing something that you absolutely cannot risk having fall from the wall, like a cabinet or a bookcase, try to anchor it to studs. Find the first stud by tapping the wall with your knuckles. Where it sounds most solid start drilling a parallel row of tiny holes no more than 1½" apart until you drill into a stud. Chisel away a narrow parallel slot to expose its full width. Then you can measure 16" from its center to the center of any adjacent stud since studs are usually 16" center to center.

However, studs never seem to be in the right place when you want them—although if you're going to hang vertical slotted standards to which bookshelf brackets attach, there will be a lot of weight if your bookshelves are extensive. You should plan to locate the standards so that at least one of them is securely screwed into a stud.

Expansion plastic anchors (the strongest are nylon) should be purchased with the exact screws they are specifically designed for. The wrong size screw-anchor combination may not hold. You simply drill a hole the proper size, tap the anchor into it, and *hammer* in the screw. This makes the anchor split inside the wall. With it in place you can remove the screw with a screwdriver to insert it through the object you're fastening.

You enjoy this same advantage of being able to take the screw out of the anchor and replace it when you use a Molly. Drill a hole just big enough to accept the slit metal sleeve that surrounds the screw. Once emplaced it expands against the back surface of the wallboard when you tighten the screw. There are various lengths of Molly.

Where strength is a prime requisite, as for hanging a heavy picture frame, cabinet, or towel bar, use toggle bolts.

There are many kinds of expansion anchor for fastening things to a solid wall. Concrete is very difficult. The hole has to be chiseled out with a so-called star drill or with a heavy (rented) electric drill with a carbide-tipped bit. But don't hesitate to fasten a screw or bolt to a brick or light-aggregate (cinder) block wall. You can purchase a special bit that drills the hole in jig time with a ¼" electric drill. Just be sure to buy—and only from a hardware dealer who really knows his stuff—the proper-sized anchor for the screw or bolt you choose and the proper-sized masonry bit for the anchor. Each must fit the other for a tight grip.

How to Repair Floor Covering

Usually, you don't really "repair" a floor tile, you replace a damaged one. But it is possible to repair an unsightly gouge or dent in a floor tile if you were foresighted enough to have saved some spares when the floor was laid, or can find an exact match at a flooring outlet—or, in a pinch, care to roll the refrigerator away from the wall and chisel a corner off a tile that will never show. Here's the how-to:

Clean out the gouge or dent first with sandpaper and slightly roughen its inner surface. Scratch some of the surface off the scrap piece and pulverize the scrapings.

Mix this powder into clear epoxy resin glue and lay it into the gouge. Epoxy self-levels itself smooth as it cures, and when hardened, is more rugged than the tile itself.

The adhesive with which all tile floors are laid today can be softened by heat. If the edge of a tile curls up, soften the adhesive underneath it by application of a hot iron laid over a wet piece of cotton cloth. Don't

put the iron directly on the tile—you may do more harm than good. Leave the iron in place or move it around only long enough to soften the adhesive, then roll the tile back and spread a thin layer of adhesive on both the undersurface of the tile and on the place where it will lie.

Let the adhesive set up; the kind most widely used is creamlike and turns clear when it is ready to stick. This way you avoid the risk of possibly having the adhesive ooze up between the tiles to play havoc with the floor surface. Press the tile into place. Lay a board over it and set something heavy on top until you're sure the adhesive is dry.

Use heat to loosen a damaged vinyl floor tile you want to replace. Applying heat with a very hot iron over a wet cotton cloth isn't as swift an approach as using a propane torch to soften the underlying adhesive, but it is inherently safer. If you have a number of damaged tiles to remove, or if you want to remove one of the thicker, heavier floor tiles, the safest source of heat is an infrared bulb. The problem is, you risk unsticking neighboring tiles if you get too near the edges when warming a damaged tile's underlying adhesive. Solution: heat up only the center area of the tile, chisel out a tri-

angular section in the middle and, cutting with a chisel or prying with a putty knife, carefully lift off the rest of the tile in pieces. Scrape away any adhesive left in the space the damaged tile occupied to make sure the underlayment is perfectly smooth.

Dry-fit your new tile before sticking it down, trimming it with a matte knife and straightedge or with sandpaper over a block if you find it necessary. If you have any doubts about the type of adhesive to use, check with your floor covering dealer, taking the tile in to show him. Apply the right amount of proper adhesive. Hold the new tile well above one of the top burners of your range to warm it sufficiently to make it pliable for laying. Once in place, lay a board over it and put weights on top.

A worn or damaged area in sheet floor covering such as vinyl or linoleum is easy to patch by making an inlay. Tape down over it a scrap of the sheet material several square inches larger than the worn or damaged area in such a way that it exactly matches the pattern of the flooring. Using a straightedge and matte knife (preferably one fitted with a brand-new blade), cut out a rectangle surrounding the damaged area.

Drive the knife blade straight down through both the patch piece and the laid flooring at the same time. You may have to make several passes with the blade. Remove both pieces and discard the worn or damaged rectangle. Scrape away any residue of adhesive in the hole you've cut. Dry-fit the patch piece to make sure it slips exactly into place. Apply flooring adhesive and inlay the new piece. Place a board over it and weight it with something heavy.

How to Replace Ceramic Wall Tile

Resetting a ceramic tile that has come loose requires two materials, a waterproof adhesive made for the job, and so-called "grout," the white filler applied to the cracks between the tiles. It comes ready-mixed but it's cheaper in the familiar powder form, which you simply mix with water.

Scrape and chip away all the old cement clinging to the back and edges of the tile. Apply the cement to the back of the tile, coming no closer than ½" to the edges of it, and set the tile in place. Wait a full 24 hours before grouting—which is no more complicated a procedure than mixing the material to a creamy consistency, pressing it into the cracks around the tile with a forefinger and rubbing it smooth. Let it dry about a half-hour, then wipe off any excess on the face of the tiles with a damp rag. Let grouting dry overnight before exposing it to water.

If a tile's been broken to smithereens or lost for good, replacement can be bothersome because colors tend to go out of style and a perfect match is often impossible. Come as close as you can in color; it will be less noticeable than you expect. Or consider replacing the tile with a decorative one such as tile dealers now sell in many modern designs and reproductions of antique tiles.

A replacement tile that has to be cut to fit does not present a formidable problem. For a straight cut, measure carefully and score the tile surface with a common inexpensive glass cutter held against a straightedge. Then lay a spike on the floor, place the scoremark over it, and press on both sides of the tile at once. It should snap in two.

Curved cuts are quite easily saber-sawed with a fine-tooth blade specifically made for the purpose, with the replacement tile marked for the cut and held in a vise. Lacking a saber saw, mark the curved line on the face of the tile. Use a glass cutter to score its face with a closely-worked crosshatch of lines filling the area to be removed. Protect your eyes with a plastic face shield or goggles. Then nip out the waste area with pliers. Break off small bites with the ends of

the pliers, working up to the rough outline of your cut, and finish off with a rounded file.

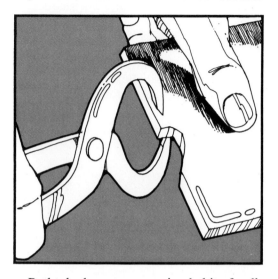

Bathtubs have an annoying habit of pulling away from the ceramic tile walls that surround them. The crack requires a flexible filler. Use waterproof butyl caulking; it comes in a squeeze tube or cartridge for a caulking gun and is a much more effective solution to this recurring problem than grout. Left unchecked, the breach will let water get at walls, floors, and substructure.

How to Mend a Window Screen

A small hole in metal or fiber-glass screening in which only one or two wires or fibers have parted is easily repaired. Realign the ends and dot the breaks with fast-setting epoxy glue. Use acetone glue for nylon screening.

The neatest way to patch a large hole in any screening is to cut the hole to an even rectangle and lay a patch of matching material over it a couple of inches wider in both dimensions. Weave a single strand of the material over and under overlapping strands on all four sides. You can thread a needle with nylon thread or filament and sew a patch in place—or just "darn" a small hole.

A simpler but more obvious way to close a small hole in metal screening is to trim the hole to a rectangle, then cut a patch an inch larger than the trimmed sides of the hole. Remove the three outer-edge wires from all four sides of the patch piece and bend the free ends of the wires down at right angles over a block of wood, forming a little open-topped "box."

Place the patch over the hole with the wire points sticking through the screening. Have someone on the outside hold it in place with something flat as you bend the ends of the wires in toward the hole, each one lying in the same direction as the wires in the screening. Be sure not to use patches of dissimilar metals to avoid setting up an electrolytic action that would cause corrosion.

The quick way to close a large hole in nylon screening is first to dismount the screen and lay it flat. Cut a patch of nylon screening or mosquito netting 2″ larger in both dimensions and lay it over the hole. Then simply paint a band of shellac around the overlap. Let it dry in place, turn the screen over, and coat the overlap on the other side.

All patches, however, should be considered temporary because they always show. Besides, rescreening is quite easy.

How to Rescreen a Window

If you don't own a staple gun but have only one or two wooden frames to rescreen, a hammer and tacks will do for fastening, but borrow or rent a staple gun if you decide to tackle a number of screens.

Check for loose corner joints of wooden frames and strengthen them with angle irons or flat mending plates or with wood screws sunk through the corner end of one member

into the end of the adjacent side. Countersink screws and fill holes with wood plastic before repainting.

There used to be a variety of screening materials to choose from, but metal shortages have reduced commonly available stock to aluminum and nylon or fiber-glass. The non-metallic materials are easier to install since you can stretch them tight by hand. The strands are so fine they are easy materials to see through, yet being resilient they withstand impact well. But they don't last as long as aluminum screening.

Pry the moldings off a wooden frame carefully, so you can re-use them, by working with a putty knife or an old chisel from the center of a molding toward its two ends. If you have several screens to do, cut a rectangle of heavy plywood a little longer but the same width as your screens and tack a 1x1″ length of wood at each end of it the same distance apart as the shorter end members of the screens. Now you can lay each screen atop these 1x1's and bow it down in the middle with a C-clamp on each side; when you finish and release the C-clamps, the unbowing will draw the screening taut.

Buy screening at least 1″ wider than the outside dimension of the molding of wood screens. Non-metallic screening should be folded under for tacking or stapling; let metal screening extend ½″ beyond the molding on both sides.

Working on a wooden frame, fasten one end of the screening down first. Draw it tight over the other end of the frame, align it carefully and start fastening from the middle out to each edge. Undo the clamps, move the frame onto a flat surface, and tack down first one long side then the other, pulling the screening taut and fastening from the center out to each end.

Trim or snip off the excess, using a matte knife or tin snips or, with nonmetallic screening, a single-edged razor blade. Replace the molding, countersink the brads that hold it down, fill the holes and paint.

On aluminum frames the screening is held in place with neoprene splines that fit tightly into grooves. The screening should be cut to extend to the outside dimensions of the frame. Snip off the corners leaving enough material to sink into the grooves.

Align the screening atop the frame and hammer the spline into its groove along one long side first. It's worth whittling a tapered

block for this operation if you have several screens to do; otherwise use a large-size screwdriver to tap the spline in place. Drawing the screening taut with one hand (some persons need help here), sink the spline into the opposite long groove. Do the ends last. Then, trim off the excess screening.

How to Fix a Window Shade

The spring mechanism needs tightening inside a shade that rolls up sluggishly. It's easy to do. Pull the shade halfway down and dismount by lifting the flat-pin end of the roller out of the slotted socket or bracket. Roll up the shade by hand and remount it. If this doesn't tighten the spring enough, repeat the process. If there's no tension at all, the spring is shot and can't be fixed; replace the roller.

If the shade has too much tension, roll it all the way up, dismount it, unroll a foot or so, and put it back up. This should solve the problem for you.

A shade that rolls up crookedly has probably been mounted on the roller improperly. Dismount it, unroll it completely and pop out the staples by which it is attached to the wood. Use a carpenter's square to mark a straight line across the paper or fabric near its end. Stabilize the naked roller on a level surface with a heavy weight and scribe a mark at each end of it exactly where it touches the surface. Line up your two scribe marks with the two ends of the straight line you've marked across the screen and tack on at line. Unless your brackets are off-level with one another, the shade will now roll and unroll straight.

Shades that fall from the window frame can usually be fixed by bending the brackets closer together if the brackets are mounted on the outside of the frame. For smooth operation of the shade, however, avoid bending the brackets too much; sometimes one of the brackets has to be unscrewed and moved slightly closer to its mate to keep shades from falling down.

Brackets mounted within the window recess are handled differently. If too close, making the shade bind when it's rolled up or down, first try hitting both brackets an easy whack with a hammer to dent them closer to the frame. If this doesn't work, you'll have to dismount the shade and remove the metal cap in which the round pin is mounted. It slides off easily, exposing the wooden end of the roller. Remove some wood off the end with a wood rasp or with coarse sandpaper, replace the cap, and try it again to see if it fits.

If a shade wobbles annoyingly when it's rolled up or down, the round pin is bent. It can easily be straightened with pliers.

When a window shade refuses to catch, the trouble is usually inside the flat-pin end; something is clogging the pivoting tongue (or tongues—in some shades there are two of these little arms) that drops into the notches in the ratchet wheel. Clean around it with the point of an awl or a toothpick and lubricate with a drop of oil or a puff of powdered graphite.

A shade that's badly worn or too dirty to clean at its lower end can be unrolled, untacked from the roller and switched end for end. There's usually enough extra to trim off the worn part before stapling or tacking it back on. Get it on straight, however (see above), or it won't roll up evenly. Make a sleeve for the stick by pressing a hem into the material and gluing its edge to the back of the shade with white glue.

A window shade that's too dirty to turn end for end can be coated with a good-quality latex-base paint, provided you can cover completely with no more than one coat, or it will crack when it's rolled. *Window Shade Primer* is a 14-page booklet you can send for illustrating imaginative ways of using shades to decorate windows. It includes directions on measuring, adjusting, and cleaning shades: send 25¢ to Window Shade Manufacturers Assn., 230 Park Ave., NY 10017.

How to Patch a Worn Place in Carpeting

If your carpet has fairly long pile and you were foresighted enough to save a piece of it when it was laid or can still buy the same material, you can patch it. Lay the new piece over the worn place, tack it down temporarily so it won't move, and cut straight down through both thicknesses with a new blade in a matte knife held against a straightedge. Then pry out the tacks and substitute the new piece for the old. It should make an undetectable inlay. Apply double-faced tape with adhesive on both sides where the edges butt; floor-covering cement will do the trick, too.

Unless you can make your cut lines (through patch and carpet simultaneously) follow some irregular lines in the carpet's design, a patch in carpeting with short pile may be objectionably obvious. Cigarette burns, however, can be eradicated with a cookie cutter-like device that slices a sharp-edged circular hole out of the carpet as it lies in place. Then a disk, cut from a scrap of the same carpeting with the tool, pops into the hole. These gadgets can sometimes be borrowed or rented from carpet dealers —if you are careful not to let them become convinced you're in the market for new carpeting.

But what to do about a badly worn area in an otherwise serviceable carpet when there are no replacement pieces available at your dealer's or squirreled away at home?

The answer may lie in a simple, inexpensive tool called a punch needle (instructions for use come with it), but first you must lift up one corner of the carpet and check out the backing. A majority of all modern carpeting is made on tufting machines and the backs are heavily latexed, often with an added layer of scrim. A punch needle won't work with such carpets. But if the backing appears to be uncoated, you might make this test: push the point of an awl or an ice pick straight into the back of the carpet. If it passes through to the other side without difficulty, chances are you can swiftly and easily cover the worn area with some big flowers or radiating stripes, or any design of your own choosing by punch-needle hooking them directly into the old carpet itself.

If the rug is heavily latexed, you can still make a whole new hooked rug and inlay it into the carpet (as explained above).

How to Repair and Maintain Blacktop

Patching a driveway is easy unless there are a great many potholes to fill. It's a simple matter of prying up the loose blacktop, digging out the loose soil beneath, and if the hole is deep, filling it with gravel to within a couple of inches of the bottom surface of the paving. Next the hole is filled with cold-mix asphalt, about $3.25 per 75-pound sack. This is then tamped with one end of a piece of 4x4, more asphalt mix is added and tamped until the surface is flush with the rest of the driveway. Driving the family car back and forth over the patch solidifies it.

Blacktop sealer, $7-$12 in five-gallon drums, easily brushed onto a dry, clean driveway with a coarse push-broom, extends the life of blacktop paving. It protects mainly against penetration into cracks in the paving of water that freezes in winter, expanding, splitting and destroying the blacktop. But it also protects from the subtler ravages of sunlight and wear. A five-gallon drum is enough to coat 200 to 300 square feet, depending on the permeability of the paved surface. It's worth applying two coats, the second two days after the first.

Easy Do-It-Yourself Home Improvements

With housing and mortgages facing such uncertain futures, it is a strong possibility that most people who now live in a house are in their permanent home whether or not they had hoped to move on to a bigger and better one.

As this home-for-life reality has come clear, Americans have been trying to take much better care of their houses. The average family spends about 1.5% of the value of its house each year on maintenance and repairs. That's $525 annually for a $35,000 house. Some families trim this figure considerably, of course, by doing their own home improvements.

If they can't get it all done themselves, do-it-yourself families find that relatively inexpensive unskilled labor is well worth using for tough jobs like scraping the exterior of a house in preparation for painting. Local high schools and colleges often have part-time job placement facilities. A one- or two-line classified ad in the local newspaper will elicit a choice of applicants willing to work for less than half what trained professionals charge.

If you decide to hire semi-professional labor to help you with a job—and even more importantly if you are hiring skilled labor —you will probably save money if you buy materials that make the job go faster, even if these cost somewhat more than materials that take longer to install or apply. Gypsum wallboard, available universally in four-foot-wide sheets of a number of lengths, provides a good example: When you have help you can hang much longer sheets just as quickly as the standard 4x8-foot ones. You'll have less taping to do as a consequence; sometimes a long sheet hung on its side (the easier way to tape) will perfectly span a wall.

Another good example is the use of factory pre-hung doors that come in their own frames. These are much easier and take far less time to install than all the trimming, fitting, shimming—and swearing—required to build a frame and hang a door yourself.

Even if you are lucky enough to salvage a whole truckload of brick from a tumbledown house, it will cost you more—for labor —to lay them up (although bricklaying isn't hard to learn) than the same construction in purchased concrete block. It's the *installed* cost you should be concerned with.

Once you are started on a do-it-yourself home improvement, however, if you should find it not going as well as you had anticipated, don't hesitate to call up a professional and ask his advice. Most specialists expect potential customers to turn to them when a project becomes too complicated. You might offer to pay him a small amount to advise you if you run into an "impossible" snag. He'll probably be glad to break away for a few minutes after work or on a weekend to come by and help you get straightened out.

There are times, moreover, when you *should* hire a professional. Some building codes restrict anyone but licensed professionals from making certain types of repairs and installations; in any urban or suburban community, major plumbing and electrical work must be performed by pros. You can't afford to have electrical wiring in your house that was installed illegally if it should be proven to have caused a fire; your insurance probably wouldn't cover you. And while you can easily repair a simple leak in a pipe or fitting, a plumber should be hired when water lines or soil pipes are being substantially altered, because a technical mistake you might make can conceivably damage the entire system, particularly when you're faced with old corroded steel pipe.

For a project that calls for electrical wiring or alterations to plumbing, heating, or air-conditioning, you may be required by your local ordinances to turn over certain parts of the job to a licensed tradesman and still be allowed to cut costs by doing much of the preliminary work yourself. Some communities allow you to install wiring (fixtures, outlets, and switches), then call in an electrician to check it out and hook it up—for a considerable saving.

How to Insulate Your House

Hardest hit by the mid-seventies' oil crisis have been families in colder regions who heat by oil, many paying as much as $500 to $600 a year to heat their houses and hot water. Some who used to pay by the delivery have gone on a budget plan— 12-month payment schedules, rather than the more common 10-month plan that omits July and August. In 1975 No. 2 fuel oil for home use cost twice what it cost in 1973. Families living in older houses with poor insulation and old converted furnaces that burn oil excessively have been especially troubled. Perhaps hardest hit have been renters in houses that may have no insulation. Even people living in multiple dwellings in larger cities have been affected indirectly, as landlords have raised rents to pass on higher heating costs.

Families who heat by electricity, natural gas, or propane have also had steep rises to contend with; the jump in propane was especially sharp. On a national basis, electricity and gas shot up 28%.

Some 20% of all energy used in the U.S. is used in homes. Of that, house heating consumes the most, 27%. Water heating is second, 13%; followed by air-conditioning, 12.5%, according to the Tennessee Valley Authority. Warm air leaking out and cold air leaking in from inadequate insulation (and inadequate caulking and weatherstripping) can cause a 15%, even a 30%, increase in your heating fuel bills, according to a report by the Office of Consumer Affairs. With insulation your first priority in cutting fuel costs, here's an idea of how much you can save by insulating your house:

In a moderately cold climate, a typical two-story, one-family house of wood frame construction with 1,500 square feet of living space, a pitched roof with an unheated attic, and a window area covering 25% of the exterior walls could save 62% on heating fuel by the installation of 6'' ceiling insulation; 3½'' outer-wall insulation; storm windows, storm doors, and complete weatherstripping and caulking. (The possible hot-weather energy saving, if this house were centrally air-conditioned, would be about 42%.) The same house, if it were already equipped with storm windows, storm doors, and weatherstripping plus caulking, could save 19% on heating fuel by the addition of 6'' ceiling insulation alone.

The bonus in an adequately insulated house is *snugness*. The warmer the interior surfaces—walls, windows, ceiling, floor— the less your body radiates heat toward those surfaces. In a warm room, when the outdoor temperature is hovering around zero, an uninsulated ceiling would be about 60°. Installing 6'' of insulation would raise its temperature well above 70°. Your body would stop playing "radiator," and you would discover you are comfortable at surprisingly low thermostat settings.

If there are no ill or elderly people or infants in your household and your family dresses warmly (arms and legs covered) and gets enough daily exercise to maintain adequate blood circulation, you may find yourselves perfectly comfortable with the daytime thermostat setting in the low 60's. Depending on the efficiency of your heating plant, lowering the thermostat in winter generally results in savings of more than 3% per degree, according to the National Bureau of Standards.

How much insulation do you need? It is so relatively inexpensive you are best advised not to try to save money on the purchase of insulation, because the optimum thickness, where winters are cold, will pay for itself in a year or two. Except in the frigid northern-border Plains states, insulation 6'' thick is considered optimum. In those places where the temperature periodically goes below zero and stays there, homeowners install extra layers.

Most people use foil-surfaced batts or rolls of fiberglass insulation. Cost: 19¢ to 20¢ per square foot. The standard tract house built since World War II has a 3½'' thickness of foil-surfaced insulation stapled between the ceiling joists, with at least a ¾'' air space between its foil surface and the top surface of the gypsum board ceiling. That dead air space contributes to the insulating factor; if the foil surface were touching the ceiling its value as a thermal barrier would be destroyed.

Most homeowners increase their insulation to the optimum 6'' thickness by staple-gunning the same 3½''-thick foil-faced insulation to the top of the ceiling joists up under the roof. Since the staple flanges are on the foil side of the batts or rolls, they have to be stapled foil side up, but this provides a thermal barrier against summer heat that keeps the house a few degrees cooler in summer. Additionally, a second dead-air space is trapped between the top of the originally installed insulation and the bottom surface of the newly installed batts or rolls—which increases the insulation factor.

If you don't care about a thermal barrier (one foil side should always face the heated part of the house), you can purchase friction-fit batts or rolls that are simply wedged between the joists, but better opt for the 6'' thickness.

Fiberglass and mineral wool are essentially the same. They are made from slag, rock, or glass extruded into fine fibers that entrap air and prevent its passage. Because they are fireproof they have long since taken over from cellulose fiber insulation.

Be sure to shop for insulation. In 1975, 4''-thick fiberglass batts, enough to cover 50 square feet, were priced anywhere from $4 to $6.50 among building supply dealers within one 10-mile radius.

Installing insulation: Professional fiberglass insulation installers wear clothing with smooth, impenetrable surfaces to which the tiny particles that break off do not cling. But you should wear old clothes and gloves when you install it and throw them away when you finish, because the little fibers don't wash out and can set up a dreadful itching. What's more, medical researchers have warned people installing fiberglass insulation to wear a dust respirator to keep the particles out of the lungs and a face shield or tight-fitting goggles to keep them out of the eyes.

In a house with an unfinished attic, insulating is relatively easy, but it's extremely important to do a careful job because heat will travel along the insulation seeking any holes it can find and escape at a much greater velocity than you might imagine (the "chimney effect" insulation contractors speak of).

In all likelihood your ceiling joists are 16'' on center, and you can buy the standard 15''-wide batts or rolls. (Lumber dealers also carry 23'' widths for prefabricated truss roofs whose joists are 24'' apart.) You can rent a staple gun for about $4 a day from hardware stores, building supply dealers, or rental centers, or buy one for $10 to $12. Drive a staple every 8'' and check your job when you're done to make sure you haven't left any gaps or bulges. Where the flange doesn't lie tightly at any point, drive in a few more staples.

If your attic is floored, temporarily remove floorboards at strategic places and (since floorboards run across the joists) you will be able to shove and haul batts or rolls between them. If the attic is an old one filled with wires running in all directions, making the installation of batts or rolls difficult, you can buy bags of expanded vermiculite—so-called "loose fill" with which you will have an easier job of completely sealing off the area, particularly in and around wires—although loose fill is more expensive than batts or rolls.

When you have no space for do-it-yourself insulating between the ceiling of the top floor of your house and the roof, either because it is a flat roof or shed roof or because the attic is completely remodeled into living quarters, you can call in professional insulating contractors for estimates on blowing in loose fill. Get written quotes for the exact specifications of the job and check the reputation of the contractor you select beforehand with your utility, building supply dealer, and Better Business Bureau.

There are insulating contractors who will blow in loose fill between the walls of a house. It is not a worthwhile investment because, what with fire stops and wiring and ductwork, there are so many blockages to impede even flow of the featherweight nodules it is almost impossible for them to properly occupy the cavity. In fact, some insulation experts strongly recommend against it because the ordinary and quite-necessary venting of the walls is blocked. Water vapor can turn the blown-in insulation sodden and make it worse than ineffective. Unless fuel prices shoot completely out of sight, it is probably not worth increasing the insulation of your walls. Concentrate your efforts on the ceiling.

And since heat rises, there is not so much heat loss through the floors of a house as

How Insulation Materials "R" Rated

A standard rating system is used by the insulation industry to specify thermal resistance of various materials. Most manufacturers stamp the "R" rating on their products. All you have to remember in buying insulation is that the higher the "R" factor, the better the insulating efficiency of the product. It's worth checking: one manufacturer's 3"-thick batts may have an R12 rating, while another manufacturer's 3" batts may have only an R10 rating. Here are the average "R" ratings of various materials:

Material	"R" per inch thickness
BATT OR BLANKET	
Wood or cellulose fiber with paper backing and facing	4.00
Mineral wool	3.80
LOOSE FILL	
Mineral wool	3.30
Vermiculite, expanded	2.08
BOARD OR RIGID	
Expanded Urethane, foamed, sprayed, or preformed	5.88
Polystyrene foam, extruded or expanded	4.50
Glass fiberboard	4.34
CONSTRUCTION MATERIALS	
Wood fiberboard, laminated sheathing	2.90
Plywood and softwoods	1.25
Plaster, stucco, or brick	0.20
DOORS	
Solid wood, 1" thick	1.56
Solid wood, 2" thick	2.33
WINDOWS (glass area only)	
Single glazed	0.88
Double glazed with ¼" air space	1.64
Single glazed with storm window	1.89

there is cold-air infiltration. Floors over a cellar that's not used for habitation should be insulated and the cellar left unheated. Usually the hot-water boiler and the furnace serve to take the edge off the cold and prevent the pipes from freezing, except, perhaps, in the coldest climates. Batts or rolls of insulation should be wedged into the spaces between floor joists and supported in place by crisscrossing them with light wire laced between nails struck into the lower edges of the floor joists above. Fit insulation against the header joist that rests on the plate at either end of the joists.

Insulate the floor over an unheated, ventilated crawl space similarly, but use foil-face batts or rolls. If you prefer to staple them up, it doesn't make much difference having the foil facing down (as will have to be the case, because the flanges for stapling are only on the foil side of the insulation). The floor would be kept only slightly warmer with the foil side up. If the crawl space is enclosed with a masonry wall, the vents can be plugged to cut cold-air infiltration, as long as you don't customarily experience a drainage problem in wintertime.

Dampness from the crawl space can be eliminated in the house by installing 6-mil continuous-sheet polyethylene film over the entire ground area, overlapping its joints and sealing them with duct tape. Bring the edges of the sheeting up the walls at least part way and seal them in place with more duct tape.

If your house is built on a slab and you suspect that it may not have been properly insulated, there's little you can do about the lack of insulation *under* the slab. But you can make a significant improvement in heat retention by insulating the *edges* of the slab. Dig a trench two feet or more deep (below the frost line) around the perimeter of your house and apply foam insulation board directly against the foundation. That part of the insulation not covered up when the soil is replaced should be weatherproofed with a layer of asbestos board and flashing inserted under the bottom row of siding protruding out over the edges of the insulation to protect it from rain. If you have a perimeter drainage problem around your slab, be aware that when and if insulation becomes soaked its insulating value drops to zero.

A concrete basement floor well below ground level, however, needs no insulation.

How to Install Storm Windows

It has been estimated that storm windows and doors pay for themselves in six to eight years, depending on the severity of the winters. A study made at the University of Illinois disclosed that 10 windows of 15 square feet each, unprotected by storm sash, let enough heat escape during the course of an average temperate-climate U.S. winter to consume 100 extra gallons of fuel oil—as against protecting the same windows in that house with storm sash.

Even if your house is well insulated, without storm windows as much as a quarter of your heat loss may be through glass even if only as little as 10% of the vertical square footage consists of single-glazed windows.

Glass is a poor insulator. Heat from a warm indoor source, such as a person, will always stream toward a cold windowpane and continue to flow toward it. This is why people feel chilly in the winter in a room without storm windows, even when the indoor air temperature may be in the seventies. The process is called *conduction,* and storm windows or double glazing reduce it. In a comfortably heated house, when the outside temperature drops to zero, the temperature of the inner surface of the window unprotected by storm sash is a mere 17°. Install a storm window and that same indoor surface of glass rises to 45°. Double glazing *plus* a storm window raises the temperature of the interior glass surface to 57°, with the outdoor temperature at zero.

Storm windows should be installed over as many windows of your house as you can afford—every window for the most dramatic fuel economy. But if your budget is tight, you'll still lower your fuel bill by installing them on the storm side of the house first, the side buffeted by prevailing winter winds, and add them on to the rest of the house when you can.

The cheapest expedient: You can make extremely inexpensive and effective temporary storm windows with polyethylene flexible sheeting, available at lumberyards. Kits costing about 75¢ per window include plastic, tack strips, and brads.

Sheets of film plastic can be installed either on the outside of the window, using tack strips, or—less unsightly but just as effectively and more easily—on the inside, using (adhesive-on-both-sides) double-faced tape. Polyethylene film, however, is not only far from completely transparent, the sun's ultraviolet rays deteriorate it so swiftly it lasts only a single season. More expensive and somewhat more transparent is flexible vinyl film. It distorts the image but lasts three years on the outside and as long as six years mounted indoors.

Now on the market is an all-plastic storm sash called "Weather or Not" that comes in kit form, each kit providing a sheet of vinyl film measuring either 39" or 51"x44" plus tough extruded vinyl channels in 3-, 4-, and 5-foot lengths. You merely hacksaw the channel strips to the right length without mitering and attach them together with right-angle corner pieces that snap into place. The clear sheet vinyl is clamped into the completed sash by a pressure-fit section that snaps into a channel in the sash like "pop beads". You wind up with something so lightweight you can install it with doublefaced tape either on the outside or inside of the window.

The sash can easily be converted to screens in the summer by popping out the pressure-fit channel and replacing the vinyl sheet with fiberglass screening. Or if you're air-conditioned you can replace the clear winter vinyl with tinted vinyl to cut down penetration of the sun's infrared thermal rays. The kits sell for $8 for the smallest-size standard window, which isn't exactly cheap. But the saving on labor in being able to put these storm sashes together and install them may make the difference.

Aluminum storm windows: Extruded aluminum storm sash is obtainable in three finishes—untreated (so-called "mill" aluminum); anodized; and baked-on enamel. Mill tends to corrode; anodized resists corrosion; enameled aluminum gives you a choice of colors and the most durable finish of the three. The most popular style is triple-track, featuring an inner track for screens and separate outer tracks for upper and lower storm window sections. These allow you to leave the storm sash and screens in place all year.

Triple-track mill-finish storm windows for standard-size window openings cost approximately $25 installed. Anodized ones cost $5 more. Baked-on enamel may run as high as $40 per window installed.

By far the greatest number of storm-and-screen sash is installed in the U.S. by contractors, but there are so many fly-by-night operators, it is wise to purchase only from a reputable firm whose references can be checked out. When you inspect the windows you intend to have installed, look for the AAMA label of certification indicating that the windows comply with specifications established by the American National Standards Institute and enforced by the Architectural Aluminum Manufacturers Association.

Most storm window contracts include aluminum storm doors, but if you live where the winters are severe, be aware that aluminum is much too efficient a conductor of heat, and a wooden storm door, properly weather-stripped, does a much better job keeping the heat in and the cold out.

Build your own storm sash: Buy aluminum sash at a hardware store; it is pre-fitted with soft plastic glazing channels that seal the glass in place when you build the frame. Special right-angle corner locks slip into the mitered ends of the sash members and hold the frame rigid. Take your measurements against the outer blind stop of the window. If the square-foot area is under nine square feet, a single storm sash of doubleweight glass will suffice. Anything over nine square feet should be a two-pane sash. To allow for warped window frames, a one-pane sash should be ⅛" shorter and ⅛" narrower than the space it will span; a two-pane sash should be ¼" smaller all around.

Double-strength glass costs so little more than single-strength it is well worth the difference, especially for windows that are put up and taken down every year.

Most storm windows are hung from a pair of overhead brackets attached to the top jamb of the permanent window. These enable you to mount and dismount upper-story windows from inside the house, saving dangerous twice-annual ladder climbing. Casement windows opening out, however, have a projecting hinge that often makes mounting of conventional outside storm windows impossible, necessitating interior-mounted ones, preferably covering the entire window, not just the casement. The kind that merely cover the casement opening, held in place by the same clips that grip the screen, leaves half the window unprotected from the elements.

If you are assembling a number of windows, you might want to purchase an inexpensive miter box to make the necessary 45° cuts easier. The only other tools you'll need are a matte knife or single-edge razor blade, hacksaw, combination square, file, hammer, and screwdriver, plus a drill for mounting the top-jamb brackets.

Check by measuring, but usually glass fits accurately if cut $1^1/_{16}''$ smaller each way than the outside dimensions of the frame. If your window openings are all the same size, it is suggested you first make up one frame and take it with you when you go to buy the glass. Have your dealer measure it and cut one sheet, then assemble the storm sash on the spot to make sure the size is accurate before having him cut the glass for the rest of the windows.

Before you start to build an aluminum storm sash, remove the glazing channel and install it around the glass this way: Set one side of the glass in the channel and tape it in place with masking tape. Before you bend it to fit over the adjacent edge of the glass, make a cut in the channel on both sides extending from the corner of the glass toward the exact center of the sheet. Now bend the channel over the corner and tape it to the adjoining edge. To miter that corner, make another cut in the channel exactly over the first one on both sides of the glass. Repeat this procedure at all four corners and set the glass aside.

For accurate, rigid fabrication of the frame, use a combination square to scribe 45° corner angles. Then use a miter box (or a dead-accurate eye) to cut exactly on the scribed lines with a very fine-toothed blade in your hacksaw. File the cut edges smooth so the corners will fit accurately.

Mitered corners of the sash are joined by corner locks that fit by friction and are locked by a simple hammer-tap on a $3^1/_2''$ spike. If the locks are hard to push into place, tap them gently with a length of 2x4, but not with a hammer, which can dent the sash irreparably.

Storm windows, whether aluminum or wood, should be weatherstripped. The simplest type to install is $3/_4''$-wide foam plastic, which self-adheres to the edge of the inner face of the storm sash and makes an excellent draft barrier compressed against the window frame's blind stop when the storm window is drawn tightly against it.

Innovation in storm windows: As a storm sash glazing material, rigid sheet plastic has a number of advantages over glass and

only one significant drawback—it scratches. But rigid sheet plastic is a 20% better barrier against cold than glass of the same thickness. If they are to be mounted on the outside of the window, single sheets of rigid plastic need only be $1/_8''$ thick up to three feet by four feet, or $3/_{16}''$ thick up to four feet by six feet. The material is impact-resistant. Much less frangible than glass, when it does break it doesn't shatter into deadly sharp-edged flying shards like glass, but into near-harmless low-velocity chunks. Mounted on the exterior of a house, rigid sheet plastic storm windows protect the glazing from a variety of hazards.

You save money, if you're making a number of windows, by buying big sheets of plastic and cutting them with a circular saw or saber saw. Leave the masking paper on to protect the surface and reduce friction and gumming behind the blade during fabrication. A steel cross-cut blade of the type recommended for finish-cuts on veneers should be used, six teeth to the inch, with all teeth the same shape, height, and point-to-point distance apart. Set a circular saw blade just slightly higher than the thickness of the sheet plastic to prevent chipping and do not force-feed. Sand edges with medium-grit abrasive paper to remove saw marks and assure maximum breakage resistance.

A panel of rigid sheet plastic for storm sash should be cut slightly smaller than the opening it will fill to allow for thermal expansion of the material. Measure the opening, then subtract $1/_{16}''$ from measurements of 12″ to 36″; subtract $1/_8''$ from measurements of 37″ to 48″; subtract $3/_{16}''$ from measurements of 49″ to 60″.

The sheet can be mounted against the outer blind stop with either $3/_4''$ quarter-round molding drilled and screwed to the window frame, or with metal mirror or storm-door clips one foot apart, which make for easier post-wintertime dismounting.

Or the sheet of rigid plastic can be framed in channeled aluminum or wood molding and hung from top-jamb hangers in the window opening. Don't neglect to weatherstrip the edge of the face of the storm sash with self-adhering foam plastic that will compress against the window when the storm sash is drawn against it.

Being a better thermal barrier than glass, rigid sheet plastic mounted unconventionally on the inside of windows makes for a snugger interior environment in bitter weather than glass-glazed storm sash. Single sheets of the least expensive .080″ thickness can be used over the inside of very big windows, but big sheets that thin are hard to store standing on their edges as they should be. With interior mounting you can increase the maximum span of ⅛″ thickness to four feet by six feet and ³/₁₆″ thickness to six feet by eight feet.

If there is no stop on the inside of the frame to rest the sheet of plastic against, one can be created from ¾″ quarter-round molding attached to the inside of the frame over a bead of butyl caulk to make it weathertight. Then a ¾″-wide strip of self-adhering foam weatherstripping is attached to the facing edge of the molding. The panel of plastic is held against it with a second strip of ¾″ quarter-round, also faced with weatherstripping bearing against the plastic.

If the inner molding is screwed rather than nailed in place the plastic panel can be easily (but carefully) removed and stored at winter's end. This is the simplest interior installation, but rigid sheet plastic can be mounted in aluminum storm sash just like glass and set in the opening if you want to go that (more expensive) route.

Cast acrylic sheet plastic such as Plexiglas (about $1 per square foot in the .080″ least expensive thickness) is optically perfect and absolutely invisible as storm window glazing. Extruded rigid acrylic sheet plastic such as Caroglaze (approximately 85¢ per square foot in the .080″ thickness) is 15 percent cheaper but not as high quality optically; there is some distortion of image. Householders may prefer to use it on windows through which the view is not inviting, installing Plexiglas on the important windows of the house.

There is an Abcite-coated scratch-resistant acrylic made by duPont, but it is not recommended for residential use because it is more expensive than its scratch resistance warrants. (The highly impact-resistant, near-unbreakable rigid sheet plastic called Lexan, ideal for "burglar-proof" glazing, is much more expensive than Caroglaze.)

For removing scratches in rigid sheet plastic, you can buy a buffing kit that includes a 4″ muslin wheel for use on a 1″ or ½″ spindle in an electric drill and a tube of buffing compound, plus instructions that tell how to obliterate a scratch.

How to Weatherstrip Windows and Doors

In past years, before heating fuel got so expensive, weatherstripping was a casual autumn chore for reducing "drafts" on the back of people's necks when the wind blew in winter. Today, adequate weatherstripping can represent a good many dollars saved on fuel, especially if you live where winter winds blow hard and cold.

If you experience any air infiltration around windows when storm windows are in place, the first phase of your weatherstripping should take place before the storm windows are put up for winter (unless you have permanent storm-screen sash). Every window in the house that does not have to be opened for any reason until spring should be sealed on all sides and across all gaps with inexpensive caulking cord, such as Mortite (about 3¢ a foot), which is a flexible putty-like material that unwinds from a coil and is easy to install by simple fingertip pressure. It works equally well on wood and steel sash.

If your storm windows are the type that fit against a perimeter stop on the outside of the window frame, install self-adhering strips of pressure-sensitive plastic foam all the way around the edge of each storm

Foam weatherstripping materials from left to right: ⅛″-wide adhesive-backed foam strip; vinyl tube gasket with foam inside; and ¼″-thick foam with adhesive back.

window on the side that faces the house. It comes in ¼'' thickness, ⅜'', ¾'' and 1'' wide and costs about 18¢ a foot, which is not cheap. But its tiny air cells make it an almost perfect barrier against strong winter winds. It will last several seasons, and thus is just about as economical as sealing the storm windows with caulking cord each year. And of course storm windows that have to be opened can be if edged with compressible foam stripping.

Those windows that must be able to be opened, as in bedrooms, are another matter. If your windows are loose you can install sash channels, which are spring-metal strips that fill the space between the sash and the frame by pressure. These necessitate removing the sash and are effective, but a fairly difficult installation.

Far easier is tubular vinyl gasket, a stripping with a nailing lip (about 8¢ or 9¢ a foot). It's very durable but difficult to nail in place on the outside parting strips and along the bottom rail of the lower sash. It is far easier to staple-gun this material in place. A more expensive version of the same thing incorporates resilient live sponge rubber molded to woven wire and fabric and coated with neoprene. These gasket weatherstrippings provide the additional bonus of stopping the rattling of loose-fitting windows and reducing infiltration of outdoor dust and noise.

The same material can be used around the perimeter of doors outside the jamb, but there are more attractive weatherstrippings for doorway application. An easy-to-apply favorite is wooden molding, tapered along one edge. Its other edge is foam plastic or foam rubber that bears against the door. Foam rubber lasts longer but foam plastic compresses more easily, making for a more weather-resistant fit.

There is, additionally, an aluminum channel version of this molding with a vinyl gasket that lies against the door. It lasts longer than either of the other two but does not compress quite as effectively to seal uneven gaps. Either the wood or aluminum ones costs $4 to $5 per door.

Molding-type weatherstripping must not be nailed too tightly against the face of the door or it will be hard to close. The technique is to cut the two side and top strips with a fine-toothed saw to fit. Now,

with the door closed, first lay down a thin bead of a permanent caulk like butyl, then temporarily tack the three strips in place with the nails sticking out and a slight compression of the foam material. Now try opening and closing the door. If it closes too easily, adjust the strips to compress a little more tightly. Try the door again and drive the nails home. Foam-edged wooden molding can be painted, but be careful to keep the paint off the foam, or you will destroy its effectiveness. Bonus benefit: door slam is deadened.

Much less expensive is felt weatherstripping that can be tacked or stapled around the door frame, but it has little resiliency for filling variations in the gap. Cost: around 3¢ a foot.

Felt and cloth weatherstripping materials from left to right: hair felt; wool and cotton felt; and a gasket type made of fabric sewn around a cotton yarn core.

The most functional door weatherstripping is the most expensive: interlocking aluminum or steel channel fitted all the way around the door's perimeter. A special threshold is installed that mates with a strip of metal attached in a rabbet to the bottom of the door. But door and frame have to be rather intricately rabbeted out to accommodate the system, and this is a job for a professional, who will probably charge you $30-$35 a door installed.

A home handyperson proficient with a block plane can dismount the door and plane down its side and top edges and install spring-metal strips that compress when the door is closed. This is also a permanent installation; it costs approximately $3 a door and creates a tight seal.

For sealing the all-important gap at the bottom of the door, easiest to install is an aluminum channel with curved vinyl facing that compresses when the door is closed.

The width of the thickness of the standard door, it lasts longer if attached to the bottom edge of the (dismounted) door than if installed as a threshold that people will be tramping on, but it works about as well either way. Cost: $1.50 to $2 per door.

More expensive is aluminum-and-vinyl hinged molding that attaches to the lower outside face of the door, along with a little roller that is screwed into the hinge side of the frame. This roller flips the molding's vinyl flap up out of the way when the door is opened and brings it down again when the door is shut—an effective solution to the problem of thick carpeting interfering with door closing.

Don't forget to weatherstrip your garage door bottom (see photo at top of next column). Permanent weatherstripping that seals the gap and cushions the slam is a rubber double lip that nails to the bottom of the door; $3.75 to $4 per 9-foot span.

As with windows, consider sealing exterior doors that you don't expect to use in winter with caulking cord, but don't seal up any doors that would serve as fire exits.

Remember to weatherstrip storm doors. Self-adhering foam strips that compress when the door is closed do the trick.

Keep in mind too that you can increase thermal barrier effectiveness at windows by lining draperies with insulation lining, either foam or reflective. Draperies should be closed at night in cold weather but opened during the day to allow as much solar radiation as possible to enter the house and give the heating system a free boost from the sun.

How to Soundproof a Door

It is not difficult to turn an old paneled door or hollow-core door into an adequate sound barrier. If appearances are paramount, simply buy a solid-core door and exchange it for the existing one.

New door or old, surround it with foam-edged weatherstripping-type molding, which can be painted the same color as the

door frame, and install an aluminum-and-vinyl threshold, the kind in which a flexible piece of vinyl presses against the bottom of the door when it's closed, sealing the gap. Where there's no space for such a threshold you can use an aluminum-and-vinyl door sweep to accomplish the same thing.

If you don't want to go to the trouble and expense of installing a new door—a solid-core door costs approximately $25—take a measurement of the back of the (closed) door, the side that does not swing out, and cut a piece of hardboard to fit. Fill the spaces in the paneling, if the door is paneled, with sheets of foam plastic or scraps of foam rubber underlayment. Or lacking either of these, fiberglass or mineral wool insulation makes a good sound-absorbent material between the door and the hardboard. The panel of hardboard you've cut need not be nailed in place. It can be dry-fitted, then glued in place with contact adhesive. Make sure it adheres all the way around close to the edge.

Somewhat more expensive, ½"-thick Technifoam will do a somewhat better job of soundproofing. It is a foil-backed rigid foam plastic; millions of tiny air bubbles inhibit the passage of sound.

Gluing on or tacking on indoor-outdoor carpeting over the back of the door makes quite an efficient sound barrier.

But whatever method you select, seal up all holes and cracks around the door. An incredible volume of sound, especially at certain frequencies, can leak through even a hole as small as a keyhole—so don't neglect to plug it up too.

How to Lay Carpeting

Strips called "rolls" are fast becoming the most popular do-it-yourself carpet installation because they are so swift and easy to lay. Where there's a choice, the wider rolls are usually more expensive; the most popular six-foot width is the least expensive.

Carpet rolls are cut to order to the nearest inch—but always add 3" *to each dimension* to allow for trimming and any irregularities in the room. (Measure your floor in several places to find the widest and longest dimensions.) Carpeting is usually priced by the square yard, but carpet rolls are sold by the running foot.

To find out how many square yards you are going to need, multiply the length of your area by the width in feet and divide by nine. To find out how many running feet of six-foot-wide carpet roll you'll require, divide your square-yard total by .66.

Carpet tiles: Although carpet rolls are less expensive than the same expanse of carpeting cut in 12" x 12" or 18" x 18" carpet "tiles," the difference is only a nickel or two per square yard. For a complicated floor area, you may find it easier to lay carpet tiles (or a combination of rolls and tiles—though you risk that rolls and tiles may not be exactly the same color, having almost undoubtedly come from different dye batches).

If you have priced carpet tiles and want to know how many it will take to cover your floor, multiply the length of the area by the width in feet for the number of 12" x 12" tiles you'll need. Divide the same figure by 2.25 to find out how many 18" x 18" tiles to buy. For areas like alcoves, measure separately and add to your total. Allow extra tiles for fitting and as replacements for any that get damaged in the future. To make sure of a true color match, buy all the tiles for one job at the same time.

For do-it-yourself installation, roll or tile, a moderate shag hides the seams between pieces of carpet best of any pile and keeps them hidden longer as the carpet wears. Shag is somewhat more expensive than the same fiber in a loop pile; nylon shag is twice as costly as polypropylene flat mat (originally introduced as "indoor-outdoor carpeting").

To stick or not to stick: Self-stick do-it-yourself rolls or carpet tiles, with a foam

How many tiles will you need?

Feet:	12"x12" tile	18"x18" tile
9x6	54	24
9x10	90	40
9x12	108	48
10x12	120	54
10x15	150	67
12x15	180	80

backing that does away with the need for separate cushion underlayment, come with an instant stick-down feature. To install, you merely peel off a protective layer of paper and press the adhesive-backed roll or tile in place. The carpeting cuts easily with a $3 carpet knife, so there's no great problem in fitting it around pipes and into odd corners.

But self-stick carpeting has one drawback that renters especially should be wary of: It may be difficult to unstick when you want to move or change carpets. If the floor has been shellacked, the self-stick coating may combine with the floor surfacing and make it almost impossible to remove without destroying its backing. Self-stick is not recommended for foyers or damp basements either, because it not only sticks too tenaciously where it is subject to dampness, but some brands tend to acquire an unpleasant odor under such conditions, according to reports of homeowners.

Wall-to-wall: The alternative is cushion-backed wall-to-wall carpeting that is not self-sticking. Double-faced tape, about $3 per 30-foot roll 2″ wide, holds cushion-backed carpet flat. But most cushion carpeting made today doesn't need to be fastened down, except at doorways, and here a three-foot strip of metal doorway edging, $1, is all you need to keep people passing through from kicking up the carpet.

Least expensive wall-to-wall is the very short (⅜″) pile polypropylene carpeting back-coated with moisture-resistant latex, an extraordinarily durable floor covering. It can be purchased a few inches longer and wider than the area to be covered and trimmed in place merely by pressing it into the floor-wall joint and cutting it carefully with a sharp carpet knife or heavy carpet shears. (Though a matrix, *see box*, is never a bad idea if you want a dead-sure fit, no matrix is really necessary.) Installed, its edges can be held down with double-faced tape.

This, the famous indoor-outdoor carpeting, is available in 6-, 9-, 12- and 15-foot widths and costs under $50 to cover a 12x12-foot area. Foam underlayment makes it more resilient to walk on. Many kitchens have been carpeted with it—but carpeting a kitchen is not considered a good idea

How to fit carpeting exactly

The surest, if not the quickest, way for the home handyperson to cut wall-to-wall carpeting or sheet floor-covering dead accurately is to make a matrix out of long sheets of heavy wrapping paper taped together with masking tape.

Construct your matrix (after the underlayment, if any, is down) a few inches larger than the floor area. It is a temptation simply to press the edges of the matrix against the right-angle where floor meets wall and trim with a single-edge razor blade or a carpet knife, but there is a much more precise way—and perfect fit is what you want: Crease the paper tightly into the floor-wall joint with your thumbnail. Then, pressing firmly with a pencil, mark this crease on the paper. Now, lifting this edge of the matrix as you go, cut right along the pencil line around the entire perimeter. At hard-to-get-at places, as around pipes and at doorway moldings, snip out small pieces of paper and tape them in place. Leave a cut line leading straight from the wall to the center of the back of any interruption like a radiator pipe. When you're done, mark the word "FACE" across the matrix before you roll it up to avoid confusion later on.

Roll out the carpeting or sheet flooring *face down* on a larger floor—even if you have to "borrow" a neighbor's family room or deck—and weight it in place. Roll out your matrix *face down* atop the carpeting or sheeting (you must not be able to read your word "FACE" now) and tape it in place at several points.

You might think you could just go right ahead and cut along the edge of the matrix, but if you do you risk having it slip out of position as you cut through one after another of the hold-down tapes. It's much surer to mark the edge of the matrix and remove it before cutting. If the undersurface (facing up at you) of the material you're cutting is light colored, use a wide-tipped felt marker, making sure part of the broad ink line falls over the edge of the matrix to give you a die-straight line to cut against. If the material you're cutting is a dark color, use a skirt marker ($2.25 at Singer sewing centers) to puff a line of powdered chalk along the edge of the matrix; when you take it up you'll have a sharp white edge to cut along.

unless your household is extremely spill-proof. Spills, especially those containing milk, must be scrubbed up immediately with detergent and rinsed, or in a comparatively short time kitchen carpeting acquires an unpleasant odor.

If you live near a big metropolitan center, you may be able to find a carpet outlet to which you can bring a paper matrix of the exact area your carpet will cover *(see box)* and have it cut for you on the spot. When you get home it will roll right into place.

Determine the number of square yards you need based on the widest and longest dimensions. Whatever you have to cut away for projections into the room like a fireplace or built-in cabinetry should be saved to use later as inlay patches in case the carpeting gets damaged *(see page 117, How to Patch a Worn Place in Carpeting)*.

Unless you live on a farm or some place where people are constantly tramping in with dirty boots, wall-to-wall carpeting throughout the house (except in the kitchen) is the most serviceable floor covering in terms of care, particularly if you install a low-shag pile with a multi-colored mixture of yarns that include dark colors. Regular vacuuming is all that's required.

Foam-backed wall-to-wall carpeting is good insulation, especially on a first floor that has no cellar under it. Although the pile may be of nylon, polypropylene, polyester, acrylic, wool, or a cotton-and-manmade fiber mixture, nylon and polypropylene seem to have the edge in durability at reasonable cost per square foot. Each fiber, however, has its special benefits and drawbacks.

How to Lay Floor Covering

Most do-it-yourselfers prefer floor tiles to sheet floor covering because tiles are so foolproof to install. The self-adhering kind are more expensive than plain-backed ones, but a householder who would not attempt to install floor tiles at all if he had to use spread adhesive (and would hire someone to do the job), saves money with self-stick tiles, which are undeniably swift and easy to lay. You just peel off the paper backing and press them in place.

Asphalt is the least expensive of the three basic floor tile materials—asphalt, vinyl-asbestos, and solid vinyl. But asphalt stains and is not nearly as durable or easy to maintain as the others.

Vinyl-asbestos is only a few cents more per tile. Its asbestos content makes it extremely rugged, but it should be kept waxed. Otherwise traffic pulverizes the surface, and there is more than a suspicion that the dust so created contains tiny particles of asbestos, which are carcinogenic.

Solid vinyl tiles are the most expensive of the three types, but come in the greatest variety of colors, patterns, and textures. The darkest and the lightest, especially in solid colors, tend to show the dirt more than patterned medium colors. For a heavy traffic area, consider buying the more expensive longer-wearing ⅛" thickness. It is more economical in the long run than the cheaper, thinnest .080" gauge, which is not particularly durable. Although textured tile floors are somewhat harder to sweep, dirt is "protected" by the texturing from acting as an abrasive when people walk on it.

There are five basic steps to installing a non-self-adhering tile floor—preparing the underfloor, laying out the room, spreading the adhesive, laying the tile, and cutting-in the border tiles.

Installing the underlayment: The surface on which the tiles will lie must be smooth, firm, and clean. If you're laying tile on concrete, smooth off any rough spots and fill cracks with a patching material. Latex-base paint in good condition does not have to be removed, but oil-base paint on concrete lying directly on the ground must be sanded off with a drum sander (rentable and not hard to use). Before laying the tiles all traces of grease, wax, and dirt must be removed with cleanser and/or solvent to ensure a perfect bond. The concrete must be absolutely dry when the adhesive is applied.

Wood floors usually present more problems. Never install floor tile over a wood floor that does not have at least 30" of ventilated space between it and the ground below. A smooth double wood floor in good condition, with all boards down tight, merely requires a layer of 15-lb asphalt-saturated paper before tiling. Apply the cement; lay the felt paper *across* the floorboards, butting its edges together, and roll it flat immediately with an ordinary rolling pin.

Tile manufacturers advise against installing floor tile directly over an old double wood floor that is very uneven from wear, or not absolutely firm, or has floorboards 4″ wide or wider. Instead, first nail down, or preferably screw down, all loose boards, replace broken ones, and patch small holes and cracks with water-soluble wood dough smoothed on with a putty knife. Any loose nail should be driven deeper (and the hole filled) or pried out and replaced with a longer flat-head nail or wood screw.

Then, if the floorboards are less than 4″ wide, install ¼″-thick underlayment-grade hardboard, smooth side up. It is less expensive than plywood and just about as durable. (Do not use tempered Masonite.) If the floorboards are wider than 4″, lay a thicker hardboard underlayment. The material comes in standard panels four feet wide in 8-, 10-, and 12-foot lengths. It is easy to cut, smooth side up, with any saw.

Nail it down with special cement-coated or annular-ring underlayment nails. They hold it tighter to the old floor than common nails. Drive a nail every 3″ along the edges and 6″ apart all over the entire expanse, starting in the middle of each panel. You'll need 50 to 75 nails per 4x8 sheet. Such lavish nailing, however, is the secret to floor tiling that stays in place. To allow for ordinary expansion and contraction of hardboard, each sheet should be laid about the thickness of a nail apart from its neighbors on all sides, and joints should be staggered.

Can tiles be laid over an existing tile or sheet floor covering? It's done but it's risky,

because the new tiles may not adhere successfully. The old surface must be rock-hard; if it is textured, coat it with a special latex for the purpose to make it smooth.

Laying out a tile floor: Never start at a wall or corner. Work from the center of the room out. To find that center starting point, first find the center of two opposing walls in the room. Tap in a nail at each point, tie a string taut between the two protruding nails and rub it with a piece of chalk. Now pick up the string and snap your first guideline.

Next measure to find the center point of the chalk line you've just snapped. Place a carpenter's square on the chalk line, at that point, and use the right-angle of the square to draw a pencil line perpendicular to the chalk line. Using this pencil line as a guide, snap a second chalk line intersecting the first at a perfect right angle, thus dividing the room into four quarters. (Lacking a carpenter's square, lay two tiles either side of the center point of your first chalk line and use them for drawing the perpendicular pencil line that determines where the second chalk line should be snapped.)

Although the intersection of the two chalk lines is the exact center of the room, this is not necessarily where you start laying tiles since you will want an even border of partial tiles all around the room. For best visual effect, borders should be at least half a tile wide, and here's how to achieve that: Dry-fit a row of loose tiles along both chalk lines

in one quarter of the room. If the space between the edge of the last tile and the wall is less than half a tile wide, slide the entire row away from the wall until the border space is a half-tile wide. Then move to the center-room end of the same row and snap a new chalk line parallel to the end-of-the-row edge of the center-room tile in the row you've just slid. Similarly, if the border width is less than half a tile at the end of the other row in the quarter, slide the entire row and snap a new right-angle guideline. The two new intersecting chalk lines (obliterate the old ones) will ensure even borders on all four sides of the room.

Spreading the adhesive: Various kinds of floor tile require different kinds of adhesive to adhere properly. Your dealer should have sold you the correct adhesive for the tiles you purchased, depending on whether you're laying them over concrete, or on floorboards, underlayment, or old sheet or tile floor covering.

One reason vinyl-asbestos tiles are so popular is that the adhesive appropriate for this tile can be applied with a brush or roller just thickly enough to grip the tiles without squeezing up between them when they are laid. Troweled-on adhesives are much more difficult to spread the proper even thickness.

Begin spreading adhesive at the intersection of your adjusted chalk lines, covering one-quarter of the room at a time.

Laying the tiles: Lay the first two rows against the two right-angle chalk lines and build out from these two rows until whole tiles are laid over the entire quarter. Then lay each of the other three quarters, leaving the border for last. It's all right to kneel on tiles you've just laid as you pyramid them out with each succeeding row.

Fitting the border: At the end of each row lay a loose tile squarely atop the last glued-down one before the gap. Then using a second loose tile as a template, lay it on top and slide it against the wall (see photo following). Its edge *opposite* the wall is now a straight-edge against which you can scribe a line across the face of the first loose tile. Cut along that scribed line for a perfect border fit.

To make a straight cut across asphalt tile, score it deeply with the point of an awl or ice pick. The tile should snap off along this line if you follow the procedure shown in the photo opposite. Smooth the edge of the tile

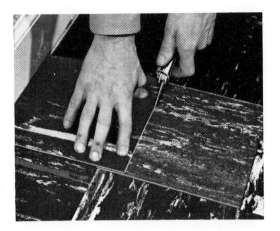

with sandpaper. For irregular cuts, asphalt tile should be heated until it is pliable, then cut with metal snips or strong shears. Similarly, vinyl-asbestos and solid vinyl tile can be cut by being warmed in an oven heated to 200° *and turned off*, then trimmed with metal snips.

Cutting-out to fit around door jambs is most accurately accomplished by making a small paper matrix of the exact shape of the door frame and transferring it to the tile. But a neater way is to make a simple cut with a carpenter's saw, removing about ⅛" of the base of the frame—the jamb is not a structural support. You will then be able to slide your border tile right under the jamb against the wall, eliminating the need for cutting the tile to fit.

Around pipes fitting is easier with a matrix. Make a straight cut in the tile from the

hole to the edge that abuts the wall. Then when you get the tile warm and pliable it will open at the cut, allowing the tile to slip into position around the pipe.

Note on laying sheet floor covering: On a floor that is washed frequently, sheet floor covering is obviously preferable to floor tiles, which do tend to come unstuck if water is allowed to seep down between the joints.

The installation of costly cemented-down sheet floor covering is perhaps best left to a professional installer because the job is so easily botched by anyone lacking the necessary training—although sheet floor covering will be a sure fit if you take the time to make an accurate paper matrix first. But laying foam underlayment, then laying inexpensive sheet linoleum or the somewhat more expensive sheet vinyl, is quite easy for a reasonably handy householder. Edges of both the underlayment and the sheet material can be held down with double-face tape. Most do-it-yourselfers, however, combine floor surfacing and resiliency by installing the somewhat more expensive cushion-backed sheet floor coverings.

Tip: When you trim sheet floor covering, save the scraps. They are useful for inlays if the material ever gets damaged (*see page 112, How to Repair Floor Covering*).

How to Cover a Wall with Fabric

The most popular do-it-yourself wall covering for walls in fair-to-good condition is self-adhering sheet vinyl. It is dimensionally stable, very durable, completely washable, and the patterns are endless. It's easier to apply than wallpaper—which is not for the inexperienced handyperson—because you butt the edges of vinyl together instead of overlapping them.

Panels of burlap, felt, or any relatively heavy fabric can be applied directly to a smooth wall with a clear, water-soluble adhesive called Glutoline 77 (about $2, enough for an average room). Extremely slippery before it dries, this adhesive allows you to slide the fabric into position after you get it on the wall, giving you wide latitude for correctible error in lay-up.

Staple-gun wall covering, however, is less messy than the brush-and-glue routine. Astonishingly swift and easy, staple-gun decorating is the only way to hide a wall that's too cracked and uneven for direct fabric (or wallpaper) application. Staple guns cost around $7, or you can rent one at a rental center for $3 or $4 a day.

A wide choice of printed designs in wrinkle-resistant synthetic-and-cotton fabric are available in 54″ and 70″ bolts; you can even use bed sheets. Select the design in the width that's easiest for you to handle. Then follow these directions:

Cut fabric into panels of desired length, leaving an extra 1″ at top and bottom (unless you're using bed sheets or felt). Be sure to have enough extra fabric to match patterns in proper sequence.

(If you suspect your ceiling is not level, lay a carpenter's level against your ceiling where it meets the wall. If your ceiling turns out not to be level, hang a heavy object from one end of a wall-height string stapled to the edge of the ceiling at the top of the wall the same distance from one corner of the room as the width of the fabric you're using. This will give you a true vertical.)

Start at the upper corner, running a line of glue along the top edge for extra tautness and ease in hanging. Turn under a 1″ excess of the upper edge of the fabric and staple it at the ceiling line, pulling it taut as you go. When the top edge is secure, draw the fabric tight toward the bottom, turning the 1″ overhang under, and staple along the baseboard or floorline. Staple down both side edges from top to bottom.

For invisible seams between panels use "backtacking": Place the second panel face-to-face against the first, using a couple of staples to hold it temporarily in place at the top. Staple a strip of ½″ upholstery tape or ½″-wide cardboard against the vertical common edge. Use plenty of staples. Now remove the temporary staples at the top of the second panel and draw it tightly over the tape or cardboard strip, hiding it, and resulting in a smooth, "invisibly" stapled seam. Staple top, bottom, and side of this second panel and continue adding new panels the same way. You may want to glue down the last edge of the final panel to keep the staples from showing.

Get the best out of your staple gun by holding it flat and snug against the fabric as you fire the staples into the wall. To assure full power, don't let it jump or recoil.

How to Restore Furniture

Few do-it-yourself families have to hear this, but the most beat-up piece of furniture, if its lines are pleasant, can be repaired and refurbished like new by any of a choice of processes. A carpenter-handyperson in the family can easily repair joints in cabinetry, sticking drawers, or broken legs.

Tying Springs

Sagging springs is a simple repair, a mere matter of turning the chair over, removing the cloth that hides the springs, hunting inside with a directed light for the loose or broken tie that should be holding the spring in place, and retying the spring with strong new cord in a tight knot. Usually rewebbing is a good idea when springs have to be tied—also an easy task. The material is so inexpensive, it pays to buy the best, which is identified by the woven-in red stripe. Visit an upholstery supply outlet, where you may also want to purchase an upholsterer's needle and twine for easiest stitching of torn upholstery. Or get these materials by mail order from Minnesota Woodworkers Supply Co., Rogers, Minnesota 55374.

Repadding

Padded chair seats are quickly dismounted by removing a few screws. Repad with foam rubber; it is simple to cut with a saw (or electric carving knife) and trim with shears. New fabric is stretched evenly over it and staple-gunned or tacked to the inside edge of the seat frame—an easy and rewarding do-it-yourself project, especially if you can pick up some inexpensive mill ends of beautiful fabric for new covering.

If you're getting into furniture refinishing, you can benefit from perusal of catalogs available free from Minnesota Woodworkers Supply Co. *(address above)* and Albert Constantine & Son, Inc., 2050 Eastchester Road, Bronx, NY 10461.

Instant Resurfacing

Very faint scratches in a clear finish often can be hidden simply by thorough cleaning and waxing. Slightly deeper ones that are more visible, usually because they are lighter than the surrounding surface, can be safely smoothed away—but never with sandpaper, rottenstone, or pumice, because these can cut through a clear finish too easily. Here's the right way, and it's swift:

Whether varnish, shellac, or lacquer, the surface should be cleaned of old wax or old furniture polish with mineral spirits, also known as paint thinner, a less expensive substitute for turpentine. Anything that stays on the surface after a thorough rubdown with a rag soaked in mineral spirits can be removed with water. Now rub the piece, following the grain, with 000 (fine) steel wool in straight strokes pressing hard, keeping the steel wool saturated with mineral spirits. This removes the infinitesimal top layer of the clear finish and results in a like-new look after it has been rubbed with wax and buffed.

For deeper scratches and gouges, touch-up sticks are available at paint and hardware stores in a variety of colors to match various woods and stains. You merely rub them across the scratch until it is obliterated. If you can't find exactly the color you want in touch-up sticks try dye stains or mix the exact match with very much thinned oil paints from an art store. Dry the touch-up with a hair dryer. Before waxing use a fine-pointed artist's brush to paint a thin coat of varnish over the exact area of the scratch after touch-up.

Stripping Down to Bare Wood

If you've tried it then you know: it takes far less effort than most people imagine to restore an old piece of furniture to new beauty by stripping, the complete removal of varnish, shellac, or paint, a drastic and time-consuming but inexpensive process. (It is often worth removing all old wax and dirt with mineral spirits first, however, to see if the underlying finish—unless it's too dark for your taste—can be restored before embarking on stripping.) Carefully read every word of the label instructions on any chemical paint-varnish remover you buy. Some removers dissolve only surface coatings and leave underlying penetrating stains in tact. Others contain bleach or other lighteners. Dyed wood usually can be lightened with a mild wood bleach of oxalic acid, found in paint stores, or stronger bleaches if this one doesn't work. If you get the wood too light, you can stain it to the shade you desire, first testing on some hidden part of the piece.

Some oak, mahogany, or walnut may have been finished with wax or oil alone. There's no point in stripping such a piece—nor should you bother stripping if you are going to paint a piece of furniture unless the surface is impossibly rough or too many coats hide desirable detail.

It's much easier to strip and refinish furniture if you remove all the hardware—handles, hinges, and knobs—before beginning, and it produces a neater job.

Wear rubber gloves for removing an old finish with paint-and-varnish remover. Experienced refinishers prefer a fast-acting liquid remover, but because beginners find they have to work too fast to keep up with it, a paste remover is better for them; it is slower drying.

How much remover should you buy? One quart is sometimes enough for stripping a chest of drawers, other times it takes much more. It all depends on what the piece was coated with and how many coats it's had. Follow the directions on the label to the letter. Some removers require a water washdown, others can simply be wiped or scraped clean. A wire brush is handy for stripping details.

A stripped piece should be rubbed down with steel wool and mineral spirits and

wiped clean with soft rags. Avoid sandpaper, which can scratch a fine old surface and destroy its patina.

Subsurface Preparation

Make all required repairs before applying a new finish—fill holes, cracks, and tighten loose joints. An excellent tool for this is Constantine's glue injector, a device that resembles a steel hypodermic needle. A small hole is drilled into a loose joint in furniture, preferably from a concealed angle, and glue is squeezed into the weakness with the injector. This obviates the need for disassembling or clamping in many cases.

Shallow dents and bruises can be made to disappear from bare wood by laying several thicknesses of damp woolen cloth over them —felt is fine—and pressing with a hot iron. Moisture causes the wood to swell and rise to normal height (do not try this on veneer).

If the surface is very rough, save smoothing time and effort by buying the more expensive but far ruggeder, and thus more economical, carborundum paper rather than common "sandpaper." An orbital-vibrating sander (which rents for about $5 per day at rental centers, paint, and hardware stores) greatly reduces the effort.

To make abrasive paper last longer, brush it off with a stiff nylon brush once in a while to unclog the grit.

Use a coarse grade only to level the surface. To smooth it, begin with medium 1/0 to 3/0-grade—always sanding with the grain, never across it.

If you want a high-gloss finish, steel-wool the job after sanding is completed to get the smoothest surface possible.

Clear Finishing

Your choice among hard-surface clear finishes is shellac, about $2 per quart; lacquer at various prices, all of them expensive; varnish, around $4 per quart; and polyurethane, also about $4 per quart.

Cheapest is oil, considered a clear finish too; although instead of adhering to the surface it penetrates the wood and hardens. Perfectly adequate is a mixture of one-half boiled linseed oil and one-half turpentine. Oils for both softwood and hardwood finishing are also available clear or in colors in modern hard polymer coatings, like Watco's Danish Oil. An oil finish is one of the easiest, most satisfying ways to give furniture a water-, alcohol-and-heat-resistant surface over smoothly sanded or stripped wood. Apply it weekly, rubbing it in with a clean dry rag in one hand and rubbing off the excess with another rag in the other hand—no brushes or spray cans to lay out money for. The furniture can be used during the period you're working up an oil finish. The more coats you apply over the course of a few months, the richer and more satiny it will turn out. Best of all, an oil finish can be renewed at any time, even years hence, by simply recoating with oil, as long as no wax or other non-compatible coating has been applied over it.

Shellac is the easiest hard-surface clear finish to apply, but it tends to chip, water turns it white, and it dissolves if alcohol is spilled on it, so it is not recommended for counters or tabletops.

Lacquer leaves a harder finish than shellac, but it too turns white when water gets on it, and it is difficult to apply.

Varnish, the hard-surface clear finish most refinishers had been using until the polyurethanes came along, goes on easily but bubbles (as the polyurethanes do not). A good grade of interior varnish (not "spar" varnish, which is for outdoor use and doesn't dry as hard) resists water, alcohol, heat, and abrasion. Two coats are enough for any surface not subject to much wear; three to five coats are not too many for counters and tabletops. The first coat should be thinned half-and-half with whatever solvent the label recommends. Varnish should be floated on rather liberally to hold down the bubbling. Brush with the grain in short, even, slow strokes, going back over a previously covered area as little as possible, because that roughens the otherwise self-leveling surface. Let the first coat dry for at least two days, then rub it smooth with fine 000 steel wool (the bubbles should disappear) and dust carefully before applying the second coat. Leave a minimum of four days, preferably a week, between succeeding coats, smoothing each with steel wool and dusting before applying the next. The more coats you apply, the more satiny the final sheen if you rub each one smooth before applying the next.

Polyurethanes, bubble-free and much easier to apply than varnish, are clear or colored, matte-, satin- or glossy-surface plastic coatings. They are very hard, chemically stable, and highly resistant to moisture and detergents, alcohol, and abrasion. They can be used to cover and enhance the appearance not only of wood but also of metal, ceramic, plastic, and glass, but are not recommended for softer surfaces, such as sheet linoleum or floor tiles.

Outdoor metal furniture can be coated with most polyurethanes, except aluminum, which requires a special treatment first, such as United Paint Company's "Alluma-grip," duPont's "Imron," or Finch's "Catalast." Polyurethanes normally dry dust-free in up to 30 minutes and can be recoated at six-hour intervals. Brushing qualities are similar to enamels, and spraying them on raises no special problems.

Glossy polyurethane is becoming recognized as the longest-wearing, most corrosion-protective surface yet discovered, and is currently being used to coat high-performance jet aircraft. Most polyurethanes are not compatible with waxes or stearates, such as are normally found in popular wood stains and sealers like Minwax. (The manufacturers of Minwax have introduced a newly formulated polyurethane coating compatible with its products.) Always verify compatibility, either by checking the label instructions or by testing on scrap materials.

No special procedures are required for coating new wood with polyurethane. Simply clean the surface of wax, grease, and dust, then coat as with any enamel. Old wood surfaces, however, should be treated as potential problems. Verify the soundness of old coatings by scraping. If firmly attached to the wood, sand the surface lightly to provide purchase for the polyurethane. But it is extremely important that a wax-free, grease-free clean surface be provided. Old stains must be removed by stripping the surface and sanding to a new-wood condition. Use polyurethane-compatible stains to tone the wood.

Zap It with Paint

Nothing brings a shabby piece of furniture to life faster than paint. It too is easier than you may imagine, thanks to a great range of simple-to-apply pre-mixed colors.

1. Before painting, test the old surface by running the back of a knife hard across an obscure place. If it doesn't chip or flake, the paint merely needs cleaning before painting (if it does chip, the old paint should be stripped with paint-and-varnish remover, closely following label directions for use).

2. The surface must be perfectly clean or the paint won't adhere. You can scrub with a cleaner like Spic & Span, using a household cleanser for stubborn places, and thoroughly rinsing with ammonia in clear water; the piece should dry for a day. But it is far easier simply to wipe the surface clean with a commercial degreaser such as Pre-kleano (about $7 per gallon at auto body shop supply stores; see your Yellow Pages). A degreaser causes much less grain raising and staining than washing. It can be used for other purposes, like the cleaning of tile

floors for rewaxing, but wear rubber gloves, the stuff is strong.

3. Painted furniture should have a hard smooth finish. If the old finish has only a few chipped places, these can be smoothed with abrasive paper. But a finish that is badly chipped, cracked, sticky, rough, or has had too many coats of paint should be stripped.

4. Fill holes and cracks with an oil-base filler, such as wood dough or "wood plastic." (A water-base filler doesn't hold well in large holes and gouges, because the water in the filler may swell the wood around it, which when it dries, shrinks and pulls away from the patch.) Apply it with your finger or

a putty knife and smooth it with fine-grit abrasive paper. Waterproof silicone carbide abrasive paper, 240A (very fine grit) and 320A (extra fine grit), is best.

5. For a smoother, better adhering paint job, use an undercoat or "primer." Best is a pigmented shellac that will grip bare wood or old paint and provide a better surface in turn, for enamel to adhere to. Sometimes it is necessary to apply a second coat of primer to cover a dark surface adequately. A primer should be allowed to dry for 24 hours or more—but long before using it on whatever you intend to paint, check the primer and final paint for compatibility on a piece of scrap material.

6. Wet-sand the primer and each succeeding coat except the last. Wet-sanding is preferable to dry-sanding because waterproof paper does not load up, and the slurry of paint and water created contributes to a very smooth surface at far less effort than dry-sanding. Waterproof paper lasts much longer too. On flat surfaces a child's blackboard eraser makes a perfect sanding block. Always sand in one direction, usually with the grain. On hard-to-get-at places switch to fine steel wool. Remove sanding dust with a clean, lint-free rag.

7. On pieces that don't get much wear you might as well use cheaper, easier-to-apply latex-base semigloss paint. (The top of a chest can be covered with a coat of gloss or matte polyurethane to protect the latex surface, but be sure to check for compatibility of the two before you opt for this ploy).

8. Rather than painting furniture with a brush, which inevitably leaves brush marks, consider a painting pad. Costing about $4, it is a plastic-handled device that holds cleanable, replaceable, fuzzy-surface foam pads. These are less messy to use than a paint roller, which tends to "pull" enamel.

9. With the prime coat smoothed and dusted, you are ready for your first coat of semigloss (also known as "satin") or high-gloss oil-base enamel—the choice of most people who paint furniture. The latter, with its reflectant luster, is tougher than semigloss enamel; it can be washed many times.

10. Stir enamels slowly but thoroughly. Speedy stirring creates bubbles that are hard to get rid of. Apply it to a small section at a time, working rapidly, going back over a just-painted section as little as possible, except to remove excess paint, so that it will self-level. If you're using more than one color, let the piece dry overnight before applying the second color.

11. Before the final coat, the surface must be "cut" with extra-fine-grit abrasive paper to make "tooth" for the last coat.

12. Apply the final coat the same as the preceding ones, then let the piece dry several days to two weeks, depending on the humidity. If a satiny finish is your goal but you have used high-gloss enamel for its toughness, the final painted, dried and cured surface can be rubbed with FFF or FFFF pumice powder in lightweight lubricating oil (like 2-in-1). Rub it on with a rag on curved surfaces. On flat surfaces, sprinkle a little pumice, then dribble a few drops of oil on top. With a new blackboard eraser or clean felt pad, rub in the direction of the grain until you get the satin finish you want. Wipe the surface with a clean, dry rag to remove every trace of oil. Then wax and buff.

Check it out before you chuck it out

Much of the furniture produced two or three generations ago was of better basic quality—solid wood—than much of the mostly veneered furniture manufactured today. Unsightly finishes and multiple coats of paint often hide the fact that an old piece nobody wants is actually solid oak, walnut, hickory, maple, or any of a number of fruitwoods.

There's excitement and suspense for the do-it-yourselfer in stripping away an opaque finish to discover some beautiful wood grain just waiting for a couple of coats of modern clear finish to accentuate its quality. Stripping often reveals a lovely patina that only time and long use could have produced.

In considering an old piece for refinishing concentrate on the basic shape, keeping in mind that details have often literally been stuck on and can be pried off quite easily if they offend the eye. Tables and chests of drawers too tall for contemporary tastes can be lowered by careful shortening of legs; a chest may look best sitting smack on the floor with no legs at all.

Where to find old furniture for refinishing? Look over your own and your relatives' attics and basements first. Check suburban and small-town newspapers for notices of flea markets, garage sales, and auctions of country property—prick up your ears at any mention of the term "barn sale" taking place in some remote county.

A secondhand store masking behind the sign "Antiques" is usually worth exploring. So are Salvation Army and Goodwill Industries "showrooms" of reconditioned furniture. Since the refurbishing mainly takes the form of cleaning, many a fine candidate for stripping has been turned up in such places. In or near cities you'll find that building wreckers sometimes have quantities of old furniture. Finally, in New York City and many other metropolitan areas across the U.S., the department of sanitation has a specific day of the month for collecting large items of refuse. People set out on the sidewalk the night before pickup day the most amazingly strippable treasures.

How to Paint the Inside of Your House

Before you reach for that paintbrush . . . *a survey has disclosed that 50 percent of American families refinish the interior of their homes on an average of once every three years, and that many waste money repainting instead of cleaning the walls. Except for those few that are wallpapered, almost all the walls in U.S. houses are coated with flat paint. When it is washed, part of the protruding pigment that makes it non-shiny breaks off. This is practically unnoticeable on flat white or pastel colored walls (but makes flat dark walls virtually unwashable). Before going to the expense and bother of repainting a room previously coated with a light paint, try washing a small area out of sight behind a piece of furniture. Scrub on a strong solution of household detergent (such as Spic & Span or Soilax) with a sponge and rinse with clear water. When it dries it may look as fresh as new. If you then elect to wash the walls instead of repainting, make the job easier by applying the detergent solution over at least a four- or five-square-foot area and letting its chemical action work before going back over it to remove the grime. Thorough rinsing is imperative to ensure continued long life of the paint surface.* But if you decide to paint, here's how to paint a room.

What You'll Need

The paint: Water-base flat latex interior paint is the home handyperson's near universal choice, and for good reason. It is self-leveling, lap marks don't show, application is easy, and cleanup a cinch. It doesn't get thicker in the can as you paint, precluding the need for thinner. Latex dries so quickly that, one coat or two, you can usually paint a room in a day. Its thick creaminess reduces splatters and drips. (Any paint spots are easier to clean up when they are wet, except on glass—these come off more easily, after they dry.)

Some latex paints cover in one coat, but few homeowners are satisfied with the results. When painting over a contrasting color with white or a pastel, better count on two coats with most brands of paint.

The brush: Natural bristles used to be the criterion, but nylon bristles replaced them. A nylon brush works well with oil-based paints, but only fairly well with latex because the water base tends to soften the bristles, and a soft brush does not distribute the paint as evenly as a firm one. DuPont now makes a (so-called "Orel") fiber bristle of polyester that is better than either natural or nylon and remains firm when wet with water, thinner, or alcohol. The polyester brush is recognizable by its brown bristles.

A good brush has lots of bristles; it is really thick. You can check by the size of the wood plug inside the circle of bristles; the smaller the plug the more bristles in an otherwise same-size brush. If you look closely as you run your fingers from the heel of a quality brush gradually down to the tip, you will see many shorter bristles that make it taper. Tapering allows the paint to flow off the end smoothly; brushes with bristles all one length do not release the paint evenly. A good brush should bend in an even arc when you press it against a hard surface and there should be little if any spread at the tip. An inferior brush bends abruptly in the middle and spreads broadly at the tip, given the same test. Look closely at the tips of the bristles. Split ends may be anathema to the ladies, but they are just

---

What size paintbrush

The most useful size, both for interior and exterior painting, is a 4″-wide brush. Sure, professional painters use 5″ and 6″ brushes, but their muscles are used to it. A 3″ brush is often used for exterior trim, but save the money and learn to use a large brush for narrow surfaces by propelling it along edgewise.

To make a paintbrush last

You must *always* clean a paintbrush immediately after you finish using it (although if you're just taking a lunch break, you can seal a wet brush in a plastic sandwich bag with masking tape to keep it from drying out before you get back). Wash a brush used for latex paint in water with a strong concentration of detergent. A small stiff brush helps. The rule is five washes and five rinses, with a final rinsing in cold water until absolutely every trace of pigment has disappeared, then wipe and hang up the brush. Never stand it on its bristles. A brush used for oil-based paint should be washed with paint thinner (much cheaper than turpentine) in a clean can. Sozzle the brush up and down in small amounts of fresh paint thinner several times, wiping it on old newspapers in between to remove all pigment. Finally, wash it in detergent and water, shake it out and hang it to dry.

what you want in a quality brush; such so-called "flagged" tips leave fewer brush marks and help to carry more paint.

You'll also need a roller paint tray, standard 9″ roller with screw-in extension handle, five-foot stepladder, and a dropcloth (plastic-backed ones are the best buy).

To Figure How Much Paint to Buy

Multiply the floor-to-ceiling height in feet by the width of each wall and add the results to get the vertical square-foot area. Don't deduct for doors and windows unless they take up a lot of the wall space. Multiply the length of the room by the width to get the square-foot area of the ceiling. Determine how many gallons you'll need by dividing your total square feet figure by the number of square feet one gallon covers.

For kitchens and bathrooms choose a gloss or semigloss latex paint. Although more expensive than flat, these can be washed much more often and more effectively, lengthening the time between paintings and lowering your long-range cost for interior refinishing.

Painting with semigloss, the speed you get with a roller may be no match for the better hiding quality of a brushed-on finish. The roller cover, in any event, should be mohair or its equivalent. High-gloss paint must be brushed on. Oil-based (alkyd) high-gloss paints, still on the market, can stand the hardest scrubbing of all and are still the best bet for kitchens. But do-it-yourselfers shun them because they take longer to dry and require thorough ventilation during and after painting to evacuate their strong odor. As they are being applied, they must be thinned with the appropriate thinner, which also has to be used for cleanup—and raises the cost.

Previously unpainted wallboard or plaster soak up considerably more paint than a painted surface. You save by applying a primer, which your dealer can recommend to go under the paint you intend to use. One prime coat is usually sufficient over previously flat-painted surfaces of uneven porosity that you are going to paint with latex gloss or semigloss; a gloss or semigloss that dries unevenly (over a prime coat) needs a second coat to put things right. If a ceiling or walls are stained (as from a water leak), pigmented Haeuser's Enamelac keeps stains from bleeding through the new coat.

If you have just moved into an old house or an apartment in an old building, however, you should know that the ceilings may originally have been coated with water-soluble calcimine over which later coats of oil-based paint were probably applied. If you try to paint such a ceiling with latex, the water base in the paint can work its way through cracks in the old coats of oil paint until it reaches the calcimine. Then your paint job may peel off in great sheets right before your eyes. Test, if you're not sure, by laying on a roller stroke of latex and wait overnight. If by the next day the latex is blistered or loose, use an oil-base paint on the ceiling, and save yourself some grief.

Color It What?

Selection of color is a personal choice, but don't buy paint by the color charts and chips you find at the paint store, because lighting conditions there are likely to be entirely different from those in the room you intend to paint. Since colors can change radically under artificial light, be sure to look at color samples at home both in daylight and at night.

Paint generally dries lighter and looks either darker or more vivid when a whole wall is painted with it. Get a swift preview of the final effect by purchasing the least amount you can of the color you choose and paint a section of wall. Let it dry before deciding if it's what you want for the whole room.

Can paint save energy? Consider the savings in electricity when you're deciding what color to paint a room. At night by artificial illumination, or even in late afternoon on a gray day, white or pastel colors bounce much more light around the room than dark colors and make it brighter.

Light colors tend to make a room seem larger; dark colors tend to make an overly big room appear smaller.

You can "lower" a too-high ceiling by painting it darker than the walls. But painting the ceiling white (except in all-white rooms) is going out of style since most people have come to prefer ceilings painted the same color as the walls, or a slightly lighter hue, for an integrated effect.

Save money buying latex (or oil-base) so-called "ceiling paint," which is always white and flat and a few dollars cheaper than white wall paint.

Preparation for Painting

Before you paint an old wall, inspect the surface for cracks and mars. Small hairline cracks can be filled with spackle mixed to a creamy consistency brushed on or applied with a fingertip. Use a putty knife to fill larger cracks with spackle mixed to the consistency of peanut butter, but be sure to rake out any loose material with a screwdriver first, making the base of the cavity slightly wider than the surface opening, so that spackle pressed into the channel will be wedged in place when dry. A 4″-wide spring-steel putty knife is the right tool for heavy spackling. Powdered spackle is much cheaper than ready-mixed. It's easy to mix (following the directions) if you add small amounts of water intermittently as you stir vigorously until you get exactly the right consistency for the application it is intended

for. Be sure to wet wider cracks and holes with water before applying spackle. Countersink projecting "popped" nailheads slightly and fill each depression with spackle. If your spackling job cracks as it dries, sand, dust, and respackle. Prime newly spackled areas, particularly if you intend to try to cover with only one coat.

Spackling completed, wash off any obvious soil smudges, grease, or wax marks with household cleansing powder and rinse clean. Run a clean dry rag over the rest of the walls to remove dust and surface dirt. Kitchen walls and ceilings are usually covered with a condensed film of vaporized cooking grease, which may extend to the walls and ceilings of adjoining rooms. Bathroom walls and ceilings may have steamed-on soil. These surfaces must be washed with a detergent (such as Soilax or Spic & Span), or new paint will not adhere—unless you can't spare the time or haven't the stamina. Instead of washing, you can coat them with Haeuser's Enamelac and paint right over the dirt, but it's a dreadful waste of money if the surfaces are not too filthy. Sand old peeling paint and seal with a primer. Rent an electric vibrating sander for removing cracked or alligatored paint from broad areas.

Old gloss or semigloss surfaces must be "cut" to dull the shine so the new paint can get a firm hold. For best results run over them with fine sandpaper (even an entire glossy wall) and wipe them down to remove the dust. You can buy "liquid sandpaper," but regular sandpaper is quicker and cheaper and takes very little more effort since you are merely roughening the surface. A small scraper will remove blisters and chipped areas around windows and doors; feather the edges with 80-grit sandpaper. Seal bare spots with primer or with an extra coat of the paint you are going to use.

Woodwork that is flaking or was varnished should be sandpapered with 120-grit paper to remove flakes and gloss. Test a small area of stained wood to see if the stain will leech through your paint. If it does, Haeuser's Enamelac is the remedy as an undercoat.

Remove all furnishings from the room if you can; otherwise stack them at one end covered with dropcloths or newspapers, because no matter how carefully you work you're bound to splatter a little paint. Dismount light-switch and outlet plates and shine or paint them before replacing—or paint right over them to make them "disappear." Absorb spatters with a coating of vaseline over fixtures and doorknobs that can't be dismounted, or cover them with newspaper held in place with tape.

Laying on the Paint

Even "odorless" paint should be well ventilated when you work. Ventilation will also shorten drying time. Paint when the temperature is between 60° and 70° if possible. Using an extension handle screwed into the handle of your paint roller and placing the roller pan at your feet, begin by painting the entire ceiling while standing on the floor, climbing the stepladder only for touching up the edges. It's the professional way and it's quicker. Dip the roller in the trough of the pan and roll it out on the tray until it is uniformly covered. If it drips when you lift it, the roller is overloaded. If you're using an inexpensive ceiling paint, get an even coat by working across from side to side the width of the ceiling, starting each new lap before the previous one dries. If you're painting the ceiling with latex wall paint, roll it on in all directions. Because paint "hangs" on ceilings, often one coat will suffice. Paint acoustical tiles with slightly thinned flat paint (thinned with water in the case of latex paint) to keep from plugging up the holes. If any do clog, punch them out later with a toothpick.

Next, paint the wood trim. A gloss or semigloss is best for kitchen or bathroom trim. In other rooms semigloss is appropriate for woodwork. However, except for kitchens and bathrooms, many householders now paint the entire interior, ceilings, walls, and trim, with the same flat latex paint.

Use a combination of roller and brush for swiftest trim painting. Paint window frames with a narrow sash brush. Do the center of double-hung windows where the sashes meet first, then raise the bottom and lower the top to paint the remainder. Be sure to open both sashes a little wider before the paint dries completely to avoid having them

stick. Jam a wedge under a door to keep it ajar until the paint has dried.

Finally, holding a good-sized rectangle of cardboard in one hand to protect the floor and sliding it along as you go, roll the trim paint onto the baseboard. Use your brush to touch up the moldings afterward.

Be sure to wipe up spills and spatters immediately when laying on any paint, because it dries so hard within an hour it may be annoyingly difficult to remove if you wait—a water-wet rag for latex, a rag dipped in thinner for oil-base paint.

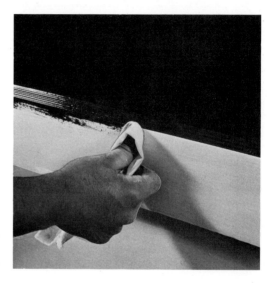

Before you begin roller-painting the walls, use your brush to "cut in" a strip of paint about a foot wide along the ceiling line. If you are right-handed, cut in the left-hand edge of the wall all the way to the floor with a foot-wide strip (southpaws go to the other edge). Apply the paint moderately slowly to the rest of the wall rolling on a big three-by-three foot W, then filling it in with long, even, back-and-forth strokes of the roller. Resort to your brush again at the bottom of the wall to cover whatever the roller may have skipped. But don't go over and over any one place with the roller; as latex dries it tends to adhere to the roller and pull back off the wall.

Equipment used for painting with latex should be washed out immediately after you are done. Any leftover paint can be saved in a labeled jar to be used for touch-ups.

How to Paint the Outside of Your House

A fresh paint job on the outside of your house is not only the least expensive and easiest way to improve its looks and make its "hide" impermeable but one of the best ways to preserve its value. The popular tendency to paint the exterior every three or four years, however, may do it more harm than good. Ideally, if you use a top-quality paint, you should not paint a wood exterior more often than once every six years, according to tests made by the U.S. Forest Products Laboratory. Painting it more often than that may build up too heavy a film. Blistering can result due to reliquification of the old paint underneath.

If the surface is dirty, first try washing it with a strong detergent like Soilax. You may discover that under that soot the paint coating is perfectly satisfactory.

But if your house does need painting, you don't need to use up a whole two-week vacation on the job. Consider using an annual long holiday weekend instead to paint just one side each succeeding year. Start with the west (usually the most weathered) side and proceed around to the south, east, and north. If there's any color difference from one side to another in doing this, the eye will never detect it, because no two sides of the house are ever seen from the same angle or with the same light reflectance. Paint the gutters, leads, and trim the fifth (or first) year. Then take the sixth one off to sit back and admire your handiwork.

How much should you pay for paint? It's poor judgment to try to save money with poor quality paint. A paint that maintains its presentability a full six years is a factor in your annual home maintenance budget.

Determine how much paint per coat to purchase by multiplying the height of your house from the foundation to the eaves, times its circumference to get the total area in square feet. Then merely divide this figure by 500, the average square-foot coverage of one gallon of house paint. If you are painting the trim a different color, a six- or eight-room house probably won't require more than a gallon.

Preparing the Surface

It's a waste of money to paint over a film that is not going to adhere to the house. You should budget the time and make the effort to carefully remove all old scaly or peeling paint. The tool most homeowners use is a hook scraper with a four-sided replaceable blade; as one edge wears down, you loosen a screw and turn to a fresh edge. Scrape the entire exterior with a firm enough pressure to convince yourself that you are removing every trace of loose and potentially detachable old paint. Make less work of this with an electrically-operated *paint-remover siding sander,* which rents for about $6 a day in most suburban communities (plus $5 for a couple of carbide disks, enough to do a house). It's a professional tool that leaves a much more uniform surface than hand scraping and gets the job done in a fraction of the time. Adjustable guides on either side of the spinning disk hold it a specific micrometric distance from the wood as it cuts away paint.

Grease or oily soot can be removed from an old surface with paint thinner. If it doesn't need sanding or scraping, old paint should nevertheless be brushed off and dusted down, or preferably, washed with a strong detergent and rinsed thoroughly with the garden hose. (The surface can be slightly damp when you paint with latex but must be dead dry when you paint with an oil-base paint.)

Then hammer in protruding nails ¼″ deep and fill in the holes as you patch any

cracks or breaks in the wood. Water-soluble compounds available at hardware stores are much cheaper, and just as durable as pre-mixed "wood plastic" if you have a lot of this sort of repair to do. Replace any rotten sections and spot-prime bare spots.

Before painting siding that contains any knots or sap streaks, clean these with paint thinner and seal them with a good knot sealer to prevent staining and cracking of the finish coat. The U.S. Forest Products Laboratory recommends the application over new wood of a water-repellent preservative containing pentachorophenol before priming. It should dry for two warm, sunny days before a prime coat is applied.

Why a Prime Coat?

Most manufacturers recommend a solvent-base primer underneath latex paint, but

don't use anything as a primer that leaves a glossy surface (such as unpigmented shellac), or your finish coat will alligator. A solvent-base pigmented primer can be painted right over a dirty or greasy surface if you haven't the time or the gumption to wash it; it kills stains, and it leaves a flat surface to which latex paint adheres perfectly. Allow the primer to dry longer than the manufacturer's label directions in humid weather, then apply the finish coats.

Caulk You Must

An important preparatory step to painting, one that is often overlooked, is the sealing of all open joints with caulking compound. It is done after the prime coat. To determine whether you need to recaulk, probe with a screwdriver. If the old compound crumbles and falls away, new caulk is required. Dig out the holes and brush it out.

Disposable cartridges of caulking compound fit into trigger-activated caulking guns; you just squeeze. Caulking seals up cracks and seams in the house against winter cold, at the same time keeping out water, insects, and rodents.

Oil-base caulk is the most commonly used and least expensive, although it bleeds through most paints. *Latex-base caulk* dries faster, shrinks less, doesn't bleed, and is not much more expensive. Use it under either latex or oil-base paints. *Polyvinyl acetate caulk* is highly mildew resistant; it does not need painting-over, but it is somewhat more expensive than the other compounds.

Caulk around windows and doors at all open places in trim and siding, at any point where two kinds of exterior siding join, at the base of wooden columns resting on concrete, and at any gaps where the wood part (plate) of the house rests on the foundation (see the photo in the following column). When applying caulk, bead laps onto both edges of the surfaces while holding the gun at a 45° angle. Force enough into the crevice to leave its surface slightly protruding rather than concave.

The Finish Coat

For new wood—such as an addition to your house—the rule is three coats, a primer and

two finish coats. But if you are short for time, ask your dealer about the possibility of a two-coat system; properly applied, the right paint over the primer intended for it will give long service. Old surfaces in relatively good condition that merely need a little sanding and dusting require only one finish coat. If the old paint is very thin, however, two top coats are recommended.

Do-it-yourselfers have long since decided that water-base latex exterior paints are so easy to use and so durable that 95 percent of American houses are painted with them. The three in general use are vinyl, acrylic, and oil-emulsion. All dry rapidly in anywhere from one-half hour to 12 hours, and most contain a mildewcide (check the label). Latex acrylics are the fastest drying, easiest to apply, and give the best results, but shouldn't be used where people will brush against them. Apply the glossier oil-emulsion-base latex at those places.

Use latex paint just as it comes, without thinning. Don't have it shaken at the store, or it will foam and may dry bubbly. It is purposely thick to be laid on with one stroke of the brush without spattering. Since it can go on over a damp surface, you don't have to wait as long after a heavy rain for the house to dry; a sudden shower or a rise in humidity while you're underway won't affect the success of the job. The quick-drying feature of latex minimizes the effect of dust or insects becoming embedded in the wet surface; but best of all, it allows you to lay on two coats the same day.

Most homeowners painting with latex use the same paint for the trim; sometimes, of course, in a contrasting or complementary color. The house paint can be used as the finish coat on downspouts, gutters, and other exterior metal work, but a primer like Rust-Oleum should be applied first on galvanized steel, the bare metal of which has become exposed or was never painted. Use house paint, aluminum paint, or exterior trim on steel or aluminum window sash. There's a special window-screen enamel, best applied with a piece of carpet glued to a block of wood and scrubbed on.

Concrete or wooden porches and steps can be painted with porch-and-deck paint. On wood, a prime coat is applied first. On concrete, an alkali-resistant primer is recommended. If you're painting entry steps that people are going to have to be using, either paint every other step and let them dry so that people (with long legs) can still use the stairs by stepping on alternate treads. Or, paint one side first, then move the traffic over to paint the other side.

When You Paint

Hold off until the weather is clear and dry and the temperature between 50° and 90° for best results; never try to paint below 40°. Wait for a windless day, preferably one when the insects are not too thick. If they get into the paint just leave them and brush them off after it dries.

On opening a gallon of paint, pour half into another container for easier handling.

Dip the brush only about one-third of its bristle length and tap off the excess against the inside of the can rather than scraping the brush against the rim, which is bad for its bristles.

The Correct Procedure

Painting begins with windows. Start with the dividing members in the window sash—and here you may prefer a narrow brush—then paint the frame, trim, sill, and apron,

in that order. Don't worry about a little paint spattering on windows. After you finish the job, a single-edge razor blade held on its side quite flat to the pane removes spatters without harm to the glass.

If the trim is to be a different color, paint all the upper parts, like dormers, before moving down to the walls. Begin painting siding high up under the eaves, either corner, it doesn't matter which, because you'll be painting with both hands on the higher parts of the house. Paint all you can reach (without leaning your belt buckle beyond the rails of the ladder) from top to base, then come down and move the ladder. Coat one wall completely before moving on to another. Save porches and steps for last.

Paint with the grain of the wood in long sweeping strokes, trying to maintain an even pressure on the brush and applying the paint from both sides of the brush with each dipping. Finish each stroke with a quick lifting motion.

As you apply paint to an unpainted area, work back into the wet edge of the pre-viously painted section. When you complete coverage of an area go over it quickly with light, long strokes to remove brush marks and even out the film.

Safety rules for painters

- Be aware that working on a ladder or scaffolding is dangerous. A fall from even a seven-foot height can result in a broken bone or spinal cord injury.
- Check out your ladder carefully to make absolutely sure that there are no weakening defects.
- Raise a long ladder by setting its feet against the base of the house, lifting the far end, and walking it up hand over hand, rung by rung until it's vertical. Then move the feet of the ladder out from the house one-fourth of the distance from the base of the house to the point of support. Position the rails firmly and evenly both on the ground and against the house. On a soft surface, place your shoes on either end of the first rung and jounce your weight evenly downward to set the feet. If the ground is wet and slippery, use a wide board under the feet of the ladder. To keep them from slipping, tie the first rung to a stake hammered into the ground a couple of feet in from the base of the ladder.
- Never climb higher than you can go and still be able to hang onto the ladder, which usually means the third rung from the top; that's as high as you should ever stand.
- Always face the ladder when climbing up or down, holding on with at least one hand, preferably with two. It's safer to haul your paint up by a string if you are working very high.
- Lean toward the ladder and keep one hand gripping it while you work. Do not overreach. Move the ladder rather than risk a fall. If the ladder is steady and secure, it is considered safe procedure to hook one knee over a rung.
- Keep a safe six-foot distance between you and any electrical wires running to your house—this is especially important in the event that you happen to be using a metal ladder.
- Wear hard-soled shoes with heels when painting for long periods on a ladder to ease the pressure on your instep from the ladder rungs.

Gearing Up for Remodeling

In a strangled housing market, house-hopping "mobile America" has slowed to a crawl. Families who had counted on improving their environment by eventually moving to a new house now have no choice but to recycle the old one. As never before, Americans are involved in remodeling, from basement to attic and beyond. In consequence, so many houses have been individualized and improved through remodeling, entire communities of built-alike tract houses have been upgraded in some areas of the U.S. For many families the motivation for "moving up" has receded; the roots are down in the old neighborhood anyway.

Remodeling an out-of-date house made up of many small rooms, "departitioning" it into fewer but larger ones, can make an old house seem new and modern. Eliminating a second-story room, floor and all, above a living room, for example, and adding new fenestration with glass soaring two stories high, can turn a cramped, suffocating living room into one of airy elegance. A relatively expensive remodeling project of this sort can make such a dramatic improvement in its standard of living, a family may feel it's worth skimping on everything else for a while to afford it.

Work with What You've Got

You will almost always find it more economical to remodel underused space than to expand your house. But try to avoid moving walls. *Re*partitioning swiftly increases the cost per square foot. And see what you can accomplish without relocating or adding a window, which can cost as much as $300 installed; or an exterior door, which can set you back $300 to $350.

Granted the bathrooms in most houses are too small, there are remodeling improvements that can make them seem larger and function better without moving walls or fixtures. A translucent hanging ceiling; a counter with a big wall-mounted mirror; or built-in shelves and cabinets.

As long as the sink is not relocated (extensive moving of water and drain pipes is costly), a kitchen can be totally made over at modest cost—with new (or refinished) doors for existing cabinets, new counters, new floor covering, new lighting—the nation's most popular home improvement and one increasing numbers of homeowners are taking on themselves. If you intend to remodel or install a bathroom or kitchen, you may pick up some ideas visiting the showrooms of suppliers of fixtures and kitchen cabinetry located in most large cities.

By the time you come to the conclusion that you are never going to be happy with a room arrangement, you have probably been experimenting in your mind with changes. As these occur to you scribble them down, even in the crudest sort of sketch. Renovating and remodeling examples that appeal to you in shelter magazines such as *Better Homes and Gardens* should be clipped and kept in a folder or mounted in a looseleaf notebook. Such sketches and clippings are useful when the time comes for you and your family to sit down together, with or without a contractor or an architect, to make final remodeling decisions.

Remodeling, Still a Good Buy

The housing industry's near-standstill has spawned one benefit: The prices of most remodeling materials have not risen as steeply as many other living costs. Although anything derived from petroleum is increasingly expensive, the cost of most home improvement materials is still reasonable. Lumber, after two years of steady increases that pushed prices up 70%, dropped sharply in 1974, in some cases to a point lower than when the 1970's spiral began.

The average do-it-yourself interior conversion can be accomplished in a series of weekends if the materials for each step are ordered, delivered, and installed before you go on to the next step. You not only spread out the workload this way, you spread out the cost—avoiding a loan. Materials for later steps are never in your way as you work.

Figuring the Costs

You'll get the quickest cost estimate for your remodeling project from a building materials supplier if you are able to tell him how many board feet of which grades of lumber you need, how many running feet of molding, how many sheets of which grade of plywood or hardboard, and how many sheets of which size and thickness of gypsum wallboard or paneling you need.

(For a big job like an addition to your house, you may be asked if your foundation is laid and you're ready to build. If you answer no, you'll probably be asked to come back when you're ready, because the cost of materials, as this is written, is fluctuating so erratically there's no point in his giving you an estimate until you're ready to go.)

But if you don't trust your skill as an estimator you can bring in a carefully drawn detailed plan of your project, and the dealer will estimate from that. Using a scale of 1″ or ½″ = 1 foot, mark all measurements in feet and inches (plus fractions of inches); graph paper is a big help. Starting in one corner of the space for remodeling, measure to the nearest window or door, taking your measurements at waist height. Continue around the room, not forgetting the height of the room and the heights and widths of windows and doors. (Show which way doors swing with curved lines made with a simple school compass.) Then add everything up to make sure the total of the individual measurements equals the overall dimensions.

You can get estimates from electrical and plumbing suppliers the same way. Just show them your scale drawing and describe your needs. They'll tell you what your local building code requires.

An expedient way to estimate costs of hardware, floor coverings, cabinets, fixtures, and appliances is to look up the prices in a Sears or Ward's catalog. There's no reason, unless you're in a great rush, not to order through the catalogs, incidentally. You'll save some money, except perhaps on exceptionally heavy items, the net cost of which may be lower locally if you can pick them up yourself and avoid shipping charges.

But catalog prices are usually a little below local merchants' prices for stock items. Where there's no difference, however, consider that if you buy locally you keep the money circulating in your own home town.

How to Hire a Contractor

On the supposition that you don't have time or the skill to tackle a major home improvement yourself, if your project is relatively straightforward, if you're sure of what you want and there are no structural complications involving load-bearing walls, should you try to be your own contractor? Only if you have the expertise and time to handle the job. Since some big remodeling projects require the services of many tradesmen, you may be better off leaving it to a professional, or you risk increasing your total cost.

A general contractor is what you need. Ask around among your neighbors for the names of good ones; ask building supply dealers; call a bank that specializes in home improvement loans. The general contractor takes on the responsibility for the complete project, dealing in proper sequence with the various subcontractors—carpenters, masons, electricians, plumbers, roofers—coordinating their efforts to make the job go smoothly and swiftly. He also knows the local building ordinances and will see that the subcontractors adhere to them.

Once you've narrowed down your choice, get estimates from two or three contractors, being careful that each bidder is given exactly the same set of specifications. Before choosing one, check his references—a couple of suppliers with whom he deals, his bank, some former customers. Make certain he has contractor's insurance; ask to see his certificate. It should cover not only workmen injured on the job but personal liability and property damage.

When you work with a contractor, you and he sign a contract that lines out the project in specific detail—the kind and quality of materials to be used, payment schedule and timetable of progress, phase by phase, from date of beginning to date of termination.

Once you've signed the contract, avoid making changes; they can shatter your budget. But put any changes in writing, along with costs involved. Such a contract should release you from liability on the long chance that the contractor might go bankrupt before he has finished your job. Otherwise, you can be held responsible for any funds he owes subcontractors or suppliers for materials intended for use on your project. Before you sign with a contractor or tackle a major improvement yourself, there are two major responsibilities you should not overlook:

To make sure that no change you are making will void any aspect of your insurance, call your (homeowners) insurance agent and tell him what you are planning to do. A rider to your existing insurance contract probably can extend your coverage.

Read over your mortgage contract to make sure the bank does not require its permission before you make an improvement on your property. If you are required to do so, you are not likely to have any trouble getting the OK from the bank, but this is a formality that should not be evaded.

The half-and-half contract: If you plan a major change to your house and believe in your ability as an amateur carpenter, you might consider having only the most difficult parts done by a contractor—building the forms yourself to have a slab floor poured by a concrete supplier directly from his delivery truck, for example. You may be able to construct the framing and install the roofing, flooring, and sheathing yourself (preferably with family help), then have a contractor take over the difficult business of joining the new roof to the existing one and blending the new exterior walls into the old. You should work this out with the contractor at your planning stage—and sign a detailed contract with him, of course.

If you build some of it yourself you will undoubtedly do a more airtight job than the average subcontractor, because you can make sure you install adequate insulation between beams, joists, and studs in an absolutely draft-impenetrable fashion, and you can carefully caulk each seam in underlayment before installing roofing, flooring, or siding. A word of warning, however: hanging a door is one of the more difficult jobs in remodeling and probably should not be attempted by any but the most experienced carpenter-handyperson equipped with excellent instructions. If the door is not

trimmed absolutely true and hung plumb, it will not fit correctly and be a constant source of irritation.

Of course, you can have the entire addition constructed for you by a contractor as a shell and still save considerably, as a "half-and-halfer", by doing the partitioning (made easier with pre-hung doors) and interior finishing yourself.

Convert to an Apartment?

Today, with mortgage money so tight, many young people getting married are having great difficulty starting a home of their own because it's so hard in most places to find a decent, affordable place to live. As a consequence, it is predictable that many, if not most, major home improvement projects in the seventies will be conversions and additions to houses—separate apartments with separate facilities but shared utilities.

Although actually a very small percentage of the total U.S. land mass is zoned for one-family housing, most suburban areas on the peripheries of cities are zoned that way. (In or near commercial districts, usually, many cities and towns have large areas of two-family zoning where carving out an apartment is not a problem.) But legal or not, it's a fact that apartments are being converted in, and added onto, existing one-family-zoned dwellings all over the country. Some communities appear to be more sympathetic to the idea than others—with officials often looking the other way. So-called "mother-in-law apartments" are usually acceptable; as soon as kitchen facilities are added, the whole house is converted, technically, into a two-family dwelling. What can happen? The occupants won't go to jail, and it's not even likely the authorities will find out unless a neighbor informs, but the owner *can* be required to rip out the entire installation—no ifs, ands, or buts—and dispossess the tenants.

In most communities, what is more, the owner is supposed to get a building permit before beginning any remodeling worth more than $200 or $300; it's a violation to remodel without one.

Some of the pitfalls thus having been made clear, suppose you still decide you want to convert space into an apartment. What's your best bet?

Many houses were built after World War II with the garage extending from the main structure. A second story can rather easily be added atop such a garage. But this is a project for which homeowners should call in a building engineer for professional advice as to whether or not the existing garage can support the addition or will have to be strengthened. Only a homeowner who is an experienced amateur carpenter should undertake an expansion of this sort, however.

Any two-car garage is an ideal (usually 20x20-foot) space for conversion into an apartment. The roof, walls, and floor are all there and the plumbing, heating, and wiring connections are usually a simple matter of tapping through the wall into the basement. The garage door can either be closed up—it faces the street in most cases—or replaced with a sliding glass wall hidden from the street by shrubbery enclosing a private patio.

(Foreseeable is the re-emergence of the carport as a home improvement for sheltering the evicted car, which is not going to be allowed to sit out in the elements and rust since cars have become so expensive and, for suburban families, a vital necessity.)

Resources for Planning

If you are seriously considering a conversion or an addition, estimating costs is a major problem. A valuable guide to the subject, newly updated in 1975, *How to "Guesstimate" Remodeling and Home Improvements,* by Peter H. Johnson, an experienced contractor, is available directly from him for $5 to: Box 226, Hasbrouck Heights, NJ 07604.

How to Renovate a Ceiling

Removing an old cracked plaster ceiling and replacing it with gypsum wallboard (Sheetrock) is a difficult and very strenuous undertaking, but not outside the realm of the accomplished home handyperson. Purchasing long sheets that span the width or length of the room greatly reduces the effort expended in taping, the most tedious part of the job. You will need help in installing big sheets of wallboard against ceiling joists.

Most do-it-yourselfers prefer to redo their ceilings with ceiling tile. Although more costly per square foot than wallboard, ceiling tiles are available at many prices depending mainly on whether or not they are sound-absorbent "acoustical" tiles, but also on texture and design.

Tiles can be cemented directly onto a ceiling that is in good condition. If it isn't, all you need is a hammer and nails to attach wood furring strips to the edges of the floor joists above—unless you select the more expensive system of hanging metal grids into which larger ceiling panels slip without fastening. A hanging ceiling of this sort is used when you want to hide pipes, ducts, or wiring—those that you still may want to get at in case of repair or remodeling.

Whatever width of tile you select, furring strips should be laid up that same width apart center to center, using 2½" nails, two into each joist. Tongue-and-groove tiles can be nailed up, but are much more easily staple-gunned against furring strips. A stapling gun rents for $3 to $4 per day, or you can buy one for $10. Tiles are stapled through the tongue at the exposed corner, then each new tile's grooves are slid over the tongues of previously emplaced ones—a very simple, swift procedure.

If you select acoustical tiles to deaden the sound in a room, don't be misled into thinking they will "soundproof" it from the rest of the house. They merely entrap reverberations within the room. On the other hand, stereo sound buffs say too much sound deadening—a combination of acoustical tile ceiling, for instance, and deep carpeting in a small room—can rob a fine hi-fi system of its "live" quality.

How to Install Wallboard

Familiar as "sheet rock," gypsum wallboard is by far the least expensive wall finishing material on the market. It is universally used to look like plaster-over-lath. A sandwich of heavy paper with a fire-resistant core of plaster-like material, its white outer surfaces are impact-resistant and durable. The standard 4-foot width comes in 8-, 10-, 12-, 14-, and 16-foot lengths in ⅜", ½", and ⅝" thicknesses.

The facing edges of panels are tapered to make room for wallboard joint compound and perforated tape, which is pressed into it with a 4"-wide putty knife to hide the joints between panels. Since relatively little

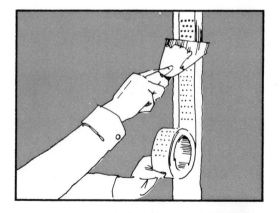

is used, one gallon of ready-mixed taping compound is sufficient to "tape" a moderate-size room. Two thin applications feathered at the edges, sometimes three, are required to make joints completely invisible.

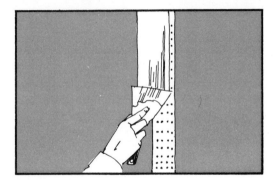

Hanging and taping wallboard is not difficult for the average home handyman. Hanging big sheets on a wall is easier with a helper.

After July, 1976, taping compound may no longer be made with carcinogenic asbestos, but there's no knowing what the manufacturers have replaced it with, so *wear a respirator when sanding wallboard joints.*

Professionals score wallboard with a sharp matte knife held against a straightedge and snap the material in two, but the surer way is to trim wallboard with a saber saw. Fit never has to be perfect, because gaps can be obliterated with compound or are covered by molding, which is one of the main reasons wallboard is such a popular remodeling material—minor mistakes are easily hidden.

So-called "annular-ring" nails (of the proper length for the wallboard thickness)

have ridges around their shanks that help them hold tightly in studding. A crown-head hammer is the preferred tool for driving the nails—a final blow slightly dimpling the surface, so that afterward a quick swipe of taping compound fills in the dimple and hides the nail heads.

Under most conditions, you save time and money laying up wallboard horizontally: if you have an eight-foot wall to span, two 12-foot panels fill the bill, eight feet (or a little more) being the standard height of walls in most houses. By laying up the first panel butting the ceiling, and the second one below it, any area not covered at the bottom is overlapped by the baseboard. The lower panel can be pressed tightly up against the long horizontal edge of the previously hung upper panel by laying a short length of wood over a block and stepping on it to lever the panel into place. Then the nails are driven in. Taping horizontal joints is easier than taping vertical ones, because you can stand on the floor and work back and forth at the four-foot level, in preference to taping up and down as you must when wallboard is hung vertically. Thus you have only the one joint, across the wall at the four-foot level, if you use molding where the wall meets the ceiling.

Corners are taped by creasing a length of perforated paper tape along the score line that runs down its middle. You can use it on both inside and outside corners. Since the latter are somewhat more difficult, however, some home handymen buy special metal corners for emplacement with taping compound; they are more resistant to impact than taped corners.

Although gypsum wallboard is undeniably the least expensive way to cover interior walls, the additional cost factors should be taken into consideration. You have to pay out for compound and tape (if not for labor). It needs a surface coating of paint, vinyl, paper, or fabric. Yet it has one long-term advantage over paneling that should not be overlooked. That's the ease with which wallboard can be repaired without a trace of damage if a hole is cut or punched in it.

How to Panel a Wall

A favorite American home renovation, wall paneling used in houses today is plywood, pressed wood, or hardboard in a variety of thicknesses, sizes, surfaces, and prices. Good-quality plywood paneling runs $5 to $25 more per 4x8-foot sheet than pressed wood or hardboard paneling. The latter are manufactured in a greater variety of colors and textures. But you have a choice of a true wood veneer or a tough vinyl facing in all three types of paneling.

What you see is not always what you get, however. Simulated wood grains, photographically reproduced either directly on the panel or printed on paper or vinyl film and laminated to it, look extraordinarily like real wood veneer. Some are even embossed to feel like wood. The more expensive paneling faced with a true wood veneer is generally reserved for living and dining areas of the house; hardboard and pressed wood paneling with washable finishes are appropriate for kitchens, bathrooms, and recreation rooms.

You can use the adhesive method to panel any smooth, flat interior wall. All you need to assemble in the way of tools is a saber saw (rentable for about $5 a day; buy a couple of veneer blades where you rent it), tape measure, hammer, chalk and string, square, level, two ¼″ shims you can easily make, caulking gun and panel adhesive in tubes. With these almost anyone can install wall paneling. Most manufacturers make color-coordinated moldings for corners, openings, and top and bottom of paneling. Check your lumberyard to be sure these are in stock before buying your panels. It's also smart to pick up the appropriate installation instructions from your supplier for the brand of panels you purchase so that you will install them according to the manufacturer's recommendations, thereby satisfying the provisions of the guarantee.

Old moldings should be removed. The surface must be clean; new gypsum wallboard should be sealed. You begin by snapping vertical floor-to-ceiling chalk lines at four-foot intervals around the room. Then run a continuous ribbon of adhesive about ½″ inside each chalk line. Horizontally, at 16″ intervals down the wall, apply 3″-long horizontal strips of adhesive 6″ apart from each other. To assure a ¼″ clearance at top and bottom for normal expansion, each panel is rested on ¼″ shims and checked with a level along its side to make

sure it's plumb before gluing. The top edge is lightly nailed and the panel pressed against the adhesive. Some 10 or 15 minutes later, with a fabric-covered block of wood between hammer and panel, it is hammered all over to ensure adhesion.

You can use the same method to panel a masonry or uneven wall, first applying vertical furring strips to the wall four feet on center over a vapor barrier, then nailing horizontal furring strips 16″ on center between the vertical ones. Continuous ribbons of adhesive are squirted onto those furring strips against which the outer perimeter of each panel will rest; strips of adhesive 3″ long and 6″ apart are squirted onto the horizontal furring strips. Then the panel is applied in the same manner as for a smooth wall, as detailed above.

Wall panels can be nailed up, but nailing is not recommended for even the most sure-eyed home handyperson because of the inevitability of surface damage to prefinished paneling from "near misses" with the head of the hammer. But if walls are too rough and uneven for the much faster, easier adhesive method, you can nail up paneling by driving the nails through the plaster or wallboard into 16″-on-center studs—one nail every 4″ around the perimeter of each panel and one every 8″ into alternate studs.

A new alternative is the Swingline Whammer, $20, a staple gun that drives 1¹/₃₂″-long 18-gauge galvanized brad-type nails that come with heads in a choice of four colors to match paneling: off-white, light, medium and dark wood tone. Whammer nails are made in continuous strips of 100 that slip into the gun like staples. They can be countersunk, but driven flush, they hardly show in paneling of near-matching color, eliminating setting and filling. The device operates on the lever principle, an internal ram driving each nail with great force with a single blow—making nailing-up of paneling much faster, with little likelihood of surface damage. Trim can be installed with the same device.

Converting an Attic

If you live in an old house with an attic, it probably isn't worth converting unless there already are stairs running up to it and unless the floor joists (ceiling joists of the room below) are strong enough to support furniture and people. If there isn't enough seven-foot headroom and the occupants would continually have to duck to get around, it probably isn't a good bet. But before discounting attic space as being too cramped, consider adding dormer windows or a single long shed dormer on the side of the roof that gets the most light. This, with a window at each end, will provide all the air circulation necessary, except in hot weather, when a small fan installed against a roofpeak vent is a consideration.

Except for dormer installation, a job that usually calls for the services of a carpenter, an attic conversion is well within the abilities of most homeowners.

Converting a Basement

Though basement rec rooms have lost favor to ground-floor family rooms, a room in the basement can be useful for a workshop; a reading, relaxing, and study retreat or office; a guest room; or a laundry.

In converting a basement, partitioning should be installed before furring strips (and insulation) are attached to concrete basement walls. The fast, easy, sure way to attach them is to rent a power stud driver, also called a "stud gun." This is an exceedingly handy professional tool for fastening furring strips to concrete quicker and more securely than by any other means—but it is a very dangerous tool and you must be

carefully instructed in its use or you risk life and limb. Special so-called "Remington Fasteners" are actually fired like bullets through the wood into the concrete, three to a furring strip—top, middle, and bottom —by separately loaded .22-cal. power-loads, special black cartridges the rental agency will sell you ($7 per 100) along with the fasteners ($14 per 100). It takes about five seconds to reload the stud driver.

New wiring and outlet boxes should be installed and heating system extensions completed before hanging the wallboard or installing the ceiling.

Adding ductwork to extend a forced-air system is not too difficult for the handy householder, a matter principally of joining prefabricated standardized parts that slide together. Your oil supplier can give you the name of a heating engineer who will come and tell you if your furnace is adequate for supplying heat for an additional room or two. Most forced-air systems are powerful enough for heating additional space, but you should make certain the blower has the strength to push hot air the added distance required of it. A hot-water system is somewhat more difficult for the householder to extend, though tools and equipment can be rented for the job. But you should know what you're doing, and have a heating engineer assure you your boiler has the capacity.

A lot of existing piping and ductwork crisscrossing the top of a basement calls for a hanging ceiling, for which you can buy special hardware—metal channels into which panels of gypsum board or acoustical tile are simply placed without fastening. Such a ceiling enables you to install translucent rigid sheet plastic under fluorescent lights. A hanging ceiling, however, requires a height of at least eight feet from the basement floor to the lower edges of the floor joists above.

If your basement floor is always dry and was laid smoothly, your best bet is vinyl-asbestos floor tile installed directly on the concrete, but if it's the least bit damp at any time of the year, it's better to cover it with a vapor-barrier plastic sheeting and install a heavy marine plywood floor resting on 2x4 sleepers. Then this plywood surface can be covered with tiles, sheet floor covering, or carpeting.

Add On to Get More Living Space

Problem: You need a bigger house. But the high costs of mortgage money, selling charges, and moving expenses make a new house too costly.

Solution: Add on. If your present house is structurally sound and the location warrants the investment, an expansion might well be the most practical answer for you.

An architect can translate your ideas into a room or apartment that meets local building codes. A remodeling contractor can save you money because he knows the most efficient tradesmen, methods, and materials to use for your project. If you have the skill and time to take it on yourself, you can get help from your building materials dealer. Often he's an authority on additions to housing. Adding-on can take many forms—rooms, wings, second stories, separate structures.

Inside or out, an addition need not match the design or style of the original house. Roof lines and siding may blend, but new full-story or clerestory windows and skylights in an expansion can provide a pleasing contrast to the usual double-hung casements of the original older house.

Today's additions often combine a sliding glass wall with a deck or patio. You can get great impact for relatively modest cost by "bumping out" part of a wall, or extending an end wall, without adding a lot of expensive square footage. Architects consider a foundation unnecessary for a projection of less than three feet, because the existing floor can so easily be cantilevered out from the structure. Zoning boards are more apt to authorize a variance, if one is required, for this type of addition than for one involving a foundation. But adding a few feet to the end of the house—and such a project definitely calls for, at the least, a contractor and quite likely an architect—may enable you not only to add new windows on the sunny side of your house to help cut the heating bills, but may let you move one or two non-load-bearing partitions to effect a radical improvement in the interior.

When to Hire an Architect

For an important expansion of your house or a significant structural change, consider hiring an architect. He charges between 10% and 15% of the cost of the project, but he earns his fee by suggesting solutions that may not have occurred to you and by preparing detailed drawings and specifications from which you (or a contractor) can get the job estimated and executed swiftly and precisely. Instead of your addition looking stuck on, an architect can assure that it will blend into or complement the existing structure, changing an ordinary house into something perhaps more dramatic, enhancing not only its appeal to you but possibly increasing its resale value. He won't charge for preliminary discussions unless those entail sketches and estimates. He can arrange for construction and take care of such legal matters as obtaining a building permit. He may even drop by from time to time to check on progress.

Find one through the local chapter of the American Institute of Architects or check the Yellow Pages. In choosing an architect, get him to show you plans and photographs of his most recent projects.

How Local Regulations Affect You

Even a small addition, with or without a deck, is likely to come under local building codes and zoning regulations. Some towns merely require that you obtain a building permit, which is hardly ever a problem, but the rules usually specify setback requirements that let you know how far your house is permitted to extend toward your property lines and toward the street. Of course, you have to know your boundaries.

Zoning regulations and building codes are usually available in pamphlet form for a small charge at your town hall. Lot-line restrictions are often a problem with a house standing on a small plot if expansion is desired at either end of the house, but an addition is usually feasible on the back of the house where setback requirements seldom limit construction.

However, the septic tank and drainage fields must be taken into consideration if your house is not connected to a town sewer, because you can't build over a tank or field or within certain code-specified distances from them. If you have no plan of your property showing the septic system, check the point where the largest pipe in your basement pierces the wall; the septic system will be in that direction outside the house. A septic tank installer can find the exact location.

Don't be discouraged from planning an addition that does not meet local zoning regulations, especially if you are restricted by setback rules. There's a good chance you can go before your town zoning board and get a variance if your proposed expansion does not detract from the neighborhood and your neighbor has no objection.

If you do go before the board, it pays to arrive well prepared with excellent arguments, as well as a familiarity with the zoning regulations that apply to your case. The board will be impressed if you have done your homework. You will probably be asked to submit detailed plans and specifications of your proposed expansion.

Building codes, as distinct from zoning regulations, apply mainly to structural considerations, load-bearing limits, framing lumber dimensions, foundation materials, and construction methods. Some go further, setting limitations on minimum room size and window size, roof pitch and other aspects of building that you should be aware of in the planning stage.

In some localities patios and paved terraces come under the code, but usually only if attached to the house so that they could conceivably become the foundation of an addition at some future time. A poured concrete slab projecting from one side of the house is likely to come under the code; a patio of bricks laid in a bed of sand probably would not. But check the code before you begin. You can often do so by phone.

If you intend to tackle a project yourself and find the code does not cover the construction method you want to employ, be sure and consult the town engineer or building inspector before you start the job. He can help you in making sure that all you put into your project will not be wasted, that you will not be asked to do it over.

In truth, the code may be helpful in planning a remodeling, even a deck you intend to construct yourself. It will give tables of minimum widths, thicknesses and spacing of floor joists, for example, depending on how broad a space they will have to span and on how much weight the floor may have to carry. This can run to a number of tons when you add up the weight of construction, furniture, and a crowd of people at a party.

Including a deck in an expansion, even a small one, invariably makes it look as if the house had been changed much more than it actually has. There are excellent suggestions for deck design in a book titled *Decks, Porches, and Patios* published by Meredith's Creative Home Library in association with *Better Homes and Gardens*, 1974.

When Do You Need a Building Permit?

Although building codes vary from town to town, you may need a building permit:
• if a conversion changes the "occupancy" of your house from a one-family to a two-family dwelling;
• if you extend or add a room;

• if you convert your garage to an apartment (with or without cooking facilities);
• if you add on a garage or a carport;
• if you install plumbing or electrical wiring and connections inside or outside the house;
• if you attach a deck to your house or intend to enclose a porch;
• if you build a retaining wall more than four feet high;
• if you install a pool more than two feet deep;
• if you build a barbecue with a chimney higher than six feet;
• if you install an underground sprinkler system for your lawn.

Your project may have to be inspected before it is finally approved. In applying for a building permit you may be asked to estimate how much your addition will cost; someone from the tax assessor's office may come out to check the job to make sure your estimate was reasonably on the beam. The value of your addition will be added to the assessed value of your house, and your taxes will rise accordingly—usually by not very much.

Putting Your Dream on Paper

The point of departure in any remodeling project is a simple sketch, a floor plan of the area as it presently exists, on which careful measurements are marked. It should show the placement of windows, doors, closets, and those built-ins that will remain in place. For even a fairly simple project it's usually imprudent to settle for the obvious solution without first exploring various creative possibilities. Consider making a scale drawing. You can use a large piece of graph paper; one inch or one-half inch should equal two feet. With a scale drawing to study you are unlikely to discover too late you have installed a window in the only logical place for bookshelves, or hung a door where it creates an inconvenient traffic pattern. You can snip out small rectangles of colored paper in the same scale as your sketch to represent the furniture that will occupy the remodeled space, trying them in different juxtapositions until you achieve what you want (see sketch in next column).

If you are seriously considering adding a room, send $1 to Information Services Division, American Plywood Association,

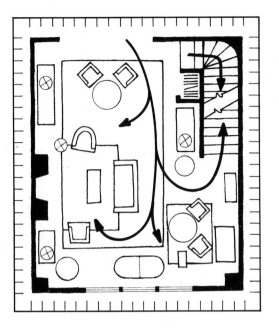

Tacoma, WA 98401 for its W605 *Add-A-Room* kit. It tells you how to research your project, finding out about codes, site limitations, and about the way your home was built—essential information preparatory to starting the design. Then it leads you by the hand in the process of developing the new space to do what you want it to in a way that harmonizes with the existing structure and permits efficient construction. For this phase the kit includes a number of inch-to-the-foot floor plan work sheets printed on heavy tracing paper, so that you can build up your final design from a rough sketch. Finally, there are work sheets that spell out in detail exactly how the construction process is accomplished; these include step-by-step photographs of an actual addition.

Save By Scheduling

Try to schedule a home improvement project for which you've hired tradesmen during what amounts to their off-season. Spring is the peak period for remodeling, fall running a close second, when good craftsmen are usually swamped with work. Winter is the time to hire—some contractors even charge less then than at other times of the year. Incidentally, if you've hired tradesmen to work on a remodeling, make certain that all the required materials have arrived before the workmen show up. Shortages will continue to delay deliveries. Check out shipments for damage and count the items the moment they arrive.

How to Buy Wood

In the strange world of lumber, you do not get what you pay for. Length remains a constant—if you order a six-foot board, it will be six feet long. But width and thickness will be the so-called "nominal" dimensions of the board after it was sawed from the log but before it was milled. Thus if you order a six-foot 2x4 you will receive a six-foot piece of lumber that is only 1½"x3½" (it used

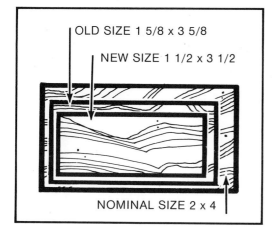

OLD SIZE 1 5/8 x 3 5/8

NEW SIZE 1 1/2 x 3 1/2

NOMINAL SIZE 2 x 4

to be 1⅝"x3⅝"). This is the "actual" size, so-called. *Nominal* and *actual* dimensions are standardized.

Following are nominal and actual dimensions for the more widely purchased sizes:

Nominal	Actual
1x2	¾x1½
1x3	¾x2½
1x4	¾x3½
1x6	¾x5½
1x8	¾x7¼
1x10	¾x9¼
2x4	1½x3½
2x6	1½x5½

There are three grades of *select* and five grades of *common* lumber. *Select* lumber is of top quality intended for use where appearances are paramount; *common* lumber, which has various defects, is appropriate for construction wherever a few knots and other irregularities are of no consequence.

The unit commonly referred to in purchasing lumber is the "board foot", which represents the amount of wood in a one-foot piece 12" wide x 1" thick. To figure board feet multiply *nominal* width and thickness in inches by the number of feet, then divide the result by 12. For example, the number of board feet in a piece of stock 9 feet long, 8" wide and 2" thick would be:

$$\frac{9 \text{ ft. x } 8'' \text{ x } 2''}{12} = \frac{144}{12} = 12 \text{ board feet}$$

Molding (and sometimes furring strips and 2x4s) is sold by the "linear" or "running" foot. This merely means that the item is sold strictly by its length; neither its width nor its thickness are of any concern in estimating costs.

Ways to save on lumber

• If you need clear lumber without blemishes or knots, look over the selection of common grade first. Most lumberyards will let you pick and choose if you don't take too long about it. Some parts of all pieces of common lumber are clear. By purchasing enough common you can cut away the blemished parts and wind up with as much good clear as you need. You may have to haul home twice as much wood to get enough clear for the project you are working on, but you'll still save a considerable amount. Clear lumber costs three times as much as common.

• Save a couple of dollars on each panel of so-called "shop" plywood, stamped with the word SHOP, meaning it's imperfect—a gouge, broken corner or two, or "sand-throughs" in the veneer. If you cut away the damaged parts you may have enough plywood left for your project. As much as 90 percent of the panel might be all right.

• When you have a small project look over the pieces of plywood in your lumberyard's cut-up bin. You may have to pay the same price per square foot as for a full panel (ask for a discount), but you won't have any unused material left over after you complete your project.

• You can often buy prefinished panels that have been damaged at the edges at a discount. These were destined for wall paneling, but you can use them for other projects.

How to Drive Your Car for Less

If you're at all typical, transportation costs now are the third largest component of your cost of living. They are surpassed only by food and shelter, and amount to 12-15 percent of your usual expenditures (excluding taxes).

Of transportation costs, car ownership is the largest item. You can restrain this hungry budget-eater with care and knowledge, and it has become urgent to do so. By 1976, the average cost of owning and operating an intermediate-size car had reached $1,831 a year for 10,000 miles—18.3 cents a mile. Back in the cheap old days of 1965, the cost was $1,177 a year or 11.8 cents a mile, and that was for a full-size car.

Where does that money go? The American Automobile Association had a cost breakdown computed by Runzheimer & Co., auto accountants, based on what it takes to own and operate a 1976 eight-cylinder intermediate-size car. Costs of gas and oil, maintenance, and tires came to $645, or an average of 6.45 cents per mile for 10,000 miles. Insurance—fire and theft, collision, property damage, and liability coverage—amounted to $383, and $30 was alloted for license and registration fees. Depreciation, the greatest single expense, was $773.

Those costs don't include finance charges, which typically can add another $250 a year, nor do they include the yield foregone on any cash investment.

This section of the book tells you how to cope with those and other costs of car ownership; what you can do to counteract the high cost of gas; how to choose a competent auto repair shop, and how to beat high repair costs; and finally, what you need to know when you shop for a new or used car.

How to Save on Gas

Americans were more than merely startled when the price of gasoline skyrocketed in the mid-1970's. We've become dependent on cars not only for travel and community life but even to reach jobs and essential services. Thus, genuine anxiety has developed over the high cost of fueling what has become, probably more than it needed to, an essential part of living.

Obviously we can expect gas prices to remain high as long as world energy demands continue to outrun the supply, likely to be a long-term condition. At the same time that the tag on gas has risen, modern cars consume more, mainly because of increased use of accessories such as air conditioning and power-assisted controls, all requiring larger engines.

In fact, in the mid-1970's for the first time, fuel surpassed depreciation as the main car expense for many owners.

How much gas you use depends on a host of factors, many of which are controllable to at least some extent:

1. The weight of the car
2. The size of the engine
3. Optional equipment
4. Where you drive
5. Your driving habits
6. The design of the car
7. How you maintain your car
8. How much you use your car
9. Type of tires you have

Car Weight

An analysis of mileage tests by the U.S. Environmental Protection Agency indicates that weight is the single most-decisive factor. In general, 500 pounds more weight can slash gas mileage 14-20 percent. Other factors equal, a 3000-pound car may get 30-40 percent more mileage than one weighing 4,000. Carrying unnecessary heavy objects in your car also can reduce mileage.

In general, and as the table in this chapter shows, compacts and sub-compacts usually get about twice the mileage of full-size cars; 26 to 33 miles per gallon (mpg) compared to 14-18. In between are the intermediates, usually averaging 18 to 25.

If you own a large car, and drive 10,000 miles a year, you can figure that you may use 600-700 gallons a year at an annual cost of about $400.

Engine Size

Big engines usually enhance performance but reduce mileage. If performance is a main consideration, often you can save money by buying the top model of a manufacturer's lowest-price line rather than the smallest size engine in his next highest line.

But don't buy a bigger engine than you really need. As one example, government tests found that one six-cylinder model yielded 18 mpg in city driving and 20 on the highway. In comparison, the eight-cylinder model of the same make yielded only 13 in the city and 20 on the highway. An overly big engine in a small car even may cancel the gas economy of lower overall weight. Thus, one compact-class car with a 140-cubic engine yielded 18 mpg in the city and 26 on the highway. But the same car with a 302-inch engine recorded only 10 in the city and 18 on the highway.

Optional Equipment

The increasing amount of optional equipment now loaded on cars, including small ones, is a factor in the steady increase in car weights to the extent that by 1976 the average intermediate-size car weighed about as much as 1972 full-size models.

Nowadays most family car buyers choose automatic shift. Manual shift is more often found on sub-compacts, compacts and sports cars. Cars with mechanical shift do usually get one to three more miles per gallon. In the case of very-small cars, manual shift can save four to five mpg.

Where You Drive

Some models give significantly more mileage in city driving; others, on the highway. If you do more of your driving in traffic, as do most people, look for a model with a higher rating in that kind of driving. If you usually rack up more mileage on highways, scrutinize the ratings for improved mileage there. Some models have a variation of as much as 11 miles between city and highway; others, as little as two.

Models from even the same manufacturer may vary. For example, in the 1976 tests the Buick Skylark got 16 mpg in the city and 22 on the highway. But the Buick Skyhawk with the same six-cylinder engine yielded 17 in the city and 26 on the highway.

You can get the most recent issues of the EPA Gas Mileage Guide at no cost by writing to Fuel Economy, Consumer Information Center, Pueblo, Colorado 91009. Some dealers also have copies of the guide. Cars sold in California may differ from the rest of the country in gas mileage because of state laws governing emissions, and so are listed in a separate booklet. Dealers are supposed to put stickers on new cars showing the mileage performance. But the program is voluntary and you may have to ask for the information.

Driving Habits

Besides conserving car use, conservative driving is the simplest way to get more mileage. Jackrabbit starts, driving unnecessarily in low gear, racing for the red light, hard braking, sudden stops—all consume more gas. Keeping an even speed helps take advantage of momentum. So does coasting to stop signs and other stops.

If you have air conditioning, don't use it unnecessarily. A government study found that at 40-50 mpg, use of the air conditioner increased gas consumption 10-15%.

Mileage drops especially sharply at speeds over 40 miles per hour. If you get 18 mpg at 40, you can expect only 16 at 50 and 14 at 60. In general, you can expect fuel use to increase about 33 percent more at 70 than at 50.

Winter usually increases consumption, especially if you live where you need snow tires. It isn't necessary to warm up before starting off. Simply drive slowly the first several miles.

Many drivers tend to pump the pedal when starting in winter. However, as every model differs, you'd better check your owner's manual for cold-start advice. You may need only to depress the pedal once.

It's especially vital to try to consolidate trips in winter. The unassailable fact is that an engine runs at maximum efficiency only when fully warmed-up. In cold weather it takes six miles of driving even to approach 70 percent efficiency. Yet, over half of all car trips are five miles or fewer.

Excessive idling is a common waster, often done in the mistaken belief that restarting the engine will use more gas. If you have to wait more than one minute, it pays to shut off the engine.

All the drivers who competed in the Mobil Economy Run used vacuum gauges in their training cars to habituate themselves to feed gas lightly and evenly. A vacuum gauge is an instrument, resembling a speedometer in appearance, which can be attached to the dashboard. The movement of the needle on the gauge shows the driver how much gas he is feeding into the combustion chamber. The gauge will show a sharp drop with erratic tromping on the gas pedal. A reading of eight or below shows that wastefully large amounts of gas are being used. If the driver can keep the needle above 12 on acceleration, and higher at constant speed, he is using gas economically.

Gauges are available at around $15, and can be self-installed or installed quickly by a mechanic.

Pollution control findings

Some dealers have claimed 15-17 percent savings on gas by removing pollution-control equipment from 1973-74 cars. Those models suffered greatest mileage loss because of pollution controls. But auto consultant George Freund has warned that owners can harm engines by removing such equipment as the air pump which recirculates gas fumes a second time. The engine is designed to work with the pollution controls; for example, by providing a lean gas mixture.

Tests by the EPA did find that removal of the controls by highly-skilled and equipped technicians resulted in mileage gains averaging 7 percent. But when the work was done by mechanics in service garages of various types, most of the cars actually lost economy even though emissions increased greatly.

Car Design

A car's design also affects fuel economy, EPA's tests have found. Even if the frontal areas of two cars are the same size, the one with the more streamlined shape will incur less drag and use less fuel.

A numerically-lower axle ratio usually saves gas compared to a higher value. Although it produces the same power, the engine runs slower for any given vehicle speed and therefore has less internal friction and throttling losses to overcome.

Fuel economy gains of more than 10 per cent during highway conditions are possible with overdrives. Other optional equipment that helps save gas includes fuel injection and electronic spark ignition.

Maintenance

Keeping a car in efficient operating condition also helps conserve high-priced gas. Proper maintenance is still only a relatively small part of a car's total expense. A tuned car will average 6 percent better fuel economy than an untuned car.

In general, the items affecting fuel economy that require periodic maintenance include air filters; the ignition system (spark plugs, distributor points, ignition timing); carburetor and proper air-fuel mixing; servicing the front wheel bearings as recommended; cylinder compression; and lubrication. Wheels out of alignment also waste gas.

Especially watch out for dirty air filters, which can cut mileage 10 percent; a slow-acting or stuck choke; engine idle set too high (but it needs to be set high enough to guard against stalling); dragging brakes; stuck heat control or thermostatic valve, and too-thick motor oil.

Amount of Use

About one-third of all auto mileage is for commuting to work. Even if you double up with just one additional commuter, your out-of-pocket expenses would be halved. Car pooling also may help you get along with just one car.

For local driving, another important saver is combining errands and combining trips with friends and neighbors, especially in winter as previously noted, but also in general. Short trips are your biggest gas users. An EPA study found that a test car's normal 13.5 mileage dropped to 11 on a ten-mile trip, and down to 5 on a one-mile jaunt due to the inefficiency of engine warmup when choking occurs.

Tires Are a Factor

Radial tires save up to 10 percent of gas, but you need them all around. You can't mix radials and bias-ply tires. But any tires get more gas mileage fully inflated. Five pounds of underinflation wastes a half gallon of gas every 20 gallons.

How to Shop for Gas

A survey by San Francisco Consumer Action offers shopping clues for families in other localities too. The survey documented the fact that stations that post prices most prominently, tend to charge least for gas. These most often were independents, and their average prices were three to five cents less a gallon than the name brands.

The consumer group found even larger differences in prices among stations selling the same brands; a range in one case of 56 to 65 cents. Actually even different brands of gas vary little. The U.S. Bureau of Mines found that gas varied more in different seasons and areas than among different brands sold in an area.

Don't buy premium gas if all you need is regular. The additional lead content is wasted if your car's compression ratio does not require the higher octane. You also pollute the air more.

You get a little more gas if you buy in the cool of the morning rather than in the hot hours when gas expands. Too, try to park in shade to prevent evaporation.

Don't let station attendants overfill your tank. Tell them to stop at the first cutoff on the automatic pump. This will eliminate any chance of the waste of spillage.

In the winter, keep your tank full to minimize condensation. But otherwise, a full tank means extra weight and extra gas consumption.

In time of high prices, it's important to be alert to tricks which may raise costs further. Observe whether the meter on the pump reads zero before it starts filling your tank.

How to Choose a Competent Auto Repair Shop

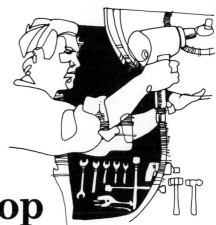

Complaints about car repairs usually are at or near the top of every agency's consumer grievance list. They usually are of three kinds: inadequate warranty service; fees which may vary sharply among different shops; and faulty repairs (sometimes even unnecessary replacement of parts).

Among the questions to ask in selecting a repair shop are:

What do others think of the shop? Ask other owners about their experience with local shops. Also note if the shop seems busy. All those people can't be wrong.

Does the shop use modern test equipment? A well-equipped shop should have and use voltmeters, engine operation and vacuum gauges, and distributor gauges.

Does the shop look well-organized? Mechanics themselves judge service shops by their appearance. They know that a clean, well-organized shop is better able to handle a car efficiently. Admittedly a dirty shop may have a top-notch mechanic. But the shop's appearance does often reflect the attitude of the owner and mechanics toward your car.

Does the serviceman diagnose carefully? A careful mechanic makes adequate tests before he will say what the trouble is. A less-skilled or less-careful serviceman is more apt to give a flash diagnosis. For example, if the difficulty is insufficient power in a comparatively new engine, a careful mechanic will use either a dynamometer (which simulates road conditions) or at least, hand instruments, and also road-test the car. Or, before telling you that you need a new battery, he'll not only test the old one but also the generator and voltage regulator. The extra time he spends will save you money.

Is the shop experienced in your make of car? While some general mechanics are highly skilled, on balance it's usually safest to use a trained specialist in your particular make or accessory. Specialists have the specific parts and are factory trained.

Does the shop use high-pressure tactics? Some shops tend to oversell to transient customers. A scrupulous mechanic will advise you on your needs but won't high-pressure you, and often may advise that you don't need something you think you want. He won't sell you a set of plugs merely because you've had yours a certain number of miles, but will test them to make sure.

Does the shop do preventive maintenance? A good shop tries to locate incipient troubles while still small. For example, it will check spark-plug gapping to make sure plugs fire properly. It will hydrometer-test your battery periodically and recommend regular lubrication. A well-greased car not only minimizes chassis wear, but saves gas and engine wear because the chassis has less friction to overcome. According to a leading repair specialist, a regularly serviced car rarely needs as many or as costly repairs as the one that doesn't come into the shop until trouble appears. Grease and oil are cheaper than metal.

Beat Those High Repair Costs

Car repair costs have jumped more than any other car expense—70 percent just from 1967 to 1975. As people hold on to their cars longer, and as repair prices pyramid, more owners are trying to do some of their own servicing.

Take a course: Adult education courses in car repairs are expanding. Some public schools now offer advanced as well as basic courses. Fees for these courses usually are under $15. In the larger cities, the auto-servicing courses often are offered at the local vocational and technical high schools.

Some courses are offered especially for women, and they've proved popular. Classes usually are a moderate 15 to 20 students. Instruction usually is 25 percent theory and 75 percent actual work on engines.

Even libraries are getting into the act. Some have established collections of auto repair manuals. One library, in Plainedge, N.Y., now has a collection of auto repair tools it lends to library members.

Do it yourself: Another trend is to do-it-yourself repair shops which provide bays, lifts, tools, and sometimes even classes and advice by experienced mechanics. Such shops often have evening and weekend hours for the convenience of working people and, in fact, are usually busiest on Saturdays. At a leading U-Do-It shop, in Long Island, New York, one researcher found that most of the users were men, with perhaps 5 percent women. The men were blue-collar workers who knew what they were doing but could use some guidance from the manuals available at each lift or from mechanics also on hand.

The mechanics advise but don't do any actual work unless engaged for jobs the do-it-yourselfers don't want to tackle or don't have time to complete.

Those who join the instruction club sponsored by the shop pay $2.50 an hour for the lift. Non-members pay $4.90 an hour for the use of a lift and a box of 50 tools.

The lifts are operated by a floorman. Parts are available at prices claimed to be competitive with the big parts catalogs such as Sears and Whitney.

The aim of the do-it-yourselfers, of course, is to beat the repair charges of $12 or more an hour, exclusive of parts. Hourly charges by 1975 were as high as $20 in some cities. The jobs car owners tackle most often are exhaust systems, tune-ups, and oil changes. An oil change may save one-third to one-half the cost of the oil, paying 60-70 cents a quart instead of 90-95. But what makes doing it yourself even more worthwhile is the chance to lubricate the car when it is up on the lift, and even to rotate tires.

Another popular money-saver at the self-service shops is batteries at below-market prices for self-installation. The procedure is simple. The car owner just unhooks the two clasps, removes the battery, and discards the old clasps which usually are rusted out. The new battery (filled with acid) is put into place and the new clasps are hooked on.

Car owners also often use the do-it-yourself shops to tighten brakes and install new brake discs or linings.

Well-equipped do-it-yourself shops also usually have wheel-alignment and diagnostic machines such as engine performance testers, usually operated only by the mechanics but with customers allowed to observe the diagnosis.

Auto co-ops: In several areas car owners have banded together to establish their own service facilities. Philip Dodge, midwest representative of the Cooperative League, reports that questions on how to establish various kinds of service co-ops have become the most-frequent question he gets. In Ann Arbor, Michigan, a group of students set up a prototype auto-service co-op offering courses in maintainance, with members learning to tune their own cars in a six-weeks class.

In Boston, members of a low-income neighborhood co-op built themselves a grease rack to do their own greasing and change oil; they also buy tires, batteries and accessories, and oil, at reduced prices.

On a much larger scale, the co-op supermarkets in Berkeley, California and Greenbelt, Maryland, own and operate their own stations, which also serve non-members.

A group of car owners in Palo Alto took a somewhat different approach. They organized the Briarpatch Co-op Auto Shop. It provides service by mechanics but also rents space to members to work on their cars, and sponsors clinics to teach how to tune up cars and do brake repair jobs.

Owner manuals: Many car owners could save on routine maintenance and protect against overcharges if they merely became familiar with their owner manuals. The manual tells you what service is needed and when, and, more importantly than many owners seem to realize, what service you *don't* need, especially on modern cars. For example, you may find, depending on your make and model, that you may need to add transmission fluid but never actually need to replace the factory-fill fluid and filter. You also may find that your manual does not recommend special engine additives which many service stations sell and that even lubrication and tune-ups may not be needed as often as formerly. Improved wheel bearing seals require less frequent lubrication.

Your manual specifies the actual maintenance your car needs and when, such as replacement of various filters and oil changes. The manual also specifies what grades of oil and types of fluids to use.

Because of the variations in recommended time intervals among various makes and models, it's no longer possible to use rules of thumb for periodic maintenance needed for all cars. For instance, intervals for oil-filter changes range from 6,000 to 15,000 miles. A table of preventive maintenance is provided in this chapter with the proviso that you need to refer to your own manual, if available, for more specific information.

Repair manuals: You can get a full repair manual for your car by requesting one in writing from the factory. They usually cost $2 to $8. All dealers have their own copies for each year and model. If your dealer is cooperative and not afraid he'll lose your

service business, he can help you get a copy through his contacts with factory zone representatives.

When you buy a new car, it's a good idea to stipulate in the contract that you will only take delivery if the dealer supplies you with the car's *complete* repair manual (there sometimes are two sections).

Such shop manuals have more technical detail than even the booklets that now come with the smaller cars, and have repair diagrams and illustrations of the various parts.

Your library probably also has copies of the general repair manuals such as Chilton's. These big books usually cover most American cars plus some foreign makes for several years. They provide repair and maintenance specifications and service procedures, with illustrations. The Chilton manual itself is $10.95 as this is written, and is available from stores, or plus postage of 94 cents, from the Chilton Book Company, Radnor, Pennsylvania 19089. The similar *Motor's Auto Repair Manual* is the same price. Petersen's Manual, *Basic Auto Repair,* was $3.95 at this writing.

While not to be considered actual service manuals, a number of useful booklets are available from industry sources. For owners who don't want to do actual repairs themselves, these booklets provide informative descriptions of the various car systems, inspecting techniques, and needed maintenance The *Handbook for Automobile Maintenance* is available for 35 cents from AIC Handbook Automotive Information Council, 666 Fifth Avenue, New York, New York 10019. Another informative booklet is *How to Get Along With Your Car,* available from Texaco dealers for $1.

Car Owning Made Easier, while promoting Ford service, is genuinely informative. It's 50 cents from Ford Parts and Service Division, Public Relations Department, One Parkland Boulevard, Dearborn, Michigan 48126. Make check payable to Ford Motor Company.

Simple Preventive Checks

Checks you can make yourself once a month or sooner, or have done when you get gas:
●Oil level in crankcase (after engine has stopped running for three or four minutes to allow oil to drain back into crankcase).

●All lights, for burned-out bulbs. If a headlight is out, the whole unit must be replaced and aligned with an aiming machine.

●Battery water level and cleanliness of terminals. Use a solution of baking soda and water to wash away corrosion—the baking soda neutralizes acid spillovers—then wipe the terminals with petroleum jelly to retard further corrosion.

●Windshield washer fluid level and condition of wiper. To restore resiliency rub the blade with a sponge dipped in ammonia.

●Water level in radiator. (Check only with radiator cold and don't overfill. While you may not need to drain antifreeze in summer, do add rust inhibitor.)

●Air filter cleanliness (see information later in this chapter).

●Condition of tires: tread depth, air pressure, any objects caught in tread, any cuts, uneven tread wear.

●Condition of radiator hoses and fan and generator belts.

Checks that you or a mechanic should make for you periodically:

●Transmission fluid. Check when it's hot, preferably twice a week.

●Level of brake fluid in master cylinder; check about once a month. If fluid diminishes, look for the cause, such as a leak.

●Fluid level in power steering. Same as above; loss may be indicated by whining sound in steering wheel movement.

●Strength of radiator coolant in very cold weather. If any loss has occurred, look for radiator leaks.

●Inspect ignition wires. Cracked, damaged or faulty wiring or cables must be replaced; all distributor cables should be clean and connected properly.

Other checks and tests you can practice in everyday driving or from time to time:

●Test brake pedal action. Cars with power brakes must have engine running. Excess pedal travel indicates worn linings or need for adjustment. Hold the brake pedal down with *moderate* pressure for sixty seconds to check for gradual "loss of pedal".

●Watch tail pipe smoke. Blue smoke means too much oil is getting into the combustion chambers. A lot of blue smoke is a warning that piston rings (also intake or exhaust valves and guides) may need replacing. Black smoke indicates too much gas in the air-fuel mixture. Your carburetor may need an adjustment. White smoke is mostly water vapor and usually you need not worry. It's especially noticeable on cold days. One other possibility is a broken head gasket.

●Check shock absorbers. Loss of shock-dampening power affects steering control and braking, also prematurely wears out tires, injures front end, transmission, and other components. Visual inspection may reveal leaks. A simple bounce test will tell whether your car needs new "shocks". There's one at each wheel; simply push down hard. A properly operating shock absorber will level out after one complete down and up oscillation. Any further movement indicates loss of holding power.

Some authorities say that an even more conclusive way to test "shocks" is to drive the car on a smooth road at about ten miles per hour while tapping the brake pedal repeatedly. If this sets up a rocking motion with front end dipping and rising alternately, the shock absorbers require replacement.

●Check wheel alignment and balance. An out-of-line wheel can increase tire wear by as much as 50 percent. An unbalanced wheel causes uneven tread wear. Have alignment and balance checked twice a year.

Easy Ways to Protect Your Car

●Save brake linings. Anticipate slowdowns. When you see you must slow down, take your foot off the accelerator slowly and let the engine's compression do some of the job. Always keep the master brake cylinder full of heavy-duty brake fluid. Also avoid running down long hills holding down your brake pedal. Shift to a lower gear.

●Don't race your engine to warm up. This doesn't help, and increases engine wear. A short period of idling followed by slow driving for the first few minutes will properly warm up the engine. Also avoid shutting off the engine immediately after a long high-speed drive.

● Wash off road salt. The body structure as well as finish can be eaten away.

● Keep chrome clean. This avoids pitting which lets in water that can cause rust.

● Fix scratches in the finish. Scratches expose metal which may then rust. Until scratches can be refinished, a dab of touch-up paint or strip of cellulose tape can help prevent rust. Clear nail polish can be used to cover scratches in chrome.

●Clean seats. Use a baking soda solution for vinyl seats, rinse and dry. This removes grease and soil without scratching. For cloth upholstery and floor rugs, use a mild soapy solution with tint dye of the same color.

●Put masking tape over locks at night. This helps prevent locks from freezing. If a lock is frozen, heat the key before inserting it.

Do-It-Yourself Repairs

How much repair and maintenance can you undertake to do yourself?

Much depends on the make of car, as well as your own knowledge, time, and mechanical ability. Some tasks that you may now have done by service garages certainly are simple enough to do on any car. These include obvious needs as adding oil yourself at 45-60 cents a quart instead of paying 90 cents or more; buying anti-freeze at stores—even now supermarkets and big drug stores—and installing yourself at typical savings of 30-40 percent; installing new air filters, and other needs some of which are described later in this chapter.

Other service needs, however, are relatively simple to accomplish on small cars, such as installing new oil filters, but are more complicated on cars with a greater clutter of additional equipment under the hood such as air conditioning, automatic controls, air pollution pumps, etc. Reconditioning or installing spark plugs is relatively simple on four and six-cylinder cars. But spark plugs on V-8's are harder to reach and require a special wrench.

Even changing oil, while basically simple, is difficult to do without a lift since the engine must be level to let all the oil drain out.

In general, most of the smaller four- and six-cylinder cars are easier to service. You may be able to do more than you realize. Often friends now get together to buy the necessary tools for tune-ups.

The increased availability of parts is an aid to do-it-yourselfers. Even some supermarkets now carry such maintenance items as minor tune-up kits and filters as well as engine oil and antifreeze. Jobbers, as well as retail auto-supply stores, recently have been more willing to sell parts directly to car owners. Don't hesitate to comparison-shop. We found differences of 10 to 15% on parts even among low-priced dealers.

The well-known Whitney catalog is especially extensive in listings of parts, accessories, tools, and manuals for specific makes. The general catalog is $1 from J.C. Whitney & Co., 1917 Archer Avenue, Chicago, Illinois 60680. Smaller Whitney catalogs of parts for specific models and years are available free.

Sears has discontinued its general catalog of auto and truck parts but extensive listings are available in both Sears' and Ward's general catalogs. Sears also has two specialized parts catalogs: *Imported Parts* and *Jeep and Scout Parts*. These are available at no cost from Sears stores or by writing to Department 628, Sears, Roebuck and Co., 303 East Ohio Street, Chicago, Illinois 60611. You also can get Montgomery Ward's imported car catalog from the Ward catalog house in your region.

Here's a summary of some of the maintenance and repairs that owners with reasonably good mechanical ability and car experience often do themselves.

Checking hoses, belts: This is one of the most important inspections you can do. A ruptured water hose can spill out your anti-freeze right in the middle of a cold spell. A loose or worn belt can affect car performance or even sideline your car. Replacements can be installed without special tools as discussed later in this chapter.

It's advisable to keep an eye on the condition of hoses, belts and even the radiator cap after two years when deterioration begins to appear.

Most belts look all right on top, even when in poor condition. But cracks on the underside are made worse by flexing and belts can break without warning. Glazing and slick, hard sides reduce battery power and cause overheating. Grease-softened undercore and slick sides cause slipping and torn rubber. Reeling or frayed undercore at the bottom corners cause the belt to run rough and fail.

While checking the condition of V-belts, make sure they're properly tensioned. A loose and slipping belt slows fan, pump, and generator, impairing cooling causing over-heating and sometimes even battery failure.

Generally, tension is proper when belts can be pushed down about ¼″ at midpoint.

Many hose defects can be spotted by looking, but also check for softening or hardening by squeezing the hose. Rubber hoses should be firm, but not brittle. Look for cracks and breaks which cause leaks that can't be stopped by tightening the clamps. If cracks go to the cords, replace the hose. Swelling or spongy ends may indicate that the hose has been ruined by oil or grease. Worn clamps should be replaced when they no longer can be tightened. If you replace a hose, it is always advisable to replace the clamps.

Antifreeze coolant: Owners who usually drive no more than 10,000 miles a year are safe in using an antifreeze solution for two years, government experts say. As noted, you would need to add rust inhibitor and also often remove the radiator cap when cold and inspect for rust and other floating particles. You or a service station attendant can measure the strength of the solution with an antifreeze tester called a hydrometer. It will show the freezing point of a sample of the solution. If temperatures in your area sometimes fall below that reading, you can drain some of the old solution and add pure new antifreeze if you are near your desired freezing point. If you replace the entire solution in very cold areas, use a fresh solution of half antifreeze and half water which will protect to −34 degrees. If you want to protect down to −12 degrees, use 40 percent antifreeze, and down to 0 degrees, 33 percent.

Because coolant capacity in modern cars is limited by the clutter under the hood, the cooling system must work harder. Thus, it has become additionally important to keep it in good condition. You can drain the antifreeze into pans before flushing cooling system with a hose equipped with a flush adapter.

If you drain the system you need to open the engine drain plug as well as the radiator drain cock, or more than half the old solution may remain.

But always consult your owner's manual. On some late-model engines you need to disconnect the lower radiator hose. A car with an air conditioner may have to be flushed while the heater is turned on and the engine running.

By adding a cleaning solution before flushing, you can clean the cooling system at the same time. If rust or loose scale is visible in the top radiator tank or in the drained coolant, you may need to use a heavy-duty cleaner.

Air filter replacement: This is one of the simpler self-maintenance tasks but an important one. It should be done about every 10,000 miles or once a year but more often in short-distance slow driving or industry areas. When the filter gets clogged, idling becomes rough because not enough air enters the carburetor. Gas mileage will drop and the car may even stall. The filter housing is the round metal container on top of the engine in most cars. Just remove the wing nut, take out the old element and replace with a new one.

It may not be worth trying to clean the element by air pressure since damage may result. Too, in replacing the wing nut don't tighten it too hard as it may distort carburetor throat and cause the automatic choke to stick and not close when the engine is cold, causing hard starting.

Oil filter replacement: While almost half of all owners change their own oil filters, they have become somewhat more difficult to replace in the growing clutter and vanishing space under the hood. The filter should be changed at every second oil change. Habitual short-distance slow driving in cold weather may require more-frequent changes since the oil collects more impurities in such conditions and breaks down quicker.

As noted, oil changes may best be done by service stations. The car must be level, the job is messy, the old oil must be discarded. The oil must be hot when changed or most of the sludge won't drain out of the crankcase, thus wasting your money. If you are having a mechanic change the oil you may as well have him replace the filter.

If you do replace the oil filter yourself, note in the manual the type required for your car. To remove the screw-on type filter you need an oil filter wrench. Before putting in the new filter, be sure to remove all oil residues—with a rag for the screw-on type and suction pump for the cartridge type. Make sure the oil filter gasket is properly seated or an oil pressure leak will occur. Double-check after installation by running the engine and observing any leaks around the top of oil filter.

Fan belt replacement: As noted, a worn or frayed or dried-out fan belt can be seen and sometimes heard. A frayed belt makes a slapping sound or if too loose may squeal when the engine is suddenly accelerated. A single belt is simple to replace. You loosen the alternator support bolts, incline the unit toward engine, take the old belt off and replace with new one, and tighten alternator back to original position (you may have to use a crowbar gently for leverage).

Dual and triple belts are much more complicated and should not be attempted by a novice. Such belts would be used in cars with power steering pumps, air conditioning compressors, and recirculation pumps.

As noted, radiator hoses are simple to replace. Just be sure to drain the antifreeze and use the right size replacement hose.

Shock absorbers: Tests which indicate the condition of "shocks" were described earlier in this chapter. Shocks are comparatively simple to replace. Usually rust remover has to be used on the old bolts, and it's best to jack up the end you are working on, and use jack stands to support the axle or frame.

Never replace just one shock; both front or both rears need to be replaced at the same time. Be sure to use the proper replacements for your model. So-called "heavy duty" shocks are satisfactory. The costlier "super duty" need only be used for habitual driving under heavy load or for light-duty trucks.

Ignition wires: Visual inspection of the wires leading from the distributor to spark plugs usually will indicate wear or cracks or actual peeling. At night with engine running, worn wires often can be seen jumping sparks.

It's safest to replace these wires one by one so the correct wire goes to the correct plug. Also make sure that connections are tight at both ends.

Heavily oiled or soiled wires should be replaced. They cause hard starting in wet or even humid weather even if the wires are not old and worn.

If the wires seem in good condition yet you have problems starting or the engine

stalls in wet or humid weather, you can try spraying the distributor housing with an aerosol moisture repellent.

Repacking front wheel bearings: Even though wheel bearing seals have been improved on modern cars, dirt and moisture gradually infiltrate, and brake heat and hot weather also break down bearing lubricants. Bearings should be repacked about once a year or every 10,000 miles. Bearing service is especially convenient to perform when brakes are being serviced; often even a precaution since bearings are exposed at this time and may collect dust particles.

Ease of repacking front wheel bearings varies among different makes. In many cases but not all, it will be necessary to remove the front brake drum or disc in order to repack the front wheel bearings and this may be difficult in some cases without letting out brake fluid or using special tools. When the fluid must be let out, it becomes necessary to bleed and readjust front brakes afterwards. Thus, the actual repair procedure for this item should be checked in the repair manual for your make of car.

Tune-ups: Because of high charges and grievances sometimes related to tune-ups, more owners have become interested in this maintenance task. You do need a tune-up manual and the proper tools (spark plug wrench, timing light, dwell meter, and a spark plug gapping tool). Good tune-up kits, including the basic tools, meters, and a comprehensive manual, range in price from $35 to $50.

You need to know how to use these tools properly. Otherwise you still may be better off finding a reliable station for tune-ups.

Need for tune-ups varies with the type of driving. *Better Homes and Gardens* automotive editors recommend a first tune-up at 12,000 miles and alternate major and minor tune-ups at least every 20,000-25,000 miles. Performance failures such as stalling, misfiring, or increased fuel consumption also may indicate the need for a tune-up.

Some owners prefer to do their own tune-ups because they feel they can extend spark plug life by cleaning and regapping while service shops may tend to replace plugs. For plug servicing or replacing you need a plug wrench. You also must know the plug gap for new plugs for your car. Look in the owner's manual or a decal in the engine compartment for this information. To reset the gap you need a gap gauge.

Spark plugs come in three heat ranges: *cold,* used for high-speed driving and heavy loads; *hot,* which has a long insulator tip and is helpful for engines that do much stop-and-go driving; *normal,* which provides ranges between cold and hot for more-common driving needs.

As well as spark plug servicing, a minor tune-up includes installing new distributor points and distributor cap and adjusting specifications for your car (also shown in the manual or engine-compartment decal).

The use of the timing light is explained in tune-up manuals. But it is important to note that owners of cars with emission control devices should refer to the test procedure on the engine compartment decal.

Also, some newer "high capacity" and "electronic" ignition systems probably need a full-trained mechanic with special equipment for satisfactory tune-ups.

PCV valve: PCV stands for "positive crankcase ventilation." The small PCV valve which recycles fumes back through the engine to be burned off needs to be kept unclogged. If clogged, rough idling, hard starting, and poor gas mileage can result.

Best time to test and either clean or replace the PCV valve is when you get a tune-up or oil change. The valve is in the line between the crankcase and the intake manifold. A special tester is used to measure the air circulation through the crankcase when the engine is idling. If the tester records pressure, the system is clogged.

As a precaution, even if no performance problem has manifested itself, the valve assembly should be cleaned every six months or 6,000 miles and more often in city traffic driving involving much idling during cold weather.

Transmission and power-steering fluids: These are simple to check. The automatic transmission dipstick is located at the back of the engine next to the metal wall between engine and passenger compartment. The fluid level should be checked with the engine running and the parking brake on. Consult your manual for exact procedures. The

AAA points out that usually the procedure calls for checking in "Park" or "Neutral" but in some cases in "Drive."

The cap for the power steering fluid is near the fan belt and also has a dipstick which will indicate the level. (First wipe and re-insert the stick.)

Brake jobs: Relining brakes is one of the big money-savers in self-maintenance with a potential saving of over half the cost; but it's also a skilled job requiring a special set of brake tools. Furthermore, if the brake drums are scored or worn they will need to be resurfaced on a lathe. Still, some relatively skilled owners feel they can save at least part of the cost by removing the drums and taking them to a brake specialist.

Adding brake fluid is no problem. You simply remove the master cylinder reservoir cap. If you can't see any fluid up to the top, add heavy-duty fluid. Or you can ask your serviceman to check the level when you are having oil changed. If the level is low, it's important to find out why. The system then should be inspected for leaks.

Exhaust systems: Muffler and tail pipe assemblies are relatively simple to install. The job requires special tools which can be borrowed or rented from the supplier, and care is needed in fitting the components together. Before you do the job, compare costs at specialized muffler shops.

Whether you make the replacement or have it done, it pays to know how to tell when the exhaust system is defective. Excessive exhaust noise always is an indication. But a system can be defective without the telltale noise. From time to time visually inspect the assembly or have your mechanic do so when the car is on the lift. Look for dents, pinholes, rust, loose clamps, other damage. You can tell if there are loose baffles in the muffler by tapping it and listening for rattles.

A Guide to Tires

In buying replacement tires, it's usually wisest, and in some cases imperative, to buy the same type and size unless you are replacing all four tires. Even then, you should follow the manufacturer's recommendation, especially if you are planning to buy a larger size than the original equipment for better traction and mileage, and perhaps greater load capacity. If you are considering buying one of the more recent wider tires, such as the "70" series, (see later in this section) make sure your wheel wells provide enough clearance so the tires won't rub against the car body.

How tires are constructed: There are three types of tire construction (see illustrations).

Bias-ply, the traditional tires with the cords running diagonally across the tires. These tires provide a relatively comfortable ride and are less costly than the other grades, but usually don't last as long.

Belted bias-ply tires are the next higher price bracket. They have additional plies or belts of, usually, fiberglass or steel cord under the tread which adds puncture resistance. These tires provide a somewhat harder ride but grip the road surface better, and usually last longer than the bias-ply.

Radial tires have the cords running straight across the tires. They cost most but usually wear longest, grip the road best, corner with least lurching, and run coolest. They are, however, the most expensive construction. Radial tires must be used only in sets of four. They "ride" a little more harshly than other constructions but many late-model cars have their suspension adapted for greater compatibility with radials.

If you drive mainly between home and work, or on short trips around town, and don't have to worry about heat build-up because of fast long-distance driving on turnpikes, bias-ply tires with a medium to heavy tread are adequate, the National Bureau of Standards has said. But if you do much long-distance driving and plan to keep your car some time, belted bias-ply and radial tires usually do more than compensate with longer wear for their additional cost.

How to be a smart tire shopper: You need at least some yardsticks for comparing tires to make sure you are getting reasonable value. The tire business sometimes seems like an Oriental bazaar with many sales, sometimes exaggerated list prices, varying grades, and even confusing ads that quote low prices which turn out on closer reading to be for the smallest sizes. Follow these buying tips:

1. Designations molded on the sides of tires can give you some clues to quality. A tire labeled "7.75-14N" means that this is a conventional tire made with nylon cord. If labeled "Poly," it is made with polyester cord. The numerals "78" in the designation mean that the tire has a 78 percent profile (the height is 78 percent of the width).

The 78 series tires are wider, with more "footprint" on the ground. Consequently, they have better cornering and traction, and also are cooler running than lower-grade tires. These may not be labeled with the profile designation but usually have an 83 percent profile.

Tires with a "70" designation have an even lower profile than the 78 series but are usually used only on certain high-performance cars.

2. The amount of excise tax, if the retailer states it separately, can give you a clue to the relative weight of a tire, which is an indication of its quality. Heavier tires carry a little higher excise tax.

3. Ask dealers to show you cross-sections of various tires to help you evaluate the construction and amount of materials used.

4. Look for deep tread with many cross-cuts. Original-equipment tires usually have a tread depth of 12/32 inch compared to the pre-1970 10/32. But replacement tires on the market may range in tread depth from 9/32 to 13/32.

5. The length of guarantee is some indication of quality although by no means a conclusive one because of the variation in guarantees. Some makers' 36-month warranties may be no better or even not as useful as the 30-month warranty provided by other manufacturers and retailers. A guarantee which provides for a pre-rate allowance on a defective tire, but bases the allowance on an inflated "list price," is of less value than a guarantee providing for exchange on the basis of the price you actually paid.

Guarantees which provide for a specified number of months of wear, including defects and road hazards, with adjustment pro-rated by months, usually are most useful for heavy users who might wear out tires relatively quickly.

Guarantees providing for adjustment pro-rated on tread wear are usually best for the low-mileage driver.

How to take care of your tires: Over- and under-inflation of tires increases probabilities of sidewall failure and also may reduce tread life. A pound or two of over-inflation prolongs tire life but too much makes a harsh ride. Under-inflation is especially harmful.

A look at the way your tires are wearing may indicate whether you have been keeping them properly inflated. Excessive tread wear on both shoulders indicates chronic under-inflation. Excessive wear in the center indicates the tire has had too much air pressure for too long a time.

Excessive wear on one edge, or erratic wear, may indicate wheels out of line.

You can get a $2 kit that will help you keep your tires properly inflated. It's called Tire Safety, available from the Tire Industry Safety Council, Box 1801, Washington, D.C. 20013.

Why have your own pressure gauge? One reason is that air-power pressure gauges at service stations are not always dependable. Surveys have often shown them to be off.

You should check air pressure at least once a month and when the tires are cool. Refer to your owner's manual for the recommended inflation.

The kit includes a tread gauge but you also can check remaining tread by inserting an upside-down penny into a tire tread. If you can see the top of Lincoln's head, the tread is dangerously low.

Most blowouts occur when a tire is down to its last 10 percent of tread. Adequate tread is especially important on snow tires.

A Guide to Batteries

Both extreme heat and severe cold are hard on batteries. In summer, they are subjected to high temperatures and charging rates on long trips, which break down the plates. In winter, when you need all the power you can get for starting, battery efficiency can drop to as little as 40 percent of normal at 0 degrees F. Battery failures are a leading source of emergency calls.

Even when it isn't completely dead, a feeble or malfunctioning battery can be responsible for many peculiarities of car behavior. For example, a battery which constantly overcharges can shorten the life of the voltage regulator, points, condenser and coil, and the battery itself, and eventu-ally cause engine failure. In modern closely-synchronized cars with their many automatic components and electrical accessories, your battery takes on extra importance.

To get maximum life and trouble-free performance from a battery, you need to:

1. Select the grade best suited to your driving conditions.

2. Give your battery the inexpensive regular care it needs to be a dependable ally instead of a somewhat treacherous stranger.

Even if you have starting difficulties, you may not really need a new battery. Good batteries are often replaced unnecessarily because car owners don't realize they can be recharged. If you can find a battery rebuilder (they're scarcer nowadays), sometimes all that's needed is a new cell.

Don't delay recharging a weak battery. It will wear out faster than one kept fully charged. Home chargers are useful for keeping a battery fully charged.

Besides starting difficulties, one clue to a weak battery is whether your lights brighten when you rev up the engine.

Before you buy a new battery, have a serviceman make sure that the charging system, including fan belt, and the ground connections and cables on your present battery are in good condition. Service stations and battery dealers sometimes fail to assure good connections and cables.

If you do need a new battery, it pays to buy at least a medium-duty grade—the equivalent of original-equipment quality. If you do much stop-and-go driving, or much over-the-road driving (which results in overcharging), or live in a very cold area, a heavy-duty battery may be desirable. Otherwise, a medium-duty battery may be satisfactory enough. *The capacity difference between light-grades and medium-duty is greater than between medium and heavy.*

How to compare batteries: The way to shop batteries is to compare the ampere-hour rating, and the cold-start or "zero crank power" rating, as some sellers call it, of various brands.

Thus, depending on the type of battery you need, light-duty batteries may have 20-hour ampere ratings of 36 to 45 amperes; medium-duty, from 53 to 60, and heavy-duty 65 to 84.

The cold-start rating (established by tests designed by the Society of Automotive Engineers) indicates a battery's ability to perform in cold weather. It shows the number of minutes the battery will deliver 150 amperes continuously at zero temperature, and the voltage after five seconds of discharge. Most medium-duty batteries have five-second voltage ratings of 9 to 9.5. Heavy-duty batteries usually have ratings of 9.6 to 10.4.

Some sellers use a "cold cranking power" rating and suggest that car owners buy a battery which will deliver a minimum of one amp for every cubic inch of engine displacement. Thus, a 305-cubic inch engine would need a 305-amp cold-cranking power battery, if the seller rates batteries this way.

You also may see batteries rated by reserve capacity. This figure indicates the number of minutes the car will still run (in 80-degree temperature) if the charging system fails. Thus, a heavy-duty battery may be rated as providing 114 minutes of reserve capacity.

Guarantees: While service stations tend to charge somewhat more for batteries than do auto-equipment chains and department stores, their guarantees may be better than those of some lower-price retailers.

Battery guarantees usually are pro-rated by the number of months used. But it makes a difference whether the replacement price will be computed on the list price or the price you actually paid. Most, but not all, service stations base the exchange price on the actual selling price. Some sellers base the exchange on the list price, which is higher and thus a less-favorable basis for the buyer.

Some guarantees also provide a longer period of full replacement if the battery fails; for example, full replacement if a battery with a 36-month guarantee fails within the first year. Some sellers may provide full replacement only within three to nine months on a thirty-six month battery.

Jump-Starting a Car

If your battery won't turn over the engine, first inspect the battery cables and the wiring to the starter. Tighten any loose connections. If the battery doesn't have enough power to operate the starter, the engine usually can be started by attaching jumper cables from your battery to that of another car. Be sure to hook up the cables correctly. Use one cable (either one) to connect the positive terminals of the two batteries. Clamp one end of the other cable to the negative terminal of the good battery and the other end to the engine or some other metal part of the disabled car to serve as a ground connection. Note that you do *not* connect this cable to the negative pole of the disabled battery. You need the ground connection to safeguard your car against damage to its electric system. Also, don't let the clamps from one cable touch the clamps on the other cable.

Remove the vent caps from both the disabled battery and the good one, and cover the vents with folded cloths to protect yourself from being spattered by acid.

Start the "charging" engine and run it a few minutes. Turn it off. Then start the disabled engine.

After starting the engine, disconnect the negative cable, then the positive, replace the battery caps and discard the cloths with care since they may have acid on them.

Your Car as Tax Saver

One small good from the big ill wind of jumping car costs is that you may be able to take a larger deduction for allowable car expenses.

For example, many families use their cars to get health care, and also for charitable purposes or while doing unpaid work for nonprofit community organizations and schools. If you itemize your deductions, as of the year 1975, you could deduct for car expenses at the rate of seven cents a mile plus any parking fees and tolls. You can deduct the same amounts for car use for medical needs if you do have enough total medical expenses for a medical deduction. You can, of course, also deduct taxi, bus, and other transportation expenses other than for a car which you incur for such qualified purposes.

The seven-cent rate also now is permitted for certain allowable moving expenses.

If you use your car partly or wholly in your work (not for commuting), the Internal Revenue Service as of 1975 increased the standard mileage rate to 15 cents for the first 15,000 miles, and 10 cents above 15,000.

Self Defense in Buying a Car

How much you pay for a car and how long you hold on to it are the main expenses of car ownership.

To help keep car costs in line, you need to (1) buy the most suitable model, both from the viewpoint of driving needs and operating economy, and (2) buy it at a reasonable price.

How to Save on New Cars

Best times to buy: There are two best times to buy. One is in midwinter, especially in bad weather when few other buyers are out looking for cars and dealers are hungry.

The other is in September just before new models are introduced. Factories usually give dealers a 5 percent rebate on unsold current-year models in order to clear them. So you usually can figure on at least that much reduction from prices earlier in the year. Price cuts may be even larger on some models with especially heavy inventory.

But does it really pay to buy near the end of the model year when even an unused car will lose part of its value? Yes, if you plan to keep the car for several years. Possibly not, if you plan to trade in two or three years.

Discounts: Most buyers now understand that the sticker or list prices on cars are really just a base from which almost everyone gets a discount, or even really just a base from which to start bargaining. How much discount should you expect?

Much depends on the list price and popularity of the model. Discounts on the small-est cars (sub-compacts) usually run about 5 percent, although there may be little on imports. Discounts on the compact and intermediate group may range from 7½ to 10 percent, and on full-size cars, 10 to 18 percent.

Trade-ins: It's wise to get quotes with or without a trade-in. If you have a car to trade, dealers may inflate the amount of the trade-in allowance but then reduce the discount they'll give you off the list price.

In general, you'll come out better selling your old car privately. The value to a dealer of an old car often is less than owners tend to think. Your credit union, bank loan officer or insurance agent usually will have on hand, and may be willing to let you consult, the auto trade *Blue Book* that shows new and used car prices, or the *Red Book* that lists values (although on the low side) for used cars in various regions. By consulting these, or observing prices on models similar to yours in ads and on used car lots, you'll have an idea of the worth of your trade-in for selling or bargaining purposes.

Car brokers: A number of plans have sprung up offering cars at only $100 or $125 over dealer's cost. Several operate nationally, such as those sponsored by United Auto Brokers, Rollins United Buying Service, and the Montgomery Ward Auto Club.

Some dealers also have arrangements with local labor unions, credit unions, co-ops, auto clubs and other groups to provide cars at a stipulated figure over cost.

But first find out what the total price would be, including options, and compare quotes among several dealers as well as a broker's plan. Note that dealers may take a larger profit on options. Also make sure that the quotations include all charges such as the new-car preparation price. It is especially helpful if the credit union or other group itself spot-checks dealers promising such special prices to make sure they live up to these claims.

A subsidiary of United Auto Brokers—Car/Puter—will provide a computer report for $10 on any model you are interested in, showing the dealer cost and list price of the car and accessories. If you want, you can order the car through one of the dealers who work with United Auto Brokers. Car/Puter's address is 1603 Bushwick Avenue, Brooklyn, New York 11207.

In buying through a broker, you may want to consider the distance you may have to go to pick up the car, and the availability of warranty service. Even though any dealer in that make is supposed to provide warranty service, if there is no large difference in the total cost including options, you may want to have the greater assurance of service through the local dealer.

Shop ahead: Don't wait until you urgently need a new car to order it. Otherwise, you may have to take a model on hand. These tend to be loaded with options you may not want, or may have a different engine, transmission, or wheel size than you prefer.

A suitable model: If all you really need is a compact or intermediate, don't buy a standard size. You'll pay more not only in initial price but in operating expenses.

If you do mainly over-the-road driving, you may not need automatic transmission which is mostly useful for city driving. Too, models vary in gas consumption for different driving needs. As discussed elsewhere in this chapter, some are much more economical on the highway. Others perform relatively better in traffic.

Make sure the contract specifically states which options will be included. Sometimes cars arrive with additional equipment or features such as vinyl roofs and side moldings, and dealers may insist that you take the extras, claiming they have no control

over the factory. But in some cases authorities have found that some such extras actually were installed by dealers themselves.

How to Save on Used Cars

Especially in buying a used car, the best time is a snowy winter day when all the owners and dealers wish the auto had never been invented. More exactly, the Government's price indexes reveal that prices of used cars usually drop sharply in midwinter. Typically, average prices fall 5-6 percent from December to February, and then jump 9 to 11 percent from March to June.

The used-car business, of course, often has been criticized for the ruses perpetrated by some dealers to get high prices for cars in poor condition. Testimony at hearings of the National Commission on Consumer Finance in the early 1970's cited examples of buyers signing installment contracts to pay $400 for old cars worth about $100, and $1,100 for cars worth $400 to $500. Today, these risks have multiplied.

Drive before you buy: Many of the problems occur because buyers fail to insist on a test drive. A reliable dealer will let you try out the car. Make certain that any paper you may sign before the test is *not* a sales contract. It's worth having an independent mechanic check the car at his shop, too.

Don't rely too much on the odometer reading. Federal and various state laws forbid turning back odometers. But these laws are hard to enforce.

However, if other signs of wear lead you to believe that the odometer has been illegally set back and you think you can prove it, a Federal law (Title IV of the Motor Vehicle Information and Cost Savings Act) provides that a suit may be brought in Federal Court even if the dollar amount is relatively small.

How to check it out: More dependable clues to the use a car has had than the mileage reading are the signs of wear shown in such places as the pedal pads, the upholstery around the driver's door latch and window handle, and at the floor boards, and whether the doors are loose.

Other clues to excessive wear or defects include: a sinking brake pedal; unusual noises in the motor or transmission; uneven tire wear; oil film inside the tail pipe; and blue exhaust smoke. Large sections of non-matching or rippled paint may indicate that the car was in an accident and had extensive damage which was repaired and painted over. Other signs of involvement in a serious accident and resultant frame damage are doors, windows and trunk lids which do not open easily.

You also should be sure that all of the lights and the horn work. The most important lights to check are headlights, taillights, stoplights, and backup lights.

Proper functioning of these items is not only a vital safety factor, but a financial one. Defective lights or horn may keep your vehicle from passing state inspections, requiring costly repairs. Too, you may find yourself collecting traffic tickets in quantity.

Should you buy a "demonstrator"? It should be noted that demonstrator cars (and sometimes even new cars) may have substantial defects. Such cars should also be carefully examined before accepting delivery. One startling example of the type of problem was reported by Calvin Zon in the *Washington Star-News*. A Maryland woman bought a demonstrator car from a dealer who told her it was "better than brand new" because it had been broken in by prospective customers. The engine was caked with mud, the air conditioner vents were broken and the left side was slightly warped. Scratches were visible on the lower part of the body. Although the woman recovered her damages, the cost in time and aggravation could have been avoided by a pre-acceptance inspection.

Before buying, also have a good idea of current market prices for models in which you are interested. You can check current prices at dealers, in ads by private sellers, and in the guide books previously mentioned.

While you sometimes can save a dealer's profit by buying from a private seller, the advantage of a dealer—if reliable—is that he'll give you a guarantee of his claims, or a warranty of the car's condition (unless sold "as is"). Make sure of the dealer's reliability by observing whether he makes exaggerated claims of value, whether prices are clearly tagged, and whether he actually has the models he advertises and his own service

department to back up his claims of reconditioning. If you have doubts, ask the Better Business Bureau whether there have been complaints against him.

Don't risk repossession: A combination of a big old car that needs expensive repairs, and high fees for financing it, often leads to the disaster of repossession. Police departments are accustomed to having people report a stolen car when actually it has been repossessed. The "repo" men, as they are called, often do their "car grabbing" at night when the car owners who have fallen behind in payments are asleep.

Can creditors do this? In most states, yes. Installment contracts usually state that the creditor has the right to repossess the property if you default, and without your permission. Lawyers call this procedure "self-help repossession." Moreover, the delinquent debtor not only loses his car but often still owes an additional amount for the remaining balance of the debt after the finance company re-sells the car.

The right of a creditor to both repossess and get a deficiency judgment may seem unfair. But this provision is permitted in most states and will be until current efforts to eliminate it from the credit laws succeed.

Financing: Sometimes it is both safer and cheaper to arrange your own financing for a used car from a credit union or bank. Credit union rates are a maximum of $6.50 per $100 of your original balance (equivalent to an annual rate of about 12 percent), and in some cases are even lower.

In contrast, dealers usually charge more to finance used cars than new; $10 per $100 of the original amount of your debt, and sometimes more depending on the age of the car, state laws and the dealer's policy. This means you pay true annual interest of about 20 percent or more.

Shop for your insurance too. Pressure to finance insurance through the dealer is another clue to a hard-sell operation.

One development that affects young buyers especially, is that most states recently have reduced the age of majority to 18. Now young people in these states not only have the right to vote but to enter into contracts, including installment contracts to buy cars. Lane Breidenstein, president of the Detroit

Better Business Bureau, has warned that in states where adults under 21 now are legally liable for their purchases, they need to realize their responsibilities.

"When you sign your name on the dotted line, you are binding yourself to meet the terms of the contract," he points out. "It is important that you know the full amount your purchase will cost; how much you must pay each month, and what can happen if you fail to make a monthly payment. Once signed, a contract cannot be changed or cancelled unless the other party agrees."

Warranties: Buyers should realize that "as is" in a contract means that the buyer has no guarantee that what he purchases will work. What you see is what you get. Even the word "guaranteed" means nothing when used by itself. A contract should specify in writing exactly what is guaranteed or warrantied and for how long. Most common, the Syracuse Consumer Affairs Unit reports, is the 30-day shared-cost warranty.

Bargain sources: In addition to potential saving of typically $400 by buying from a private seller, you also may be able to find a good buy on a repossessed car through a bank or credit union. They often have several cars on hand from which to choose. People tend to be afraid of repossessed cars on the theory that they probably didn't get good care. But while you need to inspect such cars thoroughly, some may be in relatively good condition, since default on payments usually occur within the first year.

Another source of late-model used cars is the large car-rental companies who periodically dispose of their cars. Often these are cars from corporate fleets as well as from rental locations. The larger rental companies provide a power-train warranty for twelve months or 12,000 miles.

But beware of buying used cars sight unseen from mail-order companies claiming to be "wholesalers." Sometimes these have proved to be used taxis in bad condition.

If you know cars well, or know someone who does, you also may be able to buy cheaply at auctions. There are two kinds: your own city or county police or surplus property department periodically will auction off used cars and trucks, sometimes abandoned or seized property but some-

---

Gasoline economy groupings

Following are the gasoline economy groupings of the more-widely-bought models, based on 1976 EPA tests:

AVERAGING 30-33 MPG: Mazda 808, Chevette, Datsun B210, Subaru, Honda Civic, Renault 5.

AVERAGING 26-29: Audi Fox, VW Dasher, Pinto, Toyota Corolla, Vega, Ford Mustang II, Lincoln-Mercury Bobcat, Monza, Vega Kammback, Capri II, Astre, Sunbird, VW Beetle.

AVERAGING 22-25: Fiat X1-9, Granada, Maverick, Comet, Monarch, Porsche 912E, Celica, Corona, Gremlin, Hornet, Pacer, Skyhawk, Aspen, Coronet, Dart, Starfire, Fury, Volare.

AVERAGING 18-21: Nova, Val-Duster, Century-Regal, Skylark, Camaro, Chevelle, Cutlass, Omega, Firebird, LeMans, Ventura, BMW 2002, Volvo.

AVERAGING 14-17: Matador, Seville, Coronet-Charger, Grand Prix, Corvette, Electra, Le Sabre, Chevrolet, Malibu, Monte Carlo, Cordoba, Ford Elite, Ford, Ford Torino, Cougar, Montego, Cutlass, Delta 88, Grand Fury, Pontiac, Electra, Riviera, Chrysler, Mercury, Oldsmobile 98, Toronado.

---

times also their own surplus vehicles. Call the bureau of purchases and supplies at your city or county headquarters for information on when bids may be made.

The other type of auction is sponsored by private auto auction companies, usually in the larger cities. Such auctions usually are announced in local newspapers or you can ask your bank or credit union where to find out about them. Two caveats: you are bidding against dealers, who are better able to judge the condition of the offerings. Also, here you certainly buy "as is" and need to watch out especially for cars that may have been in accidents and were rebuilt. As previously advised when buying any used car, look for ripples in the body and any difference in shade of the paint. Also rap on the body to look for a hollow sound which may indicate the use of filler for repairs.

It's important to inspect before bidding, and to have an idea of values. As noted earlier, you can consult the used-car guides.

Clothing Your Family Economically

In spite of great changes in the way we clothe ourselves in modern times, it appears that for far too many Americans of both sexes the changing styles of "fashion" are the most insidious influence on unnecessary expenditures for clothing. This continues in spite of the fact that in our democratic society, for all activities and occasions, there are acceptable modes of dress that change hardly at all from year to year. In the 1960s and 1970s, wider acceptability of more informal dress for all but the most special occasions, such as weddings and funerals, enabled Americans to reduce their clothing budgets as never before.

Work clothing—from work clothes stores where retail prices are lower than anywhere else but possibly catalog houses—have replaced "play clothes" and "sports wear" for most of the activities of daily living, with the exception of office work. Although even in big cities such as Los Angeles, Houston, Chicago, and New York, secretaries have begun wearing blue jeans to work.

This section of the book tells you how and where to buy new clothing at lowest cost; where to buy used clothing at even lower cost; how to make clothing at lowest cost of all. It instructs you in the practicalities of the *use it up, wear it out, make it do* philosophy to make your clothes last longer. And tells you how to save money in keeping what you wear clean.

The Underground Shoppers

Underground shoppers are both a type of directory and a breed of value-conscious consumers. Both have been around for years, but they've proliferated in the recent climate of high prices.

The underground books and the consumers alike are dedicated to finding real bargain places. Their sources include outlet, sample, and job-lot stores, as well as wholesale firms that also sell direct to the consumer; low-expense warehouse stores; and the lower-price discount and catalog stores. The local guides usually cost $2.

"Some of the stores may not have the service and atmosphere you may be used to," these guides typically warn. "A good many entries are manufacturers' outlets where shopping is different. In some you may not try on or return merchandise. Some accept only cash. You may not find much variety in styles or sizes. Some of the merchandise may be damaged or flawed. Occasionally it's last season's merchandise, but then again, you may be able to purchase goods before they appear in the retail stores. Savings can vary—as low as 10 percent, but as high as 80 percent and even 90 percent. Just be wary of buying on impulse."

As one guide points out, "Overloading your closets with mauve polka dot blouses just because they are 50 cents may not be so economical in the long run."

Several nationwide directories of factory outlets and sample stores (including some in Canada) also are available. One is *S.O.S.* (Save On Shopping). *S.O.S.* is a 192-page directory with state-by-state listings of selected outlet and sample stores, with many for clothing, sweaters, shoes, and fabrics but also some for pottery, ceramics, silverware, glassware, toys, bedspreads, and pillows; furniture and housewares.

S.O.S. is available at bookstores or write for current price and information on related services to the publishers, Ken and Iris Ellis, Box 10482, Jacksonville, Fl., 32207.

Another nationwide directory, *The Bargain Hunter's Field Guide,* is also broken down into state-by-state listings.

While *S.O.S.* is updated annually, it's always a good idea to phone any outlet stores listed in such directories before you set out to visit them. While some are long established, others come and go, especially in the clothing industry. In checking one directory, we found most of the listings extant but some had changed. Sue Brett, a leading New York dress manufacturer, for example, had a factory outlet in New Jersey, but had closed it and instead opened its New York showroom to retail customers on Saturdays.

Factory Outlets

Many manufacturers, especially those in the clothing and textile trades, have cut-price outlet stores in or near their factories. In New England and the South, there are many fabrics outlets; in Maine, shoe outlets at most shoe factories; pottery outlets at ceramics factories in central New Jersey, and so on.

If you live in or near a large city which has a garment manufacturing center, you often can find some manufacturers who have outlet stores or who sell at retail.

You also can find some factory outlets listed in the Yellow Pages under specific categories such as mattresses or upholstery fabrics. You also can phone manufacturers listed in the phone book in any category, such as clothing and apparel, but also even such varied goods as uniforms and storm windows, and ask whether they have retail outlets. Especially numerous are mattress factories that also sell to the public.

But be especially careful of furniture showrooms recommended by interior decorators and dealers. Often these stores have inflated "wholesale" prices set artificially high to allow for commissions to decorators, or make-believe "discounts" to consumers.

Chain Store Outlets

Most of the large retail chains have "as is" or remainder stores. Sears, for example, has "as is" stores in the Chicago area and in St. Louis. The Filene stores in Boston have a clearance center in Needham; Sloanes have clearance centers in New York and New Jersey. Wards, J. C. Penney, Lerner, and other large chains also have outlets. If you can't learn their regional location by word of mouth, you usually can by phoning the area headquarters of such chains.

Warehouse Outlets

Many department stores now offer frequent warehouse sales to clear furniture and appliances. These sales often offer fresh merchandise as well as "as is" goods and floor samples. Thus, in the New York-New Jersey area, Macy's and Bloomingdale's department stores run frequent warehouse sales; in Boston, Jordan Marsh has a warehouse clearance center; the Wards TV and appliance chain operates warehouse centers in Norfolk and Richmond, Virginia.

Specialty Outlets

Most numerous are small independent outlets devoted to one type of merchandise. Almost every town has at least one shoe outlet such as Shoe King Sam in the Long Island-New Jersey suburban areas, and the Quantico, Virginia shoe outlet where excited shoppers from all over the state often find such bargains as I. Miller shoes for $6.99, and Italian-made sandals for $1.99.

Similar values often are available in children's shoes. Needless to say, consumers need to be sure to fit carefully in outlet shoe stores, especially in children's but also in adult footwear. Complete size assortments usually aren't available in such stores and incorrect sizes can harm feet.

Fabric outlet stores are numerous. Men's clothing outlets also have proliferated in the 1970's when men's wear was subjected to sharp price hikes and became the subject of heavy fashion promotion under costly designer names.

Men's outlets often operate in lofts but also sometimes in street-level stores. Rather than specialize in the clothing of just a couple of manufacturers, outlet stores usually buy up surplus inventory or distress stocks from cash-needy manufacturers.

Outlet stores often have simplified fixtures such as pipe racks and offer no deliveries. In most cases, they don't allow charge accounts, and, by nature of their operation, have broken size assortments. They also usually charge extra for alterations which may increase costs for men who are hard to fit. But large savings often are available in these times of steep clothing costs.

Besides suits and jackets, such stores often have famous-name men's shirts and slacks, sometimes without the label, at half price and less. But consumers also should be aware that such famous-name men's furnishings often cost much more at original list prices than the house brands of the large chain stores. A reduction from the original high list prices may bring prices closer to realistic values.

Salvage Sales

Bargains in appliances and building materials also are sometimes available at freight salvage sales. Call freight forwarders, salvage specialists, and express companies in your area to learn when sales will be held. Moving-company warehouses and junk yards and house-wrecking companies also sometimes are a source of values in furniture, building materials, etc.

Thrift-Shopping for Secondhand Clothes

Anyone who can afford the high cost of clothing can dress well in America, as can anyone with a sewing machine, the skill, the impetus, and the time to use it. Those who lack such felicitous advantages and still dress well these days are likely to be wearing secondhand clothes.

The Shift to Thrift

Don't sniff. For decades, Manhattan's famous Ritz Thrift Shop right in the heart of the most fashionable retail trade district has been buying "last year's" fur coats from wealthy matrons arriving, some of them, in chauffeur-driven limousines, and selling the same coats to secretaries and housewives.

Americans spend billions of dollars on "stylish" clothes annually, much of which goes out of style while there's still plenty of wear in it, creating a veritable river of used clothing that finds its way into the secondhand clothing market.

There are several kinds of outlets for used clothing: charity thrift shops; privately owned thrift shops run for profit; resale clothing stores; church and school rummage sales or bazaars. Station wagon sales are community groups that gather weekends in vacant parking lots or open fields to sell household discards, usually with a surplus of good clothing. The ubiquitous flea markets on the other hand, sell fewer clothes than when they began to appear, because exhibitors objected to acres of glad rags flapping in the breeze. But flea markets and garage sales, tag sales, lawn sales—call 'em what you like—are very much in evidence on the suburban scene.

You'll find the best hunting, however, lowest prices, and greatest selection at charity thrift shops, especially newly established ones and little-known ones in suburban towns. Clothing almost always costs more and there's less of it to choose from at thrift shops run for profit. Resale clothing stores either purchase outright from the original owner (like the Ritz) or the store and the original owner split the sale price on a consignment basis (which means you may find yourself selling and buying on the same secondhand-clothing spree). Prices are highest in the tonier resale shops, but usually they are no more than half what the same "slightly worn" garments would have cost new in retail stores—somewhere around the wholesale equivalent. Volunteer-run school rummage sales and "exchanges," where you can trade in last year's outgrown ski boots for a pair that fits, are unbeatable sources for children's clothing.

The Joys and Rigors

Not only are many secondhand outlets extraordinary hunting grounds for perfectly acceptable clothing, but people who could easily afford to shop retail have discovered that treasure hunting can be fun. The atmosphere is more relaxed and friendly. Where once they might have kept the source of some "find" secret, today secondhand shopping is considered chic; they bring their friends along.

Plan to browse when you go secondhand shopping. Don't go looking with something specific in mind, and go when you can take your time. Your best discoveries will be pure luck. For every "possible" there will be dozens of insufferable "impossibles," and when you find something that grabs you, it probably won't be your size. The process requires patience, fortitude, and tenacity in approximately equal measure. Learn to look through a rack of secondhand clothes swiftly. If nothing catches your eye at first glance, there's nothing there you want.

Check for wear by holding garments up to a strong light, particularly the seats of pants. See if the knees and seat are "sprung" from overwear by someone sitting down; they won't regain proper shape when you stand up in them after *you've* been sitting down. Tug at seams to see if the thread is still strong in seats, under arms, around collars and cuffs. Check zippers. If they don't work, don't worry. They are cheap and easy to replace. Most dry cleaners will do the job. Worn tweed jacket elbows are easily patchable; department store notions counters sell leather elbow patches.

If something you turn up is just what you want but doesn't fit right, consider carefully. Any alterations, except dress hems and pants lengths, may require a tailor and are not likely to be worth the money—although if you're an expert seamstress you're in an altogether different ball game.

One middle-western mother of a big family rips out the seams, turns old overcoats inside out, and sews them back together again looking brand new (though usually a size or two smaller than the original). Another woman, on the east coast, buys used blue jeans for $1 (very used indeed) at a resale shop in the city where she lives. She takes them home and washes them in a strong disinfectant like Lysol (which rinses out leaving no odor). Then she patches and embroiders such imaginative designs over the worn places. Every member of her household wears her made-overs. Now she's thinking of selling her creations.

Look carefully for holes in wool and for stains in synthetic fiber blends. There's little that can be done about them; re-weaving is out of the economic question, and stains may not be eradicable. Pure wool and 100% cotton can be dyed if you're willing to settle for a darker color. It's not hard to do yourself. But don't forget the buttons usually take the dye too.

Should You Bargain?

Bargaining isn't easy for Americans. Not being an integral part of our culture, it's hard for us even to remember to try it before copping out and paying the asking price. Yet bargaining especially in the secondhand clothing world, is the best way to be sure of getting a bargain. It's easy, once you get the hang of it, and you should always try it, except perhaps in the better resale shops where you might find you were wasting your time. Once you learn the technique and have applied it successfully a few times, you may find bargaining for secondhand clothes can be fun:

Rule 1. Dress poor. *Rule 2.* Try never (except in resale shops) to pay more than 25% of your estimated price of the garment when new. *Rule 3.* Pull the rug out from under any hard-sell approach by learning to bargain with banter. *Rule 4.* Whether or not it bears a price tag, begin by flatly announcing the price you want to pay for an item, whatever its tag price, then quickly switch to reasons why the marked price is higher than you think you ought to pay— a little tear here, a button missing there, a worn place perhaps—and without down-grading the merchandise, just keep talking. This gives the person who has to sell it a chance to consider your offer and propose a counter-offer gracefully. Just be sure your original offer is low enough to allow you to make *your* counter-offer after the seller's, and eventually reach a compromise well below the marked price.

Ordering via the postal service

Although shopping by mail entails de-livery costs, which can get prohibitively high for heavy objects, you save a pretty penny buying lightweight merchandise by mail from out-of-state firms (those that have no retail outlets in your state) since you don't have any state or municipal sales taxes to pay.

The Whole World Catalog by Delphine Lyons ($5 from Quadrangle, 10 East 53 St., NY 10022) is an update of her familiar *Armchair Shopper's Guide: Mail-Order Bargains Around the World.* It's really a catalog of catalogs of firms that specialize in one or two types of merchan-dise; a large proportion are foreign clothing manufacturers. Although it's easier to shop by mail from U.S. sources, the duty and postage you pay when you order abroad are often compensated for by the much-lower-than-Stateside prices; small parcels are delivered by mail from all over the world. A good many items are unob-tainable here. You may be able to order apparel made to measure at less than you pay for retail ready-to-wear in this country. No need to know the language to order from a well-illustrated catalog, although you may want to check a word or two in a foreign-language dictionary at the library.

How to Get Started in Home Sewing

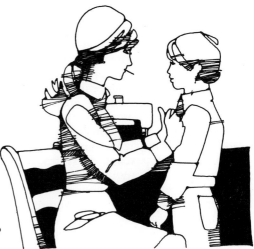

If you've about had it with the high cost of ready-to-wear—flimsy construction, inferior fabrics, rapid deterioration, and assembly-line look—one way to cope with the high cost of clothing is by learning to sew your own.

Being able to make your own clothes has always been a money-saver. Today, it's a blessing to anyone on a tight budget who wants to step out in style. If you're an average American you spend around $300 a year for ready-made clothing. Home-sewing industry experts say you can cut that cost in half by sewing your own.

A study conducted by the trade magazine *Sew Business* disclosed that a typical "medium-priced" dress using $5.84 worth of fabric and retailing for $110 costs only $21.54 home-sewn—an 80-percent saving. When you consider that for similarly spectacular savings you can make your own draperies, dish towels, pillowcases, and other household items, you can see that home sewing could save you hundreds of dollars a year.

Making something brand new isn't the only way you can hold the line with sewing, either. Think about the clothes you and your family own that aren't worn any more because they've gone out of style. And how about the clothing you've given away or thrown out because of a rip here or a hole there? Knowing how to sew enables you to reduce the volume of cast-offs by updating and repairing what might otherwise be headed for charity or the rag bag—or a costly session with the local seamstress.

Time is also money, and most home sewers don't want to spend hours laboring over intricate projects. With the scores of simple-to-sew patterns on the market as well as instructional books designed to make clothing construction quick and easy, you can put together a pair of pants in a weekend if you're slow, in a night if you're fast. If a pre-teen can learn to sew, you can, too.

You know what happens when you try to buy ready-to-wear apparel at sales prices—what you usually find is racks of plain, pawed-over leftovers. But when you sew it yourself, you don't have to sacrifice looks to thrift. Up-to-the-minute patterns are available for nearly every taste—from the conservative to the avant garde—and for every member of the family. Sewing also lets you bring your own imagination to bear on your wardrobe. Even those who aren't especially concerned about clothing costs often turn to sewing to get something they know will be unique.

Like any other craft, sewing has its good buys to watch for, shortcuts to take advantage of, and trade secrets to get in on. It also has its bad bargains to avoid and pitfalls to steer clear of. That's what the rest of this chapter is about—some straight talk on everything you need to know from first purchase to final stitch.

The Sewing Machine

Even though a sewing machine is your biggest single investment, don't assume that the fanciest or most expensive model is necessarily the best. No matter how complex your sewing projects one day become, a quality machine that meets most of your present and future sewing needs should cost between $100 and $200, depending on such variables as what extra features you choose and sales you can take advantage of. You can expect wisely purchased equipment to pay for itself in less than a year, depending on how much you use it and also on how carefully you use it.

Don't go shopping until you've done some hard thinking at home to ensure that your machine will be a hard worker rather than a dust-catcher. Ask yourself: How much sewing do I intend to do? How much time can I devote to sewing? How much sewing and storage space is available? Once you have a general idea of the kind of sewing you plan to do, your next step is to decide what kind of sewing machine best fits your needs. Here are some questions that you really should consider:

Do I want a machine that's new, used, or rented? Buy a new machine if you intend to make a sizable number (eight or more) of garments every year and household goods like tablecloths, pillows, and curtains. Also buy a new machine if you want to be assured of a long-term manufacturer's guarantee. Compare at least three different brands in your price range. Discuss the features, service availability, and parts accessibility with the dealers, independent repairmen, and friends who are experienced sewers. Also compare the prices charged and service contracts offered by several dealers (both manufacturer representatives and independents) on the same model, since sewing machines are not fair-traded. A good time to get the best buy is when major retailers or chain stores are holding sales, which will feature reduced prices on several, but probably not all, models. Sales are held at various times during the year and nearly always around the winter holidays. Installment-purchase plans are available.

Buy a used machine if your budget won't cover the cost of a new one, if you don't want to buy on time because of interest charges you'll incur, if you're not sure how much time you'll devote to sewing, or if the extent of your sewing will largely be limited to mending. As with new machines, it's a good idea to compare several different used models for prices, features, and attachments available, and availability of parts. If you buy a reclaimed or trade-in model from a dealer, he should have checked it for operation of functional parts, made any necessary adjustments or replacements, and tested it for satisfactory condition. Find out whether he offers a service warranty for the machine and check into his selling and service reputation.

Used machines can also be bought, however, in secondhand stores, from individuals advertising in newspapers or on community bulletin boards, or at garage sales or auctions. The drawback here, of course, is that there's no guarantee. Protect yourself by checking for dents which may interfere with the machine's operation, by examining the machine for missing parts or signs of wear which could mean expensive replacements or repairs, and by testing the machine in operation.

Rent a machine if most of your sewing will be done at only one time of year—say, before school starts—or if you're not yet sure how involved in sewing you want to become. Most if not all sewing-machine dealers rent as well as sell, and prices generally range from $15 to $25 a month with a deposit of $25 to $50 (depending on where you live). Representatives of several chain and independent dealers say that if anything goes wrong with the machine while you're using it (unless it's damage for which you're responsible), they'll fix it at no charge to you and extend the renting period for whatever time it was in for repairs. Usually you can rent the machine with an option to buy it or another model, and apply the rental fee to the purchase price. If you want this agreement, get it in writing. Deluxe models are not usually available for renting—your selection is limited to basic zigzags and straight-stitch models.

Do I want a machine that's straight-stitch or zigzag? A machine that sews with straight stitches both forward and backward is all you'll ever need for most sewing. It costs less, requires fewer and less expensive repairs, and is simpler to operate than zigzag models. It's a good investment for the beginner who plans to make a lot of simple garments as well as those who want to include tailoring and fine dressmaking in their sewing plans someday or those who plan to do only mending and repairing.

Attachments for various utilitarian and decorative stitches can be bought separately if and when the need arises, but the button-hole attachment is the only one most people use often enough to warrant its purchase. If you want this and/or other accessories (a zigzag attachment is also available), compare the total cost of the machine and attachments with the price of a machine in which these features are built-in.

Unfortunately, you may have to look harder for a straight-stitch machine than for a zigzag. Sewing-machine manufacturers seem to be convinced that the latter is what the public wants, and some domestic companies aren't making straight-stitchers anymore, although you may find these makers' models in some dealers' stock. Straight-stitch models still being sold by domestically-based companies start to sell at around $60. Some foreign machines are available with straight stitching; the problems to consider here are the availability of servicing (should anything go wrong with the machine before the guarantee expires) and the availability of parts after it expires.

The zigzag machine has a needle that straight stitches and swings from side to side. It's touted for the durability it builds into seams subject to strain, and for the stretch it provides when knit fabrics are being sewn. (A straight stitch will do the first job when two rows of stitching are sewn in seams subject to stress; it will do the second job on all but the super-stretchy knits when fabric is stretched slightly while sewing.)

The cheapest zigzags can be used to overcast, satin stitch, blind stitch, darn, make buttonholes, and sew on buttons; they can cost as little as $70. From there, the price goes up to over $600, depending on the number of convenience features it offers —for example, being able to make a button-hole without maneuvering the fabric and never having to lubricate the machine. Decorative stitching is another much-bally-hooed feature of zigzag machines. This feature as well as most other deluxe features take time and practice to master, often go unused, and save only a few minutes of sewing time. In short, these deluxe features aren't really essential to the funda-mental purpose for which you buy a sewing machine—to make a durable, attractive gar-ment. Ultimately, you must base your decision on whether the specialty jobs they do warrant the extra cost involved.

How can I make sure I am buying a good machine? Personally test machines you're interested in buying. You can't get a "feel" for what a machine can do or its ease of operation if you merely watch a salesperson demonstrate it. Even more important, the salesperson may not take the time to fill you in on some of the finer points about the machine and is unlikely to apprise you of its shortcomings.

Only fabrics the machine can handle well will be on hand for demonstration purposes, so take along swatches of fabrics you intend to sew most with—for example, two swatches each of a shirtweight cotton (or cotton and synthetic blend), a heavy wool coating, a sheath lining, a polyester double-knit, a chiffon or nylon tricot. Test the machine using several types of threads, including a heavy-duty mercerized cotton, a cotton-wrapped polyester-core, and a buttonhole twist. The thread that you use should also contrast sharply with your fabric swatches so that you can clearly see the machine stitching.

Check the machine on these points:
Operation and stitching
• Is it quiet and free of objectionable noise and vibration at high speeds?
• Does it change readily from one speed to another? Does it start easily? Sew slowly? Stop immediately when you want it to?
• Stitch straight and curved seams through two layers of both like and unlike fabrics. Do stitches lock within the fabric layers, or does thread loop on one side? Do in-dividual stitches form a straight line? Does fabric drift to the right or left? Is the fabric easy to guide when stitching curved seams? Do unlike fabrics—such as a heavy wool coating and a synthetic sheath lining—feed under the needle at the same rate of speed so one layer doesn't extend beyond the other when you reach the end of the fabric?
• Can both top and bobbin tensions be adjusted easily for different fabrics?

• Can the presser foot be easily adjusted to accommodate the fabric weights you'll be working with? If the presser foot is self-adjusting but can't be manually adjusted, you may not be able to sew over intersecting seams (four thicknesses) of heavy fabrics. Can the presser foot be raised beyond its normal "up" position so that you can easily slide thick fabrics beneath it?

• Are the feed dogs smooth? Do they chew up sheer fabrics? Can they be dropped if you want to use the machine for darning or embroidery? If they can't be dropped, is there a plate available to cover them? (If this attachment isn't included with the machine, don't buy it separately—use masking tape to cover the feed dogs.)

• Are there adjustable lock positions for forward and reverse stitching?

• Is the knee or foot speed control comfortable to use?

If you're testing a zigzag machine, can you switch easily to straight stitching? Do two sets of presser foots and throat plates come with the machine: one set with a wide presser foot and a wide needle hole in the throat plate for zigzag stitching, and another set with a narrow presser foot and a small needle hole in the throat plate for straight stitching?

General

• Is the machine easy to thread?

• Is the bobbin easy to take out, thread, and replace? Does it fill evenly?

• Can cover plates be easily removed, and are all parts readily accessible for cleaning and oiling?

• Is the instruction manual clear and easy to understand? Does it explain how to make tension adjustments? Buttonholes?

• Is wiring located where it won't be pinched? Is it protected against wear and dripping oil?

What else should I know before buying a machine? Understand all costs in addition to the price of the machine itself. Don't be misled by claims that you're paying only for a cabinet or service charges. The machine is included in the price.

• Buy from a reputable dealer who can give you reliable service. Ask whether he'll service the machine for you at home while the guarantee is in effect.

• Ask for a written guarantee, and study it before buying any machine. The best guarantee comes from the manufacturer—dealers can move or go out of business. Terms of guarantee vary widely, but you should be sure yours has the conventional long-term assurance (20 to 30 years) protecting specific parts against defective workmanship. The head may have a long-term guarantee, for example, but the motor may have one for a shorter period. Some parts (light bulbs, belts, needles, for example) aren't guaranteed.

• Find out what restrictions the guarantee contains. Is the machine limited to "family use" or "use by original owner"? If so, will you find this is an inconvenience in the future? Does the manufacturer guarantee that replacement parts will be available for a specific length of time? You, too, may move; find out how many service centers are available throughout the country. If you can't personally take a machine to a service center, will you have to pay the cost of shipping the machine to the factory for service?

• Find out whether the machine you get now can be traded in later if your sewing needs change.

• Pay cash if possible, rather than buy on installment, to avoid interest charges.

• Find out whether the dealer gives free lessons on how to use the machine—you're entitled to them.

Basic Supplies

You've already accumulated some of the supplies you'll need to start sewing. Others must be bought and used only for the sewing jobs they do, but altogether should cost no more than $15 for good quality. When you're at the notions counter, don't be swayed into buying more at first than you see in the list that follows; it includes all you'll ever need for any sewing project. Add to the essentials if and when you gain expertise and feel that other items would be worthwhile.

Supplies you've got on hand

• *Ironing board and iron.* Pad beneath the ironing board cover with cotton batting or a thick towel for a soft pressing surface. A steam iron is convenient since

it can be applied directly to fabric without shining it. You can use a dry iron, however, when a press cloth of muslin or other plain-woven cotton fabric is dampened and placed on the area to be pressed.
• *Tape measure*. It should be plastic or plastic-coated to prevent stretching.
• *Yardstick and ruler*. Make sure they have no ragged edges, or they may snag fabric when measuring.

Supplies to buy

• *Shears*. To cut fabric, get a pair of shears 7″ to 10″ long with a bent handle; the right length is the one that you can most comfortably hold and maneuver. Good-quality shears are made of steel and cost $7 to $10. They can also be used for clipping and slashing at the sewing machine, although a small pair of sharp nail scissors may be handier for these jobs. Never use shears for cutting string or paper, or you'll dull and nick them. Shears for southpaws are available.
• *Pins*. You'll need a lot of steel pins, so buy a box or two. Don't buy them in sheets—you pay more money for fewer pins.
• *Tracing wheel and paper*. Buy a smooth-edged wheel, which doesn't chew up the pattern tissue as a serrated wheel does when transferring pattern markings to fabric. Dressmaker's carbon paper is designed to be used on fabrics; do not use typing carbon paper. Make sure the package says the marks will wash out.
• *Needles*. For hand sewing, use needles sized 7 to 8 for heavy fabrics, sized 9 or 10 for fine fabrics. Needles for your sewing machines come in sizes 9 (for fine fabrics) to 18 (for heavy fabrics).
Some seamstresses swear by the necessity of other equipment, such as tailor's hams and sleeveboards for pressing, and dress forms for fitting. Other seamstresses never use them and get equally fine results. You may find a dress form helpful if you're not the standard pattern size and must make major alterations. Once you've sewn a number of basic or simply-styled garments and become familiar with the particular adjustments you need, you may find that a form is unnecessary. You can make some pressing equipment yourself; the *Better Homes and Gardens Sewing Book* gives instructions on how to do it.

Patterns

A pattern is to a seamstress what a blueprint is to a carpenter. A few serviceable garments and household items that require practically no shaping or fitting can be made without a pattern, but only professional designers have the training that tells them how much ease to allow for a particular design or how to design a collar so that it stands up instead of lying down.

Although some newspapers and women's magazines feature patterns for mail order, most people usually buy patterns in fabric stores, variety stores, department and discount stores that carry fabric, and some fabric manufacturers' outlets.

Pattern catalogs are issued monthly to the stores. To give a seamstress time to sew garments suitable for upcoming weather, new designs appear several months before a season begins. Basic and popular designs remain in the catalogs year after year. Catalogs are divided into sections by size and/or design; special sections are set aside for designs that are easy and quick to sew. After selecting the patterns you want from the catalogs, tell a salesperson the name of the maker, the style number, and the size of each pattern you want. If a particular design in your size is out of stock, it can be ordered.

Although patterns are available for nearly every conceivable garment from lingerie to maternity wear, bathing suits, Halloween costumes, and choir robes, studies show that the types of garments on which the greatest savings can be made are daytime dresses and children's clothing. The more expensive a ready-to-wear garment is, the greater your savings on a similar home-sewn garment. Such big-ticket items include coats and suits, evening wear for both men and women, and designer-styled clothes.

Other best buys in patterns are those that feature multiple style variations of one garment like a blouse, skirt or trousers, and those that feature ensembles that can be matched, mixed, and added to for years.

Get started with easy styles. Your goal as a beginner is to master fundamental construction techniques (such as sewing straight seams, curved seams and darts; attaching waistbands and facings; hemming), and you want to choose simply-styled patterns that will allow you to do this. As you gain experience, you can successfully tackle designs with more complicated style features and construction methods. Many seamstresses, however, continue to work with those patterns called "easy" or "jiffy" because they can be made in a short time.

Don't start out with patterns that include these design features:
• set-in sleeves
• collars with sharp points or deep curves
• V-necklines or collars
• yoked garments, especially those with curved seaming or bias-cut fabric
• in-seam (hidden) pockets
• pressed or knife pleats
• intricate details, like pin tucking, smocking, bound buttonholes, and continuous loop fastenings
• any bias-cut garments
• any garments that require tailoring or couturier techniques

Good patterns to start out with include:
• sleeveless and collarless blouses and A-line dresses
• loose-fitting kimono sleeves
• robes
• ties
• gathered and A-line skirts with waistband or waist facing

When choosing your first patterns, keep in mind that you want several different types (an A-line dress, sleeveless blouse, a softly-gathered skirt, for example) that will provide you with a variety of learning and sewing experiences. It's also a good idea to make your first pattern twice in succession, using different fabrics. This way, you'll be able to repeat and hone the skills you learned while sewing it before going on to a garment having new construction methods.

Buy the right size. Patterns are available in standard figure types and sizes. Don't assume, though, that you'll take the same size in a pattern as you take in ready-to-wear clothing. Consult the back pages of pattern books and the sales help in the sewing department to determine the correct size pattern for your measurements and body frame. Each pattern you purchase should be checked against the wearer when you get it home, to make certain of the fit.

When you must make adjustments and alterations, don't be satisfied with anything but *good* fit. Garments that don't fit properly are unattractive, uncomfortable, and not very durable. Adjustments in length and circumference are fairly simple to make on the pattern; instructions for length adjustments are given on pattern pieces where they're most often needed. Alterations for major figure problems like high, rounded shoulders or one hip larger than another are more involved than adjustments and should be made on the pattern before cutting fabric.

If your measurements are a combination of pattern sizes or you need to make other major alterations, you can speed construction of all future garments by making a master-guide garment out of a cheap muslin fabric and from what pattern companies call their "basic pattern." (To find out where to get detailed information on how to make the basic muslin garment as well as alterations for specific figure problems, see the sewing books in the bibliography at the end of this chapter.)

Give your patterns a long and varied life. Some people use patterns once, then throw them away. Carefully and imaginatively handled, patterns can last for years and be used by several people. Here's how:
1. Fuse your pattern tissue to a sturdy backing fabric to avoid tearing it. Stacy Fabrics Corp. has a fusing fabric designed for this purpose. Iron-on, nonwoven interfacing can also be used.
2. Pin, mark, and cut pattern tissue carefully. Imprecise cutting or tears or rips in your pattern will decrease its longevity. Don't pull or lean on the pattern tissue while it's pinned to your fabric. Marking darts, seamlines, etc., with tailor's tacks rips a pattern faster than lightly pressing those markings with a tracing wheel and dressmaker's carbon paper.
3. Pattern pieces can easily stray or get thrown away, so store them carefully in the pattern envelope. Fused pattern tissue pieces should be rolled and, if possible, put in a cylindrical cardboard tube.
4. Mix garments from different patterns. Expand your pattern and wardrobe's potential at no added pattern cost by combining a skirt from one pattern, a blouse from another, and a jacket from a third. Let imagination and proportions be guides.
5. Mix pattern pieces from different patterns. Suppose you don't like the sleeves

that come with a particular garment or you've used that style in several garments and grown tired of it. You can switch the unwanted sleeves with those of another pattern so long as both sets have the set-in sleeve application, the same type of curved armhole, and are set in the sleeve opening at the same angle. Dress bodices and skirts, necklines, collars, and closures can also be interchanged on a garment if certain structural similarities between them are maintained. *(Better Homes and Gardens Sewing Book* gives instructions on how to redesign patterns.)

6. Buy simple, basic styles that can be easily lengthened, shortened, or redesigned. A classic example of this is the shift pattern with sleeves. The pattern you buy may look like a housedress. But make it in a dressy fabric, add a sash of the same or contrasting fabric, and you have a daytime street dress. Or shorten it a bit, adapt the jewel neckline to accommodate a cowl collar, and it's a tunic to be worn with or without a skirt, trousers, or shorts. Make it without sleeves, and it's a jumper. Shorten it to hip or waist length, omit the sleeves, give it a V-neckline, and it's a vest. Make it floor length, adapt the bodice for a deep, round neckline, and it's an evening dress. Trousers can be similarly shortened for knickers, pedal pushers, or shorts. Blouses can be elongated into dresses by accommodating for the extra width at the hips. Robes can be shortened into bed jackets—a good gift idea for someone who likes to read in bed. To preserve your original pattern tissue, trace each garment variation onto plain tissue paper, allowing for style and length changes.

Save Money By Not Using Patterns

Gathered and unfitted, pleated skirts are the easiest garments for the average seamstress to make without a pattern. For gathered skirts, cut two to three lengths (depending on the fullness desired) of 36-inch-wide fabric on the lengthwise grain, allowing for the depth of hem needed; attach lengths at selvages with straight seams (leaving one seam open seven to nine inches at the top for the zipper); run two rows of machine gathering stitches at the top; gather; insert the zipper; and attach the waistband. Do the

same for the pleated skirt, except allow fabric that's three times the hip measurement for pleats that open on one side only and omit the gathering.

Use old clothes that are no longer serviceable as patterns for similar new garments. Carefully open the seams of the garment, then use the pieces as your pattern for a brand-new garment.

Fabric

Buying just the right fabric to set off you and your garment can be fun or a chore. The secret is to trust your taste, and not be intimidated. If you're a smart sewer, educated consumerism will also be your guide. Here's what you should know to make the best selection for your money:

What are the best fabric buys? The seamstress who wants to make a wise investment of both time and money should look for:
- Firm, closely-woven fabrics like gabardine, gingham, and percale that are easy to cut and quick to sew and press. Because they don't fray, little or no seam- or raw-edge finishing is needed.
- Fabrics in solid colors, small-scale allover prints, small checks, and thin stripes. These require little or no matching, and so less yardage and layout time are involved.
- Fabric in which the design or texture is the same on both sides, and fabrics without nap, offer the most economy.

Stay away from fabrics like these:
- Slippery fabrics like silk, synthetic sheers, satin, and tricot. They're hard to cut and sew accurately.
- Fabrics printed off-grain. Avoid them by checking to see that the print runs at right angles to the *selvage*—the finished edge that runs lengthwise on each side of the fabric.

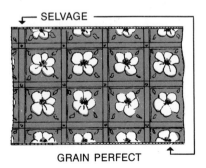

GRAIN PERFECT

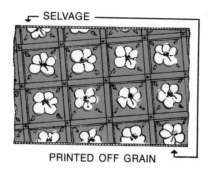

SELVAGE

PRINTED OFF GRAIN

- Loosely woven fabrics like silk, linen, and rayon with a linen look that fray and take extra time to seam-finish.
- Extremely lightweight or stretchy fabrics like tricot, chiffon, and stretchy knits which will need special machine adjustments to prevent puckered stitching.

Where can I get good fabric buys? Fabric prices range from under $1 to over $100 for a yard. Quality should be judged not by price, but by the fabric properties. Of course, fabrics that cost $1 a yard should be carefully scrutinized even if they're on sale, but more expensive fabrics can also be poor purchases if you buy only on impulse. Some studied know-how will contribute to your sewing profitably and enjoyably.

One of your first steps should be to get a sense of the fabric prices and dealer reliability in your area. There may be a slight to substantial price difference between two stores selling the same line of fabric or similar fabric. Compare the prices and quality of a printed percale, a solid-color plain knit, a lightweight wool-and-synthetic woven, and a pile lining fabric among several stores. Notice how the fabrics are displayed and cared for. Question the salespeople about the fabrics. Will they be helpful if you run into a problem on a garment as well as when you first buy the fabric? Is at least one of them an experienced sewer who can help you rework a construction mistake? What other merchandise does the store offer? What extra services does the store offer customers such as sewing clinics and fashion shows? Can you get a refund for fabric that doesn't perform as specified?

Here's where to concentrate your comparison shopping when looking for good fabric buys:

- *Chain stores,* including discount chain stores. Because they buy in bulk, they can offer lower prices than independent retailers. The salespeople may not be trained to help you, though, with questions or problems you have about sewing.
- *Independent retailers.* Although their prices for fabrics are usually higher than chain stores, they remain competitive by offering more services—for example, salespeople who are experienced sewers, "free" sewing lessons with the purchase of fabric.
- *Variety stores.* Although the selection here is usually small, you can find good buys of fabric on the bolt or in two- to three-yard lengths. If information on care or fiber content isn't available, however, these can turn out to be costly bargains.
- *Fabric outlets.* These are run by fabric manufacturers, so the majority are located in the South and Northeast. Fabric in addition to the manufacturer's own may be sold; prices are slightly to substantially below retail prices. Salespeople may be experienced seamstresses, and patterns may be available. This can be a good place to get large quantities of the same fabric at a time—for household curtains, for example. Even if you don't live near a fabric outlet, you may vacation in an area where one is located—then's a good time to stock up.

Also be sure to check out these opportunities for good fabric buys:
- *Sales.* Fabrics run in seasons, and end-of-season sales are held by most fabric stores. You'll find good buys and bad at sales. Make sure you're not buying a fabric that was made several seasons ago (is it dusty? light-faded?); manufacturer-flawed remnants cut from anywhere on a bolt of otherwise perfectly good fabric; end cuts (½ to three yards of fabric left over from the end of a bolt but with no care instructions available); off-grain fabrics; bonded fabrics in which the backing and outer layers easily pull apart. Sale goods are usually sold "as is, non-returnable and non-exchangeable," so purchase with care.
- *Remnants.* The same warnings for sale fabrics apply here. Check the fabric for irregularities; see if care instructions are available. But if a remnant proves to be a good buy, don't be dismayed that only short fabric lengths are available. You may find a matching pair of remnants which will be

enough for a garment that's made in sections. Or you may find two remnants in the same print but different colors, or a solid color and a complementary stripe—together they may be just enough to make an eye-catching four-to-six-gored skirt when the two fabrics are alternated.

• *Fabric clubs.* If you have access to only one or two fabric stores, a fabric club can expand your selection. The clubs advertise in women's and sewing magazines; joining costs about $4 to $5 a year. What membership entitles you to varies from club to club —some offer designer fabrics and notions; some send representatives to discuss their fabrics and sewing techniques; some advertise seasonal sales on fabrics; some send swatches with descriptions attached, and some send patterns and swatches that must be paired off by you. Ask to be sent a free brochure for the clubs you'd like to investigate further in order to decide which is the best for you to join. Don't join a club that fails to say whether it provides care instructions, a breakdown of fiber content, and a refund on fabric that isn't right.

• *Freebies.* Scout around your home for fabric that's going to waste—old dresses with full skirts can be torn apart and the fabric recycled for aprons, blouses, children's clothing, vests, or ties. Old sheets can be turned into work smocks, towels into bath robes, old blue jeans into vests, brimmed caps, or tote bags. An old lace tablecloth could make up into a baby's christening gown or could be used for collars, cuffs, or trim on dressy clothes. An old plaid blanket could be turned into a car coat. Make sure you get a good return on the time and energy you'll spend recycling old clothes by checking them for overall good condition. If you find any weak or worn areas or stains that are impossible to remove, maneuver your pattern pieces to avoid them. Lay all pattern pieces on the fabric to be recycled before cutting to find out if you have enough fabric for the project. Clean the fabric before cutting and sewing.

Sewing Tips

You've got your machine, equipment, pattern, and fabric—the best your money can buy. Before you start to sew, latch on to a good sewing book. Ask friends who sew to recommend the books. See if you can borrow and study them, or examine some in book stores. Study the table of contents and the index. Does the book discuss subjects you need to know about now as well as some you'll want to know about in the future? The one you want should explain every sewing process from adjustments to fine hemming, to making draperies and slip covers. It should have easy-to-understand techniques for putting your garments together. Read the section on making darts. Do you understand it? Does the book explain terms you've seen in a preliminary reading of your pattern's instruction sheet?

Although a good sewing book is an invaluable, technical guide to putting garments together, every seamstress also collects or devises her own tricks and shortcuts over the years. Some save her money. Some simplify her sewing. Others make her garments long-lasting and attractive. But why wait for years of experience? Get started right by taking advantage of these tips:

How to save money

• Don't let the margin of excess tissue paper beyond the cutting lines of your pattern lay some of your fabric to waste. When cutting fabric, overlap the margins of adjacent pieces so the cutting lines are nearly touching.

• After a garment has been cut out, save big fabric scraps for contrasting trims, appliqués, or pockets on other garments. Some scraps may be big enough for small-sized articles of clothing—belts, vests, shorts, children's clothing. Smaller scraps should be saved to patch the original garment itself should it be torn or burned or used for patchwork or stuffing for pillows.

• When a garment is finally threadbare, tear it up, using the fabric as rags. Remove any closures still in good condition—to insert in future garments.

• Instead of buying a seam-guide attachment for your sewing machine, use masking tape or cellophane tape as a guide. Cut two strips of tape about 4 to 5 inches long and lay one edge of each piece of tape ⅝-inch on one side of the machine needle (lowered into the bobbin hole for easy measurement).

How to sew a long life into your garments. Do you have trouble keeping growing children in clothes? Do you and your spouse have trouble fitting into some of your own? When you know how to sew, you and your family can get maximum use out of the clothes you have by using tricks that accommodate growing pains. Here are some growth adjustments to build into your clothes:

• *Deep hems* help you keep up with growing children and changing fashion. Simply add one or two inches to the hem allowance; then you've got room to lengthen the garment in the future. If the crease shows when you take the hem down, cover it with braid, rickrack, or lace, depending on the type of fabric used in the garment. Or take the hem down, make a horizontal tuck at the crease, fold the tuck up ¼ inch, topstitch in place and rehem as needed (this can be used for skirts and dresses, but works especially well with shorts and trousers in which a fake cuff is created). Whenever a garment would not look attractive with a deep hem (in full, circular skirts, for example), lengthening can still be accomplished by taking the hem down and adding a 2-inch strip of lightweight fabric or commercial bias hem facing.

• *One-inch seam allowances* can be cut for straight seams (side, center, and inseam) on skirts, shorts, and trousers instead of the standard ⅝-inch allowances found on commercial patterns. Let these larger seams out as needed, tapering gradually from just beneath the waistband to the point where extra fullness is needed. Seams should become no narrower, however, than ⅜-inch.

• *Hidden tucks* can be sewn into children's clothes, then let out as size changes. Two methods of making tucks, one for lengthening the waist on a dress bodice and one for lengthening a skirt, are described in *Better Homes and Gardens Sewing Book*.

• *Trims and fabric* (either the same as in the garment or contrasting) can also be used to lengthen the life of skirts, dresses, and trousers. Skirts and dress bodices can be lengthened by inserting new fabric in a contrasting or complementary color in lengths as needed at the waistline. To do this, cut the necessary width plus seam allowances and seam. Two or more bands of fabric can be added to the hem of a skirt, and braid applied over the band seams to hide them.

• *Careful pattern choice* can also help to accommodate growing pains. Some garments lend themselves especially well to weight fluctuation. Wraparound dresses, jackets, coats, and skirts can be adjusted to accommodate minor body changes. Skirts and trousers with elasticized waistbands grow or shrink with the wearer. Shifts, A-lines, and princess silhouettes will cover a small weight loss or gain. Also look for commercial patterns designed for people taking off weight.

Repairs

Sewing is one of those multi-charmed, do-it-yourself endeavors. Not only can you make your own clothes at less than half the cost of ready-to-wear, but you can also repair tears, holes, burns, and other signs of wear, adding even more to the long life expectancy your good workmanship has already built in. Now, as always, a stitch in time means fewer wardrobe replacements and more money for other needs.

Much of the equipment you use to construct garments—sewing machine, shears, pins, ruler, tape measure, iron and ironing board—is also used in mending. Other supplies which you'll need specifically for repair work should be kept in a convenient location (a large drawer, basket, or labelled boxes). The fabric scraps from your sewing projects, along with usable parts of discarded clothing such as buttons, zipper, and hook, should be stored with your equipment.

Other supplies and tools you'll want to have on hand can be bought at fabric stores or notions counters. Select from the following list those aids which will help you with your kind of mending:

• *A bodkin* is handy for replacing elastics and tapes in casings.

• *Tailor's chalk* can be used to mark guidelines for a repair. Make sure it's washable.

• *Embroidery hoops* hold fabric taut for hand or machine darning.

• *Needles* should be the long-eyed type used for crewel in sizes for both fine and heavy work. A blunt-end or round-eyed tapestry needle is best for repairing sweaters.

• *Net,* chiffon, and gauze fabrics are sometimes used as bases for darning thin spots.

• *Press-on interfacing* can be used as a backing for machine darns.

• *Tapes*—twill and bias—are used for reinforcing and finishing some garment damages.

• *Threads* should be kept on hand in an assortment of colors that predominate in your family's wardrobe. No. 150 cotton thread is used to darn fine fabrics; No. 8 to 100 for machine darning; heavy-duty mercerized thread for sewing on buttons; silk thread which can be split for fine darning; yarn for wool socks and sweaters; nylon and cotton yarn for darning other knit fabrics.

Darning: A garment area is darned when it first begins to wear thin or when a small hole or tear appears. Follow these guidelines when darning:

• Every mend should look as much like the original fabric in texture and weave as possible. Anything obvious will limit the garment's future usefulness. Remember, too, the sooner you repair a garment before wearing it again, the longer it will last.

• Use a fine needle and short length of thread. Long thread pulled across a damaged area may pull it out of shape.

• Darn on the right side of the fabric. To blend the darn, run the stitching unevenly into the cloth surrounding the hole.

• Take small stitches, but don't pull the thread tight or the darn will pucker. Too-loose stitches will make darns look puffy.

• Pull ends of darning yarn to wrong side of garment, and cut, but not too closely.

• Work so that raw edges of a tear or hole are on the underside.

• Steam-press finished darn on wrong side. If garment fabric is wool or napped, brush darn to lift texture.

The machine darn is a quick way to repair three-cornered, jagged, or diagonal tears.

1. Thread sewing machine with either silk or fine cotton thread (whichever best matches the luster of the garment fabric) in a shade slightly darker than the fabric. Place damaged area right side up on a flat surface. Straighten and trim any tangled or frayed yarns.

2. Cut a reinforcement underlay, slightly larger than the damaged area, from a lightweight, press-on interfacing. Slip the reinforcement beneath the damaged area, adhesive side up; pin edges. Comb fabric yarns into place, cover with a thin cloth, and press. If necessary, press again from the wrong side.

3. Machine stitch back and forth across the underlay, usually with the grain of the fabric and catching the edge of the garment fabric, blending stitching into an uneven border.

4. Trim away any excess reinforcement fabric, unless the surrounding area needs it for strength. Tack reinforcement invisibly to the back of garment fabric, using padding stitches (see page 198).

5. If damaged area is a three-corner tear or badly frayed, machine stitch both lengthwise and crosswise.

To machine-darn holes that can be later covered by buttons or worn spots in trousers, work clothes, or table linens, use embroidery hoop to hold fabric taut, and follow step 1 above. Then:

1. Release the pressure on the presser foot until the presser-foot lifter won't hold up the foot. Lower the feed dogs or cover them with a strip of masking tape.

2. If the damage needs reinforcement, baste a piece of thin fabric of a matching color around the hole or worn area. To hold it taut while stitching, place the area to be darned in an embroidery hoop.

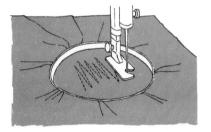

3. Slip the embroidery hoop under the presser foot. Stitch across the part to be darned, moving it back and forth until the hole is filled or the thin area is reinforced. Follow the garment-fabric grain.

Patching: Mending with patches is generally reserved for large holes and tears. Follow these guidelines:

• Patch a damaged garment that's slightly shrunken and faded with a similarly shrunken and faded patch to help hide the mend. Also shrink a patch used to mend a shrunken or washed garment, or the mend may not lie flat after laundering.

• To patch garments you've sewn yourself, use a matching scrap of fabric you've saved for just such an eventuality. To patch a readymade garment, cut fabric from a facing, hem, pocket, or sash.

• Cut patches with the grain of the garment fabric, making sure that lengthwise and crosswise yarns match.

● If the garment fabric has a design, slide patch material beneath the damaged area until the design matches. For a napped fabric such as corduroy, also match the direction of the pile.

● Use commercial press-on patches for quick mending jobs on firm fabrics, such as those used in work or play clothes. They may need replacing after several washings.

● Make these attractive, long-wearing patches out of scraps of contrasting fabric.

Hemmed patch. This sturdy patch is done by hand and is appropriate for most washable garments.

1. Mark smallest possible square or rectangle to remove damaged area, then cut it out along lengthwise and crosswise threads.

2. Clip ¼ inch deep at each corner of cut-out square or rectangle.

3. Turn under all edges of square or rectangle slightly beyond ends of clips; press.

4. Slide a scrap of fabric that's bigger than the damaged area under the cut-out square or rectangle until the pattern, if any, matches. Pin patch in place (see sketch A).

5. Turn garment inside out, then cut patch about 1 inch larger than the square or rectangle on all four sides. Baste patch in place (see sketch B).

6. Turn the garment right side out, and hem the patch to the garment with fine running hem stitches (page 198), stitching closely at the corners and just catching surrounding edge of garment.

7. Turn garment inside out. If the garment fabric is lightweight and washable, turn under patch edges about ¼ inch. Snip out bulk. Baste, and hem invisibly to garment. If garment fabric is thick, catchstitch (page 198) patch edges to garment.

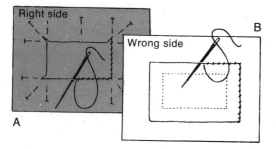

Knit-stitch patch. This isn't a patch in the usual sense that a square or rectangular fabric scrap is applied to a damaged area. Instead, matching thread is used to reknit a plain-knit garment or sweater that has been damaged. This "patch" is almost invisible and stretches in use (see directions below and sketches on page 196).

1. Make two horizontal cuts, one above the damage and one below.

2. Ravel the damaged knit to the ends of these two cuts. To prevent further raveling, run thread through the loops at each cut.

3. Thread loose ends of yarns at each side of damage through a needle and pull ends back into underside of knit. Follow the illustrations to complete patch.

Mends for typical clothing damage: Most good mends are made using both machine and hand sewing. Although fabric, type of clothing, and location and extent of damage will dictate the methods used, here are some common damages and the mends best suited to them.

Machine stitching unraveled in seam of washable trousers. Pin seam together, and restitch full length of seam, using short stitch length and strong thread. To make seam extra strong, press seam edges together and stitch again close to seam edge. Finish seam edge with hand overcasting or machine zigzagging.

Large hole in knee of dungarees. Repair this damage with a strip salvaged from a good section of discarded dungarees. With chalk, mark and section to be removed from inseam to side seam. Open inseam and side seam from ½ inch above top chalk line to ½ inch below lower chalk line. Cut out damaged section along chalk lines and, in its place, set in the salvaged strip cut 2 inches longer than the opening (this allows for two ½ inch seams stitched ½ inch above top and bottom chalk lines). Stitch, and press seams open. Restitch inseam and side seam. The same repair can be done on better trousers, disguising the patch seams with the rantering stitch (page 198). This patch is less noticeable than one with four edges showing.

Small hole in knee of dungarees. This method involves shortening leg length one inch plus length of damaged area, so use it only for small holes or for trousers that will still be worn after such shortening (if not by the original wearer, perhaps by a shorter family member). Draw chalk lines above and below the damaged area. Carefully open inseam and side seam from bottom of leg

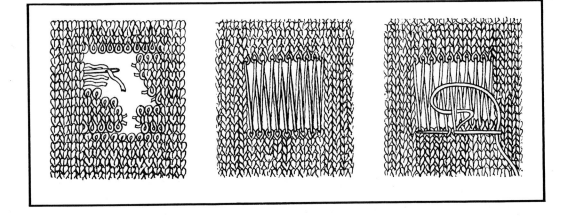

to ½-inch above top chalk line. Cut along chalk lines to remove damage. Join entire lower section of leg to upper section by machine stitching a single horizontal seam. Restitch inseam and side seam. Level and rehem lower edge of leg; shorten the other pants leg correspondingly. This repair is less noticeable than the inset patch described above for the large hole in dungaree knee because there's only one seam. The rantering stitch will help disguise this particular mend.

Round hole in girl's or boy's wool, twillweave trousers. Cut a patch from pocket facing, and baste it under hole. (Replace the hole in pocket facing with a sturdy, cotton fabric.) Using mercerized thread slightly darker than the garment fabric, machinestitch patch to garment following the diagonal lines of the twill weave.

Worn collar and band on tailored shirt. Rip collar from neckband. Machine-darn worn top collar area to interfacing. Cut away worn area on neckband. Reverse the collar so the darned portion is turned down and concealed. Press collar with the seam inside the neckband. Join the neckband to the collar with topstitching.

Ready-to-wear reinforcements Careful buying means minimal mending and long service. So run an eagle eye over every garment before you decide to take it. After all, a $3 shirt isn't a bargain if it falls apart the first time you wash it or if the buttonholes start to unravel before you've scarcely put it to use. Follow these tips to get the most for your ready-to-wear money:

• Choose types of garments that will best and longest meet your family's needs and not require exceptional care. For example, sturdy, closely-woven or knitted fabrics in dark colors stand wear better than open weaves or knits in light colors. Good clothes that can be dressed up or down for the occasion are better buys than sheer shirts, heavily trimmed dresses, or unusual colors that match only one or two outfits.

• Check size carefully. Bad fit causes unnecessary strain on garments which can cause tears later on.

• Examine style features and trims to see if they will hold up in use. Some features are satisfactory in dress clothing, but prove troublesome in work and play clothes.

• Inspect the workmanship in every garment, inside and out, to make sure it will give the service you expect. Look for generous seam allowances; finished seams; securely fastened closures; even hems; heavily stitched buttonholes. Take the time to select the best garment available; two garments, though they may look alike, have probably been made by different people who may not be equally skillful or exacting.

Give every garment you buy another double-check at home before it's worn. Some manufacturing errors and haphazard construction methods are easy to spot. Others aren't so obvious. Taking the time to look for and reinforce these potential trouble spots will avoid costlier and more extensive repairs later on:

Dangling threads. Knot, fasten, and clip off threads wherever machine stitching ends. If possible, pull threads to the inside before knotting. If threads are long, slip them through the eye of a needle and take a few fastening stitches before clipping; or pull long threads inside a hem or fold, then slide needle out through fabric but leave the threads behind.

Broken, knotted, crooked, or puckered stitching. On the inside of a garment, carefully rip out this stitching and let your machine-sewn replacement stitches overlap the end points of the good manufacturer's stitching. If the faulty stitching is on the outside of the garment, pick out bad stitches so that you have enough thread on each end to pull to the inside and tie. Replacement stitching on the outside should just meet, not overlap, and can be hand-tied by pulling threads to the inside. If faulty stitching is hard to reach by machine, replace it with hand-sewn backstitches (see opposite column).

Fraying seams. If seams fray slightly, overcast (page 198) the raw seam edges. If seams fray readily, run a row of machine stitching near the cut edges, then finish by overcasting or machine zigzagging.

Loosely stitched hems. Ready-made dresses and skirts are often hemmed with loose stitching, which can result in a sagging hem and then a torn one if a shoe heel catches in it. Rehem, using one of the secure hemming stitches on page 198.

Vents, U- and V-shaped necklines. To strengthen these openings without adding bulk, lay narrow twill tape next to the seamline or fold (on the inside), cross at the corners, and firmly stitch in place.

Pocket corners. Keep pockets on blouses or shirts from being torn by stitching reinforcement triangles at the top corners.

Plackets. Wearing and ironing can damage plackets unless they're reinforced. For a placket opening that is only hemmed and tapers to nothing at the tip of its inverted V-shape, reinforce by making a small pleat, then bar tacking by hand or machine (as shown). For lapped plackets, make a thread tack to ease wearing strain (it won't show when the cuff is buttoned).

Kick pleats. Stitching tends to break in a slim skirt at the top of a kick pleat. For short kick pleats that don't hang from the top of the waistband, tape the end of the seamline inside the skirt. On the outside, topstitch the top of the kick pleat in place in a trapezoidal shape.

Buttonholes. Rework raveled or weak buttonhole stitching with the buttonhole stitch (see sketch at bottom of page). If buttonhole is completely unraveled, machine stitch close to the hole's cut edges. Then work the buttonhole by hand.

Basic Handstitches: Handstitches work best for mends that must be soft and flexible, afford greater control than machine sewing, and can be used to make mends that are nearly invisible. Handwork helps pull damaged areas into position before darning and patching, disguises seamlines of insets or patches, and goes where a machine can't.

Here are some basic handstitches that you should practice and master. There are no hard and fast rules for using them; simply adapt them to your own tasks:

The backstitch is used for places hard to reach by machine, such as underarm seams, gussets, and plackets. It gives the appearance of machine stitching on the outside, but stitches on the under-fabric layer overlap. Begin by pushing needle through both layers of fabric and pulling thread through tautly but not tightly. Take a stitch ⅛-inch behind point where thread was pulled through fabric and bring needle out ⅛-inch ahead of the same point. Repeat by inserting needle ⅛-inch behind previous stitch.

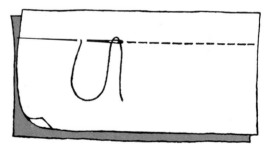

The buttonhole stitch can be used to reinforce the edges of a worn, handworked buttonhole (art A) as well as to improve the appearance and durability of machine-made buttonholes in ready-made clothing (art B).

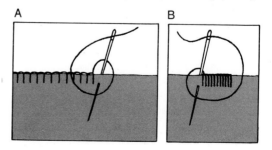

The rantering stitch is used to disguise unwanted seamlines, especially in heavy, thick fabrics where the stitches can be buried. Pinch the seamline between the thumb and forefinger, and stitch back and forth across the seamline in a V direction, picking up only one yarn on each side of the seam. Pull thread taut but not tight.

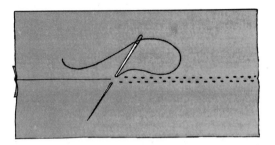

The seed stitch is a variation of the backstitch. Only tiny stitches separated by a small space appear on the right side. This stitch is nearly invisible and can be used to restitch ripped zipper plackets, where appearance matters. Carry the needle back only one or two fabric threads before inserting it through both layers of fabric.

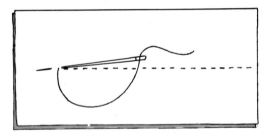

The slipstitch offers protection for garments in which the hem will be frequently rubbed by the leg, such as slim-lined skirts. Between stitches, the thread runs inside the hem fold. You may want to machine stitch the fold in this hem before slip stitching it to the garment.

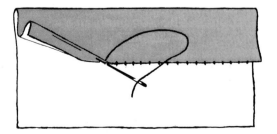

The catch stitch is used on the wrong side of a garment to hold the cut edge of one fabric next to the cut edge of another. The depth and spacing of these stitches depend on the kind of fabric and repair being done.

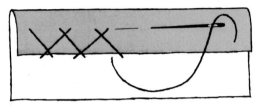

The overcasting stitch protects cut edges against ordinary fraying. It is used to finish seam edges, not to attach seams to garment.

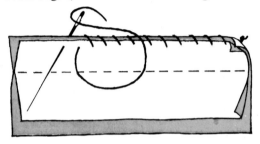

The padding stitch helps tack and hold two layers of fabric together for machine darning. It can also be used to reinforce a darn and protect against inside abrasion.

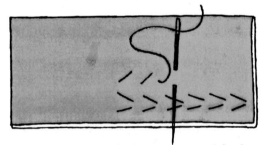

Running hem stitches are spaced farther apart than most other hemming stitches, so they work up quickly. Notice that the long, horizontal thread is slightly above and behind the hem's raw edge.

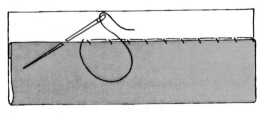

How to Save on Dry Cleaning

If you are sending clothing to commercial dry cleaners, you can save many dollars annually by letting a load accumulate and either doing it yourself at a "coin cleaners" or having it done for you by "bulk cleaning" or by the new proliferating "steam-and-clean" process.

Coin Cleaning

The machines take any amount, usually up to eight pounds, for about $3.50. You can put whatever you like into the load but you run a risk of linting and dye-bleeding. There is no way to test the latter beforehand. Best bet, if there's a coin cleaner near you, is to use it only for ruggeder clothing such as worsted suits, sweaters, and heavy outer clothing; send delicate blouses and dresses of fabrics like crepe to the dry cleaners—unless there's a bulk cleaning establishment in your area. Before coin-cleaning, try to get out stains from those fabrics from which you customarily have no trouble removing them with ordinary spot remover or plain water. Form the habit of washing off food stains as swiftly as possible before they have a chance to dry and set—but only from those fabrics unaffected by water.

Send for a copy of the government's 32-page booklet *Removing Stains from Fabrics*, Home and Garden Bulletin No. 62, 50¢, from Consumer Information Center, Pueblo, Colo. 81009. It gives specific directions for removing a wide variety of spots and stains, naming the required removers principally by their chemical terms, which helps you in comparison-shopping among spot cleaner brands since most such products use one of a number of similar chemical formulations. It pays to know clearly what you're doing before attempting to remove a stain from a delicate fabric, be forewarned, because you can make things a great deal worse, and may even ruin garments.

Bulk Cleaning

This is really ordinary dry cleaning without the pressing and with a usual 10-pound minimum for about $4.50. Garments are tagged and sorted by hardness and softness of fabric. A "silk load" of delicate fabrics gets a much gentler cleaning cycle than a "raincoat load;" dark and light, heavily and lightly soiled clothing is separated. Pre-spotting is done for you with 100-pound air pressure for super-swift drying that eliminates rings. In both coin cleaning and bulk cleaning, garments come out surprisingly wrinkle free—usually no more wrinkled than when they went in.

Steam and Clean

This process is beginning to appear in communities across the country for about 15¢ more per pound than bulk cleaning. Clothing is pre-spotted, and post-spotted as well if it needs it, and after cleaning put into a steam chamber. Here machinery shakes the clothes in an atmosphere of high-pressure steam. Wrinkles literally shake out of most garments; a hot-air cycle removes the steam. Sweaters come out looking almost as if they had been blocked, wrinkles disappear completely from knits, and most suits need only the trouser creases pressed—easily done at home, although some establishments press them in for a charge.

Men's suits, particularly summer-weight ones, however, do get wrinkled. It's relatively easy to press a man's suit with a steam iron and make it look as if it had been pressed professionally. Always fill the steam iron reservoir to capacity before beginning, however. If the water runs out and the steam suddenly stops, you may not notice it before you've scorched the fabric. And, as you probably know, scorching is disastrous with synthetic fabrics because the heat fuses the fibers together.

How to Save on Home Laundering

With water costing as much as it does to heat, families trying to trim living costs are doing the family wash in cold water, and that's that—unless there's someone sick or a baby in the house. (Washing baby's diapers is about five times cheaper than paper throwaway diapers and about half the cost of a diaper service, incidentally.)

Knowing how to use soaps and synthetic detergents is essential for best results in home laundering at the greatest economy. The choice of a cleansing agent, in turn, depends on the fabric you're washing, the kind of soil to be removed, the hardness of the water, and type of washer you have. When soiled fabric is agitated in a washer, dirt is lifted from the fabric, broken into tiny particles, each of which is surrounded and held in suspension by a film of the soap or detergent solution to keep it from settling back on the clothes.

Soap?

Whether you decide to use soap or detergent depends partly on the hardness of your wash water. In soft or softened water, soap does an excellent cleaning job for less cost than detergent. But hard water is inappropriate for soap because the soap reacts with the "hardness" minerals, calcium and magnesium, to form soap scum. This settles on clothing in gray specks. Detergents solve this problem; used in sufficient quantity they do not form scum. In very hard water (over 20 grains per gallon), however, it is more economical to soften the water and use less detergent. *Precipitating* softeners (washing soda) should be dissolved in the wash water before adding soap, because they cannot dissolve soap scum once it has formed. *Nonprecipitating* softeners (such as Calgon or Okite), also known as "water conditioners," keep minerals in solution so they can't react with soap to form scum. They also tend to dissolve soap scum already on fabrics from previous washings. In addition, nonprecipitating softeners help prevent such minerals as iron and manganese, present in some water, from staining fabrics. Always add a nonprecipitating softener to water containing iron or manganese before adding a bleach.

Or Detergent?

Because they do not react with minerals in hard water to form scum, detergents have largely replaced soaps as the workhorse of the family wash. They also contain substances that increase their cleaning power. Heavy-duty detergents such as Ajax, Duz, Fab, and Tide, are quite effective for cleaning moderately or heavily soiled fabrics.

Consider what the fabric is made of when you choose a detergent. Alkaline salts in heavy-duty detergents damage wool and silk. Wash those fabrics in nonalkaline light-duty detergents. Cotton, linen, and synthetics are not affected by the alkalinity of heavy-duty detergents.

Light-duty detergents are suitable for washing lightly soiled fabrics. Examples are Ivory, Joy, Lux, Vel, and Woolite.

Shrinkage of wool during laundering is caused by agitation in the washer, tumbling in the dryer or over-rubbing by hand—not by the type of cleansing agent used. Unless wool fabrics have a shrink-resistant or wash-wear finish, mechanical action laundering should be held to a minimum. Sweaters, in particular, look new much longer hand-washed in a cold-water, light-duty detergent such as Woolite, merely squeezed to remove soil and suds.

Items of clothing that could in some way damage other garments in washing should be separated into individual loads. When sorting, combine items of similar color, fabric, construction, and amount of soil. Always test newly acquired colored items by dipping them in a solution of hot water and detergent and squeezing them out. If the color bleeds, the item should be washed separately. If you're not sure whether an item is washable, check its label.

Old standbys

Inexpensive chlorine bleach and ammonia have many household applications that cut down on the use of more expensive detergents and cleansers. Use diluted bleach to clean and disinfect sinks, refrigerator, toilet bowls, and garbage cans. Put a little ammonia in the water washing windows, ceramic tile, tubs, basins, mirrors, and painted woodwork. (*But never mix chlorine bleach and ammonia. The two together create a toxic gas.*)

Detergent: How Much?

Some washing machines, especially the front-loading tumbler types, give much better results with low-sudsing detergents like Dash, Salvo (tablets), All, or Cold-Water All, because of the way the machines operate. In top-loading washers, either high-sudsing or low-sudsing detergents can be used equally effectively. With a high-sudsing detergent a good layer of suds should remain throughout the wash cycle, however. Low-sudsing detergents should form and maintain only a thin layer during the washing cycle.

The amount of detergent you need depends on the water capacity of your washer, size of the load, soil and greasiness of the clothes, hardness of the water, and type of detergent, of course, but the principal reason for poor washing results is underuse of detergents. If you use too little of it the colors will not be as bright as they could be and whites may become gray or yellow. Use the amount of detergent that is suggested on the label, then experiment by slowly decreasing or increasing the amount until your laundry comes through looking as you would like it to.

It helps to consult the instruction book that came with your washer in deciding how much detergent to use, but if your clothes aren't very dirty here's a money-saving idea: The now-retired originator of a laundry detergent claims he has been washing his clothes for years with only ⅛ cup of detergent per load, and they come out beautifully clean, even when the label says to use a cup or more. First he wets the clothes. Then he sprinkles detergent on the especially soiled places, like collars and cuffs, folds the garments and waits for the detergent to "act" before throwing the clothes in the washer. The trick works with straight liquid detergents, but it's best to make a paste of the granular kinds and spread it on; rub it into greasy soiled areas.

How to Remove Stains

Many fresh nongreasy stains can be removed by simple treatment: sponge them with cool water or soak them in cool water for 30 minutes or longer; some nongreasy stains require overnight soaking. If the stain remains, work a detergent into it and rinse completely. For greasy surface stains, dampen the spot and rub liquid detergent full strength or a paste of granular detergent into it. Rinse the stained area or wash the garment as usual. To remove greasy stains on some wash-wear or permanent-press fabrics, you may possibly have to rub some detergent into the stain thoroughly and let it stand for several hours before rinsing the garment.

For a deeply embedded stain, rub full-strength liquid detergent lightly but thoroughly into the stained area. Then, holding the fabric with both hands, work the stained area back and forth between your thumbs. Bend the yarns sharply so the individual fibers rub against one another. It's this bending of the yarns, rather than the rubbing of the surfaces, that effectively removes embedded stains. Go over the entire area this way, then rinse thoroughly. On rugs, heavy fabrics that can't be bent easily, or on woolen fabrics that might possibly become felted by too much bending of the yarns, it is almost always best to work the detergent into the fabric with the edge of the bowl of a spoon.

Sprinkle ease

Make a can of household cleanser last much longer by lifting off the self-stick label and repositioning it to cover all but two of the holes. You can then dispense the cleanser with much more control than when every hole is open.

Health, Education, and Your Personal Welfare

This section is planned especially to help middle-income families who need all the defenses they can muster against the sharp rise in costs of vital personal services such as health care, children's education, and even the synergistic effect of income taxes in a time of persistent inflation.

When it comes to medical care, one of the fastest-rising expenses in your cost of living, you probably aren't poor enough to qualify for government aid—and not rich enough simply to pay the ever-bouncing fees without a lot of concern.

Moderate-income families also have been hit hard in educating their children. They often have a little too much income to be eligible for the newer federal financial-aid programs but still must pay increased tuition charges. The decline in the number of students going on to college has been especially large among families with incomes from $10,000 to $15,000 a year, a 1975 survey by the American Association of State Colleges and Universities found.

Likewise, when you have to cope with legal problems, you probably can't qualify for Legal Aid and also may have trouble with fees of private lawyers. The result is that you might neglect getting needed legal advice at crucial times—and thus risk getting into even greater financial problems. So you need all the help you can get with these and similar dilemmas.

In this section you'll also find dozens of other useful ways to save—for instance, by getting together with friends and neighbors in mutual aid co-ops; where to get help with complaints; and how to cut costs of insurance, credit fees, entertaining, vacations—even haircuts.

How to Restrain Those High Medical Costs

A family determined to defend its security against high costs needs to pay special attention to medical expenses. From 1967 to 1976, medical costs rose 75 percent, led by a budget-jolting 150 percent increase in hospital room charges.

The only way to protect yourself against an inflation in medical costs is through insurance. But adequate hospital and medical insurance has become very costly.

Promotions of health insurance sold by mail have increased as these sellers try to exploit the anxieties of families worried about rising medical charges and seeking ways to supplement present insurance.

While they seem inexpensive, some mail-order policies provide little real insurance. They may guarantee, for example, ''$200 a week while hospitalized.'' This boils down to only $28 a day, while hospital charges are over $100 a day in many localities. Another loophole is the frequent two-year waiting period before you can collect on pre-existing conditions whether you know about them or not.

Types of Health Insurance

The safest way to assure your family the medical care it may need is through ''full-service'' medical insurance which provides the actual care.

There are two kinds. One is the prepaid plans which usually have their own clinics. Some 200 such group-care plans already are in existence and are expanding.

But they are not available in some towns, and enrollment often is limited to groups, such as people working for the same employer. To find out if there is one in your area, write to Group Health Association of America, 1717 Massachusetts Avenue, N.W. Washington, D.C. 20036. More such plans are becoming available. The big Blue Cross network has taken an interest and is operating an increasing number of group-practice facilities. The government is also encouraging expansion of group practice plans and other ''health maintenance organizations'' expand. Increasingly, employers are offering a choice of a group-practice plan as a health-insurance option.

You need not worry that you will be subjected to assembly-line care in group-practice organizations. In most such plans you choose a family doctor from a panel of doctors assigned to your medical center. If you don't have a doctor in mind the first time you come in, the staff may suggest a possibly suitable one. If you don't like the doctor you can change.

The other kind of full-service plan is Blue Cross, and to some extent, Blue Shield. These plans guarantee almost-full payment for hospital care and doctors' bills.

If you usually have the funds to get care for minor illnesses and won't neglect such care because it is not insured, another way to cope with rising costs is major-medical insurance.

You pay the first $100, $250, $500, or $1000 of bills (depending on the ''deductible'' amount you choose). This method holds down costs by eliminating expenses for small claims. It's usually most economical in the long run to choose the highest ''deductible'' that you could afford to pay for yourself in an illness. As one example of the difference in premiums, a middle-aged person might pay $350 a year for a major-medical policy with a $500 deductible but only $200 with a $1,000 deductible.

Another form of medical insurance is the ''indemnity'' policy which pays specified sums for various services such as surgical procedures or hospital stays. Indemnity policies usually cost less than ''service'' insurance. Unfortunately, in an inflation, the specified amounts tend to lag behind the actual rise in fees. Thus policyholders often must pay substantial additional sums out of their own pockets, especially if they live in large cities where fees usually are higher than in rural areas.

Whatever kind of health insurance you buy, it usually will cost you 20-35 percent less on a group basis. It is easier nowadays to join a group. As well as employee groups, such coverage now often can be bought through business and fraternal associations, trade unions and credit unions.

But before you buy a supplementary policy, make sure your present one doesn't provide the same coverage. Surveys have shown that many people don't know what benefits their policies do provide, and so sometimes forfeit payments.

Hospital insurance is most vital to have. It's both the biggest and fastest-rising medical expense.

Health policies vary in cost and so need to be "shopped." The Pennsylvania State Insurance Department recommends that you ask the "loss ratios" of different companies (the percentage of premiums which they pay out in benefits.) A company which pays out say, 60 percent on individual policies usually offers better value than one which pays out 30.

Other Health Care Alternatives

Families often can take more advantage of free or low-cost public health services, too. The National Committee on Health Education found that many moderate-income families fail to use immunizations, x-ray and other treatment, nutritional guidance, prenatal and infant care, family planning guidance, loan of sickroom equipment and wheelchairs, and other services available from city and county health departments.

Specialized health organizations can also provide valuable services for people with severe eye or hearing disabilities, epilepsy, kidney disease, and other ailments. A list of major voluntary health organizations is provided at the end of this chapter.

In a medical crisis the local health department may well be your first port of call. And don't overlook the health department for venereal disease checks. The service is free, and your anonymity is guaranteed. As well as direct aids the department provides, it can refer you to other services such as homemakers and visiting nurses, or the local welfare department. An ordinarily self-supporting family could become "medically indigent" in a time of severe illness and so be eligible for "Medicaid." Unlike "Medicare" which is an *insurance* program (eli-

gible people can get these benefits without regard to income), Medicaid is an *assistance* program for people in financial need.

You also can get a list of local organizations which supply homemakers and home health aids by sending a stamped self-addressed envelope to the National Council for Homemaker-Health Aids Services, 67 Irving Place, New York, New York 10003.

Veterans should know that in case of long-term disability they may be eligible for Veterans Administration pensions, depending upon their income. V.A. hospital domiciliary and outpatient care also is available for veterans.

If your dental needs become financially critical, there are several sources for help. One is your local Board of Health. Another is local dental clinics.

There are three main ways you can insure for dental care. One is through employee union plans. Other employee groups may provide a panel of dentists. Another form of coverage is through dental care policies offered by some Blue Cross plans and insurance companies.

Checklist for Health Policies

Waiting period: As noted, many commercial health-insurance policies require a two-year period before "existing" conditions are covered. But some policies require only one year; some others only six months, and most full-service plans usually require none except some waiting period on maternity coverage. Also beware of policies stipulating a general waiting period (of thirty days, for example) during which time not even new illnesses are covered.

Benefits: Compare benefits specified in the policy with actual charges for hospital room, surgical procedures, doctor's office visits, etc., in your community. The Health Insurance Institute also advises that you observe whether the policy covers related hospital expenses such as x-ray, laboratory tests, special nursing services. Note whether any limitations on amounts paid for such related expenses are so small as to be almost useless.

A relatively good policy also will provide some out-of-hospital benefits such as diagnostic laboratory tests, perhaps some nursing benefits, and costs of out-of-hospital prescriptions.

Duration of benefits: For how long a period do benefits continue? And how many hospital days?

Disability: In buying disability insurance, which pays benefits if you are unable to work, how seriously disabled must you be to collect benefits? Must you be house-bound, or only unable to work at your occupation? Too, how long would you have to wait for benefits to become effective?

Renewability: Is the policy "guaranteed renewable?" Up to what age?

Exclusions: Some seemingly-cheap policies actually cover only accidents. You need, of course, to be covered against both serious illnesses *and* accidents. Also note whether all members of your family are covered and to what ages.

Claims experience: Try to find out the company's record for paying claims. First check with your state insurance department at your state capital to see if there are many complaints of rejection of claims against the company. In any case, you will want to make sure the company is licensed to do business in your state. Otherwise, you will have no place to turn for intervention if at some future time you feel you have been treated unfairly. You can also check with your local Better Business Bureau.

Compare the "deductible": In shopping for a "major-medical" policy as well as noting the amount of deductible, compare the time periods specified for accumulating the deductible. Some policies specify that the deductible amount, for example. $500, must accumulate in a short period such as three or six months. Other policies give you a year during which the specified deductible amount can accumulate, after which you can claim benefits. The longer period is more desirable from your point of view.

Coordinating Benefits

Nowadays, a working wife as well as the husband may have group health insurance.

When each has dependent coverage for the other, the policies together often provide benefits for 100 percent of the family's medical bills once the policy's deductible—usually between $50 and $100—is met.

Insurance Companies call this Coordination of Benefits (COB). It means that after one policy has reimbursed its regular share of the expense of an illness—usually up to 80 percent—the second handles the remainder up to 100 percent (but not more).

In some cases a couple loses money that could be theirs because they are not aware of the COB provision and fail to make a claim for the extra benefits, says the Health Insurance Institute. This happens even though most employee booklets do provide this information.

It may even be worth checking past health insurance payments to be sure you did receive all you are entitled to.

Savings on Drugs

Whether drugs sold under their "generic" or common names are as safe and effective as the costlier equivalent drugs sold under trade-marked names is a persistent debate with financial significance to you.

For example, if your doctor prescribes a tradename drug for an oral penicillin, you might pay $6 to $7. But if the generic equivalent penicillin is used, your cost might be $3 to $4.

Perhaps the broadest example of price differences between generic and brand-name drugs is the tetracycline drugs. Tetracycline is the generic name for a widely-used antibiotic medicine sold under such brand names as Achromycin, Sumycin, Terramycin, etc.

Under the generic "tetracycline" name, 250-milligram tablets often retail for 15 to 20 cents. But under some of the trade-marked names prices are 20 to 35 cents.

In most states the pharmacist must fill your prescription with the brand that the doctor prescribes. Despite the potential savings, doctors tend to prescribe the better-known brands although more and more are using generic names, especially for the tetracycline drugs.

Among other reasons for the doctor's preference for well-known brands, it has been said, is that doctors tend to be more familiar with the trade-marked product and feel more assured of quality control and effectiveness.

In several cases doctors have found that lower-priced generic drugs which were chemically equivalent with costlier brands actually did not have the same degree of "bioavailability" as measured by the amount of active ingredient in the blood stream at set times after the drug is given.

Bioavailability may differ among different brands of the same drug, because the manufacturers may use different "binders" or preservatives, may press the pills too tightly or too loosely, thus affecting the rate of dissolution. Or variations in quality control in different factories may affect a drug's efficacy.

For this reason, the Food and Drug Administration is now paying special attention to testing bioavailability of some drugs in which variations have been found. Significantly, FDA has found bioavailability problems with both brand-name and generic drugs, and with big manufacturers and small ones.

The results of this testing should be reassuring to consumers, pharmacists, and doctors about the general effectiveness of generic drugs. There are few actual documented cases of differences in bioequivalence; those that do exist are now being controlled.

But even for the same drug, you may find noticeable price variations among different retailers. Thus, our comparisons found charges for 16 capsules of Achromycin varied from $1.44 to $2.90.

But be cautioned that in our experience no single pharmacy was uniformly cheapest throughout the range of prices compared. Thus, you can't conclude that a pharmacy which is lower on one prescription necessarily charges less for others. If you want to save money overall on all drugs you need to comparison-shop for each prescription. On the other hand, your relationship to your own pharmacist and the service he provides may be most important to you.

Services for Seniors

Services which help elderly people stay in their own homes are expanding. Such services include "Meals on Wheels" which brings meals to seniors unable to prepare their own. Comprehensive programs of medical and other supportive services in their own homes for oldsters, as pioneered by the Minneapolis Age and Opportunity Center, also now are being developed in other towns too.

Many of these expanding programs are organized by Senior Citizen and Golden Age Clubs affiliated with the National Council of Senior Citizens. Other community groups such as family service agencies, women's clubs, Girl Scouts, settlement houses, housing co-ops, and individual union locals, also have organized special consumer helps for the elderly such as shopping services, car pools to go to clinics, prescription collection, and legal-advice services. In some towns "Meals on Wheels" is operated by the public schools, thus utilizing the school kitchen for appropriate double duty.

Another increasing popular program is "congregate feeding." This program seeks to get elderly people out of the house and into centers where they can meet others and have recreational activity as well as a hot meal. To find out whether this program is available in your area, check with local referral agencies such as Community Chest or United Way, county offices of the aging, or area senior centers.

Another expanding service is "Ring A Day." At prearranged times, volunteers—often seniors themselves—call elderly people living alone. If there is no answer (or in case of an emergency) the caller knows which doctor, neighbor, and relatives to notify. A specialist in problems of widowhood, Dr. Virginia R. Coevering, has written a booklet, *Guidelines for a Telephone Reassurance Service,* published by the Institute of Gerontology, of the University of Michigan and Wayne State University. In the belief that such services can make a vital difference in the lives of isolated elderly people, the Institute, which is at 543 Church St., Ann Arbor, Michigan 48104, offers the booklet at no charge.

One of the most innovative self-help programs is the Jamaica, New York, Service Program for Older Adults, reports Bernard Fisher of the Community Service Society of New York.

A senior Citizen Advisory Council helped to identify what local older people themselves consider to be their primary needs and interests. The council initiated a senior citizens' crime prevention program; worked to get free checking accounts for seniors; helped sponsor health fairs, and developed a "health passport"—a wallet card with essential health data which might be needed in an emergency.

Directory of Health Organizations

The National Health Council has supplied this list of national organizations which help with specific health problems.

Your doctor or board of health can refer you to local organizations.

American Association for Respiratory Therapy, 7411 Hines Place, Dallas, Texas 75235

American Cancer Society, 219 E 42nd St., New York, N.Y. 10021. Research organizations; local affiliates can supply information on available services, sickroom supplies, oxygen, etc.

American Diabetes Association, 1 W. 48th St., New York, NY 10021. Publishes magazine for diabetics; affiliated local associations sponsor diabetes-detection program.

American Hearing Society, 1800 H St., N.W., Washington, D.C. Supplies information on hearing problems; conducts lip-reading and speech classes for children through local societies. Affiliated League of the Hard of Hearing Chapters give you a chance to try out hearing aids, provide names of specialists, other services.

American Heart Association, 44 E. 23rd St., New York, N.Y. 10010. Has affiliated local associations. Sponsors clinics to determine work capacities of cardiac patients. Provides information on cardiovascular disease and on services for cardiac patients.

American Lung Association, 1740 Broadway, New York, NY 10019. Local branches distribute information; operate clinics and sheltered workshops in some areas; supply referrals for diagnostic and health care, and aid in securing employment guidance.

American Occupational Therapy Association, 6000 Executive Blvd., Suite 2000, Rockville, Maryland 20852.

American Optometric Association, 700 Chippewa St., St. Louis, Missouri 63119.

American Physical Therapy Association, 1156 15th St., N.W., Washington, D.C. 20005

American Podiatry Association, 20 Chevvy Chase Circle, N.W., Washington, D.C. 20036.

American Speech and Hearing Association, 9030 Old Georgetown Road, Bethesda, Maryland 20014.

Arthritis Foundation, 1212 Avenue of the Americas, New York, NY 10036. Provides information on treatment; sponsors treatment facilities in smaller towns; evaluates medicines sold for these diseases.

Children's Cancer Fund of America, 15 E. 67th St., New York. Provides financial assistance after consultation with your doctor.

Epilepsy Foundation of America, 1828 L St., N.W., Washington, D.C. 20036, supplies information about services and facilities, especially directed to meet social, psychological, vocational needs of epileptics.

Eye Bank Association of America, 3195 Maplewood Ave., Winston-Salem, N. Carolina 27103.

Muscular Dystrophy Associations of America, 810 Seventh Ave., New York, NY 10019. Chapters in all large cities. Services include transportation to and from clinics, hospitals, and schools, financial assistance for therapy for needy families, and purchase of braces, crutches and wheelchairs; information booklets.

National Association of Home Health Agencies, 659 Cherokee St., Denver, Colo. 80204.

National Association for Mental Health, 118 N. Kent St., Rosslyn, VA. 22209.

National Council on Alcoholism, 2 Park Ave., New York, NY 10016.

National Epilepsy League, 116 S. Michigan Ave., Chicago, Ill. 60603. Supplies information about services and facilities especially directed to meet social, psychological, vocational needs of epileptics.

National Kidney Disease Foundation, 116 E. 27th St., New York, N.Y. 10016. Supplies information; sponsors cortisone banks which supply cortisone and its derivatives at reduced rates or without charge in cases of financial need.

National Medical Association, 2109 East Street, N.W. Washington, D.C. 20037.

National Multiple Sclerosis, 257 Park, New York, N.Y. 10010. Diagnostic services are available at local clinics and chapters; some offer rehabilitation services and booklets on this disease.

National Society for Autistic Children, 169 Tampa Ave., Albany, NY 12206.

National Society for the Prevention of Blindness, 79 Madison Ave., New York, N.Y., 10016. Chapters and field staff sponsor free vision-screening programs for preschool children, glaucoma-detection for adults; also information, referral service.

Social and Rehabilitation Service, Department of Health, Education and Welfare, Washington, D.C. 20201.

United Cerebral Palsy Associations, 66 E. 34th St., New York, NY 10016. Has local affiliates. Gives treatment through clinics and existing community facilities; guidance and psychological counseling for patients and parents, and vocational guidance.

Veterans Administration, Department of Medicine and Surgery, 810 Vermont Ave., N.W., Washington, D.C. 20420.

Visiting Nurses Association, 107 E. 70th St., New York, N.Y. 10021.

What is an HMO?

If you're more than a little queasy when you think of the drain your family's medical expenses are placing on your wallet, look to the Health Maintenance Organizations, HMOs.

Members of HMOs purchase their out-of-hospital and in-hospital care—everything from routine checkups to major surgery—with a fixed prepaid annual fee. HMOs don't create new health services for you, but they do reorganize those that already exist to help serve you better.

Of course, most Americans are now covered by some form of health insurance. But what they actually have is "sickness" insurance; they must be ill, injured, pregnant, or hospitalized, to receive benefits. Not so with HMOs.

Having paid in advance for your health care, you can see the doctor about a minor ailment. By treating your problems—and those of other patients—before they become serious, the doctor can see more patients and the cost per patient is lower. In this way HMOs attempt to focus on preventive

medicine; that is, on maintaining health.

Who operates HMOs? HMOs may be organized and run by doctors, community groups, insurance companies, labor unions, governmental units, even companies whose "business" is HMOs. Some are operated not-for-profit.

How much does a typical HMO cost? The Columbia (Maryland) Medical Plan, affiliated with the Johns Hopkins Medical Institution in Baltimore and cosponsored by Connecticut General Life Insurance Co., charges $68 a month for a family of two adults and one or more children. For most members, employers pay a large portion of this sum, leaving the average family an annual premium of $288. The fee covers outpatient care—such as visits to the "primary care" doctor and to specialists, lab tests, X rays, emergency care, eye examinations and prescriptions, immunizations, injections, and periodic reviews. There is a "gate charge" of $2 a visit for any or all services.

Drug prescriptions cost $2 each at the HMOs own pharmacy. Visits to a psychiatrist cost $2 each for the first 15 visits in a calendar year and $10 for each visit thereafter in that same year.

There is no charge for hospital care, including intensive care facilities, surgical procedures, private duty nurses when needed, blood transfusions, and all other services and supplies. Members do pay $100 for maternity care—pre- and postnatal care for mother and baby.

Home visits are provided as required with a charge of $5 for the first visit and $2 for each additional visit for the same illness. Ambulance service is free.

Provisions are also made for long-term care in a nursing home, mental institution, or at home.

Should a member require emergency care away from home, the HMO will pay the first $2,000 of his medical expenses and 80 percent of whatever is left.

For additional information, write the federal government's HMO office, in care of:
Acting Associate Bureau Director
Health Maintenance Organization Service, Room 13–07
5600 Fishers Lane, Rockville, Md. 20852.

How to Cope with the High Cost of College

The spiraling costs of college and vocational education have created an especially worrisome dilemma, particularly for families who may have several children trailing each other through the ivied walls.

Costs at private colleges by 1976 were typically $5,200 a year including incidentals, and even more at some prestige colleges.

Costs aren't really low any more even at state universities and colleges, the traditional source of educational opportunity for moderate-income families. Their costs vary considerably in different states but averaged close to $2,600 a year by 1975 for in-state students, and about $3,700 for those from out of state.

But there is no need for the anxiety that many families feel at this critical stage of family life. There are ways to pull together the money and even new and less conventional ways of getting some credits at little tuition expense; for example, by taking the first two years at one of the many community and junior colleges which have become the fastest-growing institutions.

Another recently expanded educational source is the former state teachers colleges which have converted to liberal arts schools, and the smaller state universities. These are the least-costly four-year colleges. Many are still under $2,500 a year for all costs including books and incidentals.

More students now also leave college for a while to work and then return to school at some later date. In fact, the average graduating age has risen.

Among the funds most families need to assemble are (1) some contribution from current income; (2) judicious use of family and student savings; (3) student earnings; (4) scholarship help, including some of the lesser-known sources; and (5) loans.

Contribution from Income

Most families can provide at least $1,200–$1,500 a year from current income. You probably already are spending that much for your child's food, a portion of the family's housing costs, school expenses, medical care, etc. Not all of a student's college expenses actually are added costs. But while such a contribution from parents of $1,200–$1,500 a year plus his own earnings can help a student get through a public college, it would not be enough for a private college or even some of the more expensive state universities.

Savings

If the typical 60% contribution of middle-income families is applied to the current typical costs of about $4,000 a year (averaging private and state schools), parents normally would provide $2,400 a year. The rest of the money—although usually not all—then can come from the student's own savings and earnings.

But many parents would find it almost impossible to come up with $2,400 a year out of current income, especially with other children's education to be provided for. If some savings were not accumulated beforehand, other possibilities are such "hidden savings" as the cash value of insurance policies or the equity in a home, *if* interest rates are favorable enough to warrant increasing the mortgage.

The secret of saving for college is getting an early start so that the power of compound interest goes to work for you earlier. For example, one family saves $20 a month for ten years at an after-tax yield of 4½% and accumulates $3,029. Another family saves $40 a month for five years at the same yield but winds up with only $2,693 even though both have put away the same $2,400.

Jobs

Student earnings still provide an important part of the money for college, although in times of reduced employment—students may find jobs harder to get.

The main source of earnings is summer employment. Alexander Sidar, Director of the College Scholarship Service, advised in 1975 that male students seeking financial aid from the college usually are expected to provide from summer earnings these amounts: first-year students, $500; second-year, $600; upper classes, $700. The expectation from girls often is about $100 less. Typical summer earnings were estimated in 1976 at about $600 for students who are able to find jobs.

Part-time campus jobs are a main source of earnings during the school year. They often pay $500 a year or a little more at rates of about $2.10 to $2.75 an hour. (Usually colleges participating in government college-assistance programs are required to pay at least the federal minimum wage.) Off-campus jobs as for waiters, cab drivers, clerks, typists, pay a little more but may be more available in the large cities than in small college towns. Students with special skills, as in auto and appliance service, often earn above-average pay.

A federal work-study program, administered by the colleges, provides both summer and part-time school-year jobs for moderate-income students. You can apply to the college's financial aid officer to see if you qualify for this program.

You can get a leaflet explaining this and other federal programs (*HEW Fact Sheet*) from the Division of Student Financial Aid, Office of Education, Washington, DC 20202, or the nearest regional office (see list with this chapter.)

Sample Yearly Program for Financing College		
Source*	Private College	State College
Parents' annual contribution	$1,400	$1,100
Savings (parents' and student's)	1,200	300
Summer job	600	600
School-year employment	400	400
Scholarship or grant	800	—
Loans	800	200
	$5,200	$2,600

*Your own budget would be cut to fit your own situation. Availability and amount of a scholarship will depend on both academic achievement and demonstrated need (as explained later).

Scholarships

There are other sources that families with genuine need for aid can explore. The danger is in overestimating eligibility and amounts available. A survey by Betty Lou and Wesley Marple published in the *College Board Review* found that even relatively well-to-do families were apt to overestimate the aid available in their brackets. Many believed that almost half of costs are covered by financial aid.

At some expensive colleges as many as half the students now do get some aid from college or government programs. The low-cost public colleges give fewer and smaller scholarships. In general, Sidar estimates, about one-third of students get some form of financial help from colleges or from one or more of the other sources.

The most serious result of over-optimism about scholarships is that parents tend to neglect saving for college. Over 60% had no college savings at all. Most expected to use current income as the main source of college money, and to pay for 45% of the college bill this way. While this much of a contribution may be enough for the lower-cost state colleges, various surveys indicate that a contribution from parents of 50-60%, from a combination of current income and savings, would be more realistic.

Following is a summary of college scholarship sources and information about each:

College scholarships are most numerous. Colleges usually now award scholarships or grants on the basis of financial need as well as scholastic achievement. The colleges also determine—usually through the Parents Confidential Statement (PCS) of the College Scholarship Service—whether the family has assets as well as income it can draw upon to pay for college.

College financial "aid" usually is a "package" consisting of a scholarship, loan, and job. For example, suppose that a college has determined from the PCS that a family is able to provide $2,500 a year of an estimated college budget of $4,800 from a combination of current income, savings, and student earnings. The college may provide the balance in the form of $900 in outright grant, $600 in a campus job, and $800 in a low-interest loan.

The College Scholarship Service, a facility of the College Entrance Examination Board, forwards to the colleges the information parents provide, and CSS's analysis of need. But the colleges themselves decide whether to approve the request and for how much. The CSS system takes into account special problems such as illness, recent unemployment, two in college at the same time, other dependents, and parents' ages. Sidar notes that CSS also provides a partial allowance for a working mother's earnings so the family is not penalized for going to work to help to pay for children's education.

You do not have to be really poor to qualify for scholarships. Most grants do go to students from families with incomes under $18,000, though sometimes even families with incomes as high as the lower twenties get aid when there are a number of children attending college at the same time or some other special circumstances. But the amounts get smaller.

As well as need, colleges also consider scholastic promise or other demonstration of talent in awarding scholarships.

If your application is denied the first time, you can apply again if circumstances change; for example, if family income drops or unexpected expenses occur, or another child is off to college.

State scholarships are another major source of aid. These may be either general scholarships or for specific courses. The general scholarships usually are awarded either on the basis of competitive exams or high-school grades. Actual amounts may depend on need.

Most states and the federal government also provide "war orphan" scholarships for children of those servicemen who lost their lives or (in some states) were disabled in war service.

Veterans' educational benefits are available for those who served in the Armed Forces during the Vietnam war and the period between the Korean and Vietnam wars. Some states also help Vietnam veterans by waiving tuition for them at public colleges.

And don't neglect the athletic scholarship, another form of grant-in-aid. If your offspring has a particular talent, encourage him or her to write to various schools. Some college graduates paid much of their costs running track or playing football.

Community organizations provide many, if relatively small, scholarships. These are awarded by such groups as PTA's and teachers' associations; fraternal societies; women's organizations; businessmen's and civic clubs; church, ethnic and nationality associations, and local college alumni clubs. Your high-school counselor should be able to tell you about any such awards that may be available locally.

Educational opportunity grants provided by the federal government are available to students from low-income families. The grants go up to $1,400 a year depending on how much the parents can contribute to their children's education.

As well as the federal regional education office, college financial aid offices and high-school counselors can provide information on these grants and also a supplementary program for very needy students.

Labor unions award some scholarships, usually to children of members. But some state-wide labor councils also offer scholarships open to any student. Usually these awards are based on a test or essay examining applicants on their knowledge of the labor movement.

Corporate and industry grants are a possible source of aid for students interested in specific vocations. For corporation grants, the student usually doesn't apply to the sponsoring corporation but to the colleges that administer them. If you apply for a scholarship to a particular school, the college usually will consider you for one of the corporate grants that it has available, along with its other awards.

Some industries also give aid to students interested in careers in those occupations and these potential sources of help sometimes are overlooked. Usually you apply to the trade or professional association in that industry. High-school counselors can tell you about such scholarships. Industries providing some grants include medical services and nursing; library science; journalism; hotel restaurant and retail management; printing and publishing;

pharmacy; home economics; social work; personnel and guidance, and optometry.

National merit scholarships are awarded each year to the highest scorers among high school seniors who take the tests. The amounts granted are based on the winner's actual financial need. Many universities and private sponsors also use the Merit Scholarship test results to choose candidates for other scholarships.

Loans

Loans increasingly are being used by students and their families to pay for college. But there is concern about putting too heavy a loan burden on students. They would be faced with large repayments just when they are starting careers and families.

Certainly loans need to be selected and used with care to avoid any needless accumulation of interest and heavy debt. Here are sources and costs:

National direct student loans cost least— 3 percent a year. While the government puts up the money, students apply directly to their colleges. If approved, students can take up to ten years after graduation to repay. Nor does the interest begin until after graduation. However, funds for these loans are limited, and it is necessary to show need. Each college sets its own standard of required academic performance and need. Many colleges use these loans as part of the package of aid awarded to students. Some colleges do grant these loans separately. Either way, the tendency is to reserve them for moderate-income students.

Colleges' own loans: Many colleges now use the National Direct Student Loans for long-term loans and reserve their own loan funds for short-term loans for emergency needs.

Guaranteed student loan program: This program has become one of the largest sources for student loans. The "Guaranteed" loans are partly subsidized by the government so the interest rate paid by the students is only 7% at this writing. Middle-income families usually are eligible for these loans. While subsidized by the government, application must be made to banks, savings and loan associations, credit unions, and to colleges themselves. They actually provide the loans. Students from families whose adjusted incomes are under $15,000, at this writing, also may have the interest paid by the government while they are in school.

Students who do not qualify for the interest subsidy, pay the 7% interest from the start, with the government paying the rest of the lender's actual charge. Thus, this is still a relatively low-cost loan.

Some lenders may require that you have an account in their bank. In time of tight money and high general rates, it may be necessary to try several local lenders.

Commercial loans: If you are not able to qualify for any of these subsidized loans, many banks offer their own college loans. Rates vary from 12% to as much as 20% true annual interest and more.

You may not really need a loan. Many commercial education loans merely advance the money for each semester, and you start repaying the next month. For example, an $8,000 four-year "plan" usually advances $1,000 at a time. It would cost you less to save up ahead of time the $1,000 for the first term, and pay into a savings account each month in preparation for the next term.

Another method permitted by a growing number of colleges is to pay monthly instead of at the beginning of each term. The extra charge, such as $10 a term, is much less than interest on a loan.

By pulling together such resources, families can still manage to provide higher education for their children. The critical times may come when there are two in college. Then families may need to use other ways to skin a sheep: three-year accelerated programs; five-year "work-study" programs and combinations of two-year commuting colleges and senior colleges.

Home Study

In our credential-conscious society, missing out on a college diploma can make you feel consigned to the enlisted ranks forever after. But take heart. At last, you can obtain that coveted piece of parchment without years of slogging through night classes or giving up your career to return to school full time.

Colleges all over America now make it possible for you to earn college credits—or even a degree—at your own convenience and almost without setting foot on a campus.

Basically, there are two ways by which you can earn college credits without going to college: credit by examination and independent study.

Credit by examination allows you to take a standardized test, and, if you pass, receive formal credit for your knowledge. No preparation is required, and no classes. More than 1,500 colleges in all 50 states now give credit for satisfactory performance on such tests, which are offered by the College Level Examination Program (CLEP) of the College Entrance Examination Board.

Tests are given each month in more than 500 centers across the country; cost is $15 a test, or $25 for the battery of examinations.

Many colleges offer their own tests for credit, particularly in subjects for which national tests have not been developed. Still others offer credit by "assessment," known as "credit for life experience." A government employee might receive credits for public administration, based on a faculty evaluation of his education on the job.

Former servicemen also may receive credit for service schools that they attended. Under the plan of the Commission on Accreditation of Service Experiences of the American Council on Education (CASE), any service school of more than three weeks' duration and officially listed in the services educational register carries with it the possibility of college credit.

Independent study is known by a wide variety of names—nontraditional study, external or extended-degree plans, and universities without walls.

It is not a new idea— the University of London started it in 1836. And many American programs are patterned after another off-campus British model, the "Open University," "Open U" students in Britain study on their own with the help of television and radio lectures, self-guiding study materials, correspondence with faculty advisers, periodic examinations, regular visits to an assigned tutor at a regional learning center, and finally a week's worth of classes during summer vacation.

Three American institutions—Rutgers, Maryland, and Houston—are now trying out some of the British study materials. Open University's closest counterpart in this country, however, is Empire State College of New York. Empire State has neither campus nor faculty. Students are assigned to a regional learning center near their homes where a "mentor" helps them put together an individual study package which may include some class attendance at a neighboring college, a reading list, a study guide, some on-the-job experience and often some volunteer work on a community project. Most students are expected to take about three years to earn their degree.

Colleges similar to Empire State are on the drawing boards in California, Massachusetts, Maine, and elsewhere across the nation. Florida International University is already operating and so is Minnesota Metropolitan State College.

Similarly, the "University Without Walls" enlists 20 schools from Skidmore to Chicago State which allow students to pursue personal educational goals without being tied down to a campus.

In most of these programs, the old idea of building toward a degree, credit by credit, has been dropped. Instead, a student's knowledge on admission is assessed, and then he and the institution draw up a contract, setting forth what he will achieve to earn his degree. The contracts are frequently lengthy and detailed, listing books to be read, papers to be written, and projects to be completed.

In addition some schools offer what they call "outreach" programs. Many of these are simply traditional classes located in surroundings more convenient or congenial for the student. For instance, East Los Angeles College teaches a law-enforcement curriculum entirely in the city police headquarters in the Los Angeles Civic Center.

Also, many colleges will accept televised instruction for credit. Tying into nationally telecast courses, they furnish study guides, reading lists, and supplementary materials; offer telephone and personal tutoring and counseling, and grant credit based on a final exam.

It's not cheap to get a degree by tests or independent study, although it may be less expensive than the traditional route. The CPEs cost $20 to $50 per test and can bring as many as six credits apiece; a $25 investment in the CLEP general examination battery can result in as many as 30 credits for a person. And some community-college independent study and contract programs are completely tuition-free.

Still, participants in the University Without Walls usually pay the sponsoring college's standard rate—which may mean several thousand dollars per year in some instances. Empire State charges fees comparable to other divisions of the State University of New York—$600 for freshmen and sophomores, $800 for upperclassmen.

Program for student financial aid

Here are the addresses of the regional Office of Education, Department of Health, Education and Welfare:

REGION I (Conn., Me., Mass., N.H., R.I., Vt.): JFK Federal Bldg., Boston 02203; Tel. (617) 223-6895.

REGION II (N.J., N.Y.): 26 Federal Plaza, New York 10007; Tel. (212) 264-4022.

REGION III (Del., D.C., Md., Pa., Va., W. Va.): P.O. Box 12900, Philadelphia, Pennsylvania; Tel. (215) 597-7726.

REGION IV (Ala., Fla., Ga., Ky., Miss., N.C., S.C., Tenn.): 50 7th St., N.E., Room 544, Atlanta 30323; Tel. (404) 526-5971.

REGION V (Ill., Ind., Mich., Minn., O., Wis.): 226 W. Jackson Blvd., Chicago 60606; Tel. (312) 353-5216.

REGION VI (Ark., La., N.M., Okla., Tex.): 1114 Commerce St., Dallas 75202; Tel. (214) 749-2264.

REGION VII (Ia., Kan., Mo., Neb.): 601 E. 12th St., Kansas City, Mo. 64106; Tel. (816) 374-3136.

REGION VIII (Colo., Mont., N.D., S.D., Ut., Wyo.): Room 9017. Federal Office Bldg., 19th & Stout Sts., Denver 80202: Tel. (303) 297-3733.

REGION IX (Ariz., Cal., Hawaii, Nev.): 50 Fulton St., San Francisco 94102; Tel. (415) 556-8724.

REGION X (Alaska, Ida., Ore., Wash.): Arcade Plaza Bldg., 1321 2nd Ave., Seattle 98101; Tel. (206) 442-0493.

How to Save on Insurance

Some of the quickest and greatest savings you can achieve are on your insurance—life, property, and, sometimes, auto. With a basic understanding of insurance, you might be able to improve your basic protection while spending no more or even less than you now do.

You should understand clearly that the only good reason to have insurance is to protect yourself against losses you couldn't afford to pay for—not to try to make money.

Over the long run, the average person probably can never "win" in buying insurance. The price you pay must include the insurance company's overhead and selling expense. Sometimes, this may be a relatively small amount; say, only 10 cents of your premium dollar. In other cases of high-cost forms of insurance such as credit insurance, travel insurance, and some individual accident policies sold by mail-order companies, the public may get back on average only 50 cents for each premium dollar it pays.

Insurance-Buying Principles

The best way to keep your costs down is to take as large a "deductible"—that part of the loss which you would pay—as you can afford to handle. This same principle applies to property and auto insurance, as discussed later. In fact, you may be able to dispense with some insurance entirely, such as the comprehensive portion of an auto insurance policy.

Another important principle is to buy insurance "wholesale"—meaning in large amounts rather than in a number of small policies which cost more for the same coverage. This applies especially to life insurance. Even when you want to increase your coverage, often you can add a "rider" to a present policy at less cost than buying another policy, since many insurance companies won't charge you an "acquisition" cost for adding the rider.

A third principle is to buy insurance in a group whenever possible. Depending on the type of insurance, you can probably save from 15 to 40 percent. Buying through a group plan is even more advantageous if there is any question about your health or if you are in a hazardous occupation since group coverage is often obtained without a medical exam.

Group insurance is more widely available nowadays, and often is available through small as well as large employee groups, and through professional, church, credit union, and fraternal and alumni associations.

More kinds of insurance are becoming available on group plans. Group life and hospital and medical insurance always have been widely available. Increasingly, large employee groups, and credit unions in some states, arrange for members to buy auto insurance on a group basis.

Even property insurance is starting to become available in group plans. The early instances are group purchases by members of the same housing development. Thus, the United Housing Foundation in New York has its own affiliated insurance agency, the Urban Community Insurance Co., to place insurance for its members.

Another key tip is to *cover as many "risks" as you can in one policy.*

Finally, *"shop" for the lowest rates,* sticking, of course, to reputable companies licensed by your own state insurance department and with clear records at your local Better Business Bureau. Differences in costs for the same coverage can vary widely among different companies.

The Cheapest Life Insurance You Can Buy

In moderate-income families with young children, life insurance usually should be concentrated on the family breadwinner. This is the only way a young family can really afford the big coverage it needs to supplement potential Social Security payments. "Wife" insurance usually needs to be secondary to income replacement.

"Decreasing term" is the least expensive kind of life insurance. It does not build any cash value, but it does give you the most insurance you can buy for your dollars.

A decreasing term policy can provide either a stipulated monthly income for a decreasing number of years, or a decreasing lump sum payment. The monthly-income type often is called family-income plan. For example, you can arrange for a family-income policy, or have an "income-rider" attached to a present policy, to pay your family $200 a month, $300 or whatever amount you specify for, say, 20, 30, or any number of years from the time you take out the policy.

Thus, if a breadwinner aged 35 took out a thirty-year policy to pay $200 a month, and passed away at age 50, the policy would pay the $200 for the remaining fifteen years of the original thirty-year plan.

The kind of decreasing term insurance that pays a lump sum, reduces this amount as you get older. For example, a thirty-year, $25,000 decreasing term policy sold by some insurers would pay the full $25,000 if you died the first year, $23,750 if you died five years after taking out the policy; $21,500 in the tenth year; $18,500 in the fifteenth year, and lower amounts in later years.

Mortgage insurance is another form of decreasing term insurance. It pays the remaining balance on your mortgage if you die. Mortgage insurance, in fact, is one of the cheapest ways to buy a lot of coverage for little money. (An "income-rider" attached to a policy you already have also is inexpensive.)

But decreasing term insurance *not* tied to your mortgage is more flexible. You can arrange it for a term longer than your mortgage. Nor does your insurance coverage end if you sell your house and pay the mortgage, as would usually happen with mortgage insurance.

The theory behind decreasing term insurance, and it is a sound theory for many middle-income families, is that your insurance needs decrease as your family gets older. When you have small children you need more insurance to provide income for your family for a longer period than if they are almost grown.

For example, a man of 35 can buy thirty-year decreasing term insurance with an initial first-year value of $50,000 for as little as $250–$300 a year net cost (after dividends). Such a policy could give his family as much as $250 a month income if he died in the first year, and then decreasing amounts up to about the time his wife becomes eligible for Social Security.

While decreasing term insurance usually costs least, another form of term insurance called five-year renewable term may be more flexible for some purposes, though it may cost a little more. Instead of reducing the amount of insurance while the cost remains the same, the cost of five-year term goes up each time it is renewed. You can keep the cost level by voluntarily reducing the amount of insurance you renew, so that in essence you are working out a decreasing-term insurance policy yourself. But you do have the option of keeping more of it—or even all in effect—if you find you do need more insurance at a later age.

Comparing Costs of Life Insurance

While more and more insurers have come to recognize the need of moderate-income families for a large amount of low-cost coverage by way of term insurance, some sellers contend that the kind of insurance which combines insurance with cash value is more advantageous. Such insurance usually costs about two or three times more than term insurance in the early years of a policy. Insurance which has cash value often is called "permanent insurance" as contrasted to term insurance which must be renewed at the end of each term (for example, every five years).

A typical argument is that a 35-year-old man could buy $50,000 of so-called "permanent insurance" for $724 a year. At the end of 35 years he would have $27,050 of cash value. Thus he would not only recoup his total payments of $25,340 but would have a "profit" of $1,710.

How is that possible? Can you really be protected by insurance all those years and yet recover all your payments and more?

The answer is that this calculation does not include the potential interest you lose on the higher premiums you pay for the cash-value insurance. For example, the difference between the yearly cost of decreasing term insurance and that of cash-value life insurance frequently may be about $450 a year. If you deposited that amount every year in a savings account or other fixed-value investment earning even only 5 percent after taxes, after thirty years you would have a total savings of $31,392.

Some sellers also contend when a breadwinner retires he could convert his cash value in that kind of policy into an annuity paying an income for interest in one's life. That's a reasonable argument. It's true that you can buy an annuity for a little less by converting cash value than by buying one for cash. You save the sales charge.

But the man who bought term insurance and invested the difference could still buy a bigger annuity because he would have accumulated more cash.

There are at least two times when cash-value life insurance might be more suitable: (1) for high-bracket taxpayers, since the earnings of cash-value insurance are sheltered from taxes, and (2) for people who may need the discipline of a compulsory savings plan even if it doesn't always work out that way.

If you're interested in cash-value insurance, be sure to ask for the "interest adjusted" cost. This figure will tell you the cost of the insurance over a period of years if you take into account a reasonable rate of interest the cash value could earn.

In shopping for insurance of various kinds you can get some guidance from the reports produced by the Pennsylvania State Insurance Department in the early 1970's. They include *A Shopper's Guide to Term Insurance* which has cost comparisons for over 100 companies, and *A Shopper's Guide to Straight Life Insurance,* with comparisons for these kinds of policies. These and other reports produced by the Pennsylvania department, including those on auto, health, and other kinds of insurance have been combined into a book available at $3.50 from Consumer News, Inc., 813 National Press Building, Washington, D.C. 20004. Or you can get a free copy of the Pennsylvania Department's *Shopper's Guide to Health Insurance,* by writing to Blue Cross Association, Box 4389P, Chicago, Illinois 60680.

In comparing costs of term insurance among different companies, compare the *net* cost, which is the cost after deducting dividends from the annual premium price. While dividends are not guaranteed, the record of such payouts in recent previous years is a reasonable indication of future dividend performance and realistic net costs.

While life insurance should be concentrated on the breadwinner first, if you do feel you also need insurance on a wife and children, the least-costly method is a "family" policy covering all members.

Another potential saving is to pay annually rather than monthly or even quarterly. Many small individual policies on wives and children especially tend to be monthly-payment policies. They seem cheap because of the low monthly payments but actually are very expensive for the amount of insurance provided.

More insurers now provide a "free look" or "right of return". Such policies have a clause or "endorsement" stating that the policyholder can send the contract back to the life insurance company within ten days, with a request for refund of his initial premium. In that event the policy would be void from the beginning. This privilege gives you an opportunity to withdraw from the plan at no expense if not satisfied.

In individual health insurance, the ten-day examination privilege has been available for some time.

Disability Insurance

Disability insurance, which pays benefits if you are too ill to work, also offers a form of "deductible". This is the "elimination period"—the number of weeks or months before payments start. The longer the period, the less the insurance costs you.

For example, your employer may provide two weeks' sick pay. You also may be able to manage two or even more payless weeks before you urgently need income. So in this instance, you might arrange an elimination period of four weeks or more.

Another factor affecting the cost of disability insurance is the length of time you want the policy to pay benefits. The longer the term, the more the insurance costs. Keep in mind that other benefits may be available to you in case of permanent disability. The most important is Social Security disability payments for which a covered worker too disabled to work in "substantial gainful employment" may be eligible if a disability continues beyond five months and can be expected to last at least a year. The Veterans Administration also provides total-disability payments for war veterans, depending on how much other income the veteran has.

Other benefits under specified circumstances may be available from workmen's compensation; state veterans' programs; your state vocational rehabilitation department; and any union or other employee-organization aid programs.

Property and Auto Insurance

The judicious use of "deductibles" is especially helpful in holding down costs of property and auto insurance. In some areas, the costs are painfully steep; sometimes they're difficult to get at all.

The fact of life is that insurance companies tend to "load" policies which call for almost full coverage simply because their paperwork expenses for handling, say, a $50 claim, are as much as for handling a $200 one. Thus you pay inordinately more for almost-full coverage.

In these days of rising price tags on houses, it may be more vital to keep your property up to 80 percent of current market value than to insure yourself against the first few dollars of loss which you could afford to pay yourself.

Many families now have the $50 deductible. Even a $100 deductible can provide a worthwhile saving. But the $250 deductible really saves.

For example, by switching from a $50 deductible to a $250, one homeowner was able to raise his coverage from $24,000 to $30,000 while still reducing his annual premium $28 a year. This was almost a 20 percent saving while providing more protection.

Combine coverages: The more coverages you combine in one policy, the less each costs. Thus, "homeowner" policies which provide fire, windstorm, and other extended coverage, plus property, theft, and liability insurance, have become virtually standard.

The "package" enables you to have liability insurance for little more than the expense of just fire and extended coverage. Liability insurance is the protection some families tend to neglect. It may be almost as vital as fire insurance itself. Most fires in average "protected" neighborhoods are relatively limited. But a lawsuit by someone who has been injured on your property could be ruinous.

The broader versions of homeowner policies also cover some losses away from home, eliminating the need for special policies.

Renters, too, can combine coverages. A "Tenant's Comprehensive" or "Tenant's All Risk" policy saves about 25 percent over buying separate policies for fire, theft, and related insurance. Moreover, it does make theft insurance a part of the package and thus easier to get nowadays than separate theft insurance in some areas.

While homeowner policies may vary in some states, usually there are four basic forms. Each successive form adds coverages to those provided by the preceding forms.

The Homeowners standard form is usually called Form 1 or Policy A. Generally it provides protection against damage from fire or lightning explosion; smoke; glass breakage; windstorm or hail; removal of property endangered by peril; vandalism and malicious mischief; damage from vehicles and aircraft; riot or civil commotion. This policy also includes theft insurance including, except for some metropolitan areas, personal property away from the premises. In areas where theft away from home is not covered, such coverage often can be obtained at an additional charge.

The broader forms such as Forms 2 and 3 also include coverage against building collapse; freezing or accidental discharge of water or steam from plumbing, heating system, or appliances; electrical injury to appliances, falling objects; weight of ice, snow or sleet, and rupture or bursting of steam or hot water systems.

As you can see, Form 1 protects against the most important and common potential disasters at the lowest price. Even the broadest and most expensive standard forms do not protect against several risks of particular concern in some regions, such as flood damage. These needs are now being met in part by federally-subsidized flood insurance programs. You can ask your state insurance department or a local insurance broker whether such insurance is available in your area.

In some high-risk areas, theft insurance may be difficult to get. The federal government has another program providing such insurance in some states. You can find out about its availability from a local broker or by writing to Federal Crime Insurance, P.O. Box 41033, Washington, D.C. 20014.

Another federal program, the FAIR plan, makes available fire and extended coverage for areas where private insurance companies are unwilling to sell it. You can find out about this coverage from local brokers, your state insurance department, or a regional office of the U.S. Housing and Urban Affairs Department (HUD); or write to Federal Insurance Administration, care of HUD, Washington, D.C. 20411.

As well as protecting you against personal liability for bodily injury and property which others may suffer on your property because of your purported negligence, the liability portion of a homeowner policy also protects you against injury or damage you or a member of your family, or even a pet, may cause to other people off your property (but not including auto liability).

Compare rates: Costs of homeowner and auto insurance vary among different companies, and from year to year, and even for different coverages. So don't take it for granted that rates are uniform or "standard".

Rates for property insurance especially may vary sharply among different companies; as much, in fact, as 50 percent in some localities. Rates for auto insurance may vary less nowadays, but still do vary.

In comparing auto insurance rates among different companies, note that you need to compare for a driver in your particular classification and circumstances; for example, whether you have a young driver at home or in a nearby college; or drive to work; or have more than one car; have a record of recent accidents and traffic violations; whether your car is garaged, and so on. So large is the variation in rates that one company or another in your area may charge less for a specific circumstance than others.

In comparing rates for property and auto insurance, ask for the "net" rates—the rate after subtracting recent dividends or rebates the company may have paid recently.

Also keep in mind that it's unwise to surrender present coverage until you've ar-ranged new coverage, especially for auto insurance and even property insurance in some high-risk areas. Too, if you cancel a property-insurance policy before the term is up you probably will have to pay a penalty.

Operation identification: At least one insurance company (in the Midwest) now gives policyholders a five percent discount on homeowners insurance policies if they etch identifying marks on valuable possessions to aid in recovery if stolen. Even if your company doesn't offer a discount, you get a decal which identifies you as participating in the Operation Identification program. The decal discourages thieves and serves to help recover stolen goods and aid in prosecution. The program is sponsored by the National Association of Insurance Agents. Your own agent may be able to lend you an electric pencil to etch an identifying mark.

Car pools: In a time when car pools are on the increase to save gasoline, participants have expressed concern about their insurance protection. The U.S. Department of Transportation has pointed out that insurance regulations vary among states and you may want to consult your own agent or company about whether you are protected by your present insurance for a car pool.

But in general, a car-pool passenger is like any other passenger in your car and will be covered by your insurance. An exception can arise if one member of the pool does all the driving, charging the others a flat fee that doesn't necessarily reflect a fair share of the cost. Such a driver may be judged to be operating a "public livery conveyance".

Ordinarily, however, when pool members rotate driving or otherwise operate on an actual-cost basis, standard insurance applies.

Safe driver plans: Drivers with excellent safety and traffic records often can save by signing up for the "safe driver" plans offered by many insurance companies. In these plans you start with a relatively low rate but your premium goes up progressively in the event of an accident or traffic violation.

If you really are a safe driver and use your car relatively moderately, such safe-driver plans may be worth considering. But find out to what degree rates may jump in case of accidents or violations.

Where to Obtain Low-Cost Legal Help

People in middle income brackets often have the most trouble getting adequate legal service. Those in the lower income levels may qualify for free legal aid. Those in the upper income levels can afford private lawyers. But because they fear high legal fees about which they have heard alarming stories, moderate-income individuals often live dangerously in a legal sense. They neglect getting advice before signing contracts and leases; fail to make wills on the assumption that joint tenancy and state intestacy laws will distribute their estates in the desired manner; forfeit potential tax savings for lack of skilled counsel; fail to pursue damage, injury and other claims sufficiently enough to significantly reduce losses. Couples may fail to get timely advice on matrimonial rights and responsibilities. Families sometimes delay or completely neglect to get legal help in buying and selling houses.

If you ever need help, *four types of legal "assistance" are now available:*

Legal Aid

This well-known free legal service is available only within certain relatively low income limits. To find out whether you qualify, contact the legal aid office listed in your phone book or a store-front neighborhood legal service if there is one in your area, or consult a family service agency or community action center. Legal aid and neighborhood legal offices now handle an increasing number of consumer rent and matrimonial cases as well as their traditional representation of low-income defendants in criminal cases.

Small Claims Court

This is a potentially useful way to obtain relief for certain types of claims, particularly problems with merchants who have proved intractable to mere verbal complaints. Small claims courts have several advantages. You do not need a lawyer to sue. You can fill out forms yourself without any need for legal jargon. However, you can't be too carefree. You must be careful to give the clerk of the court the exact legal name and address of the corporation, business, or individual you are suing. Then, depending on the particular court's rules, you may have to have the summons served personally on the defendant, or the clerk of the court may take care of service by mail.

The court fees are relatively low, usually no more than $3 to $15 in various states, and these fees are often recoverable from the defendant if you win your case. In some areas, related costs such as lost work time, travel and other costs also may be recovered. At the trial itself you may present your case without the need to follow the usual technical rules of evidence, and cases come up relatively soon compared to higher courts.

But small claims courts have drawbacks, too. While you don't need a lawyer to sue, and some such courts ban lawyers altogether, in others the defendant may use a lawyer. Such representation is particularly likely if the defending part is even a moderate-size business firm. Thus, the complaining consumer often is put at a distinct disadvantage. Also, the small claims court is open not only to the aggrieved consumer, but may also be utilized as a relatively uncomplicated and inexpensive way for creditors to collect consumer debts. Witnesses before U.S. Senator John V. Tunney's Subcommittee on Representation of Citizen Interests report that while consumer plaintiffs won from 85-90 percent of their cases in small claims courts in Los Angeles and Philadelphia, a number of the courts have become in effect mere collection agencies.

There is also the problem of availability. Seventeen states do not have such courts in their judicial scheme.

Further, the very nature of the small claims court may limit your recovery. The maximum you may sue to recover in small claims courts varies greatly, but is usually in the $300 to $500 range. Although you may still sue on a much larger claim in such a case, you can only recover the maximum allowed to the small claims court in your area and often must forfeit the remainder. Some courts do allow claims up to $1,000 and even $3,000, and in such states small claims courts may be a truly potent weapon in the hands of the complaining consumer, though the caveat about defendant business firms utilizing attorneys applies even more strongly in the courts with higher recovery limits.

A major problem with small claims courts has been the difficulty of collecting even when the case has been won. An investigation by New York State Attorney General Louis Lefkowitz disclosed that nearly half of the judgments in New York small claims courts are not collected. Sometimes the defendant cannot be located (one reason for the requirement of exact name and address mentioned above), or has no assets, or sometimes just won't pay. If the defendant has assets which are not too hard to locate, they may be attached. But such action requires a return to court in most cases, which is not always convenient for the consumer. Moreover, if the defendant has left the country or state or has no assets, there may be no practical way to recover which does not involve time and extensive legal costs.

Despite these drawbacks, small claims courts are still the best recourse if you have a modest claim which does not warrant hiring an attorney. Generally you will find small-claims court personnel helpful.

Group Legal Plans

This is a growing new field of legal care for moderate-income people. In California by 1975, some 350 firms offered group plans. Labor unions have been especially interested and have led in the development of group legal care, but some consumer groups such as the Berkeley, Calif. Consumer Cooperatives have helped to sponsor community-wide programs. As of 1975, Consumers Group Legal Services of Berkeley charged $30 a year for memberships which included two 30-minute consultations a year and access to legal publications along with reduced rates for legal service.

There are a variety of group legal plans providing a wide range of services at different price tags. But the core of all of the plans provides for prepayments by members of the group into a fund which is used to pay for legal expenses of the members. The payments may consist of a single or series of membership payments or under many labor union plans, allowed by a 1973 amendment to the Taft-Hartley Act, employers and employees both pay into the fund as a fringe benefit under the employment contract.

The group plan gives each member access to an attorney for a certain number of consultations, or a certain amount of time per year, either free or at a nominal rate, and often provides for reduced rates for legal advice beyond the stated benefits.

There are essentially two types of plans: closed panel and open panel. In the closed panel, favored by many unions, a number of attorneys skilled in various fields of the law are "employed" or retained by the plan, and you choose from among them. In the open panel, formed by many bar associations, you consult any attorney of your choosing and the group plan pays your fees.

Arbitration

This is a growing, relatively low-cost method for getting help, especially on consumer complaints. Arbitration panels often are sponsored by local Better Business Bureaus and offices of the American Arbitration Association. These may be found in the telephone directory. By 1976 over 10,000 businesses already had committed themselves to submit unsettled consumer disputes to binding arbitration.

Although primarily oriented to disputes between consumers and merchants, in some areas arbitration also is used to solve landlord-tenant, labor-management and other wrangles.

The arbitrators are selected by the parties from an available panel. They hold hearings with the parties. Often the meetings are held at night so neither party loses work time.

Another advantage is the low cost. In fact, the Better Business Bureaus generally pay most of the expenses. Also, the arbitration finding and award, if any, is usually reached in a relatively short time compared to most court proceedings.

How to Save on Credit Fees

In periods of inflation, a situation known as "tight money," sometimes also called a "credit crunch," appears.

It's vital to avoid playing the role of the crunchee—the one who gets crunched. "Tight money" inevitably means higher interest fees and finance charges on borrowings and installment purchases. It's not unusual for a moderate-income family—say, one with $12,000 or so income after taxes in 1975—to pay out $400 a year just in finance charges.

The trap is that many families don't pay as much attention to the amount of finance charge as they do to the size of the monthly payments—whether they can fit that amount into their budgets.

Some families also use credit more than they really need to, because they are unaware how much they pay in finance charges, and sometimes because they cherish the illusion that they can merely stop payments if the purchase doesn't work or is not as represented. Or they may reason that they may not rebuild their savings if they take out the money but *will* be forced to meet payments.

Another snare is long credit terms. This trap shows up especially in a time of inflation when high prices may induce you to take longer to pay.

Thus, higher price tags on cars have influenced banks and dealers to extend installment contracts to as long as 48 months instead of the traditional 36 and sometimes 42-month plans. At the same time banks and finance companies have raised rates.

As a result, many families buying a car nowadays may find they are paying as much as $1,000 or more just to finance it. That's more than the factory cost of the engine.

The finance rates themselves also have been creeping up during the 1970's. But even the increase in rates is not as potentially harmful to family finances as the tendency toward longer terms. Even a jump from $6 to $8 per $1,000 does not raise total finance charges as much as an increase in terms from 24 months to 36, or 36 to 48.

Very long terms on cars are hazardous in another way. A car loses about half its market value in two years. Thus, midway through a four-year contract you may find that the market value is no more or even less than the remaining balance you owe.

A family able to make a little larger down payment, even if it has to delay other installment purchases, can make dramatic savings. A four-year, $4,000 contract at $6 per $100 (the equivalent of an annual percentage rate of a little under 12 percent) will cost a total of $960 in finance charges. If you can put down $500 more and repay the $3,500 debt in three years, the total finance charge is $630. If you can make your original balance only $3,000 and repay in 36 months, your finance cost is $540 and if you can manage to repay in 24 months, only $360.

Fortunately, it is easier now to compare credit rates. The "Truth in Lending" law, which became effective in 1969, gives you a uniform method for comparing finance charges on loans and purchases. As well as stating the dollar cost of the finance charge, the lender must state in the contract the *annual percentage rate.*

But you won't get the full usefulness of the Truth in Lending law unless you ask *beforehand* what the annual percentage rate (APR) is. Some lenders and dealers may tend to avoid discussing the APR, and prefer to let you discover it for yourself in the contract—if you really *do* read the contract.

The Different Types of Credit

New car loans: Rates vary from 11-12 percent at banks and credit unions to 12-14 charged by finance companies and dealers. You can save by arranging your loan with the same bank that finances the dealer.

You don't have to be a depositor at a bank to apply for a loan, except sometimes in periods of very tight money. But you do have to be a member of a credit union to borrow from one. Credit unions are voluntary associations of people with a "common bond," such as employees of the same company, or members of the same union or fraternal group. Their maximum annual rate is 12 percent but some charge 10 or 11 percent.

If you do prefer to finance through the dealer, you may be able to negotiate a relatively low rate with him. Sometimes car dealers arrange financing through several lenders and have several rate cards that they can show to buyers. Remind the dealer that you'd like to see his lowest rate card.

Used car loans: The disparity between bank and credit union loans, and dealer financing is even greater on used cars. Banks tend to charge a little more for used-car than new-car loans, perhaps 25 or 50 cents more per $100 of loan, or about one-half to 1 percent more on the annual rate.

But finance companies operating through car dealers charge not just a little more for used-car loans, but sharply more. They usually charge annual rates of approximately 17 to 32 percent ($9 to $17 per $100 of original balance), depending on individual state regulations and the age of the car. The various state laws do allow quite high credit fees on used-car time-payment contracts, so be guided accordingly.

Home equipment: Home appliances, furniture, and other household goods usually involve higher rates, *if financed through the seller*, than do new-car loans in most states. Stores usually have two main types of plans:

1. Revolving credit, budget, or extended-payment plans, as they are called by different retailers, usually cost 1½ percent a month on the declining balance, an annual rate of 18 percent. In this type of plan, now used widely to buy relatively small items on credit, you are assigned a limit; for example, $500. You charge purchases in various departments of the store, up to the predetermined limit, and repay in monthly installments. As you pay part of the predetermined line of credit, you can make new purchases.

2. The second type is the traditional long-term installment contract, usually used for buying furniture and appliances. Such contracts require a down payment and monthly payments for one to three years, depending on the contract terms you arrange. Typical finance charges for such non-auto install-ment plans are $9 to $12 per $100 of original balance—annual rates of about 17 to 23 percent, but sometimes more.

Some stores still have the traditional 30-day charge accounts, with no credit fee at all. But while formerly such accounts could run 60 or even 90 days without a credit fee or even a delicate inquiry as to whether you have returned from your vacation, nowadays you are likely to be charged 1½ percent a month if the account is not paid after 30 days (or similar designated period). Stores that do permit long "open" charge accounts with no credit fee may charge more for the merchandise itself than the stricter stores.

Note that in some states the annual percentage rate on revolving credit and other installment plans may be less than the usual 18 percent. States where laws impose lower rates currently include Arizona, Arkansas, Connecticut, Hawaii, Minnesota, Pennsylvania, South Carolina, Washington, and Wisconsin. The maximum APR in these states usually is 12 percent. In several other states, court or legislative contracts are seeking to cut these rates below the usual 18 percent a year.

Obviously, in states where revolving charge account and installment rates are higher than 12 percent a year, the cheapest way to finance installment purchases is to borrow from a bank or credit union. You'll save at least one-third of the finance charge.

Cash loans: If you need cash for really urgent purposes, as for a medical bill or to consolidate other pressing debts, you can get a personal loan from a bank or credit union for as little as 12 percent true annual rate. Or if you aren't careful you may be charged as much as 30 and even 36 percent for a loan from a small loan company or so-called personal finance company.

Banks are not as cheap for "cash advances" they offer on their credit cards as for ordinary personal loans. They may charge annual rates of 15 or 18 percent.

Another type of bank loan is "pre-arranged," "automatic," or "open end credit." You can draw on a prearranged amount of credit by check as you need it. You repay monthly. This plan has an advantage in that you pay no interest charge until you actually use the money, and is also sometimes less costly than the retail "revolving-credit" plans described earlier. But the charges of 1 to 1½ percent a month on the balance on such accounts sometimes are higher than personal loans from the same banks.

Families who have the kind of life insurance with "cash value" have an even lower-cost place to borrow. They can borrow up to 100 percent of their cash value for as low as 5 percent on older policies.

Usually you can repay in installments or a lump sum when you wish. The company simply sends you a bill for the interest due with your premium notices.

Educational loans: National Defense Act loans cost only 3 percent per annum. They are administered by the colleges themselves and are usually used to help the neediest students. The Guaranteed Student Loan Program offers loans at 7 percent for moderate-income-families who can show need as explained in college costs, page 213.

These loans are available for vocational training as well as college. They are made directly by banks, savings associations, and credit unions. Community organizations, employers, unions, and local alumni and professional associations also often are sources for low-cost loans.

Credit Terms You Ought to Know*

ACCELERATION CLAUSE: A dangerous provision that allows the creditor to request payment of all installments at once if one or more payments are missed.
ADD-ON CLAUSE: Lets you add additional purchases to an existing contract.
ADD-ON CHARGE: The finance charge is added to the amount borrowed for the term of the contract.
ANNUAL PERCENTAGE RATE: The ratio of the finance charge to the average amount of money owed during the life of the contract. Sometimes also called the "true annual rate". Also see "Truth in Lending".
CHATTEL MORTGAGE: A document that transfers title of personal property to a creditor as security for a loan.
CLOSING DATE: The day of the month

*Based on material from New York State Education Department and other sources but more candidly restated.

on which credit accounts and monthly bills are figured.
COLLATERAL: Property put up by a borrower to "secure" a loan.
COSIGNER: A person who agrees to pay a debt if the borrower does not.
DEFAULT: Failure to pay a debt when due or failure to meet the terms of a contract.
GARNISHMENT: A court order requiring that a specified part of a debtor's wages be paid by the employer to the creditor.
INSTRUMENT: A legal document, contract, note, or any other written agreement.
LIEN: A legal right to hold a debtor's property or to have it sold or applied toward payment of a claim.
MATURITY DATE: Date when final payment is due.
NOTE: A written promise to pay a specified sum at a specified time.
OPEN-END CREDIT: An agreement whereby credit is not restricted to a specific period of time, and you pay finance charges on whatever amount you actually owe. (Also see "Revolving Credit Account.")
PRINCIPAL: The amount borrowed.
PROCEEDS: The actual amount of money you get when borrowing.
REPLEVIN: Laws giving creditors the right to seize your car or other purchases if you have defaulted on payments.
REVOLVING CREDIT ACCOUNT: The store agrees to allow a stipulated amount of credit—say, $500. You have the option of paying the entire bill when you get it within a specified time—say, 24 or 30 days—or repaying part each month.
SECURED NOTE: A note which provides that, upon default, certain pledged property may be applied in payment of the debt.
SEWER SERVICE: Illegal practice of some process servers of claiming they served legal notice when they actually didn't.
TITLE: Proof of ownership.
TRUTH IN LENDING: Popular name for Federal law requiring that lenders and installment dealers state in the contract both the annual percentage rate and the total dollar cost of the finance charge.
UNSECURED NOTE: A loan made just on your signature without further security.
WAGE ASSIGNMENT: A credit agreement you "voluntarily" enter into, that allows the creditor to collect some of your salary from your employer if you default.

Where to Get Help with Complaints

The loss of money involved in products that don't work as they are supposed to, and sometimes guarantees that don't work either, is even more serious in a time of high prices.

Under the influence of government, officials and sometimes businessmen themselves, a number of industries have instituted industry-wide "action panels" or complaint offices. Some manufacturers also have set up central offices of their own to investigate complaints.

It should be noted at the outset that the industry panels, despite their good intent and influence, don't have any actual enforcement power to settle disputes. If you have a serious complaint, the only available course may be to take it through a process starting with the dealer and then writing to the president of the company involved. You can get his name from business directories in your library or from the company itself. If you get no satisfaction from the company, then try the action panel for that industry.

If no redress is available from the industry sources, you may want to make a complaint to the government agency with appropriate jurisdiction. Sometimes the agency may be unable to intervene but may be able to refer you to another source for help. Fortunately, state and federal bureaus nowadays tend to be more aware of consumer problems and realize that complaining consumers are not necessarily cranks.

Here is a list of some of the panels established by industry sources or other trade groups:

Major Appliances Consumer Action Panel (MACAP), 20 North Wacker Drive, Chicago, Illinois 60606, is a committee of consumer experts and university professors. MACAP is sponsored by appliance manufacturers and retailers to try to resolve complaints that individual companies fail to settle.

AUTOCAP is a similar organization recently established in some cities as an experiment in settling complaints related to cars and equipment. These panels are being sponsored by the National Automobile Dealers Association, 2000 K Street, N.W., Washington, D.C. 20006. Another trade association that you might consult if you have a car complaint is the Automobile Manufacturers Association, 1619 Massachusetts Avenue, Washington, D.C. 20006. Still another is the Tire Industry Safety Council, 766 National Press Building, Washington, D.C. 20004.

FICAP is short for the Furniture Industry Consumer Action Panel, Box 951, High Point, North Carolina 27261. FICAP seeks to handle complaints about furniture products.

Complaints about carpets can go to Director, Consumer Affairs, Carpet and Rug Institute, Dalton, Georgia 30702.

The National Association of Home Builders also has established complaint procedures to help home buyers and builders "work out amicable solutions." The procedures are under the supervision of the individual area builders' association. You may be able to find the local builders' association in the Yellow Pages. If not, write to Les Blattner, Director of Consumer Affairs, National Housing Center, 15th and M Streets, N.W., Washington, D.C. 20005.

Another industry program is the Home Owners Warranty program (HOW) developed by the National Association of Home Builders with the encouragement of the U.S. Office of Consumer Affairs. The program offers consumers a warranty on new homes that includes both "early years comprehensive guarantees" and ten-year insurance against major structural defects.

Better Business Bureaus are the longtime business-sponsored organizations that often seek to solve complaints by mediation or local arbitration panels. The BBB's especially have long experience in some areas of frequent disputes such as dry cleaning, home improvements, vocational schools, investments, and others.

Local and state agencies which may be able to help you include your state attorney general; state insurance, real estate and banking department; local consumer affairs office; city or county markets or weights and measures departments.

Most major federal agencies concerned with consumer problems have regional offices in major cities. You may be able to find the regional office under "U.S. Government" in your phone book. If there is none in your area, here is a list of offices which can supply the regional office address or handle your complaint directly:

Office of Consumer Affairs, U.S. Department of Health, Education, and Welfare, Washington, D.C. 20201, can provide general advice and refer specific complaints to the appropriate government agency.

Federal Trade Commission, Washington, D.C. 20201, has jurisdiction over deceptive advertising, labeling, and warranties.

Food and Drug Administration, U.S. Department of Health, Education, and Welfare, Washington, D.C. 20201, supervises purity and safety of food, drugs, and cosmetics.

U.S. Postal Service, Consumer Advocate's Office, Washington, D.C. 20260, polices mail fraud and deception (or start with your local postmaster).

Consumer Product Safety Commission, Washington, D.C. 20207, is responsible for policing hazardous products.

Interstate Commerce Commission, Washington, D.C., 20423, has jurisdiction over interstate buses, railroads, and truckers including movers.

Your Rights As a Customer

The "Truth in Warranties" law basically requires manufacturers to label warranties on products priced over $15 as "full" or "limited." If a "full" warranty, the manufacturer must repair the product at no charge within a reasonable period, or give a refund. If the warranty is only a "limited" one the manufacturer may agree only to provide parts.

The warranty also must reveal exclusions on "consequential damage," meaning damage resulting from use of a defective product.

The law now requires that dealers have to display the warranties so you can read them before you buy.

What if you make a purchase where there's no written warranty, or you feel you have been seriously misled by the sale? You can still have certain rights as a customer.

Implied warranty: Theoretically, any purchase you make carries with it three "implied warranties," imposed by law:

1. Title. The Seller must have clear ownership of the goods and the right to sell them.

2. Merchantability. Goods must be fit to sell and meet at least minimum standards. Wash-and-wear clothes, for instance, should not fall apart as soon as you launder them.

3. Fitness for a specific purpose. The food you buy should be safe to eat; the drugs you use, safe for consumption.

The implied warranties of merchantability and fitness may be waived if you buy goods "with all faults" or "as is." Also, if you're buying a costly item and there is no guarantee, get something in writing.

Express warranty: This means a specific statement or promise made by the seller or manufacturer concerning quality, character, or performance of a product. He can be held responsible for such promises.

Sales pitch: This is an area where it's difficult to get your money back. If a salesman tells you a vacuum cleaner will do a better cleaning job than any other machine, for instance, and you find its performance mediocre, you have no comeback unless you can prove the machine defective.

"Puffing": The law does allow some leeway for salesmanship or "puffing." If an ad says a pair of boy's slacks will "wear like iron," for example, you are supposed to understand that this is mere sales talk.

Goods made to order: Say you order a suit of clothing made to your measurements. When it's finished, you're dissatisfied. The tailor won't take it back because he says he made it exactly to your specifications. Unless you can prove he disregarded your instructions, and the suit unquestionably shows it, you are legally obligated to take it. Your best protection when you contract for anything made to order is to get a written description of your specifications.

Mutual-Aid Co-Ops

In times of high living costs, there's a noticeable increase in efforts to tame high living costs by getting together in buying clubs and other mutual-aid activities. In the mid-1970's such clubs and co-ops have sprung up all over the country.

Interest in repair and service co-ops has boomed. Another phenomenon is the growing interest of students and young families. Some student co-ops even own their own residences. In Berkeley, California, students operate an apartment house and also several stores. Most large universities now have student co-ops of one kind or another, performing self-supporting services from bookstores to boarding houses.

New England and the West Coast especially have seen a flowering of food co-ops among young people, ranging from buying clubs to groups growing their own crops. Often these buying clubs use guidance and facilities of long-established larger co-ops such as the Hanover, New Hampshire, co-op and the large co-op supermarkets in Berkeley and the Washington, D.C. area.

Older people too are using the cooperative idea in some useful ways to cushion the impact of inflation on their meager resources, as in the taxi-type transportation co-ops.

Some of the older people also have their own versions of specialized food co-ops, such as the fish buying clubs which appeared in the mid-1970's in Florida.

But most of the thousands of U.S. co-ops of various kinds are comprised of families: moderate to medium income, usually with children, seeking ways to stave off the erosion of inflation by contributing some of their own labor and small amounts of capital.

These co-ops take many forms including apartment houses; food stores; repair and service co-ops; optical and drug services; medical and dental clinics; and many others.

How They Get Started

Most of these mutual-aid groups start as food buying clubs but often then look for ways to use their organized buying power to save on other needs. One of the simplest ways, although requiring continuing supervision, is to arrange with private dealers and stores in the area for reduced prices to members in return for increased patronage. Thus, the Family Buying Club in Bayside, New York, has its own food store but also has agreements with local merchants for discounts on shoes and other clothing staples, dry cleaning, and stationery, says Edna Turner, the club manager.

Whatever their main consumer-goods interest, co-op groups usually use three organizational methods to achieve them.

Informal and sometimes even temporary neighborhood associations. Such groups get together to order fertilizer and other garden supplies and equipment in bulk at low prices from wholesale or farm suppliers, or to order storm windows or other equipment jointly, or arrange with local merchants for discounts on fuel, dry cleaning, hardware, appliances, and other needs and services.

More permanent buying clubs. Some of these are as small as a dozen families; others may have over a hundred. The small ones usually have no store but dispatch members to wholesale produce and grocery warehouses, and use a member's basement or apartment to distribute the goods.

Large stores or other large services. These often are spun off by other successful co-ops. Thus, the big New York City housing co-ops such as Rochdale Village, Co-op City and ILG Houses themselves sponsor a chain of seven large supermarkets, plus drug, optical and insurance services. In Michigan, the Ferndale Co-op sponsors a credit union, housing co-ops, eye care center, and home-improvement services. Chicago's largest supermarket, the Hyde Park Co-op, operates two furniture stores.

A buying club can be useful if planned and organized realistically. Even those organized for only temporary buying objectives or that finally may not survive, do achieve some savings. The money saved through a contribution of labor at least is not taxable and adds tangibly to income.

In the Port Washington co-op, for example, consumer-education specialist Marie Bonnie found that average savings on a list of 33 food and household items was 16 percent. The list averaged $32 at the conventional supermarkets; $27 at the co-op.

Besides saving some of the usual retail margin of about 22 cents of your dollar, well-run buying clubs often are able to save additionally by emphasizing basic foods; by looking for foods in heavy supply at wholesale markets, or by limiting selections of such processed foods as dry cereals to the less-expensive brands.

Food Co-Ops

Meat is the most difficult item to handle but also the largest potential money saver. If the co-op does not have a large freezer it is necessary to have cuts wrapped and quick-frozen by the wholesaler and distributed to members immediately, Gloria Stern advises in *How To Start Your Own Food Co-op*. She reports that a Boston-area club, the Mission Hill Co-op, has a volunteer "meat person" who checks prices and advises co-op members where the bargains are.

Many of the new specialized food co-ops or "community stores" have names describing their missions, such as the Plain Old Food Co-op of West Brookfield, Massachusetts; Alternative Vittles, in Clearwater, Florida, and the Community Stomach Natural Food Co-op in Worcester, Massachusetts.

Some clubs, such as the Plainfield, Vermont, Food Cooperative operate by distributing a monthly food list. The prices are wholesale plus 10% and the members prepay, so the group operates with little capital.

Even small food buying clubs should have at least ten or twelve members in order to buy full cases of dry groceries and produce. Most often, canned goods come 24 to a case, or 48 for small cans. An organization scheme suggested by the U.S. Office of Consumer Affairs divides job assignments into coordinator or manager; buyer; driver; cashier, and sorters.

Another recent idea for mutual buying is the direct farm sales that have been arranged between farm groups such as branches of the National Farmers Organization and Farmers Union, and urban consumer groups. These often have involved basic foodstuffs that suddenly jumped to startling levels at least temporarily, as potatoes did in 1974. Such temporary truck sales had taken place in some 14 states, in 1974-75, Fairchild News Service reported. Products involved besides potatoes included ground beef, quick-frozen fruits, and cheese.

The Plainfield co-op even has sponsored its own weekly farmers market where farmers and craftsmen in the area can sell produce, handicrafts, baked goods, and other items. Cooperative crafts marketing centers also operate in several areas including Chadds Ford, Pennsylvania, and Northampton, Massachusetts. Current information on locations is available from the Cooperative League of the U.S.A. (see below). A catalog of handcrafted items is available from Community Market, Box 202, Route 5, Louisa, Virginia 23093.

Barter—The Simplest Way

Perhaps the simplest form of mutual aid is barter—the exchange of goods and services. Barter is age-old, of course, but often comes to the fore in times of recession or steep living costs. In a period when your family is subject to both pressures, the barter system can be used more often.

Thus, neighbors and friends trade garden produce, preserves, and baked goods. Vacationers in different areas trade use of their homes. A financial writer helps an oil-burner serviceman do his tax and in return gets free burner servicing. An experienced woodworker helps a skilled plumber build his boat and in return gets plumbing repairs. One man who knows how to install aluminum siding helped his neighbors; they helped him install his TV aerial. A car buff helps a friend tune his engine; he gets help with painting. One woman sews for a friend and in turn gets car transportation.

The most widespread form of barter has become the exchange of children's outgrown clothing, playthings, and sports equipment like skates and bikes. Informal exchanges have burgeoned into the more-organized "Fifty-Fifty Shops" sponsored by PTA's and church groups.

Like the savings through mutual-aid clubs, the money you make through barter is tax-free.

Preschool Co-Ops

Perhaps the fastest-growing form of mutual self-help activity is co-op nursery and play schools. By 1975, U.S. and Canadian parents were operating over 2,500 such pre-school groups in an effort to trim the charges of $700 a year then typical of many private nursery schools. The parents shared the work and usually paid $30-$35 a month —less than half the cost at private schools.

The idea spreads mostly by word of mouth, reports Barbara Cantor, editor of the *Journal of the Parent Cooperative Preschool International*. Someone who knows about the schools starts one in an area and within a few months several more schools are organized.

But careful organization and enthusiasm are needed to establish a successful parents' co-op. First steps are finding a suitable location and a trained teacher. Finding a location sometimes involves a search among churches, public agencies such as park departments, and schools, fraternal associations, and other community institutions. One Miami-area group even had to settle for a "floating school"—using a different home each week. Parents also need to buy liability insurance and satisfy other local requirements for nursery schools.

Biggest saving is from parent participation, often as teacher aides. A class usually has one professional teacher to fifteen children with two or three parents helping.

Typically, a parent may drive a car pool one day a week and then stay on to help the teacher. Classroom participation helps the parents learn about children, and the children gain too. Parents also contribute their special skills like playing the guitar and showing how bread is baked.

The co-ops also sponsor parent education programs covering a range of interests such as discipline, selection and making of playthings, behavior patterns, development of values, nutrition and eating habits, and developing respect for others.

Parents interested in forming co-ops can get help from the district vice-presidents or councils in their vicinity. There are about 50 councils in the U.S. and Canada. For the address of the one in your area, and other information materials, write to Parent Cooperative Preschools International, 20551 Lakeshore Road, Bale d-Urge 850, Quebec, Canada.

For more information: Main source of data on location of existing co-ops of various kinds, and also for material on organizing such ventures, is the Cooperative League of the U.S.A., Suite 1100, 1828 L St., N.W., Washington, D.C. 20036, or Philip Dodge, The Co-op League's Field Service Director, 456 Frontage Road, Northfield, Illinois 60093.

Other major associations include: National Association of Housing Cooperatives, care of the Co-op League; Group Health Association of America, 1717 Massachusetts Avenue, N.W. Washington, D.C. 20036; North American Student Cooperative Organization, Box 1301, Ann Arbor, Michigan 48106; Continental Association of Funeral and Memorial Societies, care of the Co-op League.

Two regional wholesale co-ops that have been realistically helpful to buying clubs are Mid-Eastern Cooperatives, 75 Amor Avenue, Carlstadt, New Jersey 07072, which services co-ops from New England to Virginia, and Associated Cooperatives, Richmond, California 94804.

Other references: Pamphlets and books you can order or which may be available from your library include: *Moving Ahead with Group Action: The Buying Club,* 85¢ from the Co-op League; *Consumer Cooperation: The Heritage And The Dream,* $1, Co-op League; *New Look at Cooperatives,* 35¢, Public Affairs Pamphlets, 381 Park Avenue South, New York, New York 10016; *National Consumer Directory,* listing of food and crafts and other clubs, and *Operations Manual Co-op Stores And Buying Clubs,* free from Caroline Ramsey, Community Services Administration, 1200 19th Street, N.W., Room 332, Washington, D.C. 20506; *How to Start Your Own Food Co-op,* a directory and guide to wholesale buying, $4.95, Walker & Co., 720 Fifth Avenue, New York 10019; *Cooperative Enterprise, the Little People's Chance in A World of Bigness,* $7.95, from the Co-op League; *Directory of Food Co-ops* and six issues of *Food Co-op Nooz,* $3, from Food Co-op Project, Loop College, 64 East Lake Street, Chicago, Illinois 60601.

How to Cut Hair at Home

Although some people seem to acquire the knack more easily than others, it really isn't hard to learn to cut hair. The woman of the house, familiar with sectioning hair from having put up her own on rollers, is probably the best prospect for family barber.

Choose Your Weapons

Home barbering, however, isn't anything like the technique trained barbers use. You don't draw dry hair out from the head and whack away at it against a long, skinny comb with long, lean barbers' shears. (You can use such shears if that's what you already own, but the shorter, straight-blade "barbers' scissors" are much easier to handle.) Instead, you snip off damp hair held taut between two fingers of your free hand, the method of today's hair stylist. Round up an ordinary comb about 8″ long with heavy teeth in one half, fine teeth in the other; some hair clips to pin longer sections of hair out of your way; and a narrow hairbrush with bristles embedded in a curved base if you intend to use a hand-held hair dryer to finish off.

Unless someone in the family still wears a butch, you can forget about clippers. Avoid those gadgets that hold a double-edge razor blade and frazzle the ends of the hairs mercilessly. Don't bother with thinning shears either, because the strands of hair they cut short tend to push the hair out and make it unmanageable as they grow back among the strands left long.

Barbers' scissors are held with the thumb and ring finger. The handle ring that slides over the thumb should lie at the base of the thumbnail and not be allowed to slide over the knuckle. Practice the technique, thumb up, by holding the stable (ring finger) blade extending from your ring finger against the palm of your other hand and move the thumb up and down to open and close the active blade. You'll soon catch on to this one-blade snipping action that greatly aids accuracy.

The Prudent Approach

If there's a boy in the family, spare your spouse when you're learning to cut hair by starting on your son. Take him to a good barber and watch closely while he gets a cut. Or better still, take him to a men's hair-cutting salon and plant yourself just out of scissors range to take a free lesson. Smile a lot and don't hesitate to move in close to observe the action—you're paying plenty. But don't let the stylist use the brush and dryer to alter the final cut into a "style" you won't be able to duplicate at home; it will just confuse you. If he uses the dryer when he completes the cutting, have him merely fluff the hair dry with his free hand, then comb or brush it into place if it's straight hair or leave it alone entirely if it's naturally curly.

Then when you get home you can ease yourself into barbering by giving your son (or your man if there's no boy about the house) a trim every 10 days or two weeks. Snip no more than ¼″ to ½″ at a time off the ends of all the strands of hair—and send him back to the barber if things get out of hand. You'll eventually get the hang of it, and your trims will eventually turn into haircuts.

Or you can take your chances, when you get home, and wait until his hair is fully grown out, then pitch in. You must be aware, however, that it is distressingly easy to cut away too much with a single careless snip and leave an irreparable hole. A haircut actually takes very few scissor cuts. Most of the clickety-snip you hear in barbershops is just to make the patrons think they're getting their money's worth.

Be smart, play it safe and cut off too little rather than too much while you're still learning. You can always go back over the head and trim away some more. Reconcile yourself to the idea that your first attempts may not be perfect and will probably take about three times longer than the same job would take a professional.

Cut It Damp

First shampoo the hair. Today's shampoos are 5% to 20% detergent. The label never tells you, but generally there's more detergent in a shampoo meant for oily hair than in one for dry hair. The detergent in the shampoo loosens the dirt and oil in the hair in about two minutes and they rinse away with water. (Soaps react chemically with minerals and salts ordinarily present in tap water to form an insoluble scum that dulls hair—and soaps simply don't get it as clean as detergents.) Rinse thoroughly. You can use a creme rinse or conditioner well rinsed out after shampooing to make the hair easier to handle as you're cutting it. With oily hair, use much less conditioner than label directions call for and rinse it off sooner. Towel-dry the hair but leave it damp. It's easier to cut when damp.

Getting Set

You should stand to cut hair. Seat the person who's getting the haircut at a height that puts your chin approximately level with the top of his head. (A board across the arms of a sturdy armchair gets a child up where you want him.) Have plenty of light on the subject. Outdoors in summertime in full sun is ideal for giving haircuts—with the snips blown away by the breeze.

Comb out the hair to make sure you're rid of snarls. Comb away from the crown in all directions, then make a part over the top of the head from ear to ear. Comb the front hair forward and slip on a hairclip or two to hold it out of the way. Comb the back hair downward. Part it vertically into three sections (see diagram) and draw them up out of the way with hair clips. Comb down the remaining hair from a horizontal line extending from earlobe to earlobe.

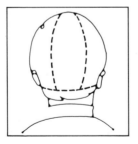

Outlining

Using the edge of your free hand to hold the hair in place, decide how much of it will extend below the natural hairline at the nape of the neck, and trim off the excess below this outline. The length of the hair you leave extending below the natural hairline establishes the length that you will now cut the back of the lower head up as far as the *horizontal* earlobe-to-earlobe line.

Pick up the scissors with the thumb and ring finger. Then, leaving the handle ring in place on your ring finger, slip your thumb out of the other handle ring and close the scissors into your palm. Now pick up the comb in the normal way, with the same hand. You'll begin at the base of the neck below the left ear and work around to the other side.

Use the comb to lift a thin (¼″ to ½″) vertical portion of hair extending 1″ to 1½″ up the scalp. Reach under the comb and grasp this hair tightly between the index finger and middle finger of your free hand, palm toward you. Swiftly transfer the far end of the comb, teeth downward, into the slot formed by the thumb and first knuckle of the hand that's holding the hair. Now pulling the hair out at a right-angle from the scalp (downward and outward at the back of the head), let it slide slowly through your fingers until it reaches the hairline-to-trimoff length you previously established. Slip the end of your thumb back into the handle of the scissors and firmly but evenly cut away the hair just beyond the back of your fingers. (If the hair doesn't cut easily, either your scissors need sharpening—never use them for anything but cutting hair—or you're trying to snip off too much at once.)

Cut the entire area this way, all the same length, from the outline at the nape to the horizontal earlobe-to-earlobe line above. Always comb the hair down after each snip to disclose any irregularities in your cutting that should be corrected.

Layering

Now unclip section 1. Working upward from the bottom of section 1, take a 1″ to 1½″ vertical parting ¼″ to ½″ thick and let it slide through your two fingers to a desired length (it's up to you)—then cut. This first cut will establish the general overall length of the rest of the haircut. If you don't trust your eye to maintain an even overall length as you continue cutting, you can lift a few adjacent strands of hair you've previously cut with each new portion of the section you're working on. This gives you a guide. As you let the hair slide through your fingers, the falling away of those previously cut strands signals the moment to tighten your grip on the hair and cut it.

Keep combing out the hair so the layers of section 1 all blend together. Cut section 2 and section 3 the same way. When you finish, comb down the back of the head with the large-tooth end of the comb. Before you go on to the front of the head, however, you may want to make a simple check to see if all the hair has been cut the same length. Do so by parting it at random here and there and lifting some hair from each side of the part. Drawing it taut straight out from the scalp, let it slide through your fingers to see how the length of the cut ends compare. If there's much variance among strands, the uneven ends should be cut to conform.

Cutting the Front

First comb out the front hair from the ear-to-ear over-the-head part forward, then part it into three sections (see diagram) by finding the natural part on one side and duplicating it on the other. Or part it at the deepest point of the natural hairline on each side. Comb the side sections straight downward

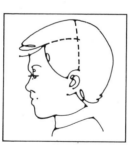

from the two parts. Draw the top section up out of your way; if it tends to flop back, pin it with a hair clip.

Both side sections are cut the same as you cut the back sections. Begin with either side, cutting the hair somewhat shorter—or longer (again it's a matter of preference)—than the overall hair length. Side hair covers the tops of the ears in today's longer hairstyles, but if he doesn't want to wear his hair that way, the conventional haircut (that older men favor) calls for an outline curving up from the nape *behind* the ears and down in front to join the sideburns.

Cut the sideburns as small separate sections, squaring them off a little below the natural hairline. (Whether he wears his hair long or short, any adult male who is wearing sideburns lower than the bottom of the ear cavity will almost undoubtedly look younger, possibly even handsomer, if they are trimmed shorter.)

Your handling of the center section can make or break the haircut—not so much with a boy, but with a man whose hair is thinning or whose hairline is receding.

A boy growing up in a family where male hairlines tend to recede early in life is best advised to train his hair forward while he's young (swinging his forelock to one side or the other) so he won't have to retrain it forward later on. To avoid the squared-off look of bangs, stand in front of him, comb the forelock to the left and trim off its ends, then comb it to the right and trim it again. Now check by combing it forward to make sure the front outline has been shortened sufficiently by this maneuver to keep the hair out of his eyes if it should fall forward, as it may.(Note: You may prefer to cut the top section first and outline it afterward.)

To cut the top, move around to his right side. Lift a few previously cut strands of section 2 from behind the ear-to-ear part to match up for length. Then, with the fingers of your left hand pointing toward his face, work forward from the ear-to-ear part to within 1″ of the front outline. Go back to the ear-to-ear part and make successive trips forward picking up thin partings of hair until the section is evenly cut. If he prefers his hair a bit thicker in front, you can easily "taper" it by cutting each ¼″ to ½″ portion at a very slight upward (toward the forehead) angle instead of parallel to the scalp. Or taper by cutting each portion you pick up slightly longer, as you work forward by increasing the space between your fingers and his head. As you work comb out the section often to reveal uneven places.

Coping With Recession

When you begin cutting your husband's hair (taking it for granted you're all practiced up on your boy), if his hair is thinning and he wants the appearance of more hair, you should cut the side section longer on whichever side of his head the hair grows thicker and comb it over the top to increase the look of fullness. If he wears it parted, the part should be located on the side of the head on which the hairline recedes the least. Leave it long enough on the top-of-head side of the part to sweep over the head and blend in with the hair on the opposite side, hiding at least half his cranial nudity.

A man with normally thick hair who wants to wear it longer to keep up to date will look better groomed if he does not let it grow too long but opts for the following alternative: The appearance of longness without the bothersome upkeep and the constant disarray can be accomplished by cutting the hair the same comparatively short, 1½″ to 2″, length all over, then trimming it off below the natural hairline by as much as 1″. Low in the back, covering the tops of the ears on the sides, parted on top or allowed to fall "casually" over the forehead, this is an easy cut for the home barber. It's a matter of simply drawing slim vertical partings straight out from the scalp and cutting all the hair a length decided upon beforehand. (If his hair is truly long now, you can keep him from going into shock by working back to shorter hair in stages, coming a little closer to his scalp with your shears each time you cut his hair.) Such a haircut is an easy-care option for any man whose hair is naturally wavy, because he can wash it and towel-dry it, then let it dry completely without applying any hair preparation at all. Each strand will curl in its natural direction; curly male hair is highly acceptable today, and more men are going this route. The truth is, a mass of curly locks can conceal such indignities as bald spots and even a receding hairline—at least for a few years.

Hair Care and Maintenance

The days of plastering the hair down with stickum are over, of course. To make hair lie in a direction it doesn't naturally grow, wash it (frequently—as often as you like), towel-dry it until it's barely damp, then brush the hair in the desired direction as you blow it dry with a hand-held hair dryer. A light unscented hair spray will keep it in place a little while longer. Properly cut, however, fairly short hair can be combed or brushed into place in the morning and left alone all day. It should fall back approximately where it belongs no matter which way the wind blows.

Shape the hair to fit the face

A round face calls for moderately long hair, swept back on the sides partially covering the ears or combed behind them. Sideburns should be trimmed fairly close to avoid the "pumpkin head" look.

A square face should have more hair at the sides and top to round out the head.

An oblong face needs more fullness at the sides and less on top. Top hair can obscure a substantial portion of the forehead either sweeping across from the part to other side or tumbled forward if the persons hair is naturally curly.

These are only suggestions. Experiment to find the most becoming style for the individual face. Some men like to wear their hair in more than one style, allowed to blow free during the day, perhaps, every hair in place on a night out.

How to Entertain for Less

Without cutting down on your guest list or your fun, you can trim party-giving costs best by controlling the two items that usually cost the most: liquor and food.

It's easy enough—and coming to be expected while times are tough—to create a festive atmosphere without an open bar or the invitation to "Help yourself!" But if you think you're going to be pressed for mixed drinks, one budget-saving suggestion is to control the mixing and pouring yourself. Or ask someone well clued into the situation to take on the job of tending bar. Use small glasses with lots of ice, keep a reasonable lapse of time between rounds, and none of your guests will consider you stingy. Set up bar in some fairly inconspicuous location where people are not apt to congregate, then make snack foods a party focal point well separated from the bar. The need to nibble will draw them away. And for goodness' sake, give your guests something to do—dancing to records is back in swing. If people are having a good time, they don't drink as much.

Remember, too, that the considerate host or hostess always makes soft drinks and non-alcoholic punches available for guests.

Low-Cost Alternatives

Save money serving a wine punch in a huge glass punch bowl encircled by punch glasses (rented from your liquor dealer if you don't own them). Your guests won't know and you don't have to broadcast the fact that there's little or no hard liquor in it. The punch bowl can be the focal point of the party, wreathed in decorations, if you like, and surrounded with tempting foods. Or you can serve a wine punch well spiked with hard liquor and still come out ahead.

Would you save by making your own wine? Possibly. Under federal law it's legal for a householder to produce up to 200 gallons of wine tax-free a year, but whatever you make must be consumed on your property. You merely file a copy of Treasury Form 1541, obtainable from the Division of Alcohol, Tobacco and Firearms Tax, Internal Revenue Service. Wine-making kits were all the rage a short while ago, but the craze died fast when neophytes discovered how difficult it is to make decent wine. For good wine you need fairly expensive equipment (available in great array from Sears), so you're unlikely to be able to make it pay for itself in less than three years' wine-making. What with storage and spoilage problems, you're probably ahead buying wine in gallon jugs (and keeping it refrigerated after you've opened it).

Beer making is illegal, in spite of the fact that a lot of quiet home brewing goes on in this country for the logical reason that better beer can be made at home than you can buy, at less than a fourth the cost. Malt extract is on supermarket shelves, but home brewers send away for brewing yeast. A free catalog of wine- and beer-making equipment, ingredients and instructions, is available from The Liberty Malt Shop, 39

Lower Floor, Pike Place Market, Seattle, WA 98101 if you live in the West, or Milan Laboratory, 57 Spring St., New York, NY 10012 if you live in the East; either if you live in between.

What to Serve When

In summer, make a splash with a wine-and-fruit punch. Consider substituting ice cream or sherbet for the cake of ice as a prelude to a smorgasbord-type luncheon or supper. Or more informally, have a keg of beer delivered (they come in all sizes). Tap it on the deck or patio where spills won't matter and let guests help themselves.

In winter, the traditional New Year's Day eggnog open house is a way of making good your past year's leftover social obligations. Just be sure to let invited guests know you're serving the real thing, not the prepared dairy imitation, and keep a freshly brewed pot of coffee ready to help those who need it to get through the tag end of the holiday season. Or some winter's weekend when the ice is good, invite friends to an afternoon skating party on a local pond and serve them doughnuts and mulled cider, hot spiced wine or steaming mugs of mocha java topped with whipped cream when they return red-nosed and frozen-toed.

At any time of year, when you've invited guests for dinner, instead of before-dinner cocktails, serve an aperitif, which might be a chilled glass of champagne or (less expensive) a dry sherry slightly chilled (50°) or an Italian Vermouth well chilled, either served in pipe-stem, V-shaped 2-oz. glasses. Or adopt the European custom of serving a wine appropriate to the first course, and ask guests to bring their goblets to the table. After dinner, serve Espresso or Café Royale, which are less expensive than liqueurs.

Feeding the Gang

It would seem the savings were self-evident in spending time preparing party foods from scratch rather than running out to buy little dainties and packaged convenience foods, but the cost-cutting route takes work and cook-ahead planning. All too often this chance is overlooked. Choose the kinds of food that can be made well beforehand. Many sorts of canapés and other hot nibbles can be readied on baking sheets or broiler pans and refrigerated, so that all you have to do is pluck off the plastic wrap at the appropriate moment and slide them in the oven. Keep in mind, however, that most cold party food is less expensive than hot; you save range fuel as well as air-conditioning energy in hot weather. But if you're determined to serve hot foods, and your big bash is only once or twice a year, chafing dishes, electric warmers and hot trays are all rentable (see the Yellow Pages). The cost is minimal compared to outright purchase.

Or you can borrow. Try church and women's groups. They feed large crowds and may be willing to lend you a giant coffee maker, glasses, cups and extra flatware, perhaps even folding tables. Reminder: a modest donation to the sponsoring organization when you return (clean) what you were loaned will be appreciated.

A meal for which each family or single guest "volunteers" to make and bring one dish is an old tradition in clan gatherings that can work equally well among good friends and friendly neighbors. It assuredly spreads out both the cost and the work load.

To halve the price on every party purchase, consider co-hosting with a neighbor, as long as your two circles of friends are compatible and your houses close enough to consolidate preparations. An amusing variation is the moveable feast in which each course is served at a different neighbor's home, guests rollicking from one to another.

White Wine Punch

> **3 bottles dry white wine, chilled**
> **3 lemons, peeled and juiced**
> **3 tablespoons sugar, or less, to taste**
> **¾ cup brandy, scotch or bourbon**
> **3 28-ounce bottles club soda**

In a punch bowl, lay a block of ice frozen in a tray without dividers. Add wine, lemon juice and peeling. Sprinkle on sugar. Stir till sugar dissolves. Add brandy and soda. Yield: 42 four-ounce servings. (To make the punch stronger, substitute sparkling wine for the club soda.)

The same recipe makes a red (Burgundy) wine punch; by adding slices of orange and lime, you have that great favorite, Sangria.

Champagne Punch

    6 lemons, sliced
    6 oranges, sliced
    1 cup sugar
    5 fresh mint leaves
    2 bottles sauterne, chilled
    2 cups brandy
    2 quarts fresh small strawberries
    6 bottles domestic champagne,
       well chilled
    1 fresh pineapple, cut in 3-inch sticks

In a punch bowl gently toss lemon and orange slices with sugar and mint. Let fruit stand till sugar starts to dissolve. Add sauterne and stir till sugar is thoroughly dissolved. Place in bowl large piece of ice (frozen in tray without dividers.) Pour in brandy and float strawberries. Just prior to serving, add champagne. Ladle into chilled punch cups with a stick of pineapple in each. Yield: 60 four-ounce servings.

New Year's Day Eggnog

    12 fresh eggs
    1½ cups granulated sugar
    1 quart heavy cream
    1 quart milk
    1 quart brandy (whiskey or sherry)
    ¼ cup Jamaica rum
    ¼ teaspoon salt
       Nutmeg

Separate eggs and refrigerate whites, covered. Beat yolks at high speed, slowly adding 1 cup of the sugar, continuing to beat until it is completely dissolved. Stir in cream and milk. Slowly add brandy and rum, testing as you stir: if rum overpowers brandy, decrease amount of rum since the two flavors should equal out; if mixture tastes too sweet, increase brandy. Refrigerate, covered, 3 to 4 hours. One hour before serving, allow whites to return to room temperature, then beat only until soft peaks form as you lift beater. Sprinkle ¼ cup of remaining sugar over beaten whites and beat just long enough to blend; sprinkle on and beat in final ¼ cup sugar similarly. Fold together yolk mixture and beaten whites in punch bowl using wooden spoon. Grate fresh nutmeg on top. Yield: 50 four-ounce servings.

Café Royale

    1 demitasse or small cup hot, strong,
       freshly brewed coffee
    Sugar cube
    Dash brandy, heated

Pour black coffee into cup. In teaspoon resting atop coffee, place cube of sugar. Saturate it with heated brandy and ignite. (Cold brandy won't light.) Just as flame is dying out, lower cube into coffee and stir gently a moment or two.

Mulled Cider

    4 quarts apple cider
    1 cup maple syrup
    2 teaspoons whole cloves
    ½ teaspoon salt
    1 teaspoon allspice
    6 sticks cinnamon
    ¼ nutmeg, fresh-grated
    2 quarts applejack, warmed (optional)

Combine cider, maple syrup, and spices in a pot, heat to boiling and simmer 20 minutes. Strain, add applejack if a kick is desired, and serve piping hot. Yield: 20 six-ounce servings (32 with applejack added).

Mocha Java

    12 cups coffee, strong, freshly brewed
    3 teaspoons Hershey's (unsweetened)
       Cocoa
    3 teaspoons Hershey's (chocolate) Syrup
    1 pint heavy cream, whipped
       Semisweet chocolate, shaved

For best results, use freshly ground beans, if possible, and wait until after your guests arrive to make the coffee, because it loses its flavor swiftly once it's brewed. Pour coffee into saucepan over low heat and stir in cocoa and chocolate syrup; the mixture must not boil. Serve in warmed mugs topped with whipped cream garnished with chocolate shavings. Yield: 10 to 12 cups.

A sprinkle of cinnamon is one option a few people like, a dash of rum is another, but fair warning, both kill the subtly exquisite 50/50 coffee-chocolate flavor of true mocha. (This same mocha java recipe is excellent in summer iced.)

Hot Spiced Wine

    2 bottles red wine
    2 tablespoons sugar
    2 lemons, sliced, a couple of cloves
        stuck in each slice
    ½ teaspoon nutmeg (fresh-grated's best)
        Cinnamon sticks

Warm wine in pot over low heat. Add sugar, lemon and nutmeg. Stir. Bring mixture almost to a boil and immediately pour into mugs, a slice of lemon afloat in each one. Serve with cinnamon sticks (which can be rinsed and reused.) Yield: About 9 six-ounce servings. A dash of brandy, whiskey or Kirsch can be added to the cup of any guest who'd like his drink strengthened.

Mock Champagne Punch

    3 cups water
    1 6-ounce can frozen orange juice
        concentrate, thawed
    1 6-ounce can frozen lemonade
        concentrate, thawed
    2 cups cranberry juice cocktail
    ½ cup sugar
    2 25-ounce bottles sparkling pink
        catawba juice, chilled

In large bowl combine water and concentrates. Add cranberry juice and sugar; stir till sugar dissolves. Chill thoroughly. Just before serving add chilled catawba juice very slowly; stir gently. Yield: 24 four-ounce servings.

Cinnamon-Fruit Punch

    ¾ cup red cinnamon candies
    ¾ cup water
    6 cups cold water
    5 6-ounce cans frozen pineapple
        juice concentrate, thawed
    3 28-ounce bottles lemon-lime
        carbonated beverage, chilled

Heat and stir candies and ¾ cup water till candies dissolve; remove from heat. Combine with the cold water and pineapple concentrate. Cover; chill. Transfer to punch bowl. Add lemon-lime beverage; mix gently. Add ice cubes or block. Yield: 42 four-ounce servings.

Amber Tea Delight

    4 cups hot tea
    2 12-ounce cans apricot nectar
    2 cups orange juice
    ½ cup sugar
    ½ cup lemon juice
    1 28-ounce bottle ginger ale, chilled
        Ice cubes

Combine hot tea, apricot nectar, orange juice, sugar, and lemon juice. Chill. Before serving, add ginger ale. Pour over ice cubes to serve. Yield: 24 (4-ounce) servings.

Decorating for a party

Unless you're planning a costume party revolving around a particular theme, and even then, decorating need not be costly. One reason the Christmas season is such a popular party time is that, with the tree up, you have a head start on decorating the house. A table centerpiece of evergreens and a swatch of greenery here and there are all you need. But you might consider hanging some bangles, baubles and bows from your houseplants.

A major transformation can be accomplished for an after-dark party any time of year simply by candlelight, with candles burning singly and in groups all over the house. Your electric lighting should be dimmed to a romantic, golden glow to fill in the shadows and soften the relative harshness of the candle flames themselves.

In summer on calm nights, a stunt for stimulating a party atmosphere as guests arrive is to border your drive or walkway with paper bags one-third filled with sand, in the center of each of which you have a candle burning. Or simply jab a pair of tiki torches in the ground either side of your doorway to say, "Welcome—the fun starts right inside!"

Another easily rigged summertime scheme is to outline and crisscross a dance area, in- or outdoors, with strings of (borrowed) Christmas tree lights, each colored bulb enclosed in a small *white* Japanese paper lantern. (These are pennies apiece at most Japanese stores, which can order them for you if they don't ordinarily stock white paper lanterns.) The effect has lovely nostalgic overtones of the Victorian era.

How to Cut Vacation Costs

If you're still wondering whether you can afford a vacation trip this year, the answer is yes. True, money is harder to come by, and worth less than a couple of summers ago, but you'll find that wise planning can shave travel costs at least as much as inflation has eroded the dollar. Follow the suggestions offered here and you'll be able to enjoy the same great vacations as usual, simply by cutting a few corners and making some concessions in scheduling and style.

House Swapping

House swapping—which costs you zero— is the ideal money-saver. You can temporarily exchange your own home for a Georgian house on a New England hilltop, a wood-and-glass construction at the edge of the sea, a Manhattan apartment, a plantation house in the South—in fact, almost any kind of dwelling you might name. And don't worry about living in a town you think nobody is interested in. It might be the destination of fond grandparents who want to visit their offspring but don't want to inconvenience them or give up their own privacy. Or maybe a business executive long since transferred from your town would like to take his kids back to see friends. Many families just want to find out what life in different parts of the country is like.

One of the beauties of house swapping is that you immediately become a member of the community, with introductions to neighbors arranged by your hosts, just as you in turn will make arrangements for them. Your children will have the same playmates throughout the vacation, and you'll probably inherit a baby-sitter list, too.

Arranging an exchange. The way to go about a swap is to join one of the home exchange clubs, all of which publish directories that list the pertinent details about available houses. If it's too late to list your home in a directory (the majority are published in the early spring), you can obtain copies of the directories and supplements, and then write to the people whose listed homes appeal to you.

Naturally, you can't be inflexible in your choice of destination. Vacation exchange clubs advise you to write to 10 or 15 prospects at a crack. You don't have to labor over individual letters—photocopies will do.

Exchanges can be arranged for periods as long as several months or as short as one weekend. Car swaps are often part of the deal—in which case you should make sure that insurance covers everybody.

Names and addresses. The Vacation Exchange Club (350 Broadway, New York, New York 10013) carries the largest number of listings. The charge for listing your home in their directory is $12; to buy a copy after press time costs $9. Adventures-in-Living (P.O. Box 278, Winnetka, Illinois 60093) charges $15 per year, including a listing. But their directory is available for half price after August 1. The Holiday Home Exchange Bureau (P.O. Box 555, Grants, New Mexico 87020), which puts out a new directory every month, charges a $15 membership fee that entitles you to receive and be listed in 12 issues.

As well as swapping houses with American families, you can exchange with people abroad—in Europe, the Caribbean, Mexico, South and Central America, Australia, even Africa. Again, the Vacation Exchange Club is biggest on such listings, but you might also try the International Hospitality Service (Suite 3, 1377 9th Avenue, San Francisco, California 94122).

Tourist Homes

Tourist homes—also called guest houses— rank high on the list of money-savers. These are private homes with extra rooms that are rented out to visitors, usually on a per-night basis. Sometimes the guest room comes complete with a private bath; other times you share facilities at the end of the hall. Sometimes the place is old-fashioned and charming, other times, ancient and rickety. Prices for a room range from as low as $4 or $5 a night in an off-the-beaten-track home where the bathtub still stands on claw legs, to as much as $20 a night in a spruced-up house in a tourist town at the height of the vacation season. Overall, the nightly charge averages about $8 to $15 for a family of four, including rollaways you might need for your youngsters.

Unfortunately, since most modern houses are not big enough to double as tourist homes, these establishments are pretty well confined to older communities. They're plentiful in small towns and medium-sized cities along the Eastern seaboard and in the South, but almost nonexistent in coastal California. You'll encounter them occasionally in the Midwest and the Rocky Mountain States. Upon request, chambers of commerce sometimes will send you listings of their community's more attractive tourist homes that you can use to make reservations. Barring that, look for signs that read "Tourists" on the front lawns of the first residential streets you hit as you drive into town. And stop early; even if the tourist homes aren't filled up, the owners want their sleep, too.

Tent Camping

Tent camping is obviously another cheap way to go. Overnight charges typically run only about $3 in state parks, $4 to $5 in private campgrounds. Your food costs should be no more than at home and campers usually spend less on entertainment than other vacationers do. A family of four can equip itself with all the camping basics for from $200 to $300, and that investment—which covers tent, sleeping bags, cots or air mattresses, stove, lantern, and cooler—can easily be amortized on one or two trips.

College Dorms

College dorms are another good deal, but only if yours is a small family. That's because they usually charge per bed, and their beds are too narrow for sharing. Rates of $4.50 or $5 per person, which are fairly standard, may seem high, but staying in university housing often makes you eligible to

eat in the school cafeteria. Breakfasts there run around $1 and dinners rarely more than $2—a considerable saving over restaurant bills.

Only a small percentage of the nation's college dorms are open to visitors, however, and those that do let rooms are apt to be open only during some special on-campus event—like a meeting, summer school, or seminar. To find out what's available, look up the locations of the schools situated along your intended vacation route in "Lovejoy's College Guide" at your library. Or write to local chambers of commerce in communities where you'd like to spend a night or more. Then contact the directors of housing at the appropriate colleges. Be sure to indicate the date you expect to arrive, the planned length of your stay, and the number of people in your party, including the ages of your children, since some schools don't take kids under six. To speed up answers, enclose a self-addressed, stamped envelope or postcard.

Several publications claim to provide reliable information on college-campus vacation opportunities, but having checked out their entries we recommend only one: "Where to Stay USA," a comprehensive reference book that also lists budget motels, YMCAs, reasonable small hotels, hostels, and student hotels (available in bookstores or from the Council on International Educational Exchange, 777 United Nations Plaza, New York, New York 10017).

Some universities abroad, especially in Great Britain and Scandinavia, rent rooms to travelers in the summer. Rates range from about $4 to $7 per person, half of what you'd pay in medium-priced hotels there. Information on tourist dorms in Scandinavia is available from the Scandinavian Tourist Office, 75 Rockefeller Plaza, New York, New York 10019. For accommodations at British universities, contact University Holiday Ltd., Box 2093, Eads Station, Arlington, Virginia 22202.

Hostels

Hostels are another way to go, but again they're a better bargain for small families than large ones because a per-person charge is usual. In most hostels, the average rate is about $3, so a family of four has to pay almost as much as in a budget motel. Moreover, sex-segregated dorms are common, so you have to give up life as a family. On the other hand, you and your youngsters may find it a lot of fun to be involved in the type of healthy communal, cooperative life that hostels foster, including cooking your meals in a kitchen shared by all of the people who are at the hostel and relaxing in a common room.

To take advantage of the establishments run by the American Youth Hostel Association and those of affiliated organizations in Europe, you must be members of AYH. This costs $10 per person per year for adults, $5 for kids under 18. Family membership, which entitles you to stay in hostels in the U.S. and Canada but not in Europe, costs $12. However, you cannot use AYH hostels just for stopovers on a car trip. Unless the hostel is in the city, you're expected to participate in the open-air activities that hosteling is all about—hiking, bicycling, canoeing, horseback riding, and so on.

Another consideration is that most hostels are closed—that is, you can't get in or out—between 10 a.m. and 4 p.m. Lights are usually turned off at 11 p.m., no alcoholic beverages are allowed, and smoking, if permitted at all, is restricted to certain areas at certain times. You must bring your own bedding in the form of a "sleeping sheet," which is simply a sleeping bag made out of a sheet with a flap at the head end to cover your pillow.

There are AYH hostels of all kinds—in schools, churches, mountain lodges, restored old buildings, revamped farmhouses. The one on Nantucket Island is in a former Coast Guard station. Rates range anywhere from $1 to $5 per person. A complete directory comes with your membership. For an application, write to American Youth Hostel Association, National Campus, Delaplane, Virginia 22025.

Independent hostels, sponsored by YM/YWCAs, church groups, and other social organizations, follow pretty much the same practices as those of the AYH, except that they don't require you to engage in outdoor activities. What's provided in the way of bedding varies from hostel to hostel, and many of them—like YMCA and YWCA hotels in many cities—have triple and quadruple rooms, not just collective dorms. Rates range from about $2 to $6 per person, depending on what accommodations are available. The lowest rate is for dorm sleeping. On the average, a family of four will pay between $15 and $22 for a private room in YMCA hotels in big cities such as San Francisco and Chicago.

Budget Motels

Budget motels rank next. Don't think for a minute they're flea bags; they're not. The vast majority are clean and comfortable, lacking only costly frills. They may not have coffee shops, but they'll be close enough to restaurants so you won't starve. The TV may not be a color set and the decor may not be luxurious, but these are hardly major problems when all you're looking for is a good night's sleep. There are any number of budget chains, some with built-in reservations systems so you can plan for your lodging ahead of time.

But low-budget rates are not limited to chains. Scattered across the country there are hundreds of independently operated establishments that offer the same economical prices, cleanliness, and modern conveniences, sometimes including a swimming pool of modest dimensions. And it isn't a big problem to find out where they're located. For $1 you can obtain a directory of these independent facilities from Budget Motels & Hotels of America, Inc., 568 Snelling Avenue North, St. Paul, Minnesota 55104.

Special Deals

Many big-chain hotels and motels offer special deals that can also save you money. At most of these facilities, rooms have two double beds, ample for a family of four. Sometimes there are extra charges for rollaways; other times rollaways are free. Most chains charge $2 to $5 for extra adults occupying your room, regardless of whether a rollaway is needed, but different chains have different rules about the age at which your child becomes old enough to be classified as an "adult."

At all Holiday Inns, children under 12 can stay free in their parents' room. A family rate for a room with two double beds—

usually only about $2 more than the regular double rate—is offered at more than half of the 1,500 Holiday Inns. And at about two-thirds of the 1,500, children under 12 can eat free from a special menu—a feature that can add up to a big saving. The Holiday Inn directory, available free at any Holiday Inn, indicates which chain members participate in the family plan. For a list of those where kids eat free, you can write to Department KEF, Holiday Inns, 3742 Lamar, Memphis, Tennessee 38118. Inns listed in both categories obviously offer the best bargains.

Almost all Howard Johnson motels let children under 18 stay free in their parents' room. Also, the chain's restaurants offer daily specials priced at $2.50 to $3, with reductions of $1 or more for children, and seconds for everyone on the house. On Sundays everything on the children's menu is 79 cents for youngsters under 13.

At Ramada Inns, children under 19 can stay in their parents' room at no charge. Sheraton Hotels and Inns offer the same saving for children under 18.

Some Marriott facilities offer special low rates for families with children under 12. At most Rodeway Inns and Imperial 400 motels, there's no charge for children under 12 years.

For specific information on big chain motels, ask WATS line information (800/555-1212) for toll-free numbers.

Package Plans

Hotel and motel package plans are often good bets for short vacations and for stop-overs on trips. Generally, the prices for the accommodations themselves are not much lower than you'd pay otherwise, but the extras cost less, sometimes much less. The question is whether these extras justify staying in what might be an expensive hotel, and whether you're willing to accept the limitations of a package—which may mean taking all your meals in the hotel restaurant, for instance. Many resort hotels offer vacation packages that include recreational facilities for which you would normally pay extra, or at least they provide reductions.

Almost every major hotel has special packages, especially on weekends in cities, but no two plans are alike, even within the same chain. The only way to find out about them is to call the specific hotel or the chain's toll-free central reservation number.

At several Dunfey hotels in New England you pay $29.95 per person for a four-day/three-night package (noon Friday through noon Monday) that includes room and breakfasts. That averages $20 a night for bed and breakfast for two. Children under 17 can come along free if they sleep in your room, but their meals are extra. If you figure breakfast for two kids for a $4 total, you have lodgings and breakfast for the whole family for $24 a day—not bad at all in a good hotel.

At the Hyatt Anaheim a three-day/two-night package (here regardless of the time of week) costs $37.50 per adult, $16 for youngsters ages 13 to 18, and $5.50 under 13, including, for each person, one free admission to Disneyland and tickets for 11 rides.

At the Sheraton Park Hotel near the zoo in Washington, D.C., you pay about $67 for a family of four for two nights, including breakfast and sight-seeing.

Timing

Simply by traveling when most other people don't, you can cut costs substantially. Even one week on either side of the official "peak" season makes a considerable difference in the amount you must pay for transportation and accommodations. Traveling at what is generally considered the "wrong" time of year is cheaper still—and not necessarily wrong at all. Florida, for instance, is a fantastic bargain during the summer and fall, and in those seasons the weather down there is probably not all that much hotter than back home. Regardless of where you go during any area's off-season or "shoulder" seasons, you'll find lower hotel rates, special lower fares, and particularly attractive package plans.

But even during the in-season, good timing can produce bargains. Most resorts, for example, offer special reduced rates from Monday through Friday. Lower midweek fares are available on trains and airplanes, too. Conversely, many big-city hotels try to stay full by cutting their rates on weekends, when the majority of business travelers have gone home.

Tax Planning to Cushion Inflation

Inflation has a pyramidal effect on your taxes. Even if your income merely keeps up with advancing prices, so that your buying power remains the same, your taxes go up faster because you keep moving into higher brackets. So, learning how to hold down your taxes becomes especially rewarding in a time of inflation.

Year-End Planning

One of the most useful techniques of managing your taxes is year-end planning. This is a device often used by large taxpayers. They arrange to pay various deductible expenses before the end of the year if they want to reduce their taxes for the current year. Or if they expect their taxes may be higher next year because of higher income, they postpone certain deductible payments.

Some taxpayers, such as professionals and self-employed people, also often can advance or delay receipt of some of their income. Wage-earners usually are not able to time the receipt of employment income but sometimes can advance or delay "taking in" gains on some investments and can advance or postpone payment of deductible items.

All this is legal. *When* you pay a tax-deductible expense determines when you take the deduction, not when you incurred the expense. For tax purposes, an expenditure occurs the day you mail the check.

To use year-end tax planning most effectively you need first to estimate whether you will itemize your deductions or take a standard deduction. If you do not have enough deductible expenses to itemize deductions in a specific year, it's wiser to postpone until the beginning of the following year the payment of whatever deductible expenses can be postponed. This is called "bunching" your deductions.

That way you may be able to take a standard deduction one year and have enough to itemize next year, or vice-versa.

Even if you usually itemize deductions anyway, pay special attention to your medical deduction. You can deduct only that portion over 3% of your income. If your medical expenses already are approaching that level, you may want to pay any outstanding bills before January 1.

Sometimes it can even be worth borrowing to pay a deductible expense before year's end. Say you owe a $500 medical or dental bill, and are in a 22% tax bracket. You'd save $110 in taxes. In contrast, the interest on a bank or credit union loan for, say, a ten-month loan of $500 would be only about $50. (Even that interest would be deductible the year you pay it.)

On the other hand, if you see that your health-care expenses this year will not reach 3% of adjusted gross income, it would save taxes to postpone whatever payments you can until after January 1 to build up a medical deduction for next year.

In addition to charitable contributions of both cash and goods, and medical expenses, other deductible payments that you can advance or postpone include:

1. Deductible work expenses such as purchase and repair of tools, equipment, safety clothing, distinctive uniforms and technical literature.

2. Interest prepaid on loans, mortgages, and installment purchases. (Up to 12 months prepaid interest usually can qualify.)

3. Employee education expenses if your employer required you to take the courses or you had to, in order to improve your skills in your present job. (Be sure you know the rules governing this deduction.)

4. You also may want to evaluate the tax consequences of selling any securities on which you have gains or losses and whether you should advance or delay cashing any E bonds (if you are planning to do so) or which bonds to cash. You may have sizable tax liability on the older bonds.

5. Families who have rental income, as from a second home or even renting an apartment, also sometimes can arrange to receive some of that income ahead of time or after the end of the year.

It's also well to prepare yourself before year's end to prove your claims for exemptions for dependents such as elderly relatives or a child at college.

Often-Overlooked Deductions

There are many tax guides on the market which provide extensive checklists of possible deductions. But those emphasized here are those that are often overlooked.

Interest you pay: As the result of the broadening of regulations in the early 1970's, you can deduct not only all the mortgage interest you pay, but *all* interest you pay on loans, credit card purchases, and installment plans.

Contributions: Keep in mind that charitable contributions are deductible in the year you make them, not the year you make a pledge. Besides cash contributions, you can deduct the "fair" market value of donated goods; expenses of performing services for tax-exempt charitable and civic organizations such as churches, schools, hospitals, Scouts, Community Chest, etc.; and costs and upkeep of uniforms for serving such organizations. You can include out-of-pocket expenses for the use of your own car or the mileage rate established each year by the IRS, plus parking and tolls.

Where taxpayers sometimes become entangled with the IRS is in deducting heavily for donated goods such as clothing and household articles. You can only deduct the "reasonable market value": what you might get if you sell the goods. For example, for clothing in good condition, one practice sometimes used is to deduct 15 percent of the replacement value. But the reaction of different IRS agents may vary.

You can't deduct the value of services you perform for community organizations, nor even payments to a babysitter to care for your children while you perform services. You can deduct an excess charge for tickets to events sold by tax-exempt organizations. But if you don't go you can't deduct the whole price.

Medical expenses: These potential deductions are often misunderstood and sometimes overlooked.

Some misunderstandings arise from the fact that the IRS permits a deduction for special foods or beverages prescribed by a doctor for treatment of an illness but only if taken in addition to the regular diet. Thus, dietetic foods for a diabetic or special foods for an ulcer diet which merely replace food you ordinarily would eat would *not* qualify for a deduction. But if a doctor recommends a daily shot of whiskey for a heart patient, he could deduct the cost.

Also deductible are over-the-counter medicines such as aspirin and cough syrup even if not prescribed by a doctor, and vitamins and iron supplements if a doctor does suggest that you take them.

You also can deduct costs of transportation to get medical and dental care. If you use your own car you can deduct the mileage rate specified each year by the IRS, plus parking and tolls.

You can deduct one-half of premiums you pay for health insurance up to $150. Any remainder can be included in your medical deduction *if* you have enough other medical expenses to itemize (over 3 percent of your adjusted gross income).

As well as non-reimbursed doctor, dentist, nurse, and hospital bills, other potential deductions include eyeglasses; cost of insuring contact lenses; hearing aids, lab fees; special equipment, even an air conditioner for an ill person; support hose; braces; and arch supports.

If you have a dependent for whom you provide more than half his support but can't claim as an exemption because he has too much taxable income of his own, you can include in your deduction any medical expenses you paid on his behalf.

Job-hunt expenses: In an era when recessions may develop even while inflation continues, a deduction for job-hunting expenses may be of some help. In the mid-1970's the Internal Revenue Service broadened this deduction to include expenses incurred in seeking a job in the same trade or business whether or not you actually get the job. But these expenses are *not* deductible if you are seeking employment in a new trade or are just entering the job market.

The IRS looks at the skill more than the business where it is used to determine if job-seeking expenses qualify for a deduction.

Thus, a waitress who becomes a stenographer could not deduct expenses of seeking that new job.

Out-of-town trips need to be related primarily to seeking a job to qualify for a deduction. Time spent on personal activity compared to looking for a job would be important in determining whether the expenses are primarily personal or for employment. But even if a trip is mainly personal, some expenses may be deductible.

Child care deduction: The government has allowed increasingly liberal deductions for care of children or disabled dependents of any age so you can go out to work. By 1976 a working couple or qualified individual could get at least some dependent-care deduction even with combined incomes of up to $44,600. This deduction also can be used by husbands with incapacitated wives; widowers; and other household heads.

The expenses must be for services provided in your home except that some costs of outside care for a child under 15 can be deducted (but not for school expenses after kindergarten).

A working wife and her husband both must work at least three-fourths of a normal work week to claim this deduction (except if the dependent is a disabled spouse).

Sales taxes: You may be able to gain a larger deduction by keeping your own records of sales taxes paid. The sales tax tables in the IRS instruction booklet may not be completely up-to-date. Taxpayers who made large purchases involving sales taxes such as cars in a particular year especially should consider estimating their own sales taxes rather than using the table amount.

Retirement accounts: Individual Retirement Accounts permitted since the mid-1970's are a valuable tax-saving opportunity for wage-earners not covered by pension plans, such as people who work for small employers or institutions without pension programs, or work on a job-by-job basis.

Such pensionless workers can establish their own retirement accounts. They can put into such accounts 15 percent of earnings up to $1,500 a year. They get two tax savers. The contributions of up to $1,500 can be deducted from gross income for tax purposes.

Moreover, the interest earned on the money in the retirement account also is tax free until the worker retires and starts drawing on the funds, at which time many workers are in no-tax or at least low-tax brackets.

If both husband and wife work each can have retirement accounts. But a worker who holds down two jobs can't have an individual retirement plan for one job if he is covered by a company pension on the first job.

Such retirement accounts can be arranged with banks, insurance companies, mutual funds, or by buying government "Individual Retirement Bonds." These earn the same interest as E bonds.

You should understand that if you withdraw funds from a retirement account before age 59½, you must report on your tax return the redemption proceeds and also pay an additional tax penalty—except if you reinvest in another form of retirement account or an employer pension plan.

Even the older "Keogh plan" for self-employed workers has not been utilized by many people who could enjoy sizable tax savings from it. The self-employed plan is even more generous. It allows you to put 15 percent of earnings up to $7,500 a year in a plan.

The self-employed plan also can help moonlighters who have part-time self-employment in addition to a regular job. They can contribute to a tax-deferred retirement plan from their sideline earnings.

As with the individual retirement plans, withdrawals are restricted until age 59½.

Custodian and trust accounts: Even moderate-income families often can use custodian and trust accounts to save taxes on the income from savings and investments.

On savings earmarked for children's education, you can minimize taxes in one of two broad ways. One is outright gifts to the child that he can hold in his own name. The other way is through custodian accounts and trusts which enable you to keep control of the transferred assets until a later date.

Under the Gifts to Minors acts in all states you can give securities to a child simply by having them registered in his name. In most states you also can have a custodian savings account. *The yield or earnings are taxable to the child but at his lower (or no) rate.*

Trusts also can be used to provide support for other dependents.

Index

A